Catalogue of
DATED AND DATABLE
MANUSCRIPTS

Catalogue of

DATED AND DATABLE MANUSCRIPTS

c.888-1600

in London Libraries

P. R. ROBINSON

VOLUME I
The Text

THE BRITISH LIBRARY

First published 2003 by
The British Library
96 Euston Road
London NW1 2DB

© P.R. Robinson, 2003

British Library Cataloguing in Publication Data
A CIP record for this volume is available from The British Library

ISBN 0 7123 4838 7 (Set)
ISBN 0 7123 4845 X (Volume 1)
ISBN 0 7123 4846 8 (Volume 2)

Typeset in England by Norman Tilley Graphics, Northampton
Printed in England by St Edmundsbury Press, Bury St Edmunds

CONTENTS

FOREWORD

The British volumes of the international *Manuscrits datés* project are hitherto the only ones to appear as separate units, not as parts of a serial publication. They nevertheless present a striking unity in conception and format. The norms established by Andrew G. Watson for the volume dealing with dated and datable manuscripts in the British Library (1979) were adopted (with one slight modification) by the same author for those of Oxford Libraries (1984) and by Pamela Robinson for the catalogue of dated and datable manuscripts in Cambridge libraries (1988) as well as for the present catalogue dealing with codices in libraries in London outside the British Library.

By concentrating on the essential features in the description of the manuscripts and renouncing long introductions dealing with the content and features of the codices and the most prominent specimens, the authors have been able to provide concise text volumes that nevertheless contain all information needed. This, together with the printing of plates in a second volume and the continuous numbering of the descriptions as well as the reproductions, makes the British volumes excellent tools for palaeographical research that are easy to handle. Pamela Robinson deserves the gratitude of the scholarly world for this, her second achievement in the field of Dated Manuscripts, which happily appears in the year in which the Comité International de Paléographie Latine celebrates the fiftieth anniversary of the launching of this project.

Albert Derolez
President of the Comité International de Paléographie Latine

ACKNOWLEDGEMENTS

This *Catalogue* has been many years in the making and in that time I have sought the advice and help of many people. Chief among those to whom gratitude is due are Dr Ian Doyle and Professor M.B. Parkes. Dr Doyle as President of the Association for Manuscripts and Archives in Research Collections (AMARC) secured funding from the Neil Ker Fund towards the purchase of photographs and has read the typescript in full. Professor Parkes has also carefully scrutinised typescript and offered his usual trenchant (but welcome) criticisms. I am also grateful to the late Professor A.C. de la Mare who advised me on all the Italian entries; even in her hospital bed she examined xeroxes of manuscripts and suggested identifications of scribes.

Others whom I must thank for help on particular points are Miss Melanie Barber, Mr Douglas East, Professor John Flood who has checked the orthography of the German entries, Dr Meryl Foster, Professor Ralph Hanna, Dr Thérèse de Hemptinne, Professor A.G. Watson, and Dr Rowan Watson. Professor Albert Derolez has kindly agreed to write the foreword.

I am also grateful to the many librarians too numerous to mention who have welcomed me to their collections and facilitated my researches. It has been a great pleasure to work in all the institutions listed here. However, I should like to offer especial thanks to Miss Helen Young, former Special Collections Librarian of the Palaeography Room, University of London Library, a model of what such a librarian should be.

Besides the funding secured by AMARC, photographs were acquired with the aid of a grant from the British Academy. The Public Record Office, the National Art Library at the Victoria and Albert Museum, and the Wellcome Library for the History and Understanding of Medicine graciously paid for the photography of their own manuscripts. Plates are reproduced by courtesy of the Chapter of the College of Arms (pls 25, 31, 36, 61, 127, 128, 141, 147, 191, 274, 275, 283, 291, 292), the Trustees of the Congregational Memorial Hall, owners of the Congregational Library (pls 39, 181), the Corporation of London Records Office (pls 27, 43, 44, 47, 97, 195, 280) and Guildhall Library (pls 37, 99, 132, 148, 188, 243), the Governors of Dulwich College (pl. 287), the Masters of the Bench of the Honourable Societies of Gray's Inn (pls 23, 88, 109), the Inner Temple (pls 34, 272), Middle Temple (pls 70, 89), and the Treasurer and Masters of the Bench of Lincoln's Inn (pls 30, 32, 33, 41, 156, 219, 220, 223, 302), His Grace the Archbishop of Canterbury and the Trustees of Lambeth Palace Library (pls 1, 2, 3, 8, 9, 10, 14, 15, 16, 17, 19, 20, 22, 26, 28, 42, 54, 56, 59, 60, 65, 68, 81, 83, 84, 85, 86, 92, 93, 96, 100, 103, 104, 108, 111, 113, 117, 125, 129, 133, 137, 140, 149, 150, 153, 154, 163, 165, 171, 172, 175, 180, 197, 198, 199, 201, 205, 208, 211, 212, 213, 237, 241, 249, 252, 258, 261, 276, 281, 295, 305), the Law Society (pl. 207), the London Oratory (pls 57, 173), the National Maritime Museum (pls 176, 269), the Public Record Office (pls 4, 5, 6, 7, 35, 38, 45, 46, 63, 75, 78, 79, 107, 114, 115, 122, 130, 226, 227) with the Secretary and Keeper of the Records of the Duchy of Cornwall (pl. 40) and the Chancellor and Council of the Duchy of Lancaster (pls 74, 82, 87), the Royal Astronomical Society (pl. 52), the Royal College of Physicians (pls 24, 138, 193, 303), the Dean and Chapter of St Paul's Cathedral (pls 229, 232), the Trustees of Sir John Soane's Museum (pl. 209), the Society of Antiquaries of London (pls 11, 13, 21, 29, 55, 73, 126, 189, 266, 297), the Rev. Michael Clifton, Archivist of the Diocese of Southwark (pls 67, 91, 247), the United Grand Lodge of England (pl. 288), University College London (pls 12, 48, 77, 143, 145, 155, 160, 161, 168, 170, 182, 217, 222, 228, 238, 242, 253, 254, 255, 277, 282, 298, 299, 306), University of London Library (pls 76, 101, 245), the National Art Library at the Victoria and Albert Museum (pls 18, 53, 58, 123, 134, 167, 186, 200, 225, 256,

260, 262, 265, 268, 284, 304), the Wellcome Library (pls 50, 51, 62, 66, 80, 90, 94, 95, 102, 105, 106, 110, 112, 118, 120, 121, 124, 131, 135, 136, 139, 142, 144, 146, 151, 152, 159, 162, 164, 166, 169, 174, 177, 178, 179, 183, 184, 185, 187, 190, 194, 203, 204, 206, 215, 216, 218, 224, 233, 234, 235, 236, 239, 240, 244, 246, 248, 250, 251, 257, 259, 263, 264, 267, 270, 271, 273, 278, 279, 286, 289, 290, 293, 294, 296, 300, 301), the Dean and Chapter of Westminster Abbey (pls 64, 72, 196), the Cardinal Archbishop of Westminster (pl. 71), the Trustees of Dr Williams's Library (pl. 49) and the Worshipful Companies of Barbers (pls 230, 231), Brewers (pl. 98), Drapers (pl. 157), Goldsmiths (pls 202, 210), Mercers (pl. 119), Merchant Taylors (pl. 221), Parish Clerks (pls 158, 192), Scriveners (pls 69, 214), and Skinners (pl. 116). Wherever possible, plates show handwriting at actual size.

Grants from the Marc Fitch Fund, the Scouloudi Foundation in association with the Institute of Historical Research, and the Vice-Chancellor's Development Fund have made publication possible. I should like to express grateful appreciation for these subventions both on my own behalf and that of the publishers.

Finally, as I dedicated my Cambridge catalogue to the memory of my father, I should like to dedicate this London volume to that of my mother, Dolly. Sadly she has not lived to see publication of a work in whose progress she always took the greatest interest.

Pamela Robinson   July 2002
Institute of English Studies, University of London

ABBREVIATIONS

archbp	archbishop
Aug.	Augustinian
B.A.	Bachelor of Arts
B.C.L.	Bachelor of Civil Law
bdg	binding
Ben.	Benedictine
betw.	between
BL	London, British Library
bld-	blind- (e.g. blind-stamped)
bp	bishop
Brig.	Brigettine
B.Th.	Bachelor of Divinity or Theology
c.	*circa*
cath.	cathedral
ch	church
Cist.	Cistercian
CLRO	Corporation of London Records Office
col (s)	column(s)
col. inits	coloured initials
d.	died
D.C.L.	Doctor of Civil Law
D.Cn.L	Doctor of Canon Law
dec.	decorated
D.Th.	Doctor of Divinity or Theology
facsim.	facsimile
FRCP	Fellow of the Royal College of Physicians, London
FSA	Fellow of the Society of Antiquaries of London
fig(s)	figure(s)
fol(s)	folio(s)
Franc.	Franciscan
GB	Great Britain
hist.	historiated
illum.	illumination
illus.	illustrates/illustration
inhab.	inhabited
init(s)	initial(s)
kal.	kalendar
Mag.	*Magister*
M.A.	Master of Arts
min(s)	miniature(s)
n.s.	new series
OCarm.	Ordo (Fratrum) Carmelitarum
OCist.	Ordo Cisterciensis
OESA	Ordo Eremitarum Sancti Augustini
OFM	Ordo Fratrum Minorum
OPrem.	Ordo Premonstratensis
OSB	Ordo Sancti Benedicti
Parch.	Parchment
Pl(s)	plates
pr.	printed
Prem.	Premonstratensian
PRO	Kew, Public Record Office
publ.	published
Soc.	*Society*
Trans.	*Transactions*
UCL	University College London
ULL	University of London Library
V and A	London, National Art Library, Victoria and Albert Museum
vol(s)	volume(s)
Wellcome	London, The Wellcome Library for the History and Understanding of Medicine

ABBREVIATED TITLES

	Carley, R.M. Thomson and A.G. Watson, *Corpus of British Medieval Library Catalogues*, 4 (1996)
Exh., *Age of Chivalry*	*Age of Chivalry: Art in Plantagenet England 1200-1400* [Catalogue of an Exhibition held at the Royal Academy of Arts, London, 6 November 1987 – 6 March 1988], ed. J. Alexander and P. Binski (1987)
Exh., *Engl. Illum. MSS 700-1500*	*English Illuminated Manuscripts, 700-1500: Catalogue [of an Exhibition organized as part of the Europalia 73 Great Britain Arts Festival in Belgium and held in] Brussels, Bibliothèque Royale Albert Ier 29 September – 10 November 1973*, ed. J.J.G. Alexander and C.M. Kauffmann (1973)
Exh., *Universal Penman*	*The Universal Penman: A Survey of Western Calligraphy from the Roman Period to 1980* [Catalogue of an Exhibition held at the Victoria and Albert Museum, London, July – September 1980], ed. J.I. Whalley and V.C. Kaden (1980)
Frere, *BML*	W.H. Frere, *Bibliotheca Musico-Liturgica: A Descriptive Handlist of the Musical and Latin-Liturgical MSS of the Middle Ages preserved in the Libraries of Great Britain and Ireland*, 2 vols (1901-32)
Gransden, *Hist. Writing*, I	A. Gransden, *Historical Writing in England c.550 to c.1307* (1974)
Gransden, *Hist. Writing*, II	A. Gransden, *Historical Writing in England c.1307 to the Early Sixteenth Century* (1982)
HBS	Henry Bradshaw Society
HMC	Historical Manuscripts Commission
Horwood	A.J. Horwood, *A Catalogue of the Ancient Manuscripts belonging to the Honourable Society of Gray's Inn* (1869)
Hunter	J. Hunter, *A Catalogue of the Manuscripts in the Library of the Honourable Society of Lincoln's Inn* (1838)
IMEP, XIII	*Index of Middle English Prose*, Handlist XIII: *Manuscripts in Lambeth Palace Library*, ed. O.S. Pickering and V.M. O'Mara (1999)
JWCI	*Journal of the Warburg and Courtauld Institutes*
James	M.R. James, *A Descriptive Catalogue of the Manuscripts in the Library of Lambeth Palace Library* (1932)
James, *Anc. Libs.*	M.R. James, *The Ancient Libraries of Canterbury and Dover* (1903)
Ker, *Anglo-Saxon MSS*	N.R. Ker, *Catalogue of Manuscripts containing Anglo-Saxon* (1957)
Kramer	S. Kramer, *Handschriftenerbe des Deutschen Mittelalters*, 3 vols, *Mittelalterliche Bibliothekskataloge Deutschlands und der Schweiz*, Supplement 1 (1989-90)
MLGB	*Medieval Libraries in Great Britain: A List of Surviving Books*, ed. N.R. Ker, Royal Historical Society Guides and Handbooks no. 3 (2nd edn, 1964); *Supplement*, ed. A.G. Watson, Royal Historical Society Guides and Handbooks no. 15 (1987)
MLN	*Modern Language Notes*
MLR	*Modern Language Review*
MMBL, I	N.R. Ker, *Medieval Manuscripts in British Libraries*, Vol. I: London (1969)
MSS datés	*Catalogue des manuscrits en écriture latine portant des indications de date, de lieu ou de copiste* (1959-)
Medieval Scribes, MSS and Libraries	*Medieval Scribes, Manuscripts and Libraries: Essays presented to N.R. Ker*, ed. M.B. Parkes and A.G. Watson (1978)
Moorat	S.A.J. Moorat, *Catalogue of Western Manuscripts on Medicine and Science in the Wellcome Historical Medical Library*, 2 vols (1962-73)
Morgan, *Early Gothic MSS*	N. Morgan, *Early Gothic Manuscripts 1190-1285*, 2 vols, Survey of Manuscripts illuminated in the British Isles, IV (1982-88)

INTRODUCTION

This *Catalogue of Dated and Datable Manuscripts c.888-1600 in London Libraries* is the fourth British contribution to an international research project established by the Comité International de Paléographie Latine in 1953.[1] The project's aim is to produce a series of catalogues describing all precisely dated and generally datable manuscript books written in the Latin alphabet from the earliest times to 1600. The project's purpose is to provide photographic specimens of precisely dated or generally datable handwriting to furnish criteria for the dating of undated manuscript books. It was Humfrey Wanley, the great seventeenth-century palaeographer and Anglo-Saxon scholar, who, recognising the need to be able to date manuscripts within close limits, first formulated the principle that one should compare the handwriting of undated manuscripts with that of dated and datable ones for the purpose.[2] The slow but steady progress in the publication of the international series of dated and datable catalogues enables scholars to apply Wanley's principle with ever-increasing confidence.

Their publication is also fostering the study of palaeography by the publication of a growing corpus of colophons.[3] Manuscripts whose copyists have informed us precisely when, where and by whom a volume was copied constitute the smallest number of manuscripts. Nevertheless, such statements, quoted as evidence for a manuscript's date, can provide evidence as to the sociology of scribes and their conditions of work. Some scribes were succinct, such as the scribe of a Sarum Office of the Dead (no. **115**) who concluded 'Scriptum est anno domini 1469' or the German scribe of a Processional (no. **141**) who finished it 'Anno domini 1497'. By contrast, Ruaidri Olachthnain, prior of the Augustinian house of Lorrha, Co. Tipperary, who signed a copy of the Clementinae at Lorrha in 1477 (no. **46**), is unusually garrulous and informative. Not only does he tell us that he wrote, illuminated, bound, and indexed the volume, but he provides a contemporary account of a Franciscan assembly at Roscrea which ended in riot.

Today colophons are scrutinised for all the information they give.[4] They can be simply formulaic, although particular formulae may prove to have been fashionable at certain times and places.[5] Colophons provide the only certain evidence that a scribe was female.[6] Thus we know that a bible (no. **186**) from the Augustinian convent of Diepenveen, near Deventer (Netherlands), was copied by a nun. A scribe's career may be traced. The German Hermann Zurke of Greifswald, one of a number of foreign scribes who sought a living in England, had settled in Oxford by 1449 where he made a copy of the *Gesta romanorum* (*DMC* no. 60), the only non-medical work he apparently copied, for an Augustinian canon of Osney. Zurke lived and worked in Catte Street (no. **81**), centre of the Oxford book trade from the early thirteenth century.[7] His principal client became Gilbert Kymer, chancellor of the University, whose 'servitor' he called himself, and in 1453 he moved to Salisbury when Kymer settled there, continuing to work for him until 1460 (*DMO* nos 80, 81, 610, 843).

How quickly a scribe could write has been established from those who dated their work on successive days. Although it depended on the script employed and the size of the book (the taller the page, the slower the scribe), the average rate of copying was between two and three folia a day.[8] The scribe of a copy of Lucan (no. **200**) began Book IX of the Pharsalia on 15 October 1471 and Book X three days and ten folios later on 18 October. As each page contains thirty-eight lines in a written space of 162 × 58 mm, the scribe worked at the average speed.

The majority of scribes, however, did not date or sign their work. What motivated those who did so?[9] Italian humanist scribes frequently dated and signed copy. Possibly, since many had been trained as notaries and became accustomed to date and sign the documents they produced, they automatically dated and/or signed any book that they copied. Yet, although he dated it, the scribe identifiable as the Florentine notary, Ser Giovanni di Piero da Stia, did not sign the copy of Matteo Palmieri's Liber de temporibus (no. **265**) that he made in 1469. In England notaries were not so routinely employed as in Italy, since the office of notary public was not recognised by English Common Law.[10] Nevertheless, notaries were important figures in the foundation of the Worshipful Company of Scriveners of London, or guild of those who produced legal instruments in the City, and from 1392 onwards every decade saw a handful of English notaries among those who subscribed to the Scriveners' Company 'Common Paper' (no. **38**).[11] Only in 1417 did it become regular practice for everyone, notary or not, to date their subscriptions. In 1487 a William Duryvale subscribed; by 1491 he was Clerk of the Worshipful Company of Merchant Taylors for which he copied, signed and dated its 'Book of Oaths' (no. **111**).

Fifteenth-century German scribes also frequently dated and signed copy. A recent study of colophons in German manuscripts suggests they were signed when their copyists intended them for their own use or that of a close relative or member of their religious community.[12] Students producing volumes for personal use, such as Johann Lindner at Leipzig who took three years to copy Aristotle's works (no. **212**) or Julian Osuelt from Zerbst who copied a collection of logica (no. **176**), possibly felt pride and satisfaction at the end of their task. Michael Suter of Wurzen who copied John of Sacrobosco's Opusculum sphericum 'laboribus ac diligencia' (no. **250**) appears to have felt relief. Whatever such scribes' motives might have been, it is obvious from the catalogues published so far that English scribes were far less inclined to sign and date their work than scribes of other nations.

* * *

The nature of the entries varies from catalogue to catalogue. In marked contrast to its British predecessors, the present catalogue contains few manuscripts written before 1100. Whereas *DMBL* records fifty-five manuscripts dating before the twelfth century, and *DMO* and *DMC* thirty-six manuscripts each, this volume records only four. They are the 'MacDurnan Gospels' (no. **97**), possibly written *c*.888 at Armagh, and later presented by King Athelstan (924-39) to Christ Church Canterbury; a manuscript of Old English sermons (no. **87**), written at Exeter Cathedral during the episcopacy of Bishop Leofric (1050-72); and the Great and Little Domesday books (nos **126**, **127**), probably compiled between 1086 and 1088.

DMBL and *DMO* record mainly non-English manuscripts (*DMBL* 818 out of 953 entries, *DMO* 603 out of 882 entries) in contrast to *DMC* and the present volume. Only 148 out of 394 entries in *DMC* were written elsewhere, while nearly half (141) of this catalogue's 285 entries were written in England. Three, possibly four, manuscripts come from Ireland (nos **46**, **78**, **97**, **118**) and three from Scotland (nos **56**, **73**, **160**). Nearly all the continental manuscripts included here are from three collections: University College London (where Robert Priebsch, d. 1935, had been professor of German and to whose enthusiasm the collection is largely due), the National Art Library at the Victoria and Albert Museum (where illuminated manuscripts and fine bindings were acquired as a resource for students of art and design[13]), and the Wellcome Library for the History and Understanding of Medicine (with its large collection of manuscripts written by German and Italian physicians). Most of these date from the later fifteenth or the sixteenth century.

One hundred and twenty-five of the English entries are dated or datable before 1526, the date of William Chell's collection of musical treatises (no. **85**), copied in London or Oxford from a compilation made in 1500 by John Tucke, Fellow of New College, Oxford (*DMBL*, no. 25). Of those to which a specific place of origin can be assigned, many were copied in religious houses: in the Benedictine cathedral priories of Christ Church Canterbury (nos **48**, **58**, **80**), Ely (no. **82**), and Rochester (no. **53**), abbeys of Abingdon (no. **45**), Bury St Edmunds (nos **5**, **100**), Chester (no. **30**), Dover (no. **68**), Gloucester (no. **121**), Malmesbury (no. **65**), and Peterborough (nos **61**, **62**, **146**, **149**, **150**), and Tutbury Priory (no. **8**); the Cistercian abbeys of Buildwas (no. **55**), Furness (no. **123**) and Stanlaw (no. **88**); the Augustinian houses of Barnwell (no. **3**), Lanthony Secunda (nos **67**, **119**, **120**), Lesnes (no. **192**) and Newstead, Notts (no. **9**); and in the Bridgettine house of Syon Abbey, Middlesex (no. **140**). A single manuscript each comes from the secular cathedrals of Exeter (no. **87**) and Lincoln (no. **66**). University book production is witnessed by one manuscript written in Cambridge (no. **43**), and six manuscripts written in Oxford (nos **28**, **57**, **75**, **76**, **77**, **81**), all but two (nos **28**, **81**) bought or partly copied there by the Augustinian canon Richard Calne, while he was a student at the University 1412-21, and taken back with him to Lanthony Priory.

Only two manuscripts are stated to have been written in Northern England: a copy of the Legenda Aurea at Crich, Derbyshire (no. **64**) and a copy of John Mirfield's Florarium Bartholomei at Swine, Yorkshire (no. **142**). The theological miscellany from St Werburg's Abbey, Chester (no. **30**) was probably written in-house, and the historical collection (no. **2**), given by Friar John Erghome to the Austin Friars of York, was perhaps written locally. Manuscripts from Southern England include a copy of Osbern Bokenham's Dialogue between a Secular and a Friar, possibly written at Bury St Edmunds (no. **14**), a cartulary from Daventry, Northampton-shire (no. **124**), a breviary possibly written at Lichfield (no. **156**), a psalter from Salisbury (no. **139**), Michael de Massa's Vita Christi copied at Salle, Norfolk (no. **89**), a manuscript of astronomical tables possibly written at Stonehouse, Devon (no. **135**), John Rous's Latin roll chronicle of the town of Warwick (no. **15**), and the 'Winton Domesday' from Winchester (no. **152**).

The largest number of manuscripts of known origin was written in the metropolitan area (including nos **70**, **281**, **282**, and possibly nos **60** and **280**, from Westminster). Some books from the medieval City of London and Westminster are still in the possession of the institutions for which they were written, others are witnesses to lost medieval libraries. Ecclesiastical and religious institutions represented in this catalogue are St Paul's Cathedral (nos **42**, **95**, **99**), the Augustinian priory of Holy Trinity Aldgate (no. **47**), the Franciscan convent (no. **83**), and the parish churches of St Margaret's Bridge Street (no. **32**) and St Peter's Cornhill (no. **36**), as well as Westminster Abbey (nos **60**, **280**-**282**). City institutions include the medieval Guildhall (nos **18**-**24**) and the Crafts of Barber-Surgeons (no. **1**), Brewers (no. **39**), Drapers (no. **25**), Goldsmiths (no. **27**), Mercers (no. **110**), Merchant Taylors (no. **111**), Parish Clerks (no. **37**), Scriveners (no. **38**), and Skinners (no. **145**). Four books (nos **126**, **127**, **129**, **130**) were kept in the Royal Exchequer at the Tower of London, one of which (no. **129**) includes a list of five other books kept there (see pl. 46).

These entries represent not only a fraction of the books such places once probably owned but also a fraction of the institutional collections of books or libraries once existing within the metropolis. Besides several large monasteries, friaries and nunneries within the city or on its outskirts, there were thirty-four hospitals and almshouses in medieval London and its suburbs. Moreover, within its boundary there were over 100 parish churches.[14] All required books, although surviving manuscripts are few. By 1500 the Inns of Court had 'nascent libraries' but lawyers mostly owned their own books.[15] *MLGB* and its *Supplement* record surviving books from only twenty 'major' libraries (including Gray's Inn and Lincoln's Inn) and eight parish churches. Only a few catalogues or inventories survive to supplement the meagre tally of extant manuscripts. What follows is an overview designed to show what little survives or we know of books from medieval London's libraries. (For brief histories of London's post-medieval libraries, see below p. 11.)

* * *

St Paul's Cathedral: Only thirty manuscripts are known to survive from Old St Paul's, yet ample docu-mentation establishes that the cathedral possessed a substantial collection in the Middle Ages.[16] One hundred and twenty-six books, including three works of Bede 'in Anglico', were left in 1313 by Ralph de Baldock, bishop of London 1304-13.[17] Not all the volumes Ralph meant to bequeath could be identified by his testators, who substituted other works for them. The only book of Ralph's known today is a copy of Alexander of Hales, alienated from the cathedral by the mid-fifteenth century when Thomas Gascoigne (d. 1458) gave it to Oriel College, Oxford (MS 30). However, Gascoigne, who had briefly been rector of St Peter's Cornhill, gave three or four other books to St Paul's.[18] By 1458 when an inventory was drawn up of the volumes to be housed in 'noua libraria', built at the expense of Walter Shiryngton, formerly Chancellor of the Duchy of Lancaster and canon of St Paul's (d. 1449), the cathedral owned some 170 volumes.[19] The collection, which included works given by Shiryngton, contained grammar, philosophy, history, medicine, canon and civil law, and a volume (formerly Shiryngton's) containing the Letters and Natural Questions of the younger Seneca, Cicero 'in rethoricis', and Virgil's Bucolics. This and a copy of Suetonius, *De vitae Caesarum*, were the only classical texts in the new library. It was otherwise heavily biased in favour of biblical studies and sermon collections, as befitted what was evidently a working library intended to meet the pastoral needs and concerns of the cathedral clergy.

One has to look to the choristers' school for a collection of books by classical authors. The books there, left by the cathedral almoner, William de Ravenstone, under the terms of his will, dated 16 July 1358, included Virgil's Georgics and Horace's Satires in one volume, Statius and Claudian in another, two copies of Juvenal, and copies of Ovid's Metamorphoses, Lucan, and Persius.[20] Ravenstone's will itself simply refers to 'all the items listed below', but attached to it is a detailed indenture, listing his goods and chattels and books. Both documents were folded over at their feet, so that the indenture sat inside the turn-up of the will. Slits were then made in the double turn-up for the insertion of two parchment tags to which the seals of Ravenstone and the cathedral chapter were appended. He could hardly change his mind about his bequest. The indenture lists forty-three volumes (some with multiple contents) containing grammar (including six copies of Alexander de Villa Dei's *Doctrinale* for eight pupils, three copies of Priscian, and a Donatus), the classical texts, and two old psalters, along with the chest in which they were stored.

Inventories also survive of service books housed in the treasury in 1245, 1255, 1295, and 1486, as well as one of the Lady Chapel in 1445, where sixteen music books were kept.[21] They describe a number of handsome volumes in detail: thus that of 1486 contains 'Item psalterium pulcherimum habens coopertum rubeum cum xiiij folijs decenter ornatis cum ym\a/ginibus auri et kalendario sequente ante psalterium 2° folio a nobis iugum ipsorum'.[22] Many items in the earlier inventories would have become outdated when the cathedral adopted Sarum Use in 1415 and hence are likely to have been discarded even before the Reformation.[23]

While old service books were no longer required, the library of the canons of St Paul's was not dispersed at the Dissolution.[24] Nevertheless, the cathedral today possesses few manuscripts (now mainly deposited in the Guildhall Library). Some soon strayed after 1540, including two volumes of history both known to John Bale and Archbishop Parker, and both of which became part of the foundation collection of Lambeth Palace Library. One (no. **42**) is a manuscript of the works of Ralph of Diss, dean of St Paul's 1180-1201, compiled under his supervision and containing revisions to text. This and a lost copy of his Postils on Ecclesiasticus and Wisdom, listed in the 1458 inventory, were the only manuscripts of Ralph's works the cathedral apparently owned, although he had been dean. The other history (no. **95**) is a fourteenth-century copy of the Flores historiarum, continued by a series of annals, regularly updated, relating to the cathedral sacristy. However, it was only in 1647, after the parliamentary forces' defeat of Charles I in the First Civil War, that most of its manuscripts were removed from St Paul's to the seventeenth-century foundation, Sion College, where all but three were seemingly burnt in the Great Fire of London, 1666. Two of these survivors cannot be traced but the third, a copy of Avicenna, has returned to the cathedral (MS 3). The flyleaves of a copy of Peter of Blois (MS 4), not itself a medieval acquisition, are from an otherwise lost volume of sermons. The library was only refounded in the early eighteenth century and its present manuscript collection is largely post-medieval.[25] Two such acquisitions are no. **140**, copied by Thomas Betson, librarian of Syon Abbey, Middlesex, d. 1516, and no. **141**, a German Processional.

The fate of its manuscripts contrasts with that of the cathedral's muniments. Many of the deeds listed in a catalogue of them, drawn up on the orders of Dean Thomas Lyseux, in 1447, are still owned by St Paul's.[26] However, a booklet containing the statutes of the chantry of Thomas More, dean of St Paul's (d. 1421), is now at Lambeth (no. **99**) and a copy of the cathedral's statutes, drawn up in 1450 on Lyseux's orders, is in Cambridge (*DMC*, no. 26).

Religious houses: The only two houses represented here are the Augustinian priory of Holy Trinity Aldgate and the Franciscan convent. Only three volumes are recorded in *MLGB* and *Supplement* from the former.[27] They include the 'Liber revelationum' of Prior Peter of Cornwall, d. 1221, probably compiled under his supervision (no. **47**). This book, however, points to a once substantial collection since it bears the fourteenth-century shelfmark 'De vj^{to} ordine .xlij.' The nine volumes recorded from the Franciscans, however, include an autograph manuscript of the humanist friar, Lorenzo Guglielmo Traversagni di Savona. This was written in the house for William Waynflete, bishop of Winchester and founder of Magdalen College, Oxford, and probably belonged to Magdalen (no. **83**). Besides the survivors, we know the convent owned at least forty-four other works which John Leland (d. 1552) reported there.[28]

This evidence is typical of a context of fitful survival and poor documentation. Booklists compiled by Leland supplement our knowledge of the books formerly belonging to the Austin Friars, Carmelites, and Dominicans. At the Austin Friary he noted thirteen volumes, none corresponding to its seven extant manuscripts. He noted a further sixteen volumes at the Dominican convent in addition to the thirteen which have survived. (Thirteen more were recorded there by John Bale from a fourteenth-century catalogue of its library that he had seen). But the fullest evidence Leland provides is for the library of the Carmelite convent. His remarks show it contained at least ten double-sided bookcases, in which he recorded sixty-one titles. Only three of them correspond to the eighteen known manuscripts.[29]

Leland's booklists, however, were not designed to be comprehensive catalogues of the collections he had visited. His aim was to collect material for a catalogue of British writers, and, since his interests were primarily historical, texts in other areas (except theological and legal works) were rarely listed.[30] Moreover, while some libraries he saw, from *c*.1533-40, were still intact, others had already been devastated by the monastic commissioners. Books other than those recorded in *MLGB* may well have survived, as perhaps one of the surviving English copies of the *Doctrinale* of the Carmelite writer, Thomas Netter of Walden, may have belonged to the London Carmel, but they cannot be assigned to a particular house.[31]

Elsewhere, seven books are known from the Crutched Friars, one of which has a prayer for its donor on the flyleaf recording that he gave it 'et vltra triginta alios libros' in 1496.[32] Two books and a leaf from a third survive from the Cistercian abbey of St Mary of Graces, where the only mention of books dates from 1430 when the stationers John Robert and William Barwe valued nine of them in an action of debt against the abbot. Their valuations ranged from 13*s* 4*d* for a psalter to 8*d* for 'unus liber vocatus sintillarum' (probably Defensor of Ligugé's Liber scintillarum).[33] Four lists survive of books sent in the fifteenth and sixteenth centuries from the Charterhouse of the Salutation to other Carthusian houses but no catalogue or inventory of its own collection.[34] Twenty-six manuscripts are assigned by *MLGB* to the house, including the 'Liber spiritualis gracie S. Matildis', copied by John Whetham in 1492 (*DMC*, no. 27), but the two English Carthusian collections in the present catalogue (nos **79, 284**) come from unknown Charterhouses.

Only one book is known from the Augustinian canonesses in Holywell (Shoreditch), and six from the Minoresses, without Aldgate.[35] Not surprisingly, half these books are in the vernacular. There are only two known survivors from Whittington College, the college of priests endowed by Richard Whittington (d. 1423), while one book survives from the collegiate church of St Michael, in Crooked Lane. None is known from St Martin-le-Grand, although an early-sixteenth-century inventory exists of its (mainly service) books.[36]

Two manuscripts survive from Elsyng's Spital (or Hospital of the Blessed Virgin Mary near Cripplegate): a copy of Pseudo-Aristotle, 'Secreta secretorum', and a compilation of works by Ambrose and others.[37] However, an inventory made in 1448 lists sixty-three books 'in libraria' and forty-three service books kept in the sacristy.[38] Evidently the library was intended for the Austin canons there, since only one of its books 'liber galieni et ypocratis' was medical (Galen's commentaries on Hippocrates were part of the Articella). Biblical commentaries, Gregory the Great's Homilies and Dialogues, works by St Augustine, saints' lives, and canon and civil law, were among the rest. Rather than the *Breviarium Bartholomei*, a medical compendium by John Mirfield (d. 1407) of St Bartholomew's Hospital, it owned his 'floriarum bartholomei', a collection of theological distinctions. Neither of Mirfield's works is known to survive from St Bartholomew's itself.[39] Eight books are extant, including a bible worth £16 recovered with five service books from the effects of the deceased master John White (d. 1423).[40] At the Hospital of St Thomas of Acon, Cheapside, whence seven manuscripts survive, chain staple marks on the pastedowns of two permit us to infer the existence of a chained library.[41] Only one book survives from the Hospital of the Blessed Virgin Mary, without Bishopsgate.

Parish churches: The two books from City churches here (nos **32**, **36**) come from the churches of St Margaret Bridge Street (New Fish Street) and St Peter Cornhill. Both are cartularies, preserved for their value as evidence to the churches' properties. Two other manuscripts also survive from St Peter's: a bible and a copy of Higden's *Polychronicon* (BL Royal 13.D.i), an imposing volume written at the end of the fourteenth century.[42] Its appearance suggests a library book to be read at a lectern desk. Although it might seem a surprising volume to find in the possession of a parish church, Higden appealed to the educated clergy, and copies also survive from the Austin Friars, the Franciscans, and the Hospital of St Thomas of Acon.[43] Nonetheless, martyrologies, missals, lectionaries and bibles were among the books more usually owned by a parish church.[44]

Such books have been lost in great number. *MLGB* and *Supplement* record only nine volumes from eight churches: a martyrology from All Hallows the Great, a missal each from St Botolph Aldersgate, St Botolph Aldgate, St Lawrence Jewry, St Margaret Lothbury, a lectionary from St Margaret Aldermanbury, a processional from St Sepulchre Holborn, and the bible and Higden from St Peter Cornhill.

This makes the inventory of books found in the cartulary of St Margaret Bridge Street (no. **32**) all the more noteworthy. While none of them is known to survive, the church in 1472 was not only well provided with service books but had a small chained library. This contained not only service books (three portos or breviaries, and two psalters) but also a copy of the *Catholicon*, a volume of St Bernard (2° folio 'tabor'), the *Compendium theologice veritatis* of Hugh Ripelin of Strasbourg, and 'a boke of the Prik of concience secundo fo "whan" cheyned'. This poem, which survives in more manuscripts than any other Middle English text, was popular with the secular clergy for whom it provided an invaluable source of didactic and homilectic material, and was probably acquired for that reason.[45] The titles suggest a small reference library which is unlikely to have been unique. St Christopher-le-Stocks seems also to have had one, of which all we are told is 'Item on the south side of the vestrarie standeth a grete library with .ij. long lecturnalles theron to ley on the bokes'.[46] Other churches may also have had libraries of which all trace disappeared in the Fire.

However, the few other inventories of City churches generally list only the required service books, as at St Peter West Cheap (1431), St Martin Orgar (1469), St Margaret Pattens (1470), and St Christopher-le-Stocks (1488).[47] Other kinds of books are rarely mentioned. St Martin Orgar only acquired its copy of Robert Holcot on Wisdom early in the sixteenth century.[48] The books of St Martin Ludgate at the end of the fourteenth century included John of Genoa's popular dictionary, the *Catholicon*;[49] St Mary's at Hill in 1432 'a boke of lawe is callyd decretallis';[50] and St Nicholas Shambles in 1457 copies of Hugutio of Pisa, the manual for a parish priest, *Pars oculi*, and a 'legende in english ycheyned in þe qwere of dyuers seintis lifes begynnynge in þe .iij de. lef. for Sara'.[51] St Stephen, Coleman Street, in 1466 also owned the *Pars oculi*, while All Hallows Barking in 1452 had John de Burgh's later revision *Pupilla oculi*, 'cheyned in the quere'.[52]

Mention of a chained book is infrequent. At St James Garlickhithe, the only two such books in an inventory of thirty-seven volumes, drawn up in 1449 by the parson, William Huntingdon, are 'Item a bible in Frenssh 7 cheyned pris xls Item anoþer boke of holy wryte compilid in frensshe \also/ cheyned pris xxs'.[53] The high price of the first suggests a copy of the Bible historiale, although Huntingdon does not mention any illumination. He described the illustration of the opening leaves of other items, however, as a way of distinguishing between different copies of a service book.[54]

The paucity of records, combined with the wholesale disposal of books at the Reformation, permit only speculation as to what libraries other city churches might once have had. Even earlier they had sold off their books. Thus in the 1470s the churchwardens of St Andrew Hubbard sold a copy of the decretals and an Old Testament to John Pye, the London stationer, for £3 and 26*s* 8*d* respectively.[55] While the Act against Superstitious Books and Images, 1549-50, was directed at service books,[56] the Edwardian inventories of 1552 show churches indiscriminately selling their old books by weight. John Day, the printer (1522-84) bought all the Latin books of St Peter West Cheap for £2 10*s*, while books had been sold at St Lawrence Pountney ('to hartwell the Stacyoner ccxl ˡᵇˢ of olde bookes at ob. the lb. xs'), St Mary Staining ('solde Bookes by weight whiche weyde a C iij quarters and xiiij lb. at iij fardynges the lb. Summa xiij s'), and St Swithin London Stone ('receyued for ijᶜ xxˡⁱ of olde Bokes xxvs iijd').[57] Since parchment afforded the binder an excellent material, such books were often cut up and recycled in bindings.[58] Four of the Edwardian inventories themselves are bound in covers made from manuscript fragments. These fragments, however, are not necessarily from books formerly owned by the church in question. The inventory of the church of St Leonard Foster is bound in two leaves from a thirteenth-century York antiphonal.[59]

Guildhall: The library built adjacent to the chapel of the medieval Guildhall, with moneys from the estates of Richard Whittington and William Bury (will dated 1422/3), predates that of St Paul's, built in the 1450s. Mistakenly claimed as the first public library in England, the Guildhall library more probably served the college of priests (founded in 1356 to serve the chantries established in the Guildhall chapel) and the poorer members of the London clergy.[60] In 1444 one of Guildhall's chaplains, John Clipstone, was appointed 'custos librarie' for life.[61] Neither Whittington nor Bury had made specific provision for a library, and it was probably due to John Carpenter, chief of Whittington's executors and Common Clerk of the City 1417-38 (d. 1442), that one was built.[62] It was he who 'saw in Guildhall chapel an opportunity to foster a college where religion and learning could go hand in hand'.[63] Carpenter's interest in the new library was such that he desired two of the executors of his own will, William Lichfield and Reginald Pecock, to select from among the residue of his goods such 'boni vel rari libri' as they thought should be chained in it for the profit of students there and those addressing the common people.[64] Judging by the books Carpenter left to specific legatees, he favoured devotional and theological works, for they included a copy of St Anselm's prayers and meditations, Prosper of Aquitaine's *De vita contemplativa*, Vincent of Beauvais, *Speculum morale*, and Roger Dymmok's *Liber contra XII errores et hereses Lollardorum*. Books like these would have been appropriate in a theological library, but no catalogue of the Guildhall library survives. Carpenter also owned books of professional interest to a town clerk: copies of the works of Alan of Lille (in vogue amongst readers interested in rhetoric in the first quarter of the fifteenth century), and booklets ('libellorum siue quaternorum') on how to engross documents. These were left to his former clerks, as was a copy of Richard de Bury's *Philobiblon*.

MLGB and *Supplement* assign a dozen volumes to the medieval Guildhall, but only two can be said to have belonged to its medieval library: an early fourteenth-century copy of Aquinas on the second book of Sentences (BL, Harley 32, with the late-fifteenth-century *ex dono* on what was a pastedown (fol. 253) 'liber emptus pro xx s do hunc librum cathenandum in libraria de gyldhalle civitatis Londoniensis') and an early-thirteenth-century copy of Petrus Riga, *Aurora* (Guildhall 3042, bought back in 1926). A copy of the *Chroniques de France* (Guildhall 244), borrowed from the Guildhall by the chronicler, Robert Fabyan (d. 1513), was kept, certainly after its return in 1516 until 1869, with the archives of the Corporation. The remaining manuscripts were not library books. Since they contain laws, local history, and city ordinances, they were useful reference works for the Mayor and Aldermen when they sought to determine the city's rights and privileges. Nos **21** and **24** were among volumes thus consulted early in Henry VI's reign.[65] As today those still in the City's possession are kept in the Corporation of London Records Office (nos **18-24**), so in the Middle Ages they were kept with its Letter Books and other administrative and judicial records, probably in an upper chamber at the Guildhall.[66] It was there that John Carpenter requested his handbooks on engrossing documents should remain after the death of his clerk Robert Brown (to whom he had left them for term of his life),[67] and it was there that the records entrusted in 1462 to the then Common Clerk (William Dunthorne) were stored in a chest.[68]

In January 1549 the library was 'borrowed' by Lord Protector Somerset. It soon became clear that the books would not be returned, and by November of the same year the City had decided not to re-establish the library. It was only refounded in the 1820s and the present collection of manuscripts is the result of later acquisitions. Thus Fabyan's own copy of the Great Chronicle of London (no. **35**) was not acquired until 1933. The City was more fortunate with its records. Although three of its custumals (nos **20-21**, **23**) had been alienated in the sixteenth century and acquired by Sir Robert Bruce Cotton, he was persuaded to restore one, the sixteenth-century 'Liber Fleetwood' (no. **23**), in its entirety and substantial parts of the other two, fourteenth-century, volumes.[69]

Inns of Court: Although three of the four inns (Gray's Inn, the Inner and Middle Temples) were in existence by 1388, their medieval records do not survive.[70] Despite this lack, we know that Gray's Inn (whose records date from 1569), received a bequest in 1488 of a Statute book and five non-legal books to be chained in the library.[71] Only Lincoln's Inn, in existence by 1422, has fifteenth-century records. These show that in 1475 the Treasurer paid Roger Towneshend 30s 'pro bibliotheca' (presumably a working library or collection of books); thirty years later (1505) they refer to 40 marks left by John Nethersale (admitted 1482) to build a library.[72] Yet only a single manuscript each has been assigned to either society. Medieval lawyers had their own books, and the entries in the present catalogue from Gray's Inn, Lincoln's Inn, and the Inner and Middle Temples are all post-medieval donations.

Westminster Abbey: At nearby Westminster the monks once owned a large collection of books, for which a library was built in the 1450s. After the death at Avignon in 1376 of Cardinal Simon Langham, once abbot and later archbishop of Canterbury 1366-68, seven chests containing ninety-one volumes were sent to the abbey.[73] The inventory of them includes works on theology, canon law, and ecclesiastical history. At least two items, a copy of Eusebius's Ecclesiastical history and 'Item actus et exilium sancti Thome in quaternis', appear not to have been delivered since it is noted against them 'creditur esse Cantuarie'. Ten more of Langham's books arrived in 1378 while another ten and three maps were left by a former prior, Richard Exeter, in 1396/7.[74] None of these donations has yet been traced.

Although forty-nine books are known to survive, the present library contains only five manuscripts which belonged to the abbey in the Middle Ages.[75] Three of them would not have been housed in the library, since they are service books. Thus, the abbey's best known manuscript, Abbot Litlyngton's Missal (no. **281**), is recorded in an inventory, drawn up in 1388, of service books kept in the vestry.[76] It was still owned by the abbey in 1540 but apparently strayed after the Dissolution only to be returned in 1663 by Dean Dolben.

Some manuscripts may already have strayed in the Middle Ages. A twelfth-century volume containing the letters of Gilbert Foliot, bishop of London 1163-87, which had belonged to the abbey in the thirteenth century, by the fourteenth belonged to Belvoir Priory, Leicestershire (*DMO*, no. 661). A fourteenth-century copy of David of Augsburg's De exterioris et interioris hominis compositione, given to Hereford Cathedral by John Bayly, canon and precentor 1460-79, has the earlier (and erased) *ex libris* of Westminster Abbey.[77]

The library suffered heavy losses after the Dissolution, despite the abbey's becoming a secular foundation. This may not have been solely because works no longer considered acceptable were removed, but also because the canons of the new foundation might have had no concern to keep their old books. Even new acquisitions found only a temporary home in the library. A manuscript of historical texts once owned by the Cistercian abbey of Sawley, Yorkshire, was seen by John Bale at Westminster Abbey but had passed into the hands of Matthew Parker by 1567 (*DMC*, no. 133). Whether deliberately or through neglect, the manuscripts of the medieval library were soon dispersed. A fifteenth-century copy of Egidius Romanus, De regimine principum, now at Lambeth and formerly belonging to the abbey, was owned in the early seventeenth century by one of the new prebendaries (no. **60**). The present small collection is largely of post-medieval acquisition.[78]

* * *

It is noteworthy that while the dispersal and loss of manuscripts from St Paul's and Westminster Abbey make it impossible to illustrate the activities of a scriptorium at either foundation, entries in the present catalogue demonstrate that City institutions employed their own secretariats. We know that by the thirteenth century the cathedral retained a *scriptor librorum*,[79] and that by the end of the fourteenth the book trade was already well established in its vicinity.[80] A community of those involved in book production (parchmeners, scribes, illuminators, bookbinders) may already have been emerging earlier. Not only would the cathedral canons have provided a market, but also those who attended the local schools at St Paul's, St Mary's-le-Bow and St Martin-le-Grand.[81]

Thus the fair copies of the works of the dean, Ralph of Diss, produced under his supervision, are now thought more likely to have been written by scribes working in the neighbourhood rather than by a group of canons in an ecclesiastical scriptorium. Ralph's own collection of his histories (no. **42**) is, like other manuscripts produced for him, a handsome imposing volume. Professor Parkes has identified one of its scribes as the scribe of two presentation copies Ralph had made, one for William de Longchamp, chancellor of England (*DMBL*, no. 401), the other for Hubert Walter, archbishop of Canterbury (*DMC*, no. 129). The three differ strikingly from the manuscript made for Bishop Foliot of his letters (*DMO*, no. 661). Ralph was aware of what Parkes calls the 'emblematic' qualities of a script, and the scribe, who was probably hired as a specialist, wrote a large formal bookhand employed for the statement it made about the status of the texts copied and, in the case of the presentation copies, the status of their *destinataires*.

Ralph's concern for the look of the book is highlighted by the untidy appearance of the Foliot manuscript. This compilation of booklets, written by several scribes, was probably produced for London's bishop by members of his household. Their small informal hands lack a disciplined house style, nor do the scribes collaborate. Only one, who was responsible for putting the volume together, appears throughout it adding letters at the ends of quires in an everyday cursive hand. The hand of this compiler is that of three documents issued in Gilbert's name, and hence he at least must have been one of the bishop's *familia*.[82]

Westminster's twelfth-century monks presumably had been as desirous as monks elsewhere to acquire a collection of patristica, but it is in charters produced for the house that their activity as scribes is now to be seen. Richly endowed by Edward the Confessor (d. 1066), the abbey ceased to enjoy the patronage of his successors. Its lands and possessions were subject to loss and depradation. The monks consequently embarked on what has been tactfully described as 'a vigorous policy of self-help, namely to reinforce their title to their lands by judiciously augmenting their archives'.[83] Several forged charters, which the prior, Osbert de Clare, was responsible for drafting, were written by a single scribe in the 1120s and 1130s. At the same time at least five different scribes produced other, genuine, documents, including a grant by Abbot Gervase (1138-*c*.57) assigning to the precentor 8*s* from the tithes of Roding, Essex, for the repair of books.[84]

Possibly a psalter made for the abbey, between 1173 and 1220?, was produced in-house (*DMBL*, no. 860).[85] However, by the late twelfth century, monastic houses often commissioned scribes from outside to copy the books they required. Despite the 'domus scriptoriae' referred to in the customary of Richard de Ware, abbot of Westminster 1259-83,[86] when Abbot Litlyngton (1362-86) desired his new missal (no. **281**) he did not turn to a monastic scribe but retained a professional, Thomas Preston, for whose board and lodging payments are found in the abbot's Treasurer's rolls for 1382-84. Impressed by the way of life, Preston became a monk and sang his first mass in 1386-87. No other manuscript copied by him has been found, though perhaps he wrote the only other book besides the Missal described in the 1388 inventory as 'bonum', a lost Collectar also given by Litlyngton. A pamphlet (no. **280**) on the papal schism might have been written by one of the monks, since Westminster sent its monks to study at Oxford.[87] Although not noted for their scholarship, their keen interest in this topical issue is witnessed by several *determinationes* on the subject (delivered at the University *c*.1396) which Leland saw in the library.[88] In the late fifteenth century the monk bailiff, Thomas Clifford, asked William Ebesham, who also worked for Sir John Paston and who had sought refuge from his debts in the Sanctuary, to produce a new cartulary (no. **282**). Ebesham also wrote for the abbey the best copy of its history by John Flete.

Conversely, scribes or *clerici* were employed full-time at the Guildhall. When Carpenter died in 1442 nine who had worked for him were named in his will. Some of these individuals may have copied the 'Liber Albus' (no. **24**), produced during Carpenter's first year as common clerk of the City. In the late sixteenth century Thomas Weston, clerk, received £5 and promotion for copying 'Liber Fleetwood' (no. **23**). However, the oldest of the City's books, the 'Liber de antiquis legibus' (no. **18**), was compiled and mostly written by one of the aldermen. Arnald Thedmar's handwriting is an example of the cursive script that had developed by the mid-thirteenth century from the current handwriting of documents. The adoption of this cursive hand as a bookhand reflects the growth in literacy among the urban bourgeoisie, men like Thedmar, who had learnt to read and write the documentary hand in order to transact their daily business.[89] Thedmar was not an expert scribe; his letter forms are spiky, as if he stabbed at them rather than forming them with a controlled movement of the quill (pl. 27).

Some forty years later, however, when the fishmonger Andrew Horn compiled 'Liber Horn' and 'Liber Custumarum' (nos **19** and **20**), he employed scribes and artists.[90] 'Liber Horn' is a small book, written in Anglicana, which originally opened with a page (now fol. 206) displaying a large illuminated historiated initial and full-page decorated border which incorporates a coat of arms depicting a fish and the saltire cross of St Andrew. 'Liber Custumarum' is a much more imposing tome. Twice as large as no. **19**, its scribes employed an elevated version of Anglicana, Anglicana Formata. The more formal script served to enhance the status of its contents: copies of the City's rights and privileges, which it was Horn's responsibility as City Chamberlain, 1320-28, to defend. The greater concern with calligraphy is paralleled by Horn's employment of artists associated with the Queen Mary Psalter workshop, whose work is otherwise found in de luxe liturgical manuscripts.[91]

The desire to ensure the city's dignity was upheld by the suitable appearance of its custumals is clearly seen in the case of 'Liber Dunthorne' (no. **22**). In 1474 William Dunthorne, common clerk, received the sum of £115 3*s* 3*d* in order that one or two new books containing all the City's ordinances might be made. Although a major part of the money would probably have been spent on Dunthorne's research expenses, the resulting volume is over a foot tall (425 × 300 mm), written in Anglicana Formata, with gold initials and bearing the City's coat of arms and is likely to have cost a considerable amount.

The civic pride expressed by the outward form of the city's custumals is seen also in the Ordinance books of the City Livery Companies. The rules or ordinances of a guild or fraternity, often accompanied by the texts of the oaths members swore to obey and preceded by extracts from the gospels and a kalendar, were usually entered in a specially donated or purchased volume.[92] Such volumes were designed to be impressive, both in terms of script and decoration, to maintain the honour of the guild. Thus the Skinners' Book of the Fraternity of the Assumption of our Lady (no. **145**) is a deluxe volume with elaborate decoration. Even lesser misteries saw to it that the format and presentation of text in their books signified the authority and prestige of their company. The ordinance book of the Fellowship of Surgeons, for example (no. **1**), compiled some five years after the erstwhile rival Barbers and Surgeons had settled their differences, was written in Textura, a script more commonly employed in liturgical manuscripts. The choice of script in such a book was surely intended to convey a statement about the importance of the texts it contained, as well as perhaps lending an air of antiquity to the company. The Parish Clerks' Bede Roll of the Fraternity of St Nicholas (no. **37**) records the annual lists of members, both living and death, in Textura. Each list of names is introduced with an illuminated decorated initial and border. When Queen Elizabeth Woodville became a member of the company in 1480, her name was entered in letters of gold. Like 'Liber Dunthorne', such books represent a considerable investment on the part of the authorities.

By the fifteenth century most companies employed a salaried clerk, such as William Porlond, clerk of the Brewers' Company (no. **39**), or William Duryvale of the Merchant Taylors' (no. **111**). Duryvale subscribed the Scriveners' Company 'Common Paper' (no. **38**) in a small splayed Secretary hand but when he wrote the Company's 'Book of Oaths' he adopted a larger, more upright, module of the script. Preserving as it did its traditions, his ordinary business hand was clearly felt to be inappropriate in such a volume. The copy of the English ordinances of Richard Whittington's Almshouses (no. **110**), was also written in Secretary but only bound in limp vellum. Nevertheless, the Mercers' Company which administered Whittington's trust engaged the master William Abell to supply a frontispiece to the text. The colophon suggests a clerk with literary tastes for he bursts into verse, begging the masters of the company to accept the manuscript favourably. The scribe's envoy somewhat incongruously begins 'Go litel boke go litel tregedie ...'.[93]

* * *

With the losses of the medieval libraries of St Paul's Cathedral, Guildhall, and Westminster Abbey (see above), entries in the present catalogue mainly come from libraries established between the sixteenth and twentieth centuries. Hence, in general, their medieval manuscript collections were not formed as part of a working library but were acquired as the result of post-medieval benefactions or bequests. Of the earlier libraries only the manuscript library of the College of Arms was formed with a specific focus (on heraldic materials), other collections reflecting the interests (antiquarian, aesthetic or literary) of individual donors.

College of Arms: Although the college was first incorporated by a charter of Richard III in 1484, the library was not finally established until 1597. This was primarily due to the annulment of all Richard's acts by his successor, Henry VII (1485-1509), whereupon the heralds lost the house Richard had granted them. Here they are said each to have 'had his place several for his own library', as well as to have owned some books in common. What happened to these 'office books' became a matter of dispute between Thomas Wrythe, Garter King of Arms 1504-34 and Thomas Benolt, Clarenceux King of Arms (1511-34); see most recently, L.R. Mooney, 'A new manuscript by the Hammond scribe', *The English medieval book; studies in memory of Jeremy Griffiths*, ed. A.S.G. Edwards, V. Gillespie, and R. Hanna (2000), pp. 113-23. Given a new charter and new home by Philip and Mary in 1555, the heralds were directed in 1568 by the Earl Marshal, Thomas Howard, Duke of Norfolk, to establish a library. Little seems to have been done about this until the late sixteenth century, and disputes continued to arise between heralds over the ownership of books; see P.M. Selwyn, '"Such speciall bookes of Mr Somersettes as were sould to Mr Secretary", the fate of Robert Glover's collections', *Books and collectors 1200-1700; Essays presented to Andrew Watson*, ed. J.P. Carley and C.G.C. Tite (1997), pp. 389-401.

Once established, heralds and others began to leave the library their books. However, the major collection of fifty-four medieval manuscripts was not acquired until 1678, when Henry Duke of Norfolk was persuaded by the antiquary William Dugdale, Chester herald, to present to the college that part of the manuscript collection formed by his grandfather Thomas Earl of Arundel (1585-1646), which dealt with history and heraldry. Many of Thomas's manuscripts had formerly been owned by his step-uncle Lord William Howard of Naworth Castle, Cumberland (1563-1640), who began collecting manuscripts in the 1580s. No catalogue of William's library survives, so the identification of his books depends on his *ex libris* (nos **2, 3**), a pen and ink sketch of his arms of lion rampant (no. **5**), or annotations (nos **4, 7**). The Arundel manuscripts are described by Black, along with ten non-Arundel volumes; for other manuscripts, see Campbell and Steer. For the library's history, A.R. Wagner, *The records and collections of the College of Arms* (1952), and R. Dennys, *The heraldic imagination* (1975).

The history of the libraries of the Inns of Court effectively begins in the sixteenth century, although the societies themselves are medieval foundations. Their libraries remained small until the seventeenth century and were not at first exclusively legal. Likewise, the library of the Royal College of Physicians was not at first confined to medicine. The manuscript collections of these institutions are chiefly the result of seventeenth-century donations.

Lincoln's Inn: The earliest reference to a library here or at any of the Inns occurs in 1475 (see above, p. 8). The single most important collection is the bequest of Sir Matthew Hale, 1609-76, Chief Justice of the King's Bench, for whom see E. Heward, *Matthew Hale* (1972). Hale was friend and executor of the antiquarian John Selden, 1584-1654, from whom he inherited some volumes, including nos **102**, **106**.

Gray's Inn: Although the society has no extant records before 1569, we know of bequests made to a library in 1488 (see above p. 8 and n. 71), and in 1555. It slowly grew from this time and after 1646, when it was discovered that an unspecified number of books had been removed, a library keeper was appointed and the books chained; see W.R. Prest, 'Law, learning and religion: gifts to Gray's Inn library in the 1630s', *Parergon*, n.s., 14 (1996-7), 205-22. Although Prest refers to MS 21, a copy of Bracton given by John Godbold, Reader 1634, he otherwise discusses only the donation of printed books including one given by John Bostock, Barrister 1636. He seems unaware of Ker's suggestion (*MMBL*, I: 50-51) that twenty of the twenty-four medieval manuscripts belonging to the Inn were given to it by the same John or his father Richard. Seventeen of the 'Bostock' manuscripts contain annotations in the same sixteenth-century hand as twelve manuscripts Richard Bostock donated to Shrewsbury School in 1607. The annotator would appear to have been 'a displaced monk [of Chester] who collected books from the neighbouring religious houses immediately after the Dissolution', since many of the books concerned come from Chester Abbey. Brief mention is made of the library's later history in F. Cowper, *A prospect of Gray's Inn*, 2nd revised edn by J. Geldart (1985).

Inner Temple: The first reference to a library at the Inner Temple dates from 1506. The chief manuscript collection is that of William Petyt (1637-1707), Keeper of the Records in the Tower of London and Treasurer of the Inner Temple 1701-2. For a detailed history of the library, see Conway Davies, I: 1-167.

Middle Temple: Robert Ashley, 1565-1641, bequeathed his library along with an endowment for its upkeep after an earlier library had disappeared. Two of the four medieval manuscripts the society owns were given in 1677 by Elias Ashmole, for whom see *Elias Ashmole 1617-1692: the founder of the Ashmolean Museum and his world*, catalogue of a tercentenary exhibition, ed. M. Hunter (1983).

Royal College of Physicians: The College of Physicians was founded in 1518 to regulate the practice of medicine within London, and ultimately came to exercise a national function as the Royal College of Physicians. For the College's founder and first President, Thomas Linacre, see *BRUO* 1147-49; C. Webster, 'Thomas Linacre and the foundation of the College of Physicians', *Essays on the life and work of Thomas Linacre c.1460-1524*, ed. F. Maddison, M. Pelling and C. Webster (1977), pp. 198-222; and for his own library, G. Barber, 'Thomas Linacre: a bibliographical survey', *Essays on the life and work*, pp. 331-36. The original library, established at the same time as the college, was destroyed in 1666, and only ten manuscripts were saved, including no. **137**. The library of Henry Pierrepont (1606-80), Marquess of Dorchester, was given to replace it. See further E. Boswell, 'The library of the Royal College of Physicians in the Great Fire', *The Library*, 4th ser., 10 (1930), 313-26; G. Davenport in *The Royal College of Physicians and its Collections: an illustrated history*, ed. G. Davenport, I. McDonald, and C. Moss-Gibbons (2001), pp. 70-95.

The seventeenth-century libraries of Lambeth Palace, Dulwich College and Sion College acquired manuscript collections from their foundations, although that of Sion College was almost totally lost in the Great Fire.

Lambeth Palace Library: The library was established by the terms of the will of Richard Bancroft, archbishop of Canterbury 1604-10, a catalogue of whose books includes 472 manuscripts. These and the manuscripts left by Bancroft's immediate successor, George Abbot (d. 1633), form the nucleus of the collection of medieval manuscripts. During the Commonwealth, 1649-60, the archiepiscopacy was suppressed and the library removed to Cambridge University Library. The books were returned to Lambeth after the restoration of the monarchy, where they were re-catalogued by William Sancroft, archbishop 1678-90. Sancroft's own books were left to Emmanuel College Cambridge. See further A. Cox-Johnson, 'Lambeth Palace Library 1610-1664', *TCBS*, 2 (1954-58); M.R. James, 'The manuscripts in the library at Lambeth Palace', *Cambridge Antiquarian Society*, Octavo Publications no. 33 (1900), 64; James's posthumously published 'The history of Lambeth Palace Library', *TCBS*, 3 (1959-63), 1-31; and N.R. Ker, 'Archbishop Sancroft's rearrangement of the manuscripts of Lambeth Palace', *Catalogue of the Manuscripts in the Lambeth Palace Library MSS. 1222-1860*, ed. G.G.W. Bill (1972). For details of more recent *fonds*, see M. Barber, *Handlist of Catalogues and Indexes of the Archives and Manuscripts in Lambeth Palace Library* (1998).

The library now includes all but four of the manuscripts formerly belonging to Sion College (see below).

Dulwich College: The college was established by Edward Alleyn (1566-1626), the Shakespearian actor who founded the Fortune Theatre, as the College of God's Gift at Dulwich. For an account of the foundation and school, see S. Hodges, *God's Gift, a living history of Dulwich College* (1981). Alleyn bequeathed to it his books and personal papers, including those of his wife's stepfather, Philip Henslowe (*c*.1555-1615), owner and manager of the Rose Theatre. His gift was augmented by others over the years. For a brief history, see G.F. Warner, *Catalogue of the manuscripts of Alleyn's College of God's Gift at Dulwich* (1881).

Sion College: The college was founded by Dr Thomas White, rector of St Dunstan-in-the-West and founder of the Oxford chair of Moral Philosophy, d. 1624, as a meeting place for London clergy. The library itself, opened in 1630 and chained until 1720, had a strong Presbyterian bias. The college acquired eighteen manuscripts of its own between 1629 and 1664, a collection that was increased during the Commonwealth period by the transfer to the college of the manuscripts of St Paul's Cathedral. This combined collection was almost totally destroyed in the Fire of London, 1666. Nos **142**, **143** were among nine Sion survivors. Subsequent donations increased Sion's collection to thirty-four manuscripts. For a brief history of the library and its benefactors, see E. Edmondston, 'Unfamiliar Libraries IX: Sion College', *The Book Collector*, 14 (1965), 165-77.

Four of the manuscripts described in 1969 (*MMBL*, I: 263-91) were sold in 1977: MSS Arc. L.40/2/L.9, Suetonius (now San Marino, Huntington Library HM 45717), L.21, Suetonius (Oxford, Bodleian Library, Lat.class. d.39), L. 28, Hugo de Folieto (Los Angeles, Getty Museum, Ludwig XV.3), and E. 23, *Canterbury Tales* (Tokyo, T. Takamiya, MS 22). The remainder were transferred to Lambeth Palace Library on the college's closure in 1996.

The remaining libraries represented in the catalogue are:

Society of Antiquaries: Although some trace the society's origins to *c*.1586, the intellectual climate of the court of James I did not favour antiquarian study and meetings ceased. The society was not (re-)founded until the eighteenth century, when regular meetings began to take place from 1717. The first major bequest of manuscripts (including no. **148**) was that of Charles Lyttelton, bishop of Carlisle and President of the Society, d. 1768. In 1790 the Society bought the Winton Domesday (no. **152**). See further J. Evans, *A History of the Society of Antiquaries* (1956), and on the growth of the manuscript collections, Willetts, pp. xi-xxiii.

Dr Williams's Library: The 'public library, whereto such as my Trustees shall appoint shall have access', founded under the terms of the will of Dr Daniel Williams (*c*.1643-1716), Presbyterian minister, was first opened in 1729 in Cripplegate. It moved to its present home in Gordon Square, Bloomsbury, in 1890. Dr Williams made no provision for book purchase, although he bequeathed over 6,000 volumes, and it was not until 1805 that any income from the Trust was permitted to be spent on books. The eight medieval manuscripts result from later donations. For a brief history, written on the occasion of the Library's 250th anniversary, see the library's pamphlet *The Founder and his Library*.

The Library also now owns the two manuscripts formerly belonging to New College, London (*MMBL*, I: 162-63). These were received in 1976-77 when the Governors, upon the latter's closure as a theological college, donated some 12,000 volumes. The manuscripts of the Congregational Library (see below) are also now available here.

Royal Astronomical Society: The library was founded on the society's inception in 1820. For a listing of its manuscript collection, see J.A. Bennett, 'Catalogue of the Archives and Manuscripts of the Royal Astronomical Society', *Memoirs of the Royal Astronomical Society*, 85 (1978), 1-90. It owns only three medieval volumes which have been re-shelved since they were catalogued in *MMBL*, I: 192-96. They are now Add. MSS 1 and 2. Add. MS 1 includes two separate volumes, the former QB. 7/1021 and QB. 7/1022 (no. **135**), both given in 1845 by the Rev. Charles Turnor.

Law Society: The Law Society, founded in 1825, is the professional body of solicitors in England and Wales. Its library dating from 1828 has been built up by donation and purchase. The ten medieval manuscripts described *MMBL*, I: 115-23 include four belonging to the Mendham Collection (MSS 2, 3, 5, 9). Formed by the Rev. Joseph Mendham of Sutton Coldfield (d. 1856), this collection was given to the society in 1869. It has now been deposited at Canterbury Cathedral Library and is described *Catalogue of the Law Society's Mendham Collection*, ed. S. Hingley and D. Shaw (1994).

University College London: The library dates from 1829 but grew only slowly in the nineteenth century, depending mainly on benefactions. Apart from isolated gifts, eleven medieval manuscripts were bequeathed by John Graves, professor of Jurisprudence, d. 1870. The purchase of manuscripts to develop the study of palaeography within the college was initiated by Robert Priebsch, professor of German, d. 1931. Many of UCL's German and Swiss manuscripts had once been owned by the bibliomaniac, Sir Thomas Phillipps (1792-1872). In 1953 seven manuscripts, owned by C.K. Ogden (1889-1957), were purchased with the aid of a grant from the Nuffield Foundation. For a brief history, see G. Furlong, 'University College London's manuscripts and rare books', *University College London Old Students Association* (1993), 8-14.

Congregational Library: Established in 1831-33 as a subscription library on the initiative of Joshua Wilson (1795-1875) and others, for the congregations of Independent churches which at this time were forming themselves into the Congregational Union in England and Wales. The library closed in 1866 when its original premises were purchased for railway development, and only re-opened in 1875 in Farringdon Street. The manuscripts were still there when described *MMBL*, I: 12-18, but subsequently moved with the rest of the library to Cricklewood. In 1978 it came under the Congregational Memorial Trust Ltd, and in 1982 moved again to accommodation adjacent to Dr Williams's Library in Gordon Square, Bloomsbury, where the manuscripts can now be consulted. See further J. Cressey, *The Congregational Library*, Congregational Lecture 1992.

Sir John Soane's Museum: The architect Sir John Soane (1753-1837) transferred his house and the museum which he had created to the nation in 1833. He also bequeathed an endowment to the Trustees to provide for it as the first public museum and library in Britain on architecture. For Soane and his collections, see further G. Darley, *Sir John Soane, an accidental romantic* (1999).

United Grand Lodge of England (Freemasons' Hall): The library was formed in 1837, although the history of the masons in London dates back to the middle ages, see D. Knoop and G.P. Jones, 'The London Masons'

Company', *Economic History*, 4 (1938-39), 157-66. For its collections, see A. Tudor-Craig, *Catalogue of the Manuscripts and Library at Freemasons Hall* (1938).

Victoria and Albert Museum, National Art Library: The library originated at the Government School of Design founded at Somerset House in 1837. It moved, first in 1852 to Marlborough House, to the Museum of Ornamental Art established there by Henry Cole to perpetuate the Great Exhibition of 1851, and then again in 1857 to South Kensington. A major donation of manuscripts was made in 1902-3 by George Reid. See E. Bonython, *King Cole: a picture portrait of Sir Henry Cole, KCB, 1808-1882* (1982); R. Watson, 'Educators, collectors and fragments, and the "illuminations" collection at the Victoria and Albert Museum in the nineteenth century', *Interpreting and Collecting*, pp. 21-46.

University of London Library: The library originated in 1838 but its development dates from its formal opening in 1876-77. Its first medieval manuscript was acquired in 1920. Since the description of its medieval manuscripts in 1969 (*MMBL*, I: 365-78), the library has acquired six further manuscripts, to be described in *MMBL*, V (forthcoming). Three of them come from the estate of the late N.R. Ker. On the collections, see J. Gibbs and P. Kelly, 'Manuscripts and archives in the University of London Library', *Archives*, 11 (1974), 161-71.

Oratory: The London Oratory was established in the City in 1850, and moved to Brompton in 1854 (hence it is popularly known as 'Brompton Oratory'). Its library was mainly assembled between 1854-1900 by the Fathers and benefactors. The greatest single donor was David Lewis (1814-95), a disciple of Newman whom he followed into the Catholic church. Five of its twelve medieval manuscripts were left by Lewis. See further R. Price, 'The library and its benefactors', *The London Oratory: Centenary 1884-1984*, ed. M. Napier and A. Laing (1984), pp. 85-105.

Southwark Catholic Diocesan Archives: The diocese of Southwark was formed in 1850 on the restoration of the Catholic Hierarchy in that year. Five of the nine medieval manuscripts described in 1969 (*MMBL*, I: 320-31) were the gift of Daniel Rock (1799-1871), canon of the cathedral. Since their description, MS 4 has been deposited as BL Loan 85/4. No. **158**, not in *MMBL*, is of unknown provenance. For the collections, see M. Clifton, 'Southwark Diocesan Archives', *Catholic Archives*, 4 (1984), 15-24.

Public Record Office: Established in Chancery Lane between 1851 and 1899 following the Public Records Act of 1838, the PRO has moved to Kew since the description of some of its medieval manuscripts in 1969 (*MMBL*, I: 179-92). On the collections, see *Guide to the contents of the Public Record Office*, 3 vols (1963-68).

Corporation of London Records Office: Established in 1876 to house the official archives of the Corporation of the City of London, the customals which had been retained in the Town Clerk's office since the Middle Ages were transferred here rather than to the Guildhall library. Only some of the City's customals are described *MMBL*, I: 18-42; for brief notices of others, see H. Deadman and E. Scudder, *An introductory guide to the Corporation of London Records Office* (1994), pp. 9-11.

Westminster Cathedral: The cathedral was founded by Cardinal Herbert Vaughan, archbishop of Westminster 1892-1903; its foundation stone was laid 1895. The manuscripts in the Treasury are unavailable to readers.

Westminster Diocesan Archive: The archdiocese came into existence in 1850, but the diocesan archive was not established until 1902. It contains only the one medieval manuscript. On its collections, see P. Hughes, 'The "Westminster Archives"', *The Dublin Review*, 201 (1937), 1-11.

Wellcome Library for the History and Understanding of Medicine: The library was created as part of the Wellcome Historical Medical Museum by Sir Henry Wellcome, FRS (1853-1936), founder of the pharmaceutical company Burroughs Wellcome and Co. For him, see H. Turner, *Henry Wellcome: the man, his collection and his legacy* (1980). The library was not opened to readers until 1946. Little was added to the manuscript collections in the decades after Sir Henry's death until the 1960s and 1970s when they began again to be acquired. He had been an omnivorous collector, but recent acquisitions have focused on materials for the history of medicine. The manuscripts are described by Moorat, with supplementary notices on forty-four of them in *MMBL*, I: 393-401. More recent acquisitions are described by R.J. Palmer, *Catalogue of Western Manuscripts 5120-6244 in the Wellcome Library for the History and Understanding of Medicine* (2000).

   The collection now includes the manuscripts of the Medical Society of London (*MMBL*, I: 148-52) bought for the Library in 1984.

National Maritime Museum: Opened in 1937 as the National Museum of Maritime History, the Caird Library – so named in honour of Sir James Caird, shipowner and major benefactor (1864-1954) – contains the manuscript collections. These are mainly post-medieval and were largely developed under Caird and the Museum's first director, Sir Geoffrey Callender (d. 1946). For brief listings, see R.J.B. Knight, *Guide to the manuscripts in the National Maritime Museum*, 2 vols (1977-80).

City Livery Companies: Despite the medieval origins of the City Livery Companies, the libraries of the Worshipful Companies of Barbers, Drapers, Goldsmiths, and Mercers are modern. Their medieval ordinance books (nos **1**, **25**, **27**, **110**, and **111**) are retained with their archives; those of the Brewers, Merchant Taylors, Parish Clerks, and Skinners (nos **39**, **37**, **111**, and **145**) are deposited in the Guildhall Library. The best general history of the livery companies remains G. Unwin, *The gilds and companies of London*, with new introduction by W.F. Kahl, 4th edn (1963).

NOTES TO THE INTRODUCTION

1. The other British contributions cover the British Library, *DMBL*; Oxford Libraries, *DMO*; and Cambridge Libraries, *DMC*.

2. Cf. M.B. Parkes, 'Archaizing hands in English manuscripts', *Books and Collectors 1200-1700: Essays presented to Andrew Watson*, ed. J.P. Carley and C.G.C. Tite (1997), p. 127. For Wanley's pronouncement, see his 'Part of a Letter, written to a Most Reverend Prelate [Narcissus Marsh, Archbishop of Dublin], in answer to one written by his Grace, judging of the Age of MSS. the Style of Learned Authors, Painters, Musicians, etc. By Mr Humfrey Wanley. London, July 11. 1701', pr. *Philosophical Transactions*, no. 300 (June, 1705), pp. 1993-2008; repr. *Letters of Humfrey Wanley, Palaeographer, Anglo-Saxonist, Librarian, 1672-1726*, ed. P.L. Heyworth (1989), pp. 166-79.

3. In addition to colophons cited in dated and datable catalogues, see also the corpus collected by the Bénédictines du Bouveret, *Colophons de mss.*

4. Thus the proceedings of the 10th colloquium of the Comité international de paléographie latine were devoted to the subject; publ. *Scribi e colofoni: le sottoscrizioni di copisti dalle origini all'avvento della stampa*, ed. E. Condello and G. de Gregorio (1995).

5. See L. Reynhout, 'Pour une typologie des colophons de manuscrits occidentaux', *Gazette du livre médiéval*, no. 13 (1988), 1-4, and also his 'A propos de la formule "Finito libro, reddatur cena magistro", essai d'intreprétation comparative', *Scriptorium*, 42 (1988), 93-101.

6. Cf. P.R. Robinson, 'A twelfth-century *scriptrix* from Nunnaminster', *Of the Making of Books: Medieval Manuscripts, their Scribes and Readers. Essays presented to M.B. Parkes*, ed. P.R. Robinson and R. Zim (1997), pp. 73-93.

7. Oxford, University Archives WPß/F/46, an early-thirteenth-century conveyance of a property in Catte Street, next door to a binder's, is witnessed by a scribe, three illuminators, and two parchment makers. For further evidence, see M. Michael, 'English illuminators c.1190-1450: a preliminary survey from documentary sources', *English Manuscript Studies*, 4 (1993), 63-68.

8. J.P. Gumbert, 'The speed of scribes', *Scribi e Colofoni*, pp. 71-9; and see also M. Gullick, 'How fast did scribes write? Evidence from Romanesque manuscripts', *Making the Medieval Book: Techniques of Production*, ed. L.L. Brownrigg (1995), pp. 39-58 and E.A. Overgaauw, 'Fast or slow, professional or monastic. The writing speed of some late-medieval scribes', *Scriptorium*, 49 (1995), 211-27.

9. See *DMC*, pp. 9-12, where I suggest some possible reasons;

also A. Derolez, 'Pourquoi les copistes signaient-ils leurs manuscrits?', *Scribi e colofoni*, pp. 37-56.

10. Cf. C.R. Cheney, 'Notaries public in Italy and England in the late Middle Ages', *Studi Senesi*, 92 (1980), 173-88.

11. C.W. Brooks, 'The histories of the London Scriveners' Company and the Notaries of London before 1700', in C.W. Brooks, R.H. Hemholz and P.G. Stein, *Notaries Public in England since the Reformation* (1991), pp. 52-75.

12. Cf. E.A. Overgaauw, 'Where are the colophons? On the frequency of datings in late-medieval manuscripts', *Sources for the History of Medieval Books and Libraries*, ed. R. Schlusemann, J.M.M. Hermans and M. Hoogvliet (1999), pp. 81-93.

13. See R. Watson, 'Educators, collectors, fragments, and the "Illuminations" collection at the Victoria and Albert Museum in the nineteenth century', *Interpreting and collecting fragments of medieval books*, ed. L.L. Brownrigg and M.M. Smith (2000), pp. 21-46.

14. For map, see *The Times London Atlas*, ed. H. Clout (1991), pp. 50-51, and on hospitals, C. Rawcliffe, 'The hospitals of later medieval London', *Medical History*, 28 (1984), 1-21.

15. See J.H. Baker, 'The books of the common law', *The Cambridge History of the Book in Britain*, III, *1400-1557*, ed. L. Hellinga and J.B. Trapp (1999), pp. 413-17. In the present catalogue a digest of case law (no. **31**) was written for Thomas Segden, Principal of Furnival's Inn, Holborn, while a copy of the Nova Statuta Angliae (no. **103**) was owned by Gregory Adgore, Serjeant at Law.

16. Twenty-seven are recorded in Ker, *MLGB* and *Supplement*, to which D. Williman, 'Some additional provenances of Cambridge Latin manuscripts', *TCBS*, 11 (1999), 443, 445, 446, has added three more.

17. Thus 'Bede in Anglico', 'Practica Bede in Anglico', and 'Donatus Bede in Anglico' cf. *BRUO*: 2147-48; also S.H. Cavanaugh, *A Study of Books privately owned in England 1300-1450*, Unpubl. PhD thesis, Univ. of Pennsylvania, 1980, pp. 64-69.

18. *BRUO*: 745-48. Gascoigne's gifts survive as Aberdeen University Library MSS 137 and 241, and Oxford, Bodleian Library, James 23; he may also have meant the cathedral to receive Oxford, Balliol College, MSS 45 and 46, a two-volume Aquinas.

19. BL Cotton Roll XIII. 11; pr. W. Dugdale, *The History of St Paul's Cathedral in London*, with continuation and additions by H. Ellis (1818), pp. 392-98.

20. Guildhall 25271/46, endorsed with a note of probate 6 May 1361; see E. Rickert, 'Chaucer at School', *Modern Philology*, 29 (1932), 257-74.

21. For the 1245 inventory and the 1445 inventory of the Lady

Chapel, see W.S. Simpson, 'Two inventories of the cathedral church of St Paul, London', *Archaeologia*, 50 (1887), 496-500; for those of 1255 and 1295, see N.R. Ker, 'Books at St Paul's Cathedral before 1313', *Studies in London History presented to P.E. Jones*, ed. A. Hollaender and W. Kellaway (1969), pp. 41-72, repr. in his *Books, Collectors and Libraries*, pp. 209-42; and for that of 1486 (Cotton Roll XIII. 24) Dugdale, op. cit., pp. 399-401.

22. Identified by Williman, 'Additional provenances', as Cambridge University Library Kk.6.14.

23. Cf. P. Baxter, *Sarum Use: the development of a medieval code of liturgy and customs* (1994), p. 34. Twenty-six leaves from a late twelfth-century Breviary which refers to St Paul's Use might be such a discard or survive from one of the City's parish churches, see J. Brunius, 'Medieval manuscript fragments in Sweden: a Catalogue project', *Interpreting and Collecting*, p. 159

24. The present library contains two psalters (MSS 1 and 2) listed in the 1486 inventory.

25. See further J.W. Clark, 'On ancient libraries', *Cambridge Antiquarian Soc. Proceedings and Communications*, 9 (1899), pp. 56-60; Ker, 'Books at St Paul's', and for the present collection of manuscripts, *MMBL*, I: 240-62.

26. Now Guildhall 25511. See further G. Yeo, 'Record-keeping at St Paul's Cathedral', *Journal of the Soc. of Archivists*, 8 (1986-87), 30-44.

27. This tally counts BL Add. 10052, 10053, and San Marino, Ca., Huntington Library HM 112 as a single volume.

28. Leland's list pr. K.W. Humphreys, *The Friars' Libraries*, Corpus of British Medieval Library Catalogues, I (1990), pp. 217-22.

29. See Humphreys, pp. 7-9 (Austin Friars), pp. 201-3 (Dominicans), and pp. xix and 178-88 (Carmelites). For Bale's extracts from the Dominican library catalogue, ibid., pp. 199-200.

30. For Leland's library tours, see the general remarks by J.P. Carley in the first of his series of articles on Leland's booklists , 'John Leland and the contents of English pre-dissolution libraries: Glastonbury Abbey', *Scriptorium*, 40 (1986), 107-20.

31. M. Harvey, 'The diffusion of the Doctrinale of Thomas of Walden in the fifteenth and sixteenth centuries', *Intellectual Life in the Middle Ages: Essays presented to Margaret Gibson*, ed. L. Smith and B. Ward (1992), pp. 281-94.

32. Westminster Abbey CC. 18, Repetitiones Lanfranci, pr. Johann Koelhoff, Cologne, 1488.

33. Pr. D.N. Bell, *The Libraries of the Cistercians, Gilbertines, and Premonstratensians*, Corpus of British Medieval Library Catalogues, 3 (1992), pp. 32-34; see also Christianson, *Directory*, p. 66.

34. Pr. E.M. Thompson, *The Carthusian Order in England* (1930), pp. 323-30. Cambridge, Christ's College 4, has been identified as one of the books sent to the Charterhouse of St Anne, Coventry; cf. Williman, 'Additional provenances', p. 429. A printed book and a flyleaf from a lost volume of sermons are assigned to the London Charterhouse in *MLGB*.

35. D.N. Bell, *What Nuns Read; Books and Libraries in Medieval English Nunneries* (1995), pp. 151-52, details two wills leaving books to the Minoresses.

36. Westminster Abbey Muniment 9487, a paper booklet of four folios.

37. Trinity College Dublin 436 (for which see M.L. Colker, *Trinity College Library Dublin: Descriptive Catalogue of the Mediaeval and Renaissance Latin Manuscripts*, 2 vols (1991), II: 866-67), and Oxford, Bodleian Library, e Mus. 113 (*SC* 3584); the first appears in an inventory of 1448 (see n. 38) but the second cannot be identified. Both volumes were given by Thomas Dye and Alice, his wife.

38. BL Cotton Roll XIII. 10; J.P. Malcolm, *Londinium Redivivum; or, An Antient History and Modern Description of London*, 4 vols (1802-7), I: 27-30 prints the list of library books but not those in the sacristy.

39. A copy of the *Florarium* survives as no. **142**. The church of St Andrew Hubbard sold a copy in 1483; cf. the church-wardens' accounts, Guildhall 1279/1 (I owe this information to Fiona Kisby). For Mirfield's medical work, see F. Getz, 'John Mirfield and the *Breviarium Bartholomei*: the medical writings of a clerk at St Bartholomew's Hospital in the later fourteenth century', *Bulletin of the Soc. for the Social History of Medicine*, 37 (1985), 24-26.

40. St Bartholomew's Hospital HC 2/1 ('Cok's Cartulary'), fol. 69. The bible, the only one among the recovered items to be extant, is Wolfenbüttel, Herzog August Bibliothek, Extravagantes 25.1, cf. A.G. Watson, 'The manuscript collection of Sir Walter Cope', *Bodleian Library Record*, 12 (1986-88), p. 296 no. 28.

41. See BL Royal 15.c.xvi (given by Henry Spicer (d. 1437), canon of Windsor, pledged as security by John Neele, Master 1432-63, to the Bonshommes of Ashridge, and restored by James Butler, earl of Ormond, 1452-61) and Royal 3.A.ix (given by William Pykenham, archdeacon of Suffolk 1472-97). The marks of a brass chain staple are visible in what would have been the bottom right corners of the upper covers of their medieval bindings.

42. See J. Crick, *The Historia Regum Britannie of Geoffrey of Monmouth, III: A Summary Catalogue of the Manuscripts* (1989), no. 111; S. Harrison Thomson, *Latin Bookhands of the later Middle Ages, 1100-1500* (1969), pl. 102.

43. Cf. J. Taylor, *The Universal Chronicle of Ranulf Higden* (1966), pp. 105-9. The Austin Friars' copy is TCD 486, the Franciscans' Oxford, Bodleian Library, Laud misc. 545, and that from the Hospital of St Thomas of Acon, BL, Royal 14. C. xii.

44. Cf. C. Wordsworth and H. Littlehales, *The Old Service Books of the English Church* (1904), p. 29, for the books a church was required to possess. On parish libraries generally, see now J. Shinners, 'Parish libraries in medieval England', *A Distinct Voice: Medieval Studies in honor of Leonard E. Boyle, O.P.*, ed. J. Brown and W.P. Stoneman (1997), pp. 207-30.

45. R.E. Lewis and A. McIntosh, *A Descriptive Guide to the Manuscripts of the Prick of Conscience* (1982) record 115 manuscripts. Wordsworth and Littlehales, p. 48 illustrate the booklist. I hope to discuss it more fully elsewhere.

46. Guildhall 4424, fol. 33.

47. See for St Peter West Cheap, Guildhall 645/1, fol. 173 (a total of 29 books); St Martin Orgar, Guildhall 959/1, fol. 2ᵛ (21 books plus later additions); St Margaret Pattens, Guildhall 4569, fols 4-6 (23 books plus later additions), pr. W.H. St John Hope, 'Ancient inventories of goods belong-

ing to the parish church of St. Margaret Pattens in the City of London', *Archaeological Journal*, 42 (1885), 312-30; and St Christopher-le-Stocks, Guildhall 4424, fols 26-29 (29 books), pr. E. Freshfield, 'On the parish books of St. Margaret-Lothbury, St. Christopher-le-Stocks, and St. Bartholomew-by-the-Exchange, in the City of London', *Archaeologia*, 45 (1880), 111-120.

48. Guildhall 959/1, fol. 15: 'a booke called holcott uppon sapience'.

49. See Guildhall 1311/1, part 1, fol. 4, pr. E.S. Dewick, 'On an inventory of church goods belonging to the parish of St. Martin Ludgate', *Trans. of the St. Paul's Ecclesiological Soc.*, 5 (1905), 117-28. The inventory is in French.

50. Guildhall 1239/1, part 1, fols 9^v-10, pr. (somewhat inaccurately) by H. Littlehales, *The medieval records of a London City Church (St. Mary at Hill) A.D. 1420-1559*, EETS OS 125 (1905), pp. 26-28. See also C. Burgess, 'Shaping the parish: St Mary at Hill, London, in the fifteenth century', *The Cloister and the world: essays in medieval history in honour of Barbara Harvey*, ed. J. Blair and B. Golding (1996), pp. 246-86.

51. See St Bartholomew's Hospital SNC 1, fols 3-4, and H. Combes, 'Piety and belief in fifteenth-century London: an analysis of the fifteenth-century churchwardens' inventory of St Nicholas Shambles', *Transactions of the London and Middlesex Archaeological Soc.*, 48 (1997), 137-52.

52. For St Stephen Coleman Street, see Guildhall MS 4456, fols 8-9, pr. E. Freshfield, 'Some remarks upon the Book of Records and history of the parish of St. Stephen, Coleman Street, in the City of London', *Archaeologia*, 50 (1887), 17-57; and for All Hallows, All Hallows RR/J/5, muniment 138, pr. M.H. Cox and P. Norman, *The parish of All Hallows Barking, part I*, Survey of London, 12 (1929), pp. 70-75 (I owe my knowledge of the latter inventory to Fiona Kisby). For the text, see L.E. Boyle, 'The *Oculis sacerdotis* and some other works of William of Pagula', *Trans. of the Royal Historical Soc.*, 5th ser., 5 (1955), 81-110.

53. Westminster Abbey Muniment 6644, a parchment roll, pr. C. Burgess and A. Wathey, 'Mapping the soundscape: church music in English towns, 1450-1550', *Early Music History*, 19 (2000), 44-46.

54. For the more usual practice of citing the opening words of the second folio as a means of identifying books, see D. Williman and K. Corsano, 'Tracing provenances by *Dictio probatoria*', *Scriptorium*, 53 (1999), 124-45.

55. Guildhall 1279/1, fol. 34^v: 'Item resceyued of Pye stacyoner for a boke called decrees to hym by vs the said wardenis sold iij li Item resceyued of the same Pye stacyoner for a boke called the half bible of the old testament by vs to hym sold xxvj s viij d'.

56. *Statutes of the Realm*, IV (1819), 110-11. On the consequences of the Act, see C.E. Wright, 'The dispersal of the libraries in the sixteenth century', *The English Library before 1700*, ed. F. Wormald and C.E. Wright (1958), pp. 148-75.

57. H.B. Walters, *London Churches at the Reformation with an account of their contents* (1939), pp. 570, 334, 460, 610 respectively.

58. See N. Pickwood, 'The use of fragments of medieval manuscripts in the construction and covering of bindings on

printed books', *Interpreting and Collecting Fragments*, pp. 1-20.

59. See H.B. Frere, ' Some fragments of illuminated manuscripts', *Antiquaries' Journal*, 18 (1938), 180-82 and pl. 51.

60. Cf. C.M. Barron, *The Medieval Guildhall of London* (1974), p. 34; also W. Scase, 'Reginald Pecock, John Carpenter and John Colop's "common-profit" books: aspects of book ownership and circulation in fifteenth-century London', *Medium Aevum*, 61 (1992), 261-74.

61. R.R. Sharpe, *Calendar of Letter-Books preserved among the archives of the Corporation of the City of London*, 11 vols (1899-1912), *Letter Book K*, p. 295.

62. Barron, pp. 33-35

63. Cf. P.E. Jones, *Calendar of Plea and Memoranda Rolls of the City of London, 1458-1482* (1961), p. ix.

64. 'Prouiso semper quod si qui boni vel rari libri inter dictum residuum bonorum meorum inueniantur qui per discreciones predictorum magistrorum Willelmi lichefeld' et Reginaldi Pecok videantur neccessarij communi librarie apud Guyhald' in profectum studencium ibidem et sermonizancium communi populo tunc volo et lego quod libri illi per executores meos ponantur et cathenentur in libraria illa sub tali forma quod visores et studentes eorumdem citius moueantur ad deprecandum pro anima mea': Guildhall 9171/4, fols 84-85^v, dated 8 March 1441, probate 12 May 1442. For an Engl. translation, see T. Brewer, *Memoir of the Life and Times of John Carpenter, Town Clerk of London* (1856), pp. 131-44. The Edwardian inventory of the Guildhall's possessions refers to the library as being appointed for students of Divine Scripture, see J.J. Baddeley, *The Guildhall of the City of London*, 2nd edn (1899), p. 96.

65. Sharpe, *Letter Book K*, pp. 90-91

66. A list of books added to one of the Letter Books includes not only the Letter Books themselves but nos **18**, **19**, **21**, and **24**; cf. Sharpe, *Letter Book D*, pp. 317-18.

67. Guildhall 9171/4, fols 84-85^v.

68. *Cal of Plea and Memoranda Rolls*, p. 28. A list of books added on the endleaf of Letter Book D includes nos **19**, **20**, and **24**, see *Letter Book D*, pp. 317-18

69. See further P.E. Jones and R. Smith, *Guide to the Records in the Corporation of London Records Office and the Guildhall Muniment Room* (1951), pp. 22-24 and 182-4, and for the manuscripts, *MMBL*, I: 18-42 and 67-87.

70. J.H. Baker, 'The Inns of Court in 1388', *Law Quarterly Review*, 92 (1976), 184-87; cf. P. Brand, 'Courtroom and schoolroom: the education of lawyers in England prior to 1400', *Historical Research*, 60 (1987), 147-65.

71. Baker, 'The books of the common law', p. 413 and n. 16.

72. *Records of the Honorable Society of Lincoln's Inn: The Black Books*, 5 vols (1897-1968), I: 59, 136.

73. Westminster Abbey Muniments 9226 (with a contemporary copy, W.A.M. 9225*), pr. *English Benedictine Libraries*, pp. 615-25.

74. Ibid., pp. 625-30 (pr. from W.A.M. 6604 and 6603 respectively).

75. Cf. *MLGB* and *Supplement*. Hereford Cathedral O.VI.7, for which see R.A.B. Mynors and R.M. Thomson, *Catalogue of the Manuscripts of Hereford Cathedral Library* (1993), pp. 41-42, also formerly belonged to the abbey.

76. Canterbury Cathedral Lit MS A. 10.

77. Hereford Cathedral O.VI. 7, for which see n. 75 above.

78. On Westminster Abbey Library, see Clark, 'On ancient libraries', 45-56; *English Benedictine Libraries*, pp. 608-33; and L.E. Tanner, *The Library and Muniment Room*, Westminster Papers, no. 1 (1933); for its present manuscripts, J.A. Robinson and M.R. James, *The Manuscripts of Westminster Abbey* (1909), supplemented by *MMBL*, I: 401-15.

79. *Registrum statutorum et consuetudinem ecclesiae cathedralis Sancti Pauli Londinensis*, ed. W.S. Simpson (1873), pp. 73, 75 n, 133, 173 n

80. Christianson, *Directory*; see also his 'A community of book artisans in Chaucer's London', *Viator*, 20 (1989), 207-18.

81. See HMC, 9th Report and Appendix (1883), p. 29, and J.H. Round, *The Commune of London and other studies* (1899), p. 117.

82. Cf. A. Morey and C.N.L. Brooke, *The Letters and Charters of Gilbert Foliot* (1967), pp. xxxv-li and 2-7, and pls II-III for their Hand I (the compiler), IV for their Hand X. *DMO*, pl. 82 (a) and (b) illustrate Hands II and III.

83. E. Mason, *Westminster Abbey Charters 1066-c.1214*, London Record Soc., 25 (1988), p. 9.

84. Mason, no. 251; and see also P. Chaplais, 'The original charters of Herbert and Gervase abbots of Westminster (1121-1157)', *A Medieval Miscellany for Doris Mary Stenton*, ed. P.M. Barnes and C.F. Slade, Pipe Roll Soc., n.s. 36 (1962), pp. 89-110 and pl. VII (c).

85. A St Albans' origin has also been suggested for this manuscript, but see R.M. Thomson, *Manuscripts from St Albans Abbey 1066-1235*, 2 vols (1982), I: 61.

86. One of the earliest references in English sources to a room specifically set aside as a scriptorium, see *Customary of the Benedictine monasteries of St Augustine, Canterbury, and St Peter, Westminster*, ed. E.M. Thompson, 2 vols, HBS 28 (1904), II: 97.

87. B. Harvey, 'The monks of Westminster and the University of Oxford', *The Reign of Richard II: Essays in honour of May McKisack*, ed. F.R.H. Du Boulay and C.M. Barron (1971), pp. 103-30; J. Campbell, 'Gloucester College', *The Benedictines in Oxford*, ed. H. Wansbrough and A. Marett-Crosby (1997), pp. 37-47.

88. For Leland's list, see *English Benedictine Libraries*, p. 632, and for the pamphlet, P.R. Robinson, 'The format of books: books, booklets, rolls', *The Cambridge History of the Book*, II, *1100-1400*, ed. N. Morgan and R.M. Thomson (forthcoming).

89. Cf. M.B. Parkes, 'The Literacy of the Laity', *Literature and Western Civilization: the Medieval World*, ed. D. Daiches and A.K. Thorlby (1973), pp. 555-77, repr. in his *Scribes, Scripts and Readers: Studies in the Communication, Presentation and Dissemination of Medieval Texts* (1991), pp. 275-97.

90. For Horn and his books, see J. Catto, 'Andrew Horn: law and history in fourteenth-century England', *The Writing of History in the Middle Ages: Essays presented to R.W. Southern*, ed. R.H.C. Davis and J.M. Wallace-Hadrill (1981), pp. 367-91. Horn borrowed a herbal from the monks of Bermondsey Priory in return for depositing with them a copy of one of Hugutio of Pisa's grammatical treatises, cf. *English Benedictine Libraries*, p. 28.

91. Cf. L. Dennison, '"Liber Horn", "Liber Custumarum" and other manuscripts of the Queen Mary Psalter workshops', *Medieval Art, Architecture and Archaeology in London*, ed. L. Grant, British Archaeological Association (1990), pp. 118-34, and Sandler, *Gothic MSS*, no. 68.

92. C.R.H. Cooper, 'The archives of the City of London Livery Companies and related organisations', *Archives*, 16 (1983-84), 331.

93. This echoes a line from Chaucer's *Troilus and Criseyde* (cf. *The Riverside Chaucer*, gen. ed. L. Benson (1987), p. 584, Book V, line 1786); and see also *The Index of Middle English Verse*, ed. C. Brown and R.H. Robbins (1943), and *Supplement*, ed. C. Brown and J.L. Cutler (1965), nos 926-31, for examples of what had become a literary commonplace.

SCOPE OF THE PRESENT CATALOGUE

The intention is to describe all precisely dated manuscript books in institutional libraries in London outside the British Library (such BL manuscripts are recorded in *DMBL*). It should be noted that libraries included here do not necessarily overlap with those included in *MMBL* I, since not all the libraries described in that volume contain dated manuscripts.

The present catalogue includes dated manuscripts from 1286 to 1600, and manuscripts from the ninth to fifteenth centuries that are generally datable to within fairly precise chronological limits. In deciding whether or not to include such a datable manuscript, I have followed the principles adopted by Professor Watson in *DMO* (I: xv). Either a *terminus ante quem* or *terminus post quem* is considered sufficient to include a manuscript written before 1200. Thirteenth- and fourteenth-century manuscripts are included only when they are datable to within twenty-five years. Before the publication of *DMO* in 1984 dated manuscripts only had been catalogued for the fifteenth century, as in *DMBL*; with *DMO* the decision was taken to include fifteenth-century datable manuscripts when they were copied by English scribes. Whereas it was common practice among fifteenth-century continental scribes (particularly German and Italian copyists) to date their work, few scribes in England did so. Consequently, the total of fifteenth-century dated manuscripts recorded in the series as a whole contained a negligible proportion of manuscripts written by English (or indeed Scottish, Welsh, or Irish) scribes, whether in Latin or the vernacular. Since there proved to be so few dated specimens of fifteenth-century handwriting from Britain, it has seemed best to include datable specimens as well, as in *DMO*, *DMC*, and this catalogue. I have not attempted to include entries for datable fifteenth-century manuscripts from the BL here because time and publication costs did not permit. Manuscripts copied by foreign scribes in or after 1400 either on the continent, or in Britain, are catalogued only if they are precisely dated.

In practice most of the thirteen entries in this catalogue datable before 1200 have proved to be datable within a span of years, the longest timespan being the twenty-three years, 1120-*c*.1143, within which no. **65** was written. I have included a few thirteenth- to fifteenth-century manuscripts that are only approximately dated: for example, no. **2** given by John Erghome to the Austin Friars of York, since the date 1372, that of the house's library catalogue, suits the appearance of the handwriting. Although a different hand to that of the main cataloguer intercalates the 220 volumes given by Erghome, it appears the catalogue was deliberately planned to include his donation. Given such latitude, doubtless many more manuscripts could have been included, but too many instances might have created an imbalance in the provision of the kind of evidence for dating which it is the aim of these catalogues to provide.

The various criteria taken into consideration when determining whether or not a manuscript is datable are those set forth in *DMC* I: 17-18. Thus:

(i) Evidence from the text. The date when a text was completed provides a *terminus post quem* for a copy, and sometimes subsequent alterations or additions to a text when datable, can suggest a *terminus ante quem* for the copying of the original text (for example, nos **3**, **54**). A *terminus post quem* may be provided by a reference to a recent historical event, or, in the case of liturgical books, by the presence of a datable feast in the kalendar. Conversely, the absence of a datable feast does not establish a firm date before which such a book must have been written, since we do not know enough about precisely how a new feast was promulgated 'at all the levels needed to make it generally effective – or accepted' (R.W. Pfaff, *New Liturgical Feasts in Later Medieval England* (1970), 3).

(ii) Where the *destinataire* of a book can be identified, this can provide chronological limits for the production of that book (as nos **51**, **107**); and the first recorded owner can provide a *terminus ante quem* (nos **19**, **20**).

(iii) In some instances the origin of a manuscript can provide evidence for the chronological limits within which it must have been copied. For example, the scribes of no. **87** worked in Exeter during the episcopate of Bishop Leofric. Richard Calne who tells us he wrote nos **76** and **77** while he was up in Oxford must have worked between 1412 and 1421.

(iv) In the case of a well-known scribe the date of his death may be known. Thus no. **65** must have been copied before the death of William of Malmesbury in *c*.1143.

(v) External references where these agree with the palaeographical features of the manuscripts in question. For example, no. **281**, is mentioned in Abbot Litlyngton's Treasurer's rolls for the years 1382-84 (Litlyngton died in 1386), while payment for no. **22** is recorded in the City of London's archives. The early twelfth-century manuscript from Rochester Cathedral Priory, no. **53**, is included in the library catalogue datable before 1124.

There inevitably remains a degree of subjectivity in the dating of a manuscript, but I have not accepted evidence afforded solely by the palaeographical features or decoration of a manuscript.

The application of these criteria has led to the exclusion of some famous books from this catalogue. A list of rejected manuscripts appears at the end of the volume (pp. 97-101).

The intention here (as in the other catalogues of the series) is to illustrate the handwriting, where possible accompanied by a sample of decoration, of manuscript books. Documents are excluded even when they were written in book hands, although I have included cartularies, formularies, and registers of writs since such items have been included in previous volumes. I have also included the City of London's medieval Customals and the Ordinance Books of City Livery companies, although it could be argued that they are administrative volumes, such volumes having been omitted from previous catalogues.

I have made no attempt to emulate the examples of the French catalogues of dated and datable manuscripts which list undated or undatable manuscripts of known provenance, or written by named scribes. N.R. Ker's *Medieval Libraries of Great Britain* records manuscripts known to have been in institutional libraries in this country during the middle ages. For manuscripts copied by named scribes one can refer to the Bénédictins du Bouveret, *Colophons de manuscrits*.

ARRANGEMENT OF THE CATALOGUE
AND LAYOUT OF ENTRIES

Libraries are listed in alphabetical order with manuscripts in order of shelfmark, and the description of a manuscript is set out as follows:

1. *Heading* consisting of collection and shelfmark, with date and place of origin in abbreviated form to facilitate quick reference. *Dates derived from a manuscript's title or colophon are given in the form in which they occur in the manuscript, i.e. no attempt has been made to change Old Style or any other form of dating to New Style.* In the case of a few manuscripts maintained annually over a long period (e.g. Lambeth Palace 413), the date is expressed as 'annual entries 1417-1481'. When a manuscript is datable, dates are enclosed in square brackets. 'Betw(een) 1473 and 1475' means that writing took place at some unknown time between those dates. Places of origin are given in their modern form, e.g. Bubeneč, Czech Republic for Wellcome Library 16. When the name of a place appears in square brackets, with or without a query, this indicates that some positive evidence other than a colophon exists for assigning a manuscript to that place; when only the name of a country appears in square brackets this indicates that that country is a likely place of origin on the basis of such evidence as script, decoration, scribe's name, ownership, or language of a vernacular text. However, it is recognised that scribes and artists travelled and that, say, an Italianate manuscript need not have been produced in Italy.

2. *Content.* Identification of the content is summary; if a manuscript contains more than one item, only the first is identified unless the manuscript consists of two or more dated booklets in which case the first text in each booklet is identified. The formula punctuated as in 'Anselmus, Epistolae, etc.' indicates that the manuscript contains other works by the same author; whereas, when puncuated as follows 'Historia Freculphi; etc' this indicates that subsequent works are not by the same author. Titles of Latin works are given in Latin, titles of vernacular works in the appropriate vernacular, except for a few descriptive titles which are given in English: for example, nos **161**, **194**, **220**, and **264**.

3. *Physical description of the manuscript.* 'Parch(ment)' is used for all membrane. 'Parch(ment) and paper' means that parchment and paper quires in the volume are separate, 'parch(ment) and paper, mixed' means that quires are made up of a mixture of parchment and paper leaves. Only the number of extant medieval leaves is given. I give the dimensions of the leaves, followed by the layout of the written space (1 or 2 columns), the dimensions of the written space, and the number of lines per page. In describing decoration I specify miniatures (illuminated or not), borders (illuminated or coloured, full-page or not), initials (illuminated, inhabited, historiated, decorated, gold or coloured). Headings are called rubrics only when they are in red ink, otherwise I specify the colour of inks used. I also specify the colour of inks used to note feasts in a kalendar. Bindings are only mentioned if they are sixteenth century or earlier.

4. *Evidence of date.* When quoting a manuscript title or colophon, I have used the following conventions in transcription: square brackets [   ] enclose editorial explanations or other interpolations into the passage

quoted; diamond brackets < > enclose words or letters lost by deliberate erasure or accidental damage, or words or letters whose reading is uncertain because of damage to the manuscript; caret marks \ / indicate words or letters inserted by the scribe or in another early hand. Abbreviated Latin words are expanded silently but expansions of abbreviated vernacular words are indicated in italics. 'Fol. 1' indicates the recto of a leaf, 'fol. 1ᵛ' the verso.

I have then noted as appropriate:

5. *Evidence of origin*. It is often stated in a manuscript's colophon where a book was written. Sometimes the origin of a manuscript provides evidence for the date at which it was written, e.g. Lambeth Palace Library 393, written when the Augustinian canon Richard Calne was studying at Oxford.

6. *Other work by the same scribe*. I have attempted to record other manuscripts copied by the same scribe or to refer to a printed source where a list of the scribe's work may be found. Sometimes a scribe known to have been working in a particular place provides the evidence for the origin of the manuscript.

7. *Evidence of later history*. In the case of a composite volume where only the dated booklet has been described, some attempt has been made to identify the content of the rest of the manuscript. Institutional owners of all periods are recorded, but for reasons of space personal owners are recorded only up to *c*.1600.

8. *Bibliography*. This is not intended to be comprehensive (such a bibliography for Domesday Book would fill a book on its own). Primarily I have given references to works which contain illustrations of the script of a manuscript, but references to works containing illustrations of the decoration of a manuscript are usually included also. Other references are to works which contain a detailed discussion of the manuscript. Reference is made where they exist to library catalogues of the various collections or to the description of a manuscript in *MMBL* I.

9. *Reference to plates*. Each entry is illustrated with the exception of nos **15**, **100**, **117**, and **283**. Some entries are illustrated by more than one plate, but it has not been possible to illustrate every hand in volumes in which many scribes participated.

THE CATALOGUE

1   **Barbers' Company**   *[c.1497] [London, England]*
Ordinance Book of the Fellowship of Surgeons
Parch. 58 fols. 230 × 160 mm. 1 col., 133-38 × 93-100 mm. 19 lines. Painted coat of arms and tinted drawing (fol. 1ᵛ), col. inits, rubrics. Kal. in red and black. Blind-tooled leather bdg over boards, with clasps.

Two booklets preceded by a kalendar. The latest date recorded in the second booklet (fols 29-42, containing a copy of the Company's amended ordinances of 1492) is that of a copy of a licence granted 1497 ('viij day of August. the ȝere of oure lord god .Mᴵ . cccc. lxxxxvij') to one Robert Anson to practise surgery. The first booklet (fols 8-28, ordinances of 1435) and preceding kalendar (fols 2-7), written by different scribes, were probably copied about the same date. In space originally left blank on fols 8-28 further ordinances added by another hand (fols 23ᵛ-24ʳ) begin 'In þe name of god amen. In þe 28 day of september þe ȝere of owre [Lord] .1503. and in þe ȝere of kyng harry þe .7 þe 19'. The kalendar is preceded by a single leaf depicting on fol. 1ᵛ the Company's arms, granted 'The ȝere of owre lorde. Mᴵ. CCCC. lxxxxij. at the goyng ovyr the see of oure souereyn lord kyng Harry the .vijᵗʰ. In to fraunsse Thes armys were geuen on to the crafte of surgeons of london the vijᵗʰ ȝere of his reyng In the tyme of Hewe Clopton mayr'. Fols 43-58, though ruled, are blank.

> S. Young, *Annals of the Barber-Surgeons of London, compiled from their records and other sources* (1890), pls illus. fols 1ᵛ and 36-38 betw. pp. 68-69; R.T. Beck, *The Cutting Edge: Early History of the Surgeons of London* (1974), pp. 124-35; J. Dobson and R. Milnes Walker, *Barbers and Barber-Surgeons of London: A History of the Barbers' and Barber-Surgeons' Companies* (1979), pp. 97-98 and figs 2, 3 illus. fols 1ᵛ, 36 (reduced).
> *Pls 230, 231*

2   **College of Arms Arundel 6**   *[c.1372?] [England]*
Historia Freculphi; etc.
Parch. 148 fols, foliated i, 1-88, 88bis, 89-146. 350 × 224 mm. 2 cols, 258 × c.145 mm. 42-59 lines. Col. inits, rubrics.

A volume of histories, the latest of which extends to 1357. Fol. 1ᵛ: 'Iste liber est Fratris Johannis de Erghom', followed by a table of contents; item 165 in the catalogue of the library of the York Austin Friars (cf. *The Friars' Libraries*, ed. K.W. Humphreys, Corpus of British Medieval Library Catalogues (1990), p. 149). The catalogue's heading states it was drawn up in 1372, in Erghome's presence (among others), but his collection of over 220 volumes is 'intercalated' by a different hand (perhaps Erghome's own) from that of the main cataloguer (Humphreys, p. xxv). The date when Erghome's books entered the library cannot be precisely determined, but, if (as Humphreys argues, p. xxx) the catalogue was deliberately planned to include them, a date of *c.*1372 or shortly thereafter would suit the appearance of the script, and provide a *terminus a quo* for the present MS. Erghome is last heard of in 1385 but may not have died until 1406-8 (cf. J.B. Friedman, *John de Foxton's **Liber Cosmographiae** (1408): an Edition and Codicological Study* (1988), pp. xvii-xix).
Fol. 1: 'Edwardus Northeus Miles' (s. xvi). Fol. 145ᵛ: 'James Necton' (s. xvi). Fol. 146ᵛ: 'John Ortone', 'Davy Hough'. Fol.

2: '[Lord] William Howard 1607'; for other MSS owned by him see no. 4 below.

> Black, pp. 12-13; A. Gransden, *The Chronicle of Bury St Edmunds 1212-1301* (1964), pp. xxxvii-xxxviii; K.W. Humphreys, 'The library of John Erghome and personal libraries of the fourteenth century in England', *A Medieval Miscellany in honour of Professor John Le Patourel*, ed. R.L. Thomson, Proceedings of the Leeds Philosophical and Literary Society, 18, pt 1 (1982), 106-23; Humphreys, *Friars' Libraries*, pl. 3 illus. fol. 1ᵛ.
> *Pl. 61*

3   **College of Arms Arundel 10, fols 39-112**
[betw. 1225 and 1232]
[Barnwell, England]
Chronicon ('The Barnwell Chronicle')
Parch. 77 fols. 265 × 180 mm. 2 cols, 180 × 110 mm. 38-40 lines. Col. inits (fols 39-91), rubrics (fols 39-98). Leather bdg over boards, with clasp (s. xiii), s. xv title 'Hec de pontificibus <illegible> legibus Angliae et <illegible> Barnwell'.

Written in one hand to the year 1220 (fols 39-92), where another scribe takes over in mid-annal, and copies annals to 1225 (fols 92ᵛ-105ᵛ). A third scribe starts copying at the foot of fol. 105ᵛ (1226) and continues to fol. 110 (1232), where a fourth scribe takes over and concludes the entry for 1232 (fols 110-12). From fol. 106 (1226 onwards) the scribes write below top line (a change in scribal practice which developed in the second quarter of the thirteenth century; see further N.R. Ker, 'From "Above Top Line" to "Below Top Line": A Change in Scribal Practice', *Books, Collectors and Libraries*, pp. 71-74, and M. Palma, 'Modifiche di alcuni aspetti materiali della produzione libraria latina nei secoli xii e xiii', *Scrittura e civiltà*, 12 (1988), 119-33). Papal and episcopal lists at the beginning of the volume (fols 1-17) were copied by another scribe who concluded the list of popes with Honorius III (1216-27) and that of the bishops of Ely with Geoffrey de Burgo (1225-28). Fols 18-38 contain a Chronicle ending 1216 (the text is closely related to that in BL, Cotton Faustina B. VII (*DMBL*, no. 530, datable between 1208 and 1215); cf. W.H. Monroe, '13th and early 14th century genealogical manuscripts in roll and codex: Peter of Poitiers' *Compendium*, universal histories and chronicles of the kings of England', Unpubl. PhD thesis, University of London, 1990, pp. 222-26) by an early-thirteenth-century copyist. The last three leaves (fols 113, 114, 115) contain brief annals 1260-1309.
On fols 81, 83 marginal notes by hands of s. xiii record the death of William Devon, prior of Barnwell (d. 1213), the election of his successor, William Bedford, and the latter's death (1214). Fol. 115ᵛ: 'J. de Wangeford frater A. de Walsok salutem' (s. xiii). No. 7 in the list of books noted by Leland at the house, *c.*1536-40 (*Augustinian Libraries*, p. 7). Fol. 1: 'William Howard 1589'; for other MSS of Howard's, see no. 4 below. Fol. iii: 'Anno domini 1590 Doctor Griffin deane of Lincoln [1585-93] was convented [*sic*] before Jhon Whitgift archbishop of Canterbury for prechenge at Lincoln before the Justices of assisses that Christ was as wicked a sinner as euer Lyved on earth For which opinion he cyted martin Luther'.

> Black, pp. 16-17; W. Stubbs, *The Historical Collections of Walter of Coventry*, 2 vols (RS 1872-3), I: xli-xlii;

Gransden, *Hist. Writing*, I: 339-45.
Pl. 25

4   **College of Arms Arundel 23**   *[betw. 1473 and 1475]*
[London? England]

Genealogical Chronicle of the kings of England from Adam to Edward IV

Parch. 8 membranes, folded concertina fashion into 55 fols, each 223 × 157 mm. 2 cols, 113 × 170 mm. Up to 25 lines. Min. (fol. 2), col. roundels surmounted by gold crowns, gold inits with borders, col. inits, rubrics.

The chronicle runs to the coronation of Edward IV (1461). The scribe drew roundels for six children, so presumably this copy was written after the birth of the king's sixth child, Richard, in August 1473, but before the birth of his seventh, Anne, in November 1475, since throughout Edward's reign it seems to have been usual to compile fresh genealogies after the birth of each of his children (cf. A. Allan, 'Yorkist propaganda: pedigree, prophecy and the 'British History' in the reign of Edward IV', *Patronage, Pedigree and Power in Later Medieval England*, ed. C. Ross (1979), p. 174). However, only four children are named, the latest being Edward Prince of Wales, born November 1470. One of a group of chronicle rolls or roll-codices copied by the so-called 'Considerans' scribe, for whose work see Scott, *Later Gothic MSS*, II: 315-16. He also copied no. 161 below in which the initials 'T N' occur beside the final set of roundels. Other MSS by the scribe include Oxford, Corpus Christi College 207 (*DMO* no. 777), illustrated by the same artist as the present copy; Bodleian Library, Lyell 33 (*DMO*, no. 637) and e Musaeo 42 (*DMO*, no. 654); Brasenose College 17 (*DMO*, no. 758); and Copenhagen, Kongelige Bibliothek, Ny kgl. S.1858 2° (*Living Words & Luminous Pictures: Medieval Book Culture in Denmark*, ed. E. Petersen, Catalogue of an Exhibition held at the Royal Library, Copenhagen, 1999, no. 147). Because of the variety of artists found working with 'Considerans' and the provincial decorative styles of some of them, Scott suggests that 'Considerans' worked in London where he sold undecorated copies, which were taken away and illustrated elsewhere. Alternatively, he may have been an itinerant copyist and provincial buyers employed local artists. For the text and its format, see A. de la Mare, *Catalogue of the Collection of Medieval Manuscripts bequeathed to the Bodleian Library Oxford by James P.R. Lyell* (1971), pp. 80-85. Fol. 1: 'Liber thomae Corsaeri presbiteri a magistro Leche pro . Oswaldo in marcum. Et sententijs allegabilibus habitus 12° martij anno domini .1543. iuxta calculum anglicanum'; 'Liber guiliel. Bocheri emptus ab eun'str [*sic*,?] anno domini 1545 et 14 die Junij preci xx [ ]'; '[Lord] William Howarde' (1543-1640), of Naworth Castle, Cumbria, son of Thomas III, 4th Howard duke of Norfolk. In the two roundels originally left blank Howard supplied the names 'Richard d of York' (and beside that drew another roundel to contain '= Anne daughter & heire of [John] Moubray', last Mowbray duke of Norfolk) and 'Anne married to Thomas [I, 2nd] Howard duke of Norffolk'. Howard also owned nos 2-3, 5 and 7 in the present catalogue. For his books, see G. Ornsby, *Selections from the Household Books of Lord William Howard of Naworth Castle*, Surtees Soc., 68 (1878), pp. lix-lx and 469-87.

Black, p. 33.
Pl. 191

5   **College of Arms Arundel 30, fols 97-190**
[c. 1285; betw. 1286 and 1296]
[Bury St Edmunds, England]

Chronicon Buriensis

Parch. 86 fols. 225 × 135 mm. 1 col., 150-58 × 85 mm. 32-33 lines. Col. inits, rubrics.

To 1268 the annals are copied by a single hand (fols 97-156ᵛ), another taking over (at the beginning of a new quire) in mid-annal and copying to the year 1285 (fols 157-73ᵛ). Thereafter annals for 1286-96 (fols 173ᵛ-90ᵛ) were probably written soon after the events they describe since a number of different hands contributed to each of the annals, presumably adding news as it became available; additions have been made in the margins (see A. Gransden, *The Chronicle of Bury St Edmunds 1212-1301* (1964), pp. xxxviii-xlii). The latter part of the MS (fols 191-204) containing the Chronicle from 1296-1301 is a fair copy by a scribe who was still at work in 1325 (fol. 204). The rest of the volume was also written at Bury and contains items mainly of local interest. Fols 5-10 are palimpsest being written over an Anglo-Saxon square minuscule fragment of Virgil's *Aeneid*, Bk V (no. 20 in L. Holtz's list of MSS, 'Les manuscrits carolingiens de Virgile (Xè et XIè siècles)', *La Fortuna di Virgilio*, Società nazionale di scienza, lettere e arti di Napoli, Pubblicazioni del bimillenario Virgiliano promosse dalla Regione Campania, 7 (1986), p. 146). Historical notes on fols 131ᵛ, 132ᵛ, are in the hand of Henry of Kirkestede (see R.H. Rouse, 'Bostonus Buriensis and the author of the *Catalogus Scriptorium Ecclesiae*', *Speculum*, 41 (1966), 484-5). According to John Bale's *Index Britanniae Scriptorum* (ed. R.L. Poole and M. Bateson, with introduction by C. Brett and J.P. Carley (1990), p. 200), the MS was owned by a 'master Bacon', for whom there are three suggested identifications (*Index*, p. xix): Thomas Becon, canon of Canterbury (c.1511-67), Sir Nicholas Bacon (d. 1578), and Thomas Bacon, master of Gonville Hall, Cambridge, 1552-9. Bale himself (d. 1563) later owned the MS (see W. O'Sullivan, 'The Irish 'remnaunt' of John Bale's manuscripts', *New Science out of Old Books: Essays in Manuscripts and Early Printed Books in honour of A.I. Doyle*, ed. R. Beadle and A.J. Piper (1995), p. 382). Subsequently acquired by Matthew Parker (fols 201ᵛ-202 bear notes in his hand), from whom it passed to his son John (S. Strongman, 'John Parker's manuscripts: an edition of the lists in Lambeth Palace MS 737', *TCBS*, 7 (1977-80), 1-27, in whose list this MS is no. 17). Arms of Lord William Howard (d. 1640) on fol. 10ᵛ; for other MSS owned by him see no. 4 above.

Black, pp. 44-57; C.R. Cheney, 'The fragment of a decretal collection from Bury St Edmunds', *Bulletin of Medieval Canon Law*, n.s., 8 (1978), 1-7.
Pl. 31

6.   **College of Arms Arundel 41**   *1571 [England]*

John Vowell *alias* Hooker, The Order and Usage of Keeping Parliament in England, with a description of Exeter.

Paper. 58 fols. 290 × 200 mm. 1 col., 233 × 147 mm. 29 lines. Arms of city of Exeter painted on separate piece of paper pasted in (fol. 36ᵛ), other arms painted in margins, fols 37-56ᵛ.

Fol. 1: 'To the right Worshipfull grate and prudent the Maior and

Senators of the most auncient and honorable Citie of Excester, John Vowell alias Hoker gent*leman* and Chamberlayne of the same, wisshethe a happy successe in goverment w*th* the longe continuaunce thereof, to the benefyt of the publique welthe and encrease of worshippes.1571'. For Hooker (*c*.1527-1601), see *The History of Parliament: The House of Commons 1558-1603*, ed. P.W. Hasler (1981), II: 333-35. The present MS was apparently used as printer's copy for the edition of ?1575 (*STC* 24887); see further R. McLeod, 'From Copy to Print: A MS of John Hooker and the Compositors', *Manuscripta*, 27 (1983), 13. Conversely, Oxford, Bodleian Library, Rawlinson B. 104, a MS of other works by Vowell/Hooker, was copied from printed editions (*STC* 24885 and 24889; cf. J.K. Moore, *Primary Materials relating to copy and print in English books of the sixteenth and seventeenth centuries*, Oxford Bibliographical Soc., Occasional Publication No. 24 (1992), p. 7).

> Black, pp. 67-68.
> *Pl. 274*

7 College of Arms Arundel 58   *1448 [England]*
Robert of Gloucester, Metrical Chronicle; etc.

Parch. 342 fols, fols 5-119 foliated by scribe fo. p°-cxxvj° (fols lxxxi-lxxxij wanting). 342 × 235 mm. 1 and 2 cols, 250 × 120-50 mm. 36-38 lines. Col. ports of kings (Conqueror – Henry VI) fols 335ᵛ-42ᵛ, illum. dec. inits. with borders, col. inits., rubrics.

The prologue ends (fols 1ʳ⁻ᵛ, in red): 'This tabel kalender of more plennarly knowlich Foluyng wᵗ a boke offe the Ful Text. All so A petegrew Fro William conquer*our* of the Crowne of Engelonde lynnyally descendyng vnto Kyng Henr' the vj in the end of thys boke' lymned in Fygurs. Thys boke wᵗ hys antecedens and co*n*sequen*s* was ful Ended the vj day offe August' the ʒere of our' lorde a Mˡ cccc . xlviij And the [ ] yere of oure souerayn lorde kyng' harry the vj aff*ter* the conquest the xxvj'. The date is written in black. Fols 1-98ᵛ and fols 304-34 (quires 1-14 (part), 40-43) are written by hand 1; fols 99-264 and 276-303 (quires 14 (part)-34, 36 (part)-39) are by hand 2 who signs the beginning of his stint 'hic incipit Robertus Moille' (foot of fol. 99); while fols 265-75bis col. a (quires 35-36 (part)) are by hand 3. Fol. 275bis col. b has been cut away and the verso is blank. Fols 335-42 (quire 44, containing the 'petegrew') are by a hand similar to that of hand 1. The current foliation omits fol. 288.

Marginal annotations throughout in the hand of Lord William Howard (d. 1640); for other manuscripts owned by him, see no. 4 above.

> Black, pp. 104-10; A.M. Hudson, 'Robert of Gloucester and the Antiquaries, 1550-1800', *Notes and Queries*, 214 (1969), 322-33; G. Guddat-Figge, *Catalogue of Manuscripts containing Middle English Romances* (1976), pp. 215-17; L. Mooney, 'Lydgate's "Kings of England", and another Verse Chronicle of the Kings', *Viator*, 20 (1989), 255-88; Scott, *Later Gothic MSS*, II: 222.
> *Pls 127, 128*

8 College of Arms Arundel 59   *[betw. 1452 and 1458]*
Tutbury, England

Cartularium

Parch. 173 fols, foliated in ink from seventh leaf x-xiiij, xiiij bis-lxxx, 81-171. 190 × 135 mm. 1 col, *c*.127 × 90

mm. Up to 31 lines. Full-page col. border (fol. xvij), col. inits, rubrics. Leather bdg over boards.

Fol. 144ᵛ (lines written alternately in black and red): 'Ordinatus est iste liber seruiturus per dominum Thomam Gedney Priorem [1433-58] in Monasterio beate Marie de Tuttebur' in Comitatu Staffordie Couentrensis ac lichefeldensis diocesis Et si quis alienauerit anathema sit faucibus illius necnon Indignacio Apostolorum et omnium sanctorum quosque satisfaciat et illic reddatur .fiat fiat.'. The latest document copied by the hand of fols xvi-lxxx and 81-163ᵛ is dated 28 January 1452 (fol. 56); the scribe also provided a table of contents, fols x-xv. Fols 164-71 contain additions by later hands. Fols 1-6 and 172-73 are endleaves.

Fol. 4: 'Sum liber Johanni Hawirth' (s. xvi). Fol. 129: 'Charles Agard'. Fol. xvj: 'Julij yᵉ third Anno Domini 1710. This Booke was Given to yᵉ Corporation of the Kings Heraults & pursivants of Armes att London: By me Michael Burton \of Wirkesworth/ son and heire of Thomas Burton late of Holmesfield and Ollercarr Parke Esq \in yᵉ County of Derby/ wᶜʰ said Thomas was yᵉ son of William Burton of Holmesfield who was yᵉ Brother of Thomas Burton of Fansham Gate Gent*leman* who were yᵉ sons of John Burton of Dronfield or Apperknowle \in yᵉ said County/ me*n*tioned in a pedigree Remaineing in the said Heraults Office. Michael Burton'. Burton also donated no. 9 below.

> Black, pp. 110-26; Davis, *MC*, no. 981; *The Cartulary of Tutbury Priory*, ed. A. Saltman, Collections for a History of Staffordshire, 4th ser., 4 (1962).
> *Pl. 141*

9 College of Arms Arundel 60   *1286 Newstead, England*
Cartularium

Parch. 215 fols, foliated 1-3, 5-216. 212 × 150 mm. 1 col., 165-75 × 110-15 mm. Up to 41 lines. Col. inits, rubrics. Leather bdg over boards, with remains of iron lock.

Fol. 5 (in red): 'Anno domini Millesimo . Ducentesimo . Octogesimo . sexto . notata sunt in hoc libro vniuersa munimenta et singula ad Ecclesiam noui Loci in Schirewode [Newstead, Notts] spectantia. tam de ecclesiis. terris. Redditibus. quam possessionibus et rebus aliis collatis eidem vel uenditis. In quo nominatur dona et nomina donatorum et etiam carte tenencium per nos feoffatorum'. By one main hand which provided the table of contents, fols 5-22. Fols 1-3 are endleaves. Many blank leaves throughout and frequent additions by later hands.

Fol. 216ᵛ: 'Thomas Freeman his booke Amen' (s. xvii). Fol. 26: 'Memorandum That this manuscript being yᵉ Leiger Booke of the Dissolued Abbey or priory of Newstead in Com' Nottingham did formerly belong to Thomas Freeman of Sutton in yᵉ Dale in yᵉ Hundred of Scarsdale and County of Derby Gent*leman* a Louer of Learneing and Antiquitys: This Sutton is yᵉ Seate of yᵉ Rᵗ Hon*ora*ble Nicholas [Leake, 4ᵗʰ] Earle of Scarsdale Vnder whose Auncestors the said Thomas Freeman had seuerall years serued in Cheifest Trusts and with greate Fidelity and Reputation in Testimony wherof the said Earles Auncesters have a Noble Anuity or Rent Charge of sixty pounds per Annum to the said Thomas and his wife for their Liues. At the request of my Learned and Hon*o*red Freind Ralph Heathcoate Clerke Rector of Morton in yᵉ said Hundred and County this Booke was given vnto me Michael Burton of

Holmesfield and Wirkesworth in yᵉ said County of Derby Esq by Elizabeth yᵉ widow and Relict of yᵉ said Thomas Freeman and at her request by me to be presented to the Honorable Society of the (fol. 26ᵛ) Colledge of Armes in London to be there Reposited as a Monument of Antiquity and for the Common benefitt & vse of yᵉ Members of yᵉ said Honorable Colledge and all other Lovers of their Countrey and yᵉ Antiquitys thereof. Which gift or present I do hereby accordingly make and Give to yᵉ said Honorable Society of yᵉ Colledge of Armes most Humbly requesting their Candid acceptance therof as a Testimony of yᵉ Greate Honor & Respect I haue and beare towards yᵉ said Honorable Society and all the Members thereof In witnesse whereof I have herevnto subscribed my Name this Eleventh day of February in yᵉ Eleventh yeare of yᵉ Reigne of our most Gratious Souereigne Lady Anne by yᵉ Grace of God of Greate Brittaine France and Ireland Queene Defender of yᵉ Faith etc. Annoque Domini :1712: Michael Burton'. For another MS donated by Burton, see no. 8 above.

Black, pp. 126-29; Davis, *MC*, no. 693.
Pl. 36

10 **College of Arms Arundel 62**   *1587 [London, England]*
The Song of Caerlaverock' (in Old French)
Paper. 34 fols, foliated 1, 4-36. 217 × 160 mm. 1 col., 135 × 95 mm. 16 lines. Full-page painting (fol. 22ᵛ), coats of arms painted in margins throughout, col. inits, ruling in red ink.

Fol. 1ᵛ: 'Exemplar verissimum vetusti cuiusdam reverendae antiquitatis Monimentj, religiose admodum transcripti, renovati, et ab iniuria temporis vindicati. Eundem fideliter cum prototipo siue originali in omnibus concordare, testatur Robertus Glouerus Somersett' fecialis regius, Armorum regi cui Norroy nomen inditum, Mariscallus designatus [Somerset Herald, 1570-88]. Qui veritatj testimonium perhibere pulchrum ducens tam hic in fronte, quam etiam in calce, manu propria nomen suum subscripsit, Tertio Nonas Februarij, Anno Christi servatoris .M.D. lxxxvijᵒ, Regni vero Serenissimae Reginae Elizabethae tricesimo. Glouer Somersett Marischal au Norroy Roy d'Armes'. See also no. 13 below, and for Glover's manuscripts, P.M. Selwyn, '"Such speciall Bookes of Mr Somersettes as were sould to Mr Secretary": the fate of Robert Glover's collections', in *Books and Collectors 1200-1700: Essays presented to Andrew Watson*, ed. J.P. Carley and G.G.C. Tite (1997), pp. 389-401.

Black, pp. 130-31; A.R. Wagner, *A Catalogue of English Medieval Rolls of Arms* (1950), pp. 30-31; N. Denholm-Young, 'The Song of Carlaverock and the Parliamentary Roll of Arms as found in Cott. MS. Calig. A.XVIII in the British Museum', *Proceedings of the British Academy*, 47 (1961), 251-62, repr. in his *Collected Papers* (1969), pp. 121-32.
Pl. 292

11 **College of Arms A. 9**   *1585 London, England*
Heraldic and historical commonplace book
Paper. 190 fols. 320 × 200 mm. 1 col., up to 289 × 130 mm. Up to 82 lines. Painted coats of arms, rubrics. Gold-tooled leather bdg, ties gone (s. xvi).

Fol. 1: 'In this booke ys contayned the names and Armes of all the kinges and quenes governynge this Realme of England, since the Conquest therof made by William Duke of Normandye, called William the Conquerer, wᵗʰ the tyme of their begynnyng and endinge and how longe they raigned wᵗʰ the names and Armes especiallye of all the barrons remaynynge or created since that tyme … written and sett in order as appereth by me Alexander Evesham begon .1583. and fynyshed .1585. in london. in the xxvjᵗʰ yere of the raigne of Elizabethe queene of England'. For Alexander (d. 1592) and MSS owned by him, see R. Watson, 'A manuscript from the library of Epiphanius Evesham', *Bulletin of the International Society for the Study of Church Monuments*, 10 (1984), 213-16.
The upper cover of the binding is tooled with the name 'Alexander' and date '1586', and the lower with 'Evesham', '1586'.

Campbell, I: 183-85.
Pl. 291

12 **College of Arms Vincent 21**   *1578 [Netherlands]*
'Genealogies, descentes, et alliances des Cheualiers de l'ordre de la toyson d'or'
Paper. 66 fols, unfoliated. 420 × 290 mm. 1 col., 373 × 238 mm. Up to 66 lines. Col. wash drawing fol. 1, coats of arms in pen and ink. Limp vellum bdg (s. xvi).

Fol. 1 (title page): 'Genealogies, descentes, et alliances des Cheualiers de l'ordre de la toyson d'or colligées avecq grande diligence par Corneille Mertin Zelandois. Anno 1578'.
Fol. 1: 'Given to the Heralds Office at London by Raphe Sheldon of Beoly in Worcestershire Esq. anno 1684'. For other MSS left by the antiquary Ralph Sheldon (1623-84), see nos 13 and 14 below, and on his library, I.G. Philip, 'Sheldon manuscripts in Jesus College Library', *Bodleian Library Record*, 1 (1939-41), 119-23.
Campbell, I: 261-62.
Pl. 283

13 **College of Arms Vincent 444**   *1572 [London, England]*
Nicholas Upton, De officio militari
Paper. 108 fols, paginated 1-216. 278 × 208 mm. 1 col., 190 × 138 mm. 27 lines. Painted coats of arms, col. drawings, col. inits, rubrics. Leather bdg over paste boards, ties gone.

P. 216 (in red and black): 'Explicit libellus vocatus de officio militari. Scriptus per Baddesworth Anno domini 1458. Transcriptus per R[obertum] Glouerum alias Somersett Heraldum [1570-88] Armorum Serenissimae Elizabethae Angliae Franciae et Hiberniae Reginae Anno Domini 1572'. Glover's exemplar was BL, Add. 30946 (*DMBL*, no. 345). For another MS transcribed by him from an earlier exemplar, see no. 10 above.
P. 1: 'Given to the Heralds office by Raphe Sheldon of Beoly Esq, who dying 24 June 1684, was buried at Beoly [Beoley, Worcs.]'. For other MSS left by him, see no. 12 above.

R. Dennys, *The Heraldic Imagination* (1975), pp. 82, 215 and pls on pp. 34, 35 illus. drawings pp. 163, 171; Campbell, I: 455.
Pl. 275

14 College of Arms Clare Roll   *[c.1456]*
[Bury St Edmunds? England]

Osbern Bokenham, Dialogue between a Secular and a Friar

Parch. 1 membrane. *c*.790 × 255 mm. 1 col of 18 7-line stanzas Engl. verse, 1 col. of 100 Lat. hexameters. Min., painted coats of arms, gold inits, rubrics.

Headed in red: 'This dialoge bitwix a seculer askyng and a frere aunsweryng at the graue of Dame Johan of Acres shewith the lyneal descent of the lordis of the honoure of Clare [Suffolk]. fro the tyme of the fundacion of the [Augustinian] Freeris at the same Honour. the yere of our lorde anno M^{lo}.CC. xlviij^{ti} and the first day of may the yere anno M^l CCCC lvj^{ti}'. Since the scribe rectified an omission and also made an erasure, A. Sutton and L. Visser-Fuchs (*Richard III's Books: Ideas and Reality in the Life and Library of a Medieval Prince* (1997), p. 25 n. 17) assume that the Clare roll was only a copy. The artist has been identified by Scott (*Later Gothic MSS*, II: 304) as her illustrator B of BL, Harley 1766, one of a group of mid-fifteenth-century manuscripts all probably produced at Bury St Edmunds. Owned by Augustine Vincent, Windsor Herald (d. 1626), who cited it in his *A Discoverie of the Errours in the first edition of the Catalogue of the Nobility, Published by Raphe Brooke* (1622); see further A.F. Sutton and L. Visser-Fuchs, '"Richard liveth yet": an old myth', *The Ricardian*, 9, no. 117 (June, 1992), 266-69. On dorse: 'Given to the Heralds Office by Raphe Sheldon of Beoly <...> 1684'. For other MSS left by him, see no. 12 above.

W. Dugdale, *Monasticon Anglicanum* (1655), I: 535-37; *Heralds' Commemorative Exhibition, 1484-1934, held at the College of Arms; enlarged & illustrated catalogue* (1936), p. 37, no. 16 and pl. XLII illus. beg of roll (reduced); A.R. Wagner, *A Catalogue of English Medieval Rolls of Arms* (1950), pp. 98-99; K. W. Barnardiston, *Clare Priory, Seven Centuries of a Suffolk House* (1962), pp. 63-69; *Richard III's Books*, pl. III illus. beg. of roll, fig. 50 its end (both reduced).
Pl. 147

15 College of Arms Warwick Roll   *[betw. 1483 and 1491]*
[Warwick, England]

John Rous, Latin Roll Chronicle of the town of Warwick

Parch. 23 membranes. *c*.7378 × 292 mm. Text of varying length under each of 64 pen and ink figures, colour washed, each figure beneath its painted coat of arms.

One of two armorial roll chronicles composed by John Rous, chaplain of Guy's Cliffe near Warwick (*BRUO*, 1596-97), giving brief biographical sketches of the founders and benefactors of the town and of the earls of Warwick, from legendary figures to Richard III. The present roll contains the Latin ('Lancastrian') version, whereas BL, Add. 48976 contains the Middle English ('Yorkist') version. Both were probably executed under Rous's direction, and some of the figures in both are by the same artist (cf. Scott, *Later Gothic MSS*, II: 360-61). Both versions were originally complimentary to Richard, and it is uncertain which was written first. They must have been finished after 9 September 1483 (since Edward, Richard's son, is referred to as Prince of Wales) but before April 1484 (after Edward had died). After Richard's death in 1485 the present roll was cut up and edited to become hostile to him and partial to Henry VII (see W. Courthope, ed., *Thys rol was laburd & finishid by Master John Rows of Warrewyk*, repr. with introduction by C. Ross (Gloucester, 1980), pp. v-xviii). Rous died 1491. Owned by Robert Arden of Park Hall, Warwick (d. 1643), when transcribed by William Dugdale (in Oxford, Bodleian Library, MS Dugdale 14). In s. xix the text was treated with a reagent in an attempt to make it more legible and it is now severely damaged.

A.G.B. Russell, 'The Rous Roll', *Burlington Magazine*, 30 (1917), 23-31 and pls I-III illus. ports; *Heralds' Commemorative Exhibition, 1484-1934, held at the College of Arms; enlarged & illustrated catalogue* (1936), p. 50, no. 39 and pls XXV, XXVI illus. ports and text (reduced); J.G. Mann, 'Instances of antiquarian feeling in medieval and renaissance art', *Archaeological Journal*, 89 (1932), 254-74 and pls II(2)-IV illus. ports; T.D. Kendrick, *British Antiquity* (1950), pp. 18-29 and pls II-IV ports; A.R. Wagner, *A Catalogue of English Medieval Rolls of Arms* (1950), pp. 116-17; C.E. Wright, 'The Rous Roll: the English version', *British Museum Quarterly*, 20 (1955-56), 77-88; A. Gransden, 'Antiquarian studies in fifteenth-century England', *Antiquaries' Journal*, 60 (1980), 75-97; Gransden, *Hist. Writing*, II: 310 and pl. XIIf illus. port.; A. Sutton and L. Visser-Fuchs, *Richard III's Books, Ideas and Reality in the Life and Library of a Medieval Prince* (1997), pp. 145-46, no. XVIII in their catalogue of Richard's books.
Too severely damaged to photograph

16 Congregational Library I.b.2   *1471 [Germany]*

Biblia, pars II (Ecclesiasticus – Apocalypsis)

Paper. 418 fols. 297 × 215 mm. 2 cols, 215 × 140 mm. 41-42 lines. Col. inits, rubrics.

Fol. 412, col. 1: 'Amen. 1471. Conradus freudenreich', then in red ink 'Finita in vigilia armorum christi'. Fols 412, col. 1 – 418^r are by the same scribe; fol. 418^v blank.
Now deposited at Dr Williams's Library.

MMBL, I: 13-14; M. Maniaci, D. Muzerelle and E. Ornato, 'Une bible ... mais encore? Le portrait des manuscrits bibliques dans la catalographie moderne', *Sources for the History of Medieval Books and Libraries*, ed. R. Schlusemann, J.M.M. Hermans, and M. Hoogvliet (1999), pp. 303-4.
Pl. 181

17 Congregational Library I.f.33, fols 1-64
1294 [France]

Gautier de Chatillon, Alexandreis

Parch. 64 fols. 173 × 125 mm. 1 col., 130 × 95 mm. 44 lines. Col. inits (fols 1, 2^v)

Fol. 64: 'Guillelmus vastel hunc librum scripsit Anno domini M° CC° nanagesimo [*sic*] iiij° mense maij post translationem sancti nichol<ai>'. Fol. 64^v, originally blank, contains scribbled notes on drunkenness and four lines of verse added s. xiii/xiv. The rest of the volume consists of four booklets, fols 65-84, 85-88, 89-102 and 103-107, written by other hands of late s. xiii.
Now deposited at Dr Williams's Library.

MMBL, I: 15-17; T. Pritchard, 'Three Oxford Alexandreis Manuscripts', *Scriptorium*, 34 (1980), 268.
Pl. 39

18 CLRO Cust. 1   [betw. c.1268 and 1274]
[London, England]

'Liber de antiquis legibus'

Parch. 167 fols. 245 × 170 mm. 2 cols, c.195 × 133 mm. 37 lines. Pen and ink drawing (fol. 123), col. inits (fols 3-36ᵛ only). Leather bdg over boards with 2 pins lower cover; straps gone.

Compiled and mostly written by Arnald Thedmar, alderman of the City of London, who had died by 10 February 1275 (will then proved, see *Calendar of Wills Proved and Enrolled in the Court of Husting, 1258-1688*, ed. R.R. Sharpe, 2 vols (1889-90), I: 22; for Thedmar, see further J.P. Huffman, *Family, Commerce and Religion in London and Cologne, Anglo-German emigrants c.1000-c.1300* (1998), pp. 189-95). Thedmar seems to have been writing at intervals from least as early as 1268; part of his continuation of the Annals of London (fols 71ᵛ-144) was written before the death of Pope Clement IV in that year (cf. *De antiquis legibus liber*, ed.T. Stapleton, Camden Soc. 34 (1846), p. 83 line 27). Thedmar's hand last appears 1274. A list of the sheriffs of London on fols 58-60, originally ending in 1271, was updated to 1273 by another scribe who collaborated with Thedmar in the latter's continuation of the London annals (from fol. 123) until 1274 and who provided the table of contents on fols iᵛ-iiᵛ. Fols 160-62, fragments of a service book (on which had been added 'The prisoner's prayer', for which see I. Aspin, *Anglo-Norman Political Poems* (1953), pp. 6-9 with reduced facsim.), also contain an addition by Thedmar (fol. 162). Fols 1-36, 52-71ᵛ, and 147-53, written in several small textura hands, may (as *MMBL*, I: 23 suggests) have been commisioned by Thedmar as the basis of his own work. Additions by other hands of s. xiii and early s. xiv have been made on leaves left blank by him and his collaborator.

MMBL, I: 22-27, 435 and pl. V illus. fol. 144 (part).
Pl. 27

19 CLRO Cust. 2   1311; [betw. 1311 and 1328]
[London, England]

'Liber Horn', in Latin and French

Parch. 376 fols. 220 × 142 mm. 1 col., 170 × c.95 mm. 32-39 lines. Illum. dec. borders, hist., dec. and col. inits, rubrics. Tawed leather bdg over boards, strap-and-pin fastenings gone (s.xiv).

Fol. 206 (in red): 'Iste liber restat Andree Horn piscenario London' de Breggestrete in quo continentur Carta et alie consuetudines predicte Ciuitatis. Et carta libertatis Anglie et statuta per Henricum Regem et per Edwardum Regem filium predicti Regis Henrici edita Quem fieri fecit Anno domini M.CCC.xj Et Anno regni Regis Edwardi filii Regis Edwardi vᵗᵒ'. Although now placed in the middle of the volume, fol. 206 appears once to have been its opening. Begun in 1311, 'Liber Horn' was soon augmented by additions in various hands and it is uncertain how much was actually written in that year. The rubric seems to cover the contents of fols 206-26 and 16-176 containing 'a conventional, if unusually exhaustive, collection

of statutes' (J. Catto, 'Andrew Horn: law and history in four-teenth-century England', *The Writing of History in the Middle Ages: Essays presented to R.W. Southern*, ed. R.H.C. Davis and J.M. Wallace-Hadrill (1981), p. 372), but it has been argued by L. Dennison ('Liber Horn', 'Liber Custumarum' and other manuscripts of the Queen Mary Psalter workshops', *Medieval Art, Architecture and Archaeology in London*, ed. L. Grant, British Archaeological Association (1990), pp. 118-34) that the date refers only to fols 206-26 and 21-41, since they were copied by a single scribe and contain the only work in the MS of her artist A. She identifies a second artist B working in fols 16-20 and 49-176 and suggests they were perhaps written later. Fols 226ᵛ-369ᵛ (unillustrated) contain copies of London documents dating from 1313-18; fols 8ᵛ-9 and 14ᵛ a table of contents which Catto suggests was drawn up by 1319. Horn died in 1328. Bequeathed to the Guildhall by Horn: item 4 of the books in his will (cf. Catto, pp. 370-71). For another item in his bequest, see no. 20 below. Front pastedown 'Liber Horn' (s. xvi).

M. Weinbaum, *London unter Eduard I und Eduard II*, 2 vols (1933), II: 91-101; *MMBL*, I: 27-34, 435 and pl. VI illus. fol. 22 (part); D. Oschinsky, *Walter of Henley and Other Treatises on Estate Management* (1971), p. 22; Dennison, pls XXVIA, XXXVB, XXXVIA-B, XXXVIIA-B, XXXVIIIA-B illus. fols 206, 174 (detail), 35ᵛ (detail), 120ᵛ, 41, 41ᵛ (detail), 46, 10ᵛ, and pl. XXXIVC illus. bdg (all reduced); R.J. Dean and M.B.M. Boulton, *Anglo-Norman Literature: A Guide to Texts and Manuscripts*, Anglo-Norman Text Society, Occasional Publications, No. 3 (1999), nos 393-94.
Pl. 43

20 CLRO Cust. 6, fols ii, 1-84, 86-102, 173-86
[betw. 1321 and 1328] [London, England]

'Liber Custumarum', in Latin and French

Parch. 116 fols. 345 × 245 mm. 2 cols, 255 × 173 mm. 39 lines. Illum. hist. and dec. inits and borders, gold and col. inits, rubrics.

Part of a larger volume, formerly known as 'Liber legum antiquorum regum', the rest being BL, Cotton Claudius D.II, fols 1-24, 30-40, 42-115, 124-35 and 266-77 + Oxford, Oriel College 46, fols 109-211; fol. 85 in the present MS is wanting. For the original order of the leaves see N.R. Ker, 'Liber Custumarum and other manuscripts formerly at the Guildhall', *Books, Collectors and Libraries*, pp. 135-42. The original volume can be identified with item 1 in Andrew Horn's will; he died 1328 (cf. J. Catto, 'Andrew Horn: law and history in four-teenth-century England', *The Writing of History in the Middle Ages: Essays presented to R.W. Southern*, ed. R.H.C. Davis and J.M. Wallace-Hadrill (1981), pp. 376-78). Written by several hands but the latest item copied by the main scribe, a list of the mayors and sheriffs of London, ends 1321 (fol. 186ᵛ). This scribe has been identified as the main scribe of a theological miscellany, now Cambridge, University Library, Gg.4.32 (cf. L. Dennison, 'Liber Horn', 'Liber Custumarum' and other manuscripts of the Queen Mary Psalter workshops', *Medieval Art, Architecture and Archaeology in London*, ed. L. Grant, British Archaeological Association (1990), p. 132 n. 62). Two quires were taken from the volume in 1419 to be incorporated with 'Liber Albus', no. 24 below, as fols 20-43 of that volume (fol. 35ᵛ illus. *Munimenta Gildhallae Londoniensis*, ed. H.T.

Riley, 4 vols (RS 1859-62), I: frontispiece). For another book left by Horn, see no. 19 above.

Alienated, along with no. 21 below, from the Guildhall in s. xvi. From William Fleetwood, recorder of London (d. 1590), both MSS passed to Francis Tate, the antiquary (1560-1616), who kept part of each volume and gave the rest to Sir Robert Cotton. Lengthy negotiations led to the restoration in 1608/9 of the parts of each most concerned with the City of London. They were then bound as one and the name 'Liber Custumarum' applied to the whole (cf. Riley, *Munimenta*, II: xvii-xxii; Ker, 'Liber Custumarum', p. 139).

> Riley, *Liber Custumarum*, I, pl. illus. fol. 6; *MMBL*, I: 20-21; Dennison, pls XXVIB, XXVIIA, XXVIIIA, XXXD and XXXIA illus. fols 1, 3, 90, 70 (detail) and 184ᵛ-85 (all reduced); Sandler, *Gothic MSS*, no. 68 and ill. 82 illus. fol. 6 (reduced).
> *Pl. 44*

21 CLRO Cust. 6, fols 103-72, 187-284
[betw. 1324 and 1327] [London, England]
'Liber Custumarum', in Latin and French
Parch. 163 fols. 345 × 245 mm. 2 cols (except 1 col. fols 103-15ᵛ), 270 × 175 mm. 42 lines. Blank spaces for inits.

Part of a larger volume, the original 'Liber Custumarum', the rest being BL, Cotton Claudius D.II, fols 116-23 + Oxford, Oriel College 46, fols 1-108. For the original order of the leaves see N.R. Ker, 'Liber Custumarum and other manuscripts formerly at the Guildhall', *Books, Collectors and Libraries*, pp. 135-42. The latest document copied by the original hand is a letter patent dated 16 June 1324 (fols 194ʳ⁻ᵛ). Other hands have made many contemporary additions, the earliest of which is a copy of Edward III's charter for Southwark, 6 March 1327 (fol. 265). Since most of its contents are derived from Andrew Horn's MSS, nos 19 and 20 above, the volume was probably produced in the Guildhall during his chamberlainship (1320-28), and it is possible he was responsible for the account of the London Eyre of 1321 on fols 224ᵛ-63ᵛ (cf. H.M. Cam, *Yearbooks of Edward II*, Selden Soc. 26 (1968), p. xii; J. Catto, 'Andrew Horn: law and history in fourteenth-century England', *The Writing of History in the Middle Ages: Essays presented to R.W. Southern*, ed. R.H.C. Davis and J.M. Wallace-Hadrill (1981), p. 379).
For the MS's later history, see no. 20 above.

> *MMBL*, I: 21-22.
> *Pl. 47*

22 CLRO Cust. 10
[c.1474] [London, England]
'Liber Dunthorne', in Latin, French and English
Parch. 462 fols. c.425 × 300 mm. 1 col., 268 × 195 mm. 36-41 lines. Full-page borders (fols 1, 19) with the City's arms (fol. 19), hist., gold and col. inits.

A custumal compiled under the direction of William Dunthorne (*BRUC* 201), Town Clerk of London from 1461. Written by a single hand, the latest item included is dated 16 November 1473 (fol. 269ʳ). Dunthorne received £115 3s 3d, 28 November 14 Edw IV (1474), 'vt scribi facit \de novo/ vnum vel ij libros continentes omnes consuetudines et ordinaciones Ciuitatis predicte ...' (Journal of the Court of Common Council 8, fol. 91). He died in 1490. Fols 463-68 contain additions in a hand of late s. xv or early s. xvi.

A.F. Sutton and L. Visser-Fuchs, 'Richard III's books: Vegetius' *De re militari*', *The Ricardian*, 7 no. 99 (1987), 546; L. Wright, 'Medieval Latin, Anglo-Norman, and Middle English in a civic London text: an inquisition of the River Thames, 1421', *De mot en mot: aspects of medieval linguistics. Essays in honour of William Rothwell*, ed. S. Gregory and D.A. Trotter (1997), p. 224 pl. illus. part fol. 337 (reduced).
> *Pl. 195*

23 CLRO Cust. 11
1576 London, England
'Liber Fleetwood', in Latin, French and English
Parch. 197 fols. c.315 × 205 mm. 1 col., 240 × 120 mm. 35 lines. Col. diagrms (fols 88ᵛ, 95ᵛ), gold inits (fol. 99), ruling in red. Bld-stamped leather bdg over boards, horn label with title 'Fletewoode', bosses gone (s. xvi).

A dedicatory epistle (fols 1ʳ⁻ᵛ) addressed 'To the right honorable and right worshipfull the Lord Maior and Aldermen of the most renowned and famus Citie of London ...' is dated 'From Bacon howse in Noble Strete nere Stayninges churche London the laste of Julie 1576' and signed 'Your good Lo. And Worships moste bounden William Fletewoode Recordator'. Fleetwood was recorder of the City of London 1571-92 (for whom see *The History of Parliament: The House of Commons 1558-1603*, ed. P.W. Hasler (1981), II: 133-38; J.D. Alsop, 'William Fleetwood and Elizabethan historical scholarship', *Sixteenth Century Journal*, 25 (1994), 155-76). The present MS was written by Fleetwood's clerk, Thomas Weston, who received for his work £5 and the reversionship of the office of one of the four clerks of the Mayor's Court, 28 September 1576 (Proceedings of the Court of Aldermen, Repertory 19, fol. 123). Subsequently fols 5-15 were added; they contain illustrations by Anthony Hall, skinner, of the coats of arms of the then Mayor and Aldermen, for each of which he received 2s in 1582 (Rep. 20, fol. 320).
Alienated from the Guildhall after Fleetwood's death in 1590, and reported to be in the possession of Sir Robert Cotton, 10 November 1607 (Proceedings of the Court of Aldermen, Rep. 28, fol. 117ᵛ). Restored 1610 (cf. H.T. Riley, *Munimenta Gildhallae Londoniensis*, 4 vols (RS 1859-62), II: xix).
> *Pl. 280*

24 CLRO Cust. 12, fols 1-18
1419 [London, England]
'Liber Albus', in Latin and French
Parch. 18 fols. c.375 × 250 mm. 1 col, 265 × 160 mm. 45 lines. Dec. init. and full page border with City's arms (fol. 1), col. inits.

According to the preface (fol. 1) this custumal was compiled '... tempore Maioratus nobilis viri Ricardi Whityngtoni Maioris dicte Ciuitatis Anno Videlicet Incarnationis domini Millesimo quadringentesimo decimo nono Regni vero Regis henrici quinti post Con<questum> septimo mense Nouembris huiusmodi volumen annuente <domino> compilatur'. Produced on the initiative of John Carpenter, common clerk of the City 1417-38, who died 1442. W. Kellaway ('John Carpenter's Liber Albus', *Guildhall Studies in London History*, 3 (1977-79), 67-84) demonstrated that the 1419 date applies only to the present fols 1-18 (Kellaway's fols i-iii, 1-15) containing preface, contents-list, and Bk I part 1; fols 18ᵛ-19ᵛ blank. Fols 44-346 (formerly fols 40-352), in contemporary hands, contain Bks II-IV which (apart from s. xvii additions on fols 122-37, formerly fols 118-33) must have been written earlier than Bk I part 1, since they contain references to it. Fols 20-43 (formerly fols 16-39), two quires abstracted from no. 20 above, form Book I part 2.

Flyleaf: 'J. Carpenter'(s. xvi). Fol. 345 (endleaf): 'By me John Brovn exet [?] x s vi d' (s. xvi); 'qui non assuescit virtutibus dum invenescit A vitijs nescit decedere quando Senescit TW' (s. xvii).

> T. Brewer, *Memoir of the Life and Times of John Carpenter* (1856), pp. 17-22; *Munimenta Gildhallae Londoniensis*, ed. H.T. Riley, 4 vols (RS, 1859-62), I pl. opp. 529 illus. fol. 264.
> *Pl. 97*

25 Drapers' Company, pp. 11-16, 19-21, 26-40
1462 [London, England]

Ordinance Book

Parch. 13 fols. 380 × 255 mm. 1 col., 274 × 175 mm. Up to 38 lines. Full-page illum. min. (p. 15), min. (p. 14), full-page borders. Col. inits, rubrics. Kal. in red and black. Tooled leather bdg (gold tooling on roll mostly rubbed away, central panel blind-stamped) with 4 corner bosses, clasps gone (s. xvi).

Bound in the order pp. 11-12, 19-20, 13-16, 21, 26-40 (pp. 17-18, 22-25 contain late s. xv and s. xvi additions). Pp. 19-20, 21 contain a copy of the Company's 1405 ordinances headed: 'In tempore Johannis Walsha Magistri artis Panariorum Bartholomei James Thome Welles Johannis Pake et Willelmi Brogreue Gardianorum xix° die mensis Februarij anno regni Regis Edwardi quarti Primo [March 1461-62, then in blue] Iste ordinaciones Fuerunt scripte in libro isto'. Two other scribes at the beginning of the volume probably worked about the same date; one copied the kalendar (pp. 11-12 and 13, adapted for London use by the addition of Erconwald and Mildred), the other the oath of a brother and ordinances headed 1418 (pp. 14, 26-40, the date 1455 occurs p. 29). Although begun in 1462, the volume has been considerably augmented: pp. 2-4 contain obits of late s. xv and s. xvi date, pp. 41-136 further ordinances and memoranda in s. xvi hands. On the endleaf (p. 1) it is noted that 'the xxj^th daye of October anno regni regis henrici viij° xxxviij° [1546] I pervsyd this boke agaynst my First quarter daye I kept & I Fownde lackyng. wch were Cutt out of this boke before I Cam' in offyce. xij levys of parchement per me William Bere [Clerk of the Company]'.

> A.H. Johnson, *The History of the Worshipful Company of Drapers of London*, 5 vols (1914-22), I: 242-82, V: 4.
> *Pl. 157 a, b*

26 Dulwich College 27
1582 London, England

John Osborne, 'Eschines answer to Demosthenes'

Paper. 58 fols, foliated [i-v] 1-49 [vi-ix]. 213 × 167 mm. 1 col., 140 × 80 mm. 27 lines. Limp vellum bdg, with stubs of 2 green silk ties.

The dedicatory epistle, addressed to Sir Christopher Hatton (1540-91), ends [fol. v]: 'And so Sir wishing you all that thankfulnes can wishe, I humblye take my leaue. London. 26 Jan: 1582 Youres most humbly to be commaunded John Osborne'. This epistle was probably copied by Osborne himself; it is in the

same hand as the MS of his translation, 'The argument of Demosthenes oration against Leptines bill', which he presented to Hatton in 1581 (BL, Add. 10059, with corrections to text). The translation in the present MS (fols 1-49) was copied by the writing master Peter Bales (1547-?1610); his initials 'P.B.' occur within a series of concentric circles on fols 24, 49. Bales later dedicated his *The writing schoolemaster* (STC 1312) to Hatton. For Bales, see further H. Woudhuysen, *Sir Philip Sidney and the Circulation of Manuscripts 1558-1640* (1996), pp. 31-37. For Hatton as literary patron, see E. St John Brooks, *Sir Christopher Hatton, Queen Elizabeth's Favourite* (1946), pp. 124-44.

[Fol. v]: 'F.7.8'; this shelfmark recurs as 'F 7 N° 8' on the upper cover of the binding. Other Dulwich MSS have similar shelfmarks. Probably remained with other MSS in the possession of the Hatton family until after 1689, the date of the collection of letters in Dulwich 35 addressed to Captain Charles Hatton.

> G.F. Warner, *Catalogue of the Manuscripts and Muniments of Alleyn's College of God's Gift at Dulwich* (1881), pp. 349-50.
> *Pl. 287*

27 Goldsmiths' Company 2524
1478, 1483
London, England

Ordinance Book

Parch. 63 fols, medieval foliation j-viii, x-xviij, xxxi-lxxvij. 294 × 205 mm. 2 cols, 183 × 135 mm. 26 lines. Col. inits, rubrics. Bld-stamped bdg, rebacked.

Fol. 10^v (singleton): 'Thys boke was made and ordeyned by Hugh Bryce Altherman Henry Coote Mylys Adys and Willyam Palmer wardens the xx day of September in the yere of oure Lorde god Ml' CCCC lxxviij and in the xviij yere of the Reigne of Kyng Edward the fourth Humfrey Hayford then Mayre of the Cyte of London. John Stokker and Henry Colett sheryffys of the same cyte'. This date applies to fols 11-18, 31-77. In 1483 a preliminary quire containing a table of contents was added, fol. 1^v: 'Thys kalendar was made and ordeyned for this boke by Henry Coote Stephen Kelke John Ernest and Alen Newman wardens the last day of August. In the yere of oure Lorde god .Ml. CCCC. lxxxiij. And in the Furst yere of the Reygne of Kyng Richard the thryd Syr Edmond Shaa. Knyght then Meyre of the Cyte of London. William Whyte. And John Mathew Sheryffys of the same Cyte'. According to the list of contents nothing is missing from the volume, though the medieval foliation suggests fols 19-30 are wanting. The volume was enlarged and continued in s. xvi (fols 78-81).

> T.F. Reddaway and L.E.M. Walker, *The Early History of the Goldsmiths' Company 1327-1509* (1975), pp. 209-74 and pls 14, 15 illus. fols 10^v, part of 14^v (both reduced); S.M. Hare, 'The records of the Goldsmiths' Company', *Archives*, 16 (1984), 376-84; M.M. Foot, 'A Binding by the Crucifer Binder, c.1505', in her *Studies in the History of Bookbinding* (1993), pp. 128-30.
> *Pls 202, 210*

28 Gray's Inn 6
[betw. c.1414 and 1432?]
[Oxford, England]

Robert Cowton, Questiones super Sententias, abbrev. Richard Snetisham, tabula by Peter Partriche.

Parch. 155 fols, foliated i-iii, 1-152. 220 × 155 mm. 1 col, except tabula fols 143-52 in 2 cols, 150 × 95 mm. 42 lines. Gold inits and borders (fols 1, 57ᵛ, 99, 127ᵛ), col. inits. Leather bdg over boards, with remains of clasp and chain (rebacked).

Fol. 144ᵛ: 'Qui scripsit carmen sit benedictus amen W. Trengof'. The scribe, Walter Trengoff, was Fellow of Exeter College 1403-18 and Chancellor of the University of Oxford 1419-21, when he became rector of St Ive, Cornwall (*BRUO*, 1896). Partriche, author of the tabula, was M.A., B.Th. by 1414 (*BRUO*, 1430); his own copy of 'Cowton abbreviatus' with tabula (BL, Royal 11.B.i) was given to Lincoln Cathedral of which he was chancellor 1424-51. R.M. Thomson, *Catalogue of the Manuscripts of Lincoln Cathedral Chapter Library* (1989), p. 214, lists several volumes, including the present MS, descended from Royal. Trengoff presumably copied Partriche's MS while both men were resident together in Oxford. He must have copied it by 1432, to which year a note in a small, almost illegible, hand on the flyleaf, fol. iᵛ, can be dated: 'Annum gracie habui in tempore Tibbert Et alium eciam annum gracie habuit eciam in tempore hals ante festum omnium sanctorum'. William Tibard (*BRUO*, 1874) was senior proctor in 1431-2 and John Halse (*BRUO*, 856) junior proctor in 1432.

Horwood, p. 5; *MMBL*, I: 56.

Pl. 88

29   Gray's Inn 8   *1433 [France]*

Henry Suso, Horloge de Sapience

Parch. 121 fols, with medieval foliation fols 1-76, 78-120. 277 × 180 mm. 2 cols, 200 × 140 mm. 35-43 lines. Col. inits, blanks left for occasional mins. Blind-tooled leather bdg over boards, with 5 metal bosses, clasps and chain staple (rebacked).

Fol. 120: 'Cy fine le liure qui est dit auloge de sapience le quel fist frere Jehan de souhaube de lordre des freres p*r*esche*ur*s. Escript lan mil iiij^c .xxxiij le samedj dapres le saint sacrem*en*t en Iuing'. Unlisted by J. Ancelet-Hustache, 'Quelques indications sur les manuscrits de l'Horloge de Sapience', *Heinrich Seuse. Studien zum 600. Todestag 1366-1966*, ed. E.M. Filthaut (1966), pp. 161-70, but see P. Künzle's further list of MSS of the French translation of Suso's work (*Heinrich Seuses Horologium Sapientiae* (1977), p. 253 no. 7). The translator, John of Swabia, was a Franciscan. Copies produced before 1450 rarely contained more than four or five pictures; cf. P. Rolfe Monks, 'Pictorial programmes in manuscripts of the French version of Suso's Horologium Sapientiae', *Archivum Fratrum Praedicatorum*, 57 (1987), 31-43.

Fol. ii (flyleaf): 'I. Pye' (s. xv), the London stationer; for other MSS with Pye's signature, see Christianson, *Directory*, pp. 145-48.

Horwood, p. 7; *MMBL*, I: 57-58.

Pl. 109

30   Gray's Inn 14, fols 23-60   *[betw. 1221 and 1231?]*
                                            [Chester? England]

Theologica

Parch. 38 fols. 300 × 215 mm. 2 cols, 247 × 168 mm. 60 lines. Col. inits, rubrics. Leather bdg over boards, with clasps and chain staple (rebacked).

Fol. 28 (rubric): 'secundum magistrum R[adulphum] de maidinstan archidiaconum Cestr' super sententias'. Ralph, archdeacon of Chester 1221-31, became dean of Hereford in 1231 and bishop thereof 1234-39 (*BRUO*, 1203-4). Part of a theological miscellany of six booklets: fols 1-22, 23-60, 61-101, 102-7, 108-23, and 124-37. As this is the only known copy of Ralph's text and as the present volume belonged to the abbey of St Werburg, Chester (see fol. iᵛ for the distinctive s. xiv pressmark 'viii° loco'), the reference to him as Chester's archdeacon may provide a *terminus a quo* for fols 23-60. The remaining booklets, copied by various hands, were all probably written about the same time. Bound with an edition of Jaime Perez de Valencia's *Cantica canticorum Salamonis cum expositione* (Paris, 1509).

Horwood, pp. 12-15; *MMBL*, I: 61-63.

Pl. 23

31   Guildhall 208   *1457 London, England*

Abbreviationes placitorum (in French)

Paper. 439 fols (contemporary foliation of fols 12-439 as i-ccccliiij takes account of now missing leaves). 285 × 210 mm. 1 col., *c*.200 × 130 mm. Up to 37 lines. Red paraphs throughout. Bld-stamped leather bdg over boards, with 'T. Segden' incised on lower cover, clasps gone (s. xv).

Fol. 11ᵛ: 'Iste liber constat Thome Segden principali de Furnyvale Inne In holborn' Scriptus per J. Lake Anno domini Millesimo CCCC lvij° Et anno regni regis henrici vj° post conquestum \xxxiiij et/ xxxv \quem idem <.> cond< >/ et finitur scriptura eius per eundem Johannem Lake \de Furnyvale Inne/ in festo sancti Martini in yeme eodem anno \xxxv/ et kalendar' est ex manu et ex abstraccione mei dicti Th. Segden etc'. The earliest dated example of an 'abridgement', or digest of case law, under alphabetical titles (a typical abridgement is that attributed to Nicholas Statham (d. 1471), printed in 1490 by Richard Pynson, *STC* 23238); cf. J.H. Baker, 'The books of the common law', *The Cambridge History of the Book in Britain*, III, *1400-1557*, ed. L. Hellinga and J. Trapp (1999), p. 418. Lake, who copied fols 12-439, may be the same John Lake who was clerk of the crown at Lancaster, 1468-80 (for whom see R. Somerville, *A History of the Duchy of Lancaster, 1265-1603* (1953), p. 486). Segden provided the index of contents, fols 1-11, and made addenda throughout.

Bound for Segden by the 'Scales Binder' who worked in London from the 1450s to *c*.1481; see further N. Barker, 'A Register of Writs and the Scales Binder', *The Book Collector*, 21 (1972), 365-67. No. 13 in Barker's list of the binder's works, to which M.M Foot, 'A Binding by the Scales Binder, 1456-65', in her *Studies in the History of Bookbinding* (1993), pp. 121-24, adds a further example.

MMBL, I: 67-8; A.W.B. Simpson, 'The source and function of the later Year Books', *Law Quarterly Review*, 87 (1971), p. 116; Barker, loc. cit., pl. VII illus. bdg (reduced).

Pl. 148

32   Guildhall 1174   *[betw. 1472 and c.1484]*
                                            London, England

'White Book' of St Margaret's, Bridge Street, London

Parch. 122 fols (fols 1, 122 are pastedowns). 310 × 210

mm. 1 col., 200 × c.125 mm. Up to 37 lines. Wooden boards, rebacked.

Fols 8-15 contain an inventory of the relics, jewels, vestments and books belonging to the church of St Margaret's, Bridge Street (later New Fish Street) 'Made the laste day of August in the yere of oure lorde M cccc lxxij and in the xij yere of the regn' of kinge Edward the iiij^th Made by hugh hunt of london gentilman'. Fols 16-95, a cartulary containing copies of grants and bequests to the church, are also in Hunt's handwriting which varies considerably; the latest deed that he copied was the will of Thomas Goldwell, fishmonger, dated 1484 (fols 93^v-95). Hunt's own will was proved 27 June 1496. As in many cartularies, space was left for additions and fols 1-8 and fols 95^v-122 are blank.

The inventory's 'Item this booke called saint Marget white booke' (fol. 14) suggests (from its use of the demonstrative) that Hunt had bought the present volume already bound. Various scribbles throughout and 'A Prayer for the Morninge' (fols 100-101), dated 1593, are in the hand of Richard Owen, who signs fols 40, 100 and 121^v. Wills dated 1625, 1634, 1639 added fols 95^v-97. St Margaret's was destroyed by the Great Fire of London, 1666.

> A. Wordsworth and H. Littlehales, *The Old Service-Books of the English Church* (1904), pl. II illus. fols 13^r-v (reduced); Davis, *MC*, no. 628; A.G. Dyson, 'A Calendar of the Cartulary of the Parish Church of St. Margaret, Bridge Street (Guildhall Library MS. 1174)', *Guildhall Studies in London History*, 1 (1973-75), 163-91.
> *Pl. 188*

33   **Guildhall 1362**   *[betw. 1290 and 1307] [Italy]*

Regula fratrum de Penitentia, etc.

Parch. 44 fols, foliated ii, 1-42. 208 × 136 mm. 1 col. Fols 1-24: 120 × 76 mm, 23 lines; fols 25-42: 145 × 85 mm, 13 lines. Col. inits throughout, rubrics fols 25-42 only. Red leather bdg over boards, clasps and metal bosses gone (s. xiv).

Two booklets, fols 1-24 and 25-42, written by two contemporary scribes, the latter booklet containing a second copy of the first item in the first, Nicholas IV's bull *Supra montem* of 1289 confirming the rule of the third order of Franciscans. The first booklet also contains (fols 11-13^v) regulations promulgated by the chapter of the Milanese province, ending: 'et hoc ordinatum est in ciuitate laude [Lodi] de anno currente. Millesimo .cc. nonagesimo. Indictione tercia' (fol. 13^v). At the end of the second booklet (fol. 42) an added record of the appointment of officials of the third order in Brescia is dated 'Millesimo CCC septimo'.

Contemporary additions (fols 20 and 42) refer specifically to the brothers of the third order at Brescia.

> G.G. Meerseman, 'Premier auctarium au dossier de l'ordre de la Pénitence au xiiie s.: Le manuel des Pénitents de Brescia', *Revue d'histoire ecclésiastique*, 62 (1967), 5-48; *MMBL*, I: 76-77.
> *Pl. 37*

34   **Guildhall 1363**   *1450 [Germany]*

Regula S. Augustini, cum expositione

Parch. 56 fols. 188 × 130 mm. 1 col., 140 × 90 mm. 24-26 lines. Col. inits, rubrics. Bld-stamped leather bdg over boards, clasps gone (s. xvi).

Fol. 55^v (in red): 'Conscripta et finita Anno domini .M° . cccc° . 1° . In die sancti Lamberti'.

An added note on the rule, fols 55^v-56^v, is in the hand which wrote the heading 'Sequitur ordinarius iuxta vsum ordinis nostri Candidi Præmonstratensis scribi [...] inchoatus anni 1593 20 Januarij per fratrem Ioannem Antonium Peltanum', fol. 56^v.

> *MMBL*, I: 77 (date misprinted as 'M° ccc° 1°').
> *Pl. 132*

35   **Guildhall 3313, fols 145-369**   *[c.1512]*
 [London, England]

Great Chronicle of London

Paper. 225 fols, foliated in red cxlv-ccxlvij, then restarts ij-cv (= fols 248-352), fols 353-69 unfoliated. 288 × 200 mm. 1 col., 185 × 125 mm. 28 lines. Inits (fols 253, 357) with col. engravings pasted in, col. inits, rubrics.

A chronicle of London affairs to 1512, the MS consists of two different portions written by three different hands. In the first portion (fols 1-144) the chronicle was begun by a mid-fifteenth-century hand which records events up to 1439; in the second (fols 145-369) two later hands of early s. xvi subsequently brought it up to date, 1512. The first of these later hands (fols 145-56 and 165-369) has been identified with that of Holkham Hall 671 + BL, Cotton Nero C.XI, the autograph volume of Robert Fabyan's *New Chronicles*. He died 1513. The second later hand who writes a single quire (fols 157-64) is contemporary with Fabyan. See further *The Great Chronicle of London*, ed. A.H. Thomas and I.D. Thornley (1938). Since the later sixteenth century Fabyan has been identified as the author of both the *Great Chronicle* and *New Chronicles*, but J.M.W. Bean ('The Role of Robert Fabyan in Tudor Historiography of the "Wars of the Roses"', *Florilegium Columbianum: Essays in honor of P.O. Kristeller*, ed. K.L. Selig and R. Somerville (1987), pp. 167-85) has noted differences between the two in their treatment of events for the years 1450-59 and suggests that they may have had different authors. Bean does not remark that the years 1450-59 are recorded in the quire (fols 157-64) not written by Fabyan.

Belonged to the martyrologist John Foxe, 1516-1587 (see Thomas and Thornley, pp. xvi-xvii), and subsequently to the antiquarian John Stow (d. 1605) who notes fol. 37: 'ye writen coppy of policronicon perteynynge to master l[aurence] nowell seythe John stowe'.

> Thomas and Thornley, pls 6-10 illus. fols 145, 157, 183^v, 235, 253; *MMBL*, I: 86-87; E.D. Kennedy, *Chronicles and other Historical Writings, Manual of the Writings in Middle English 1050-1500*, ed. A.E. Hartung, (1970-), VIII: 2651-52 and 2853-55; M.R. McLaren, 'The Textual Transmission of the London Chronicles', *English Manuscript Studies 1100-1700*, 3 (1992), 38-72; M.C. Erler, 'Pasted-in embellishments in English manuscripts and printed books c.1480-1533', *The Library*, 6th ser., 14 (1992), 185-206 and fig. 8 illus. fol. 357 (detail).
> *Pl. 243*

36 Guildhall 4158

1425, 1426 London, England

Cartularium

Parch. 286 fols (contemporary foliation of fols 15-270 as 1-11, 13-59, 100-116, 116bis-308). 216 × 143 mm. 1 col., 144 × c.85 mm. Up to 28 lines. Col. inits. Tawed leather bdg over boards, with leather straps; pins gone (s. xv).

A volume in 2 parts: (1) medieval fols 1-59 + 100-258 and (2) fols 259-308. A preliminary quire (unfoliated) contains a selective table of contents, in English, for part 1 only. It is headed (fol. iii): 'In nomine patris et filij et spiritus sancti vnius videlicet \et/ trine deitatis indiuidue anno domini Millesimo quadringentesimo vicesimo quinto et anno Regni Regis Henrici sexti post conquestum Anglie tercio prima die lune mensis Februarij Johannes Whitby Rector parochialis ecclesie sancti Petri super Cornhull' london' fecit hic inscribi per Johannem Seward scolemaiste*r* cartas et munimenta tamque concernunt Cantarias ipsius ecclesie supradicte quam que preter Cantarias suas spectant ad eandem ecclesiam ...'. For Seward, d. 1435, see V.H. Galbraith, 'John Seward and his circle', *Medieval and Renaissance Studies*, 1 (1943), 85-104; J.N. Miner, *The Grammar Schools of Medieval England* (1990), *passim*). The hand of the preliminary quire does not reappear in parts 1 or 2. Part 1, fols 1-26 are by a scribe whose hand, after fol. 15, becomes variable. From fol. 27 onwards part 1 was written by a number of contemporary hands, some of them rather amateur in appearance. Part 2, headed (fol. 259): 'Anno domini millesimo CCCC^{mo} vicesimosexto et anno Regni Regis Henrici sexti post conquestum Anglie quarto decima die mensis Aprilis Johannes Whitby Rector parochialis ecclesie sancti Petri super Cornhull' hic subscribi fecit munimenta ecclesie sue supradicte ...', was written by a scribe who seems to appear in part 1, fols 193^{v}-94^{v}. Fol. i^{v}: 'Iste liber constat ecclesie sancti petri super Cornhyll' london' et debet tradi rectori eiusdem ecclesie' (s. xv). The hand of the *ex libris* also added a deed dated 1473 on fol. ii. Fol. i^{r} note that 'Robart karpynder & katerin karpynder gave a novall Rynt to synt peters v^{d} by the ch<..>er of london of 33 s' (s. xvi). Side notes by John Stow, the antiquary (d. 1605), on Seward and Whitby, fol. iii, are so small and faint as to be scarcely visible.

HMC, 6th Report (1877), Appx pp. 407-18; P.E. Jones and R. Smith, *A Guide to the Records at Guildhall London* (1950), pl. 6 illus. fol. iii (reduced); Davis, *MC*, no. 632.
Pl. 99

37 Guildhall 4889

[betw. 1449? and 1461]; annual entries 1462-1521 London, England

Bede Roll of the Fraternity of St Nicholas

Parch. 60 fols. c.500 × 250 mm. 2-3 cols, 483 × 210 mm. Up to 86 lines. Illum. inits and borders, col. inits, rubrics.

A volume containing annual lists of members, both living and departed, of the Fraternity of St Nicholas (later the Parish Clerks' Company) copied by a series of hands to 1521. The first list to be specifically dated is that for 1462 (fols 9-11), after which all lists are dated. Preceding undated lists (fols 1-8) are believed to date from 1449, in which year John Henley and Thomas Hunt were masters, to 1461 (see J. Christie, *Some Account of the Parish Clerks, more especially of the Ancient Fraternity (Bretherne and Sisterne) of St. Nicholas, now known as the Worshipful Company of Parish Clerks* (1893), pp. 30-55).

Henley's and Hunt's names have largely been cut away in binding. The names of the living and dead were at first kept separate; thus the list, fols 1-2, headed (in red) 'Oremus specialiter et deuote pro bono statu omnium fratrum et sororum fraternitatis sancti Nicholai Londiniarum quorum nomina in hac tabula continentur', contains among the living Henry VI, John Mowbray, duke of Norfolk (1432-61), Richard Neville, earl of Salisbury (1438-60), and Robert Neville, bishop of Durham (1438-57), while that on fols 3-4 contains among the departed Cardinal Beaufort and Humfrey, duke of Gloucester, both d. 1447. Entries for 1472-74 (fols 17-19) are by a single hand. That for 1480 (fol. 25) includes Queen Elizabeth Woodville in letters of gold.

R.H. Adams, *The Parish Clerks of London* (1971), pp. 23-4 and pl. I illus. fol. 57 (reduced).
Pls 158, 192

38 Guildhall 5370, pp. 1-8, 53-162, 221-22

1392; [betw. 1392 and 1417]; [London, England] [betw. 1417 and 1425]; annual entries 1425-1600

Scriveners' Company 'Common Paper'

Paper. 61 fols. 390 × 285 mm. 1 col., 316 × 223 mm. Up to 38 lines. Bld-tooled leather bdg, with strap and buckle renewed.

An irregularly made-up volume begun in 1392 (pp. 1-8, 221-22) with a copy of the Company's ordinances, in Latin and French, by a scribe working when Martin Seman et John Cossier were presented as Masters 'Decimo septimo die mensis Maij Anno regni Regis Ricardi secundi quintodecimo' (p. 4). Each member of the Company subscribed to the ordinances on admission, and pp. 53-162 contain subscriptions from 1392 to 1600 (continued pp. 163-218 to 1627; a note p. 219 records 'Inde incepit liber nouus admissionis', pp. 223-78 being left blank). The earliest subscriptions are those of Seman and Cossier (p. 53), followed by 39 subscriptions (pp. 54-64) datable between 1392 and 1417 when John Chesham, who was first to do so, dated his subscription 'xiiij^{mo} die Junij anno regni Regis Henrici quinti graciosi post conquestum quinto'. Among the 39 is the subscription of William Grove, one of Richard Whittington's executors (p. 57 and see pl. 69). Between Chesham's subscription of 1417 and that of Walter Culpet, the next to date his entry (p. 66: 20 July 3 Henry VI, 1425), there are 6 datable examples (pp. 64-66). Both Chesham and Culpet were also Imperial notaries. After Culpet each signatory dated his subscription, and the first to date his entry by the year of Grace was another Imperial notary, John Daunt (p. 66: 1440). This became a regular method of dating in 1452 when Richard Wyse alias Hynton signed (p. 74). Pp. 66-91 contain 120 dated subscriptions from 18 Sept 4 Henry VI (1425) to 1499, pp. 93-162 351 dated subscriptions from 1500-1600. Among later s. xv signatories was William Duryvale, Clerk of the Merchant Taylors' in 1491 (cf. no. 111 below and pl. 214), who subscribed in 1487 (p. 85).

The remainder of the volume consists of (1) pp. 9-10, 15, 186, 220, 281-82, 296 memoranda in s. xv hands; (2) pp. 17-38 names of apprentices from c.1450 to 1573; (3) pp. 189-92 ordinances in s. xvi hands; (4) pp. 283-95 assessments of fines 1562-89. Other entries are by s. xvii hands. Pp. 11-14, 39-52 and 280 blank.

E. Freshfield, 'Some notarial marks in the "Common Paper" of the Scriveners' Company', *Archaeologia*, 54

(1895), 239-54 and figs 1-12, 14-26, 29-30 illus. subscriptions pp. 53, 55, 61, 64, 66, 71, 72, 86, 94, 70, 77, 80, 98, 106, 107, 117, 121, 123, 129, 133, 141, 104; H. Jenkinson and H.C. Johnson, *The Later Court Hands in England from the Fifteenth to the Seventeenth Century* (1927), I: 4-5 and II, pls I-IX illus. pp. 53, 61 (part), 64 (part), 70 (part), 72 (part), 77 (part), 80 (part), 83 (part), 87 (part), XI-XVIII illus. pp. 93 (part), 101 (part), 109 (part), 113 (part), 117 (part), 124 (part), 128 (part), 140 (part), and pl. XX illus. pp. 145 (part); F.W. Steer, *Scriveners' Company Common Paper 1357-1628*, London Record Soc., 4 (1968), xiii-xvi and pls II-III illus. pp. 96, 106 (part); C.R.H. Cooper, 'The Archives of the City of London Livery Companies and related organisations', *Archives*, 16 (1984), 323-53 and pl. 2 illus. p. 66 (reduced).

Pls 69, 214

39 Guildhall 5440   *[betw. 1418 and 1440]*
[London, England]

William Porlond's Minute Book, in Latin, French, and English

Paper. 328 fols. 295 × c.220 mm. 1-2 cols, c.240 × 180 mm. Up to 40 lines.

Although it chiefly contains accounts, this volume, kept by William Porlond, Clerk of the Brewers' Company, also includes memoranda, menus, bills and petitions, ordinances, and eulogies of several of London's Lord Mayors (partly ed. R.W. Chambers and M. Daunt, *A Book of London English 1384-1425* (1931), pp. 138-91; although they call him 'Porland', in the MS his surname is always spelt 'Porlond') . It begins, fol. 1, in the mayoralty of William Sevenoke, 1418: '<....> papir primerement escript le Moys de Nouembre <....> puis le conquest dengleterre sisme fait plener remembrance et <....> Resceitz et expens' faitz per lez Maistres pur le temps estiantz del Fraternite dez <....> Cite de Londres founde en lesglise p*a*roschiel de Toutz Seintz en la mure de Lo<ndres W>illiam <S>euenoke donqs Mair de mesme la Citee John Perneys et <Ralph> Barto<n ....> Citee et William atte Wode William Edrich Will*i*am Ferrour et John <Reyner ....> anxi lez Maistres del Frat*er*nite au*aunt*dite Et en ceste an morust John Moroy adonq <....> clerk de mesmes lez Breweres Cest assauoir le x*me* i*o*ur du moys [daugst] de Feu*er*er lan vj*me* suisdit E <...> xiiij*me* iour de mesme le mois [daugst William] de Feu*er*er William Porl<ond> fuist receu au mesme <...> l*o*ffice p*ur* estre Clerk dez ditz Breweres et le dit William ordeignast cestre liure p*ur* auoir <...>nisaunce de toutz lez choses faitz en lez mistiere et Frat*er*nite soisditz p*ar*tout le temps que le dit William fuist clerk dez ditz Breweres', and was kept up yearly. Porlond had died by Spring 1440; see two payments recorded fol. 324: 'Also to Roberd Cokat Clerk of the same crafte for iij q*uar*ters of the seid yere [i.e. from Christmas to Christmas, 18 Henry VI] xxx s Item to the wyff late of Will*i*am Porlond for here pensyoun be þe seid yere xl s'. Many of the earlier accounts (fols 1-156ᵛ) were subsequently crossed out, and some items inserted in space originally left blank. Porlond's hand is very variable and not all the entries are by him.

G. Unwin, *The Gilds and Companies of London*, 4th edn with new introduction by W.F. Kahl (1963), illus. pp. 167, 234 illus. fols 11ᵛ, 113; M. Ball, *The Worshipful Company of Brewers* (1977), pp. 45-55 and pl. opp. p. 39 illus. fol.

69ᵛ; C.R.H. Cooper, 'The Archives of the City of London Livery Companies and related organisations', *Archives*, 16 (1984), 323-53 and pl. 1 illus. fol. 11ᵛ (reduced).

Pl. 98

40 Inner Temple, Petyt 511/9   *[betw. 1285 and 1295]*
[England]

Vetera Statuta Angliae; Registrum de Cancellaria

Parch. 136 fols. 253 × 167 mm. 1 col., 190 × 105 mm. 38-40 lines. Inhab. init. and col. border (fol. 4), col. border (fol. 89), col. inits.

Two booklets, the first (fols 4-50 + 61-88) containing statutes and the second (fols 89-136) a register of writs, ending abruptly (fols 51-60, further statutes, were inserted in s. xiv). The register can be dated to after 1285 since it contains several references to the Statute of Westminster II (cf. *Early Registers of Writs*, ed. E. de Haas and G.D.G. Hall, Selden Soc., 87 (1970), pp. civ-cvii), while the latest of the statutes date 18 Edward I (1289-90). Fols 1-3 contain an index to the latter in which, at the top of fol. 2ᵛ, the date 1295 is scribbled twice: 'Anno anno domini Mᵒ ccᵒ nonagesimo quinto Anno domini mᵒ ccᵒ Nonagesimo quinto'. On s. xiii copies of the *Statuta* in general, see D.C. Skemer, 'Sir William Breton's Book: Production of *Statuta Angliae* in the late thirteenth century', *English Manuscript Studies 1100-1700*, 6 (1997), 24-51.

Flyleaf: 'Liber Johanni Byrche' (s. xviᵉˣ).

MMBL, I: 88; Conway Davies, I: 220-21.

Pl. 34

41 Inner Temple, Petyt 530 vol. A   *1569, 1570*
Burton upon Trent; London, England

John Leslie, Historie of Scotland

Paper. 196 fols. 199 × 144 mm. 1 col., 172 × 100 mm. 31-41 lines.

The MS appears to be the author's working copy. Although written by amanuenses, it contains revisions and corrections to the text in a hand which can be identifed as Leslie's own (see P. Robinson, 'John Leslie's "Libri duo": Manuscripts belonging to Mary Queen of Scots?', *Order and Connexion: Studies in Bibliography and Book History*, ed. R.C. Alston (1997), p. 66). The preface ends fol. 6: 'At [burton, *crossed out*] the [*blank*] day of Apryle 1569'. In a lengthy marginal addition on the same page Leslie records that he began the 'Historie' while imprisoned at Burton upon Trent 1569 but that he revised and extended it February-May 1570 when subsequently placed in the keeping of Edmund Grindal, bishop of London: 'At quhilk tyme being sequestrat and restranitt in ye bishop of Lundouns hous at Lundoun I entered agane to Reid our and revise these things qᶦᵏ I had collected <of> in my first restranitt and having more aboundance of Historeis because I was so nere ye libraries I thairfore corrected and reformit ane part to forme to ye veritie of ye historie. And *pro*ceidit in ye historie so lang as lasair was gevin to me'. The text itself concludes in 1570, fol. 196: 'And thus I finishe & mak end ye xxv day of m*ar*che M vᶜ lxx'. For other Leslie MSS, see no. 93 below.

Conway Davies, I: 328-29.

Pl. 272

42 Lambeth Palace 8 *[betw. 1188 and 1201]*
[London, England]

Radulphus de Diceto, Opera historica

Parch. 161 fols, foliated i-ii, 1-81, 82-158, + leaf unfoliated between 81 and 82. 425 × 320 mm. 2-3 cols, 335 × 227 mm. 43-44 lines. Col. inits, rubrics. Leather bdg over boards, clasps and chain staple gone.

Ralph's collection of his own works, with contemporary revisions to text written over erasures and new material added in the margins. Composition of the contents can be dated to between 1188 (prologue to *Abbreviationes Chronicorum* thus dated, fol. 5: '… annum a tempore gracie .m.c.lxxxviij tibi metam constitue') and 1199 (the conclusion of the *Ymagines Historiarum* with the coronation of John, 27 May 1199, fol. 139; see further W. Stubbs, *Radulfi de Diceto Decani Lundoniensis Opera Historica*, 2 vols (RS 1876), I: lxxxviii-xc and xciii-xcvi. Only one other copy of the *Ymagines Historiarum* ends at same point: BL, Royal 13. E. vi, directly copied from the present MS, which has all but one of the alterations made here; see R.M. Thomson, *Manuscripts from St Albans Abbey 1066-1235*, 2 vols (1982), I: 73-4). Ralph had died or resigned as Dean of St Paul's, London, by May 1201 (for this date see D.E. Greenway, 'The succession to Ralph de Diceto, Dean of St Paul's', *BIHR*, 39 (1966), 86-95). By several scribes, who may have worked in the cathedral's vicinity rather than in an in-house scriptorium. One of them (fols 4ᵛ, 153-54ᵛ) has been identified as the scribe of two other copies of Ralph's works, both presentation MSS: BL, Add. 40007 (*DMBL*, no. 401) and Cambridge, Corpus Christi College 76 (*DMC*, no. 129). He must have been working here after 1193 since his list of archbishops of Canterbury (fol. 4ᵛ) ends with Hubert Walter, 1193-1205. Another of the scribes also appears in BL, Cotton Claudius E. III (*DMBL*, no. 521) and is the scribe of Oxford, Bodleian Library, Rawlinson B. 372, fols 3-4, the so-called 'Domesday of Ralph de Diceto' (*ex info*. Professor M.B. Parkes).

Fol. ii: 'Cronica composita a Radulfo de diceto decano et Incipit liber a Rubrica. In opusculo sequenti trium temporum et finit et in penultimo folio in Rubrica. Comites Flandrences' (s. xiiiᵉˣ), agreeing word for word with an entry in the 1295 list of books in St Paul's treasury (cf. N.R. Ker, 'Books at St Paul's Cathedral before 1313', *Books, Collectors and Libraries*, p. 234, no. 117). Also in the 1458 inventory of books 'in nova libraria' (cf. W. Dugdale, *History of St Paul's Cathedral*, ed. H. Ellis (1818), p. 393 [F. 1]). Fol. 5: 'Liber ecclesie sancti Pauli London' (s. xvᵉˣ). Seen by Bale at St Paul's (see T. Graham and A.G. Watson, *The recovery of the past in early Elizabethan England: Documents by John Bale and John Joscelyn from the circle of Matthew Parker*, Cambridge Bibliographical Soc. Monographs, No. 13 (1998), p. 25 n. 117). Fol. 55: annotation in red crayon by Archbp Parker. Item J2.64 in John Joscelyn's pre-1567 list of writings on English history (for which see Graham and Watson, pp. 61-109).

> James, pp. 20-21; *The Year 1200: A Centennial Exhibition at the Metropolitan Museum of Art*, ed. K. Hoffmann (1970), no. 299; Gransden, *Hist. Writing*, I, pl. VII illus. part of fol. 1ᵛ (reduced); B. Smalley, *Historians in the Middle Ages* (1957), pl. 57 illus. fol. 1 (reduced).
>
> *Pl. 17 a, b*

43 Lambeth Palace 32, fols 1-257 *1385*
Cambridge, England

Thomas Bradwardine, De Causa Dei contra Pelagium

Parch. 257 fols. 387 × 235 mm. 2 cols, 317 × 187 mm. 62-65 lines. Col.inits.

Fol. 257: 'Explicit istud opus de causa dei contra pelagium et de virtute causarum dei Thome de Bradwardyna Cancellarij london' perscriptum Cantebriggie. Anno domini Millesimo CCC⁰ octogesimo quinto editum ab eodem Thoma london' anno domini Millesimo \ccc⁰ / quadragesimo quarto'. By two different hands; hand 1 copied only fols 1-60 (the first five quires) while hand 2 copied the rest of the text, fols 61-257, as well as the following tabula, fols 257-71. 6 flyleaves (2 at beginning and 4 at end) are from a civil law MS (s. xiii); fol. i, originally a pastedown, bears the green stain left by a brass chain staple.

Fol. 271ᵛ: two *cautio* notes, the first of which (having been erased) is only partly visible under ultra-violet light: 'Caucio magistri W. Gylls exposita ciste <Neel> anno domini mˡ .cccc. xxxiij < >'. The second reads 'Caucio magistri Willelmi Dyngley [*BRUC* 203 and Appx] exposita ciste [Ricardi] bylyngford [*BRUC* 61] anno domini mˡ ccccᵐᵒ xxxvjᵗᵒ \vij die mensis maij/ pro xl s'. On Cambridge loan chests, see G. Pollard, 'Mediaeval loan chests at Cambridge', *BIHR*, 17 (1940), 113-19, and R. Lovatt, 'Two collegiate loan chests in late medieval Cambridge', *Medieval Cambridge: Essays on the Pre-Reformation University*, ed. P. Zutshi (1993), pp. 129-65. Part of Dyngley's donation to Peterhouse, for which see M.R. James, *Descriptive Catalogue of the Manuscripts in the Library of Peterhouse* (1899), p. 8 (no. 111 in the medieval catalogue as pr. by James).

> James, pp. 46-47.
>
> *Pl. 65*

44 Lambeth Palace 35, fols 1-245 *1450 Rome, Italy*

Dominicus de Bandinis, Fons Memorabilium Universi, pars i-iii

Paper. 245 fols. 380 × 268 mm. 2 cols, 268 × 195 mm. 60 lines. Pen and ink drawings, diagrs, col. inits, rubrics. Bld-stamped bdg over wooden boards, clasps gone (s. xv).

Fol. 245: 'Cuius copiam fecit seu scripsit Egghardus Buck alias Nygeland clericus Bremen' dioc' pro Reuerendissimo <……> patre et domino domino dominico et sancte Crucis in Jerusalem sancte romane ecclesie presbitero Cardinali atque sumo priario firmano vulgariter nuncupato [i.e. Domenico Capranica, bishop of Fermo, d. 1458] Finitum Rome anno domini millesimo quadringentesimo quinquagesimo Cum erat annus jubileus annus gracie sue remissionis omnium peccatorum in die jouis octaua mensis januarij'. Fols 247-370 containing pars iv are by a different hand. The suggestion (James, p. 51) that Cambridge, Corpus Christi College 78, containing pars v, forms a set with the present volume should be discounted. See further A.T. Hankey, 'The successive revisions and surviving codices of the *Fons Memorabilium Uniuersi* of Domenico di Bandino', *Rinascimento*, 11 (1960), 3-49.

One of two copies of the work owned by Capranica; the other, now Vatican, Rossiana 1155-7 (for which see H. Tietze, *Die illuminierten handschriften der Rossiana in Wien-Lainz* (1911), 93, no. 150, and cf. A.V. Antonovics, 'The library of

Cardinal Domenico Capranica', *Cultural Aspects of the Italian Renaissance; essays in honour of Paul Oskar Kristeller*, ed. C.H. Clough (1976), pp. 141-59) was bequeathed by him to the Collegio Capranica which he founded in Rome.

James, pp. 49-52.

Pl. 133

45   Lambeth Palace 42   *[after 1162]*
[Abingdon, England]

'Florence of Worcester', Chronicon ex chronicis, with the continuation of John of Worcester

Parch. 155 fols, foliated i, 1-154. 370 × 245 mm. Fols 1-14 2-4 cols, 280 × 190 mm; fols 15-154 2 cols, 280 × 190 mm. 44 lines. Col. inits, title in red, green and blue capitals, rubrics.

Text and papal and episcopal lists preceding it were copied by the same scribe. The latest names in such lists were originally Pope Alexander III (1159-81) and Thomas Becket (1162-70). The list of popes (fol. 9ʳ) was later extended by another hand to Clemens III (1187-91) and that of archbishops of Canterbury (fol. 9ᵛ) to Baldwin (1184-90); a scribe of s. xiii further extended the latter to Boniface (1241-70). The text has some Abingdon interpolations closely related to the text of the first Abingdon chronicle, BL, Cotton Claudius C. IX, and it is very likely both MSS were written by the same scribe (cf. P. McGurk in *The Chronicle of John of Worcester*, ed. R.R. Darlington and P. McGurk (1995-), II: xlv; for a facsimile of Claudius, see *Chronicon Monasterii de Abingdon*, ed. J. Stevenson, 2 vols (RS, 1858), II, frontispiece). In Claudius the scribe was active after 1166, see J. Hudson, 'The abbey of Abingdon, its *Chronicle* and the Norman Conquest', *Anglo-Norman Studies*, 19 (1997), p. 184.
Fol. 15: 'Iste liber est ecclesie sancte Marie Abbendon' Quicumque ipsum alienauerit celauerit uel aliquo modo defraudauerit anathema sit. Amen' (s. xiv); *ex libris* repeated by s. xv hand on fol. 6. Fol. i (flyleaf): 'Iste est liber lxxxviij In inuentorio almarioli claustri' (s. xv). Occasional annotations by Thomas Gascoigne, d. 1458 (*BRUO* 745-48). Fol. i (below the Abingdon catalogue number): 'Iste liber pertinet ad me Edouardum Jons presbiterum' (s. xvi). Fol. 1: 'Lumley', John Lord Lumley, d. 1609, but omitted from the catalogue of his library.

James, pp. 58-60; M. Brett, 'John of Worcester and his contemporaries', *The Writing of History in the Middle Ages: Essays presented to R.W. Southern*, ed. R.H.C. Davis and J.M. Wallace-Hadrill (Oxford, 1981), pp. 101-26; *The Chronicle of John of Worcester*, II: xli-xlv and 609-15, and III: xvii.

Pl. 15

46   Lambeth Palace 46   *1477 Lorrha, Ireland*
Clementinae

Parch. 128 fols. 370 × 245 mm. 1-2 cols, 260-3 × 165 mm. 21 lines of text, 42 lines commentary. Col. inits., rubrics.

Fol. 127 (in red) 'Finit amen finit. Rodericus olacthnain Prior Monasterij fontis viui de lothra [Lorrha, co. Tipperary] regularis ordinis sancti augustinij laon' dyoc' [Killaloe]. Scripsit illuminauit ligauit tabulauit istam clementinam cum suo apparatu suo fratri carnali Tatheo Olacthnain vtriusque iuris baculario. Ac officiali Cass' [Cashel] et prebendario Cass' et laon' [for whom

see *Calendar of entries in the Papal Registers relating to Great Britain and Ireland: Papal Letters*, ed. W.H. Bliss *et al.* (1893-), XIII: *passim*] tunc Anno domini M⁰ cccc⁰ lxxvij⁰ tempore quo fratres minores congregauerunt apud Rosscreg [Roscrea] …'. Prior Ruaidrí continues with a frank account of the behaviour of the friars of Roscrea, of their rioting and looting of castles and churches. For details, see A. Gwynn and D.F. Gleeson, *A History of the Diocese of Killaloe* (1962), pp. 494-95.
Still in Ireland in 1521; cf. fol. 128ᵛ 'Memorandum quod decimo nono die mensis decembris in domo domini Willelmi de Cassell' Mauricius dei gratia Cassell' archiepiscopus [Maurice FitzGerald, archbishop of Cashel c.1504-24] conferebat et dedit primam tonsuram Rhoberto et Willelmo stapulton filijs Patricij theobaldi stapulton nec non et Redmundo filio domini donati filij Redmundi preceptoris de Clouanly et dispensauit cum quolibet ipsorum ut possit ad minores ordines peruenire et simplex beneficium optinere presentibus tunc Roberto Oflawan et mauricio filio doctoris phisice de Cloyn Philippo Oflawan et me thoma Oholy notario publico Anno domini M⁰ CCCCC⁰ xxj Ind. X. pontificati pape Leonis x Anno ix'.

James, pp. 63-64; Gwynn and Gleeson, pp. 506, 537-39; F. Henry and G. Marsh-Micheli, 'Manuscripts and illuminations, 1169-1603', *A New History of Ireland*, ed. T.W. Moody, F.X. Martin and F.J. Byrne (1976-), II, *Medieval Ireland 1159-1534*, pp. 788-89.

Pl. 198

47   Lambeth Palace 51   *[betw. 1200 and 1221]*
[London, England]

Peter of Cornwall, Liber reuelationum

Parch. 465 fols, foliated i-ii, 1-463. 353 × 230 mm. 2 cols, 275 × 175 mm. 39 lines. Col. inits, rubrics (some erased).

A collection of visions of the other world, compiled by Peter, prior of Holy Trinity, Aldgate, d. 7 July 1221 (for whom see R.W. Hunt, 'The disputation of Peter of Cornwall against Symon the Jew', *Studies in Medieval History presented to F.M. Powicke*, ed. R.W. Hunt, W.A. Pantin, R.W. Southern (1948), pp. 143-56). For recent visions Peter drew upon the testimony of personal informants, the accounts of two of whom are dated to 1200. In that year he heard of a vision of St Patrick's purgatory ('Narrauit mihi Petro priorj Sancte Trinitatis Lundonie anno m<i>llesimo ducentesimo ab incarnatione domini …', fol. 21ᵛ, col. 1), while his father told him about the vision of Ailsi ('Huius Jordani erat filius quidam Petrus nomine Canonicus et Prior sancte Trinitatis Lundon'. Qui hec que audiuit a patre suo scripsit. Anno ab incarnatione domini .m⁰. cc⁰. Qui et ipse exspectat regnum dei', fol. 26ʳ, col. 2). The present volume is a fair copy by two scribes, hand 1 copying most of Book I (fols 2-60ʳ, col. 1, 60ᵛ-130ᵛ) and a short addition to Book II (fols 340ᵛ col. 2-342ʳ col. 1, at the end of quire 43), hand 2 most of Book II (fols 131-340ᵛ, col. 1, 343ʳ-462ʳ) and a short passage in Book I (fol. 60ʳ, col. 2). They were probably working under Peter's supervision, since the text contains a few contemporary alterations and corrections, some by a hand apparently closely resembling that of the principal corrector of Taunton, Somerset Record Office, DD/AH66/17, a copy of Peter's *De reparatione lapsus*, written between 1197 and 1208 (see R. Sharpe, 'Peter of Cornwall's *De reparatione lapsus*: a "lost" work retraced', *Scriptorium*, 38 (1984), 79-81).

Fol. 2: 'De vj^{to} ordine .xlij.' (s. xiv pressmark). Fol. 337^{v} (in the margin): 'Dominus Thomas Percy Pryor' [of Holy Trinity, 1481-93]. Fol. 2: 'Arundel', Henry Fitzalan, Earl of Arundel, d. 1580, from whom the book passed to his son-in-law 'Lumley', John, Lord Lumley, d. 1609. Not in the Lumley catalogue.

James, pp. 71-85; R. Easting, 'The date and dedication of the *Tractatus de Purgatorio Sanctii Patricii*', *Speculum*, 53 (1978), 781; Easting, 'Peter of Cornwall's account of St. Patrick's purgatory', *Analecta Bollandiana*, 97 (1979), 397-416; Easting and R. Sharp, 'The visions of Ailsi and his sons', *Mediaevistik*, 1 (1988), 207-62.
Pl. 19

48 **Lambeth Palace 59, fols 1-182**   *[after 1122?]*
                                              [Canterbury, England]
Anselmus, Epistolae, etc.

> Parch. 182 fols. 350 × 242 mm. 2 cols, 225 × 170 mm. 31 lines. Col. inits, rubrics.

The manuscript consists of two parts: fols 1-159 (20 quires of eight, quire 7 wanting leaf 6) containing Anselm's correspondence, and fols 160-82 (supplementary quires 21-23) miscellaneous works of his. As R.W. Southern has demonstrated ('Sally Vaughn's Anselm: an examination of the foundations', *Albion*, 20 (1988), 191-202, 695-96; also his *St Anselm: a portrait in a landscape* (1990), pp. 459-80) the view that the letter collection in fols 1-159 was compiled under Anselm's personal supervision, and hence between 1103 and 1108, is erroneous. At the end of quire 20 (fol. 159^{v}) the main scribe was still in the middle of copying ep. 469. Rather than starting a new quire he finished it on a leaf (fol. 160^{r}) originally left blank at the beginning of a quire (quire 21) into which he had already copied other items. He then proceeded to copy three further letters, epp. 471-72 and 193 (fols 160^{r-v}), and, because of existing text, was forced to squash the conclusion of the last, ep. 193, into the bottom margin of fol. 161^{r}. For the identity of the hand of fols 160-82 with that of the main scribe of fols 1-159, see R. Gameson, 'English manuscript art in the late eleventh century: Canterbury and its context', *Canterbury and the Norman Conquest, Churches, Saints and Scholars 1066-1109*, ed. R. Eales and R. Sharpe (1995), pp. 119-20 n. 85 (and *ex info*. Mr M. Gullick). Since fols 160-82 (supplementary quires 21-23) contain a poem in praise of Anselm beginning 'Presvlis Anselmi qvem nvper obisse dolemus' (fol. 176), the scribe must have been working after Anselm's death in 1109. Southern argues that since William of Malmesbury did not use this copy when he put together his own collection of Anselm's letters in 1120-22 (no. 65 below), the present MS must post-date William's activity, and that possibly the Christ Church monks were encouraged to produce it by William's example. Fols 183-90 contain duplicate copies of items on fols 160-82 and appear to have been taken from another MS (s. xii). They form a quire which has been refolded back to front, so that its original leaves 1-4 have become leaves 5-8 (present fols 187-90). Text begins abruptly fol. 187 in the middle of Ep. 471 and ends fol. 190, leaving what had been the last four leaves (present fols 183-86) blank. A cursive hand has supplied the beginning of Ep. 471 at the top of fol. 187, and written the inscription 'Que restant modici sunt scripta manu thiderici' (fol. 190). W. Frölich ('The genesis of the collections of St. Anselm's letters', *American Benedictine Review*, 35 (1984), 249-66; 'The letters omitted from Anselm's collection of letters', *Anglo-Norman Studies*, 6 (1984), 58-7; and his tr. and edn *The Letters of St Anselm of Canterbury*, Cistercian Studies Series, 96 (1990), pp. 32-39), and S. Vaughn ('Anselm: saint and statesman', *Albion*, 20 (1988), 211-16) have mistakenly taken this to mean that the Christ Church scribe Thidericus, one of Anselm's correspondents, was responsible for the entire volume. For Thidericus, see F.S. Schmitt, 'Die unter Anselm veranstaltete Ausgabe seiner Werke und Briefe: die Codices Bodley 271 und Lambeth 59', *Scriptorium*, 9 (1953), 64-75

Fol. 1: Christ Church pressmark (s.xii); fol. i (flyleaf): 'D. ij^{a} . G. x' (s. xiii). No. 71 in Prior Eastry's catalogue (James, *Anc. Libs.*). Fol. ii^{v}: '<liber ecclesie christi cantuar' de prima demonstratione>', s. xv *ex libris* crossed out by Archbp Sancroft (1678-90) who supplied a list of contents (see no. 49 below). Annotated by Archbp Cranmer; cf. D.G. Selwyn, 'Thomas Cranmer and the dispersal of medieval libraries: the provenance of some of his medieval manuscripts and printed books', *Books and Collectors 1200-1700: Essays presented to A.G. Watson*, ed. J.P. Carley and C.G.C. Tite (1997), pp. 285-86. Fol. 1 (at foot of page): 'Lumley'; cf. *The Library of John, Lord Lumley*, ed. S. Jayne and F.R. Johnson (1956), p. 43, being item 40 in the 1609 catalogue of his library. Now bound with no. 49 below.

A. Wilmart, 'La tradition des lettres de S. Anselme: lettres inédites de S. Anselme et ses correspondants', *Revue Bénédictine*, 43 (1931), 39 and n. 5; James, pp. 71-85; *S. Anselmi Opera Omnia*, ed. F.S. Schmitt, 5 (1951), frontispiece illus. fol. 64 (reduced); Southern, *Albion*, 20 (1988), pl. I illus. part of fols 187 and 190 (reduced); R. Gameson, *The Manuscripts of Early Norman England (c.1066-1130)* (1999), p. 122, no. 581.
Pl. 9

49 **Lambeth Palace 59, fols 224^{v}-30**   *1468 England*
Anselmus, Liber de similitudinibus

> Parch. 7 fols. 350 × 242 mm. 2 cols, 320 × 150 mm. 40 lines. Col. inits, rubrics.

Fol. 230^{v}: 'Explicit Tabula Anselmi de similitudinibus completa per Johannem Marchall' Anno dominice incarnationis .1468. die Sancti Felicis martiris'. Fols 191-224 and 231-74 (other works by Anselm) copied by the same scribe are undated.
On fol. 274^{v} Marshall began to copy Augustine, *De vera innocencia*, but broke off after the first few lines leaving the rest of the page and the following four leaves (fols 275-78) blank; he restarted copying the Augustine in a new booklet (now Lambeth MS 50, fols 185-216, undated). Medieval foliation in ink establishes that the present fols 191-278 of Lambeth MS 59 were once fols 1-88 of Lambeth MS 50, and that the present fols 1-112 of the latter MS were originally fols 89-200 (medieval foliation ceases thereafter). Lambeth MS 50 thus once formed a compilation of works by Anselm and Augustine (cf. s. xv^{2} table of contents in Lambeth MS 50, fol. i^{v}, and the note on the endleaf, fol. 287^{v}: 'Opera Ancelmi byse florysshed Opera Augustini'), which were all copied probably around the same date by John Marshall and other scribes. All of Anselm's works were removed from this original compilation to the present MS by Archbp Sancroft who then supplied a list of contents in Lambeth MS 59 (no. 48 above) which included the contents of the newly introduced 88 leaves (now fols 191-278). He also annotated the original (s. xv) list of contents in Lambeth MS 50.

Letters 't ihc b' in red within initial (fol. 191) occur also in Eton College 8 (for which see *MMBL*, II: 636-37).

James, pp. 91-96 and 68-71.

Pl. 171

---

50 **Lambeth Palace 61, II** *1476 Rome, Italy*

Bullarium carmelitanum

Parch. 25 fols, foliated 118-42. 352 × 230 mm. 1 col., 252 × 180 mm. 44 lines. Enlarged capitals with pen flourishing (fol. 118).

Fol. 142: 'Datum Rome apud Sanctum petrum Anno Incarnationis dominice Millesimo quadringentesimo septuagesimo sexto Quarto kal' Decembris Pontificatus nostri anno sexto [Sixtus IV, 1471-84]'. Bulls, Nicholas III to Pius II, promulgated in favour of the Carmelite Order, copied in the papal chancery and signed (fol. 142): 'Gratis de mandato sanctissimi domini nostri pape D[idacus] Serrano', 'L[eonardus] Grifus', and 'D[ominicus] Gallettus', scribe of the present MS. For these men, see T. Frenz, *Die Kanzlei der Päpste der Hochrenaissance (1471-1527)* (1986), nos 574, 1504, 594 respectively. Grifus also signs fol. 142ᵛ: 'Reᵗᵃ apud me L. Grifum'. The arms of Sixtus are drawn in the initial, fol. 118. Fol. 142: 'Orate pro animabus patricij calinani et ane ny vo<.>the' and on fol. 142ᵛ a line of Irish. Notes in the hand of John Bale, fols 128-29: see H. McCusker, 'Books and manuscripts formerly in the possession of John Bale', *The Library*, 4th ser., 16 (1936), p. 163; W. O'Sullivan, 'The Irish "remnaunt" of John Bale's manuscripts', *New Science out of Old Books: Studies in Manuscripts and Early Printed Books in honour of A.I. Doyle*, ed. R. Beadle and A.J. Piper (1995), p. 378). Fol. 132: 'Jacobi Ussherij', Archbp of Armagh, d. 1656. Now bound up with the unrelated parts I (s. xii/xiii, Alexander Neckham on the Psalter) and III (s. xiv, sermon of Henry de Harkeley (*BRUO* 874), d. 1317).

James, pp. 97-99.

Pl. 197

---

51 **Lambeth Palace 69** *[betw. 1408? and 1416]*
[London, England]

Breviarium ad usum Sarum (the 'Chichele Breviary')

Parch. 421 fols, foliated i-iii, 1-418. 340 × 225 mm. 2 cols, 202 × 130 mm. 40 lines. Illum. hist. inits with full-page or partial borders, gold and col. inits, rubrics. Kal. in red, blue, green and black.

The arms of Henry Chichele (*BRUO* 410-12) as archbp of Canterbury, 1414-43, occur in the borders of fols 1, 209, but they appear to have been added. Since the MS belonged to him, it seems likely it was produced before 1416, because the offices of David, Chad, and Winifred (whose feasts were accepted by the Convocation of Canterbury in 1415) and that of John of Beverley (whose feast was ordered throughout England in 1416) do not occur in the proper of saints; cf. NPS, 2nd ser., II, pl. 131. Perhaps made for Chichele when he was bishop of the secular cathedral of St David's, 1408-1414, for the initial on fol. 1 depicts a bishop, without pallium, receiving a book from two groups of canons. David (though not Chad, Winifred or John of Beverley) is present (in red) in the kalendar, with nine lessons (cf. Exh., *Engl. Illum. MSS 700-1500*, no. 73). The initial on fol. 1 is signed by Herman Scheerre with his motto 'Si quis amat non laborat quo(d) herman'. His career in England has been dated between 1403 and 1419 by G.M. Spriggs ('The Nevill Hours and the School of Herman Scheerre', *JWCI*, 37 (1974), 115). On Scheerre, see also M. Rickert, 'Herman the illuminator', *Burlington Magazine*, 66 (1935), 39-40; C.L. Kuhn, 'Herman Scheerre and English illumination of the early fifteenth century', *Art Bulletin*, 22 (1940), 138-56; G.M Spriggs, 'Unnoticed Bodleian manuscripts, illuminated by Herman Scheerre and his school', *Bodleian Library Record*, 7 (1962-67), 193-203; and S.A. Wright, 'The Big Bible, Royal 1.E.ix in the British Library, and manuscript illumination in London in the early fifteenth century', Unpubl. Ph.D. thesis, University of London 1986, pp. 188-209 and 296-312). A second artist is identified by Scott (*Later Gothic MSS*, Cat. no. 30) as the 'Carmelite-Lapworth Master'. Other work by this latter artist probably includes no. 122 below (and see Scott, II: 28 for a list of MSS attributed to him).

BFAC, *Exhibition of Illuminated MSS*, no. 148; NPS, 2nd ser., II, pl. 131 illus. fol. 209; Frere, *BML*, no. 1; E.G. Millar, 'Les principaux manuscrits à peintures du Lambeth Palace à Londres', *Bulletin de la S.F.R.M.P.*, 9 (1925), pl. XLI illus. fol. 1 (reduced); James, pp. 109-12; Kuhn, loc. cit., figs 14-16 illus. inits fols 55, 1ᵛ, 4ᵛ (reduced); M. Rickert, *The Reconstructed Carmelite Missal* (1952), pl. LIIIb illus. init. fol. 55 (reduced); M. Rickert, *Painting in Britain: the Middle Ages* (1954), pl. 170c illus. init. fol. 1 (reduced); Exh., *Engl. Illum. MSS 700-1500*, pl. 36 illus. init. fol. 1; Scott, *Later Gothic MSS*, Cat. no. 30, colour pl. 5 illus. fol. 1, and illus. 127-33 illus. inits fols 209, 223ᵛ, 227ᵛ, 237, 282, 373ᵛ, and border dec. fol. 209.

Pl. 81

---

52 **Lambeth Palace 74, fols 152-95** *1390, 1391*
[England]

Walter Burley, Expositiones

Parch. 45 fols, foliated 152-59, 159bis, 160-95. 333 × 240 mm. 2 cols, 240 × 172 mm. 50 lines. Col. inits.

Fol. 174: 'Explicit liber de sompno et vigilia secundum magistrum Walterum de Bur [*sic*] Et finitus est Anno domini Mᵒ cccᵒ xcᵒ

Nomen scriptoris tu qui cognoscere queris

L tibi \sit/ primum e medium o que sit ymum' [Leo];
fol. 195ᵛ: 'Explicit tractatus Burley dei potencijs anime Iste liber erat scriptus Anno domini Mᵒ CCCᵒ xcjᵒ'. Two booklets (fols 152-74 and 175-95) both written by the same scribe and forming part of a compilation of Burley's works; fols 9-32 and 33-151 are also by Leo, while fols 1-8 are by an early s. xv hand. According to James, p. 120, an erased but partly legible inscription on fol. 1 is that of Richard Calne (*BRUO* 340), canon of Lanthony Priory, Gloucestershire. *MLGB*, p. 273, reports 'emptus per ... (R. Calne)'. Such an inscription is not now visible, even under ultra-violet light. However, the table of contents on fol. iᵛ (flyleaf) is in the same s. xv hand as that of tables of contents in other Lanthony books, including one of Calne's (no. 76 below).

James, pp. 120-22; M.J. Kitchel, 'The "De potentiis animae" of Walter Burley', *Medieval Studies*, 33 (1971), 85-113.

Pl. 68

53   Lambeth Palace 76, fols 1-147   *[before 1124]*
[Rochester, England]

Augustinus Hipponensis, Retractationes; etc.

Parch. 147 fols. 332 × 218 mm. 2 cols, 233 × 150 mm. 33 lines. Col. inits, rubrics.

Item 16 in the earliest catalogue of the library of Rochester cathedral (cf. *English Benedictine Libraries*, p. 474). This catalogue, included in part II (fols 119-235) of the *Textus Roffensis* (Rochester Cathedral Library A.3.5), has been dated between 1122 and 1123 (ibid., p. 470), since part I (fols 1-118), written by the same scribe as part II, is datable then. Thus the latest archbishop of Canterbury given by the scribe in episcopal lists in part I is Ralph d'Escures, whose death 20 October 1122 is recorded. His successor, William of Corbeil, consecrated 18 February 1123, was added by another hand (fol. 110ᵛ). However, P. Wormald ('*Laga Eadwardi*: the *Textus Roffensis* and its context', *Anglo-Norman Studies*, 17 (1994), 243-66), argues this archiepiscopal list only provides a *terminus post quem* of 1122 for the Canterbury exemplar from which it was copied. He dates part I to 1123-24 (*The Making of English Law: King Alfred to the Twelfth Century* (1999-), I: 245). Since the catalogue is part of a cartulary (part II) in which the latest deeds date from the episcopate of Ernulf, bishop of Rochester 1115-24 (see P.H. Sawyer, *Textus Roffensis, part ii*, EEMF, 11 (1962), p. 18), a date of before 1124 for the catalogue seems acceptable. The two parts were bound together at least from the fourteenth century (the date of the *ex libris* (fol. 1) attributing the volume to Ernulf). The present MS is by the same scribe as the *Textus Roffensis*. For other MSS by him, see N.R. Ker, *English Manuscripts in the Century after the Norman Conquest* (1960), p. 31; K.M. Waller, 'The library, scriptorium and community of Rochester Cathedral Priory c.1080-1150', Unpublished Ph.D. thesis, Liverpool 1980, pp. 90-94; *DMO*, no. 69; and *DMC*, nos 34, 376.

Item 22 in the 1202 catalogue (*English Benedictine Libraries*, p. 501). Fol. 1: 'Liber de Claustro Roffensi', then added 'per Laurentium de London' (s. xiv). Bound by Archbp Sancroft with another copy of Augustine (fols 148-238, also s. xii) which is perhaps no. 191 in Lanthony library catalogue of c.1355-60 (*Augustinian Libraries*, p, 59).

> R.P. Coates, 'Catalogue of the Library of the Priory of St Andrew, Rochester, from the *Textus Roffensis*', *Archaeologia Cantiana*, 6 (1866), 120-28; James, pp. 124-27; M.P. Edwards, 'Texts and their traditions in the medieval library of Rochester Cathedral Priory', *Trans. of the American Philosophical Society held at Philadelphia*, 78, part 3 (1988).
> *Pl. 10*

54   Lambeth Palace 84   *[betw. 1477 & 1479; c.1482?]*
[England]

The Prose Brut

Parch. 199 fols, foliated 1-3, 6-82, 84-108, 110-202; fols 4-5, 109-109bis are s. xvi supply leaves. 303 × 225 mm. 1 col., 215 × 150 mm. Approx. 38-45 lines. Col. drawing (fol. 10), diagr. fol. 51, pen and ink drawings in margins, col. inits (fols 1-108ᵛ only, thereafter space for inits), rubrics.

The *Brut* narrative to 1419 with a short, original, continuation copied by the scribe. This continuation contains a list of Edward IV's children (fol. 202ᵛ), naming George, born 1477, but not Catherine, born 1479. Later, the scribe returned to his MS and extensively revised the text in light of the 1482 publication of Caxton's edition of Trevisa's translation of Higden's *Polychronicon* (*STC* 13438), making interpolations both in the margins and on slips inserted after fols 19, 72, 76, 82, 85, 88, 95, 97, 119, 177, 181. See further L.M. Matheson, 'Printer and scribe: Caxton, the *Polychronicon*, and the *Brut*', *Speculum*, 60 (1985), 607-9 and 'The Arthurian stories of Lambeth Palace MS 84', *Arthurian Literature*, 5 (1985), 70-91. Fol. 203 is an endleaf from a missal (s. xiii).

Fol. 182: 'John Stoughton' (s. xv ex) 'is a littel wantton' added by another hand; fol. 201ᵛ: 'William anford' (s. xv ex); fol. 1: 'lorde haue mercye on me / christe haue mercy on me / lorde haue mercy on me / quothe Symson' (s. xvi). Fol. 1: 'Lumley': item 1022 in the 1609 catalogue of the library of John, Lord Lumley (cf. S. Jayne and F.R. Johnson, *The Library of John, Lord Lumley* (1956), p. 131).

> James, pp. 139-42; Scott, *Later Gothic MSS*, II: 67, 224; *IMEP*, XIII: 13-14.
> *Pl. 201*

55   Lambeth Palace 109   *[betw. c. 1155 and c. 1176 ?]*
[Buildwas, England]

Gregorius, Moralia in Job, libri VI-XI (fragmentum)

Parch. 52 fols, foliated i-ii, 1-50. 330 × 220 mm. 2 cols, 244 × 160 mm. 35 lines. Col. init. (fol. 12), rubrics.

One of a group of MSS (interconnected by script and provenance) produced at the Cistercian abbey of Buildwas, Shropshire, during the abbacy of Ranulf, 1155-87. The present volume contains the work of two hands, the so-called 'flyleaf scribe' and the 'master scribe' (the latter responsible here only for the initial on fol. 12); their activity is assigned to c.1160-70 by J.M. Sheppard (*The Buildwas books: book production, acquisition and use at an English Cistercian monastery, 1165-c.1400*, Oxford Bibliographical Soc. Publications, 3rd ser., 2 (1997), pp. 5-10). Both scribes also occur in Cambridge, Trinity College B.1.3. However, only in Oxford, Christ Church lat. 88, dated 1167 (*DMO*, no. 760), written and illustrated by the master scribe, is the work of either of the scribes precisely dated. The flyleaf scribe also copied the discarded folios of another copy of Gregory's Moralia used as flyleaves in the original twelfth-century bindings of London, BL, Harley 3038, dated 1176 (*DMBL*, no. 723) and Trinity B.1.3. If Sheppard's suggestion (p. 9) is accepted that these discarded leaves were rejected when it was decided to produce the Lambeth MS, it would provide a *terminus ante quem* of 1176 for the present copy.

Fol. iiᵛ (in caps, words alternately in green and red): 'Liber sancte Marie de Bildewas' (s. xii). Fol. 49ᵛ (foot of page): 'Nunc finem feci da mihi quod merui' (s. xv).

> James, pp. 184-85; N.R. Ker, 'The English manuscripts of the Moralia of Gregory the Great', *Kunsthistorische Forschungen Otto Pächt zu seinem 70. Geburtstag*, ed. A. Rosenauer and G. Weber (1972), pp. 77-89, no. 28 in his list; J.M. Sheppard, 'The twelfth-century library and scriptorium at Buildwas: assessing the evidence', *England in the Twelfth Century*, Proceedings of the 1988 Harlaxton

Symposium, ed. D. Williams (1990), 193-204 and pls 15, 18 illus. part of fol. 4 (reduced), init. fol. 12; Sheppard, *Buildwas Books*, pl. 2 illus. part of fol. 12 (reduced).
Pl. 14

56   Lambeth Palace 117   *1545 [Scotland]*
Gavin Douglas, Eneados

Paper. 426 fols. 303 × 205 mm. 1 col. 200 × *c*.90 mm. 29 lines. Penwork init. (fol. 2), col. inits, rubrics.

Fol. 426ᵛ: 'Heir endis ye buks of Virgill writtin be the hand of Johanne mudy wᵗ maist*er* thomas bellenden of auchinnovll Just*is* Clerke [1539-47] and endit ye 2° feb*ruar*ij anno etc xlvᵒ'. Bellenden (for whom see *The Scots Peerage*, ed. Sir James Balfour Paul, 9 vols (1904-14), II: 63) was the first of three generations of the Bellendens of Auchnoul to become justice-clerk, one of the principal law officers of Scotland. Mudy, who also signed and dated the MS to 1545 on fols 1, 359ᵛ, and 396ᵛ, must have served under ('with') him. On fol. 1 his monogram 'J.M' is accompanied by a scribal paraph.
Fol. 1ᵛ: 'Edmund Ashefeyld 1596'.

James, p. 192; *Virgil's Aeneid translated into Scottish verse by Gavin Douglas*, ed. D.F.C. Coldwell, Scottish Text Soc., 3rd ser., 30 (1964), 99; P. Bawcutt, *Gavin Douglas: A Critical Study* (1976), p. 25 and n. 14.
Pl. 258

57   Lambeth Palace 145, fols 1-137
[betw. 1412 and 1421] [Oxford, England]
Pseudo-Chrysostomus, Opus imperfectum in Matthaeum

Parch. 137 fols. 297 × 210 mm. 2 cols, 229 × 145 mm. 49-50 lines. Col. inits, rubrics.

Fol. 135: 'liber lanthonie iuxta Gloucestriam emptus per fratrem Ricardum Calne [*BRUO* 340] tempore quo fuit scolaris Oxonie et qui eum a predicta domo absque licencia prioris et conuentus eiusdem domus alienauerit anathema sit. fiat fiat. Amen'. Calne studied at Oxford between 1412 and 1421 and a date of purchase sometime during these years accords with the appearance of the script. Fols 135ᵛ-37 are blank. For other books Calne purchased at Oxford, see no. 77 below.
Bound in s. xvii with fols 138-256, a Chrysostomus (s. xii), items 43-9 in an early s. xiv list of authors and titles drawn up at Crowland (*English Benedictine Libraries*, p. 118), and fols 257-64, a quire from a homiliary (s. xii). Table of contents for this new volume provided by Archbp Sancroft.

James, pp. 231-34.
Pl. 83

58   Lambeth Palace 159, fols 117-84   *1507*
[Canterbury, England]
Vitae S. Anselmi

Paper. 68 fols. 294 × 222 mm. 1 col., 214 ×135 mm. 36-42 lines. Col. inits, rubrics.

Fol. 183ᵛ: 'Scriptum per me fratrem et Commonachum ecclesie christi Cantuarie Duompnum Ricardum Stone indignum. Soli deo: honor et gloria. Amen', dated by Stone in the margin 'Anno domini Mˡᵒ. Vᶜ. vijᵒ'. Fol. 184 is blank. For Stone (d. 1508), see J. Greatrex, *Biographical Register of the English Cathedral*

Priories of the Province of Canterbury, c.1066-1540 (1997), p. 293). One of three booklets written by him; the other two, fols 48-114 and 185-220, are undated. Probably to be identified with the 'quaternae noviter suscriptae de patronis ecclesiae' listed among his possessions; see C.E. Woodruff, 'An inventory of the contents of the bed-chamber of Brother Richard Stone, monk of Christ Church, Canterbury', *Archaeologia Cantiana*, 43 (1931), 103-10. Fols ii + 1-47, 221-36, 237-60, 261-75, 276-83 contain later additions by other scribes.
From Stone the MS passed to four other monks. Fol. iiᵛ: 'Liber Dompni Jacobi Hartey monachi Ecclesie Cristi Cantuarie'; he occurs 1500-22 (Greatrex, p. 190). Hartey's name was later crossed out and that of 'N[icholas] Herst [II]' substituted; he occurs 1510-40 (Greatrex, p. 198). Another *ex libris* below records: 'Modo liber Johannis Sarysbury. Ex dono Magistri Willelmi Hadley cuius anime propicietur altissimus'; Salisbury occurs 1511-40 and Hadley 1502-40 (Greatrex, pp. 276, 187). Salisbury has further noted that 'Willelmus Hadley obijt xxviijᵒ die Janvaij [*sic*] anno domini Mᵒ Vᶜ xlvjᵉ Cuius anime propicietur altissimus amen'. He also signed fol. 284ᵛ: 'Johannis Sarisberus est possessor huius libri'. Fol. iᵛ: 'Rychard Hatton in art' bacc' oxon' [*BRUO 1501-40*, 274].

James, pp. 248-56; D.J. Sheerin, 'An anonymous verse epitome of the life of St. Anselm', *Analecta Bollandiana*, 92 (1974), 104-24.
Pl. 237

59   Lambeth Palace 174   *1440 [England]*
Petrus de Crescentiis, Libri ruralium commo-dorum libri XII

Parch. 212 fols, medieval foliation in ink 1-130, 132-212, 214. 295 × 200 mm. 2 cols, 197 × 130 mm. 43-44 lines. Rubrics, blank spaces left for inits.

Fol. 212ᵛ (note by the hand of corrections to text): 'Scriptus erat hic libellus anno domini millesimo CCCCᵐᵒ xlᵐᵒ multo labore et studio quamquam non plene correctus'. Not listed by either L. Frati, 'Bibliografia dei manoscritti', *Pier de' Crescenzi (1233-1321): Studi e documenti*, ed. A. Sorbelli, Società Agraria di Bologna (1933), 259-306, or R.G. Calkins, 'Pier de' Crescenzi and the medieval garden', *Medieval Gardens*, ed. E.B. MacDougall, Dumbarton Oaks Colloquium on the History of Landscape Architecture, IX (1986), p. 159 n. 9.
Fol. 12 (in red pencil): 'E. Donyngton' (s. xv²). Fol. iᵛ (flyleaf): 'John Rauen is no knaue my Lord I would be the Trumpetter Jack Rauen' with a man's head drawn in ink (s. xvi). Fol. iiᵛ: 'Edo. Orwell 13 Julij 1586'.

James, pp. 274-75.
Pl. 113

60   Lambeth Palace 184   *1460, 1461*
[Westminster? England]
Egidius Romanus, De Regimine Principum; Petrus Thomae, Formalitates

Parch. 240 fols, foliated 1-239, + leaf omitted in foliation between 9 and 10. 295 × 203 mm. 1 col. 200 × 126 mm, 40 lines fols 1-183; 196 × 130 mm, 37-38 lines fols 184-239. Full-page border (fol. 1), illum. dec. inits with borders, gold and col. inits, rubrics.

Two booklets both written by the same scribe: (1) fols 1-183 dated fol. 179ᵛ (in red) 'Fratris Egidij Romanj ordinis fratrum heremitarum In sacratissima Theologia professoris nominatissimj De principum erudicione et Regimine liber Explicit feliciter 1461 A IESU MERCY'; (2) fols 184-239 dated fol. 239ᵛ (in red) 'Eximij sacratissime pagine doctoris Petri thome Formalitates Expliciunt feliciter:- 1460 A IESU MERCI'. From Westminster Abbey: arms attributed to Edward the Confessor impaled with the keys of St Peter in a shield added to border, fol. 1. Fol. 1 'J. Foxus' (s. xvi), probably the prebendary of Westminster 1606-23, for whom see *The Marriage, Baptismal and Burial Registers of the Collegiate Church or Abbey of St. Peter, Westminster*, ed. J.L. Chester, Harleian Soc., 10 (1876), p. 121 n. 3.

James, pp. 288-89; C.F. Briggs, 'Manuscripts of Giles of Rome's *De Regimine Principum* in England, 1300-1500', *Scriptorium*, 47 (1993), p. 69 no. 34; also Briggs, *Giles of Rome De Regimine Principum: Reading and Writing Politics at Court and University, c.1275-c.1525* (1999), p. 164.
Pl. 154

61 Lambeth Palace 198, fols 9-192
[betw. 1361 and 1369] [Peterborough, England]

Consuetudinarium, pars I

Parch. 184 fols. 270 × 180 mm. 1 col., 188 × 120 mm. 29-30 lines. Col. inits, rubrics.

Fol. 192ᵛ (foot of page, in red capitals and partly cut away): '<FINIS.> PRIME. PARTIS'. Rites to be observed at the Benedictine abbey of Peterborough from the first Sunday in Advent until Easter. The text (fol. 42, ll. 23-24) refers to the election as abbot of Henry of Overton, elected October 1361. It has been kept up-to-date with frequent additions and corrections. On fol. 135ᵛ an addition at the foot of the page by a hand other than that of the main scribe notes that a custom described in the text had recently been abolished by Overton in the 8th year of his office, 1368-69; see further A. Gransden, 'The Peterborough Customary and Gilbert de Stanford', *Revue Bénédictine*, 70 (1960), 625-38. At the beginning (fol. 9) the main scribe has written alternately in black and red ink the lines:
'Hec ascribenda Symoni sunt scripta legenda
Ex yarwel natus fuerat monacus memoratus
De solitis rebus speculum nitet hic quasi phebus
In quo consuetas elucidat ipse dietas'
Preceded by a kalendar (in a preliminary quire) copied by another scribe (with marginal obits of previous abbots, the latest being that of Henry's predecessor, Robert de Ramsey, abbot 1353-61).
Probably a companion volume with no. 62 below.

C. Wordsworth, 'Kalendarium e Consuetudinario Monasterii de Burgo Sancti Petri', *Archaeologia*, 51 (1888), 7-15, 28-40; Frere, *BML*, no. 15; James, pp. 309-10.
Pl. 56

62 Lambeth Palace 198 B, fols 18-284   *1371*
[Peterborough, England]

Consuetudinarium, pars iii

Parch. 266 fols. 270 × 185 mm. 1 col, 195 × 112 mm. 30 lines. Col. inits, rubrics.

Fol. 284, text ends in red: '... Et sciendum quod festum corporis \christi/in Natiuitate sancti Johannis baptiste ab anno domini .mˡ . cccᵒ . Septuagesimo primo. in quo anno iste liber scriptus fuit non continget. vsque ad .iiijˣˣ . annos proximo sequentes. secundum tabulam dionisii. et aliarum tabularum.', then the following verse with alternate words in red and black:

Hiis declaratis	sit scriptor. cumque beatis	
Ac ipsum gratis	sinus capiat pietatis.	Amen
Dictus erat rite.	Jon Trentham. quem deus orbis	
A tetris morbis.	saluet. det gaudia vite.	

Since fol. 18 reads 'Incipit tercia pars consuetudinarii de historiis dominicalibus inter oct' Pentecost. et dominicam primam Aduentus domini', the present MS is generally assumed to be vol. 3 of a customary of which vol. 1 is no. 61 above (vol. 2 now missing). In spite of the close similarity of their layout, A. Gransden ('The Peterborough Customary and Gilbert de Stanford', *Revue Bénédictine*, 70 (1960), 625-38) has argued that the two MSS cannot once have formed part of a set, because their contents are partly dissimilar and they are 'not apparently by the same author'. Despite Trentham calling himself *scriptor*, she suggests *scriptor* here 'means author as it seems unlikely a scribe would be allowed to celebrate his achievement with four lines of verse'. Trentham (and Simon of Yarwell, no. 61 above), was more likely a copyist. Both volumes are preceded by an identical kalendar (fols 10-16 of the present MS) but not by the same hand. Here the kalendar is an integral part of the volume, although not written by Trentham.
Fols 285-88 contain ordinances from Robert de Sutton, abbot 1262-73, to the 6th year of Henry of Overton, 1366/7, by a different hand to Trentham, with additional ordinances from Richard Ashton, abbot 1439-71. Fols 5ᵛ-7 contain further Ashton ordinances. Fol. 2ᵛ (erased): memorandum of items sold by William Qoket of Peterborough in London, 18 May 4 Henry IV (1403).

James, pp. 310-12.
Pl. 59

63 Lambeth Palace 209   *[betw. 1252 and 1267?]*
[London? England]

Apocalypsis (the 'Lambeth Apocalypse')

Parch. 56 fols, foliated i-ii, 1-54. 272 × 196 mm. 2 cols, c.95 × 153 mm. 17-23 lines. Full-page frontispiece (fol. iiᵛ), tinted drawings (fols 40-53), mins, hist. init. (fol. 1ᵛ), gold and col. inits, rubrics.

Drawings at the end of the MS, although in a separate group of quires, bear inscriptions in the hands of the scribes of the text. One (fol. 48) portrays the *destinataire* of the MS as a lady kneeling before the Virgin and child; on her undermantle she bears the arms of Ferrers and on her overmantle those of de Quincy. She is usually identified as Eleanor Ferrers who married, as his second wife, Roger de Quincy, 2nd earl of Winchester, in 1252. He died 1264. In 1267 Eleanor married Roger de Leybourne, of Leeds Castle, Kent, after which date she would presumably have borne his arms rather than those of de Quincy (cf. N. Morgan, *The Lambeth Apocalypse*, with a contribution on the palaeography by M. Brown (1990), pp. 73-82. Morgan dismisses an alternative identification of the lady depicted as Margaret, Roger de Quincy's daughter by his first marriage, who, in 1238, had become the second wife of William Ferrers, earl of Derby, because the de Quincy arms are shown on the lady's outer garment and thus are more likely to be those of her husband's family than her own). By three scribes: (1) scribe A (fols ii^v, 1-19^v, 53-53^v) whom Brown (*Lambeth Apocalypse*, p. 116) suggests was also the scribe of Oxford, Bodleian Library, Rawlinson A. 384, fol. 91; (2) scribe B (fols 20-22^v, 46^v-47^v, 48^v) whose hand is said to resemble strongly that of one of the scribes of the Gulbenkian Apocalypse (Lisbon, Museu Calouste Gulbenkian L.A.139); and (3) scribe C (fols 23-39^v).

Traditionally said to have been produced in Canterbury, but Morgan argues on grounds of stylistic and iconographical inter-relationships that the present MS was one of four Apocalypses likely to have been produced in the same London workshop. The others are the Gulbenkian Apocalypse; New York, Pierpont Morgan Library M. 524; and Metz, Bibliothèque municipale, Salis 38 (destroyed in 1944).

Fol. 54: 'Pignus Willelmi de Barton' (s. xiv). Fol. ii: 'Lumley'; item 27 in the 1609 catalogue of John, Lord Lumley's library, cf. *The Library of John, Lord Lumley*, ed. S. Jayne and F.R. Johnson (1956), p. 42.

> S.M. Kershaw, *Art Treasures of the Lambeth Library* (1873), pp. 47-54, pls 2-3 illus. mins fols 8, 39; Pal. Soc., 2nd ser., pl. 195 illus. fol. 21; BFAC, *Exhibition of Illuminated MSS*, pl. 73 illus. fols 39^v-40; E.G. Millar, 'Les principaux manuscrits à peintures du Lambeth Palace à Londres', *Bulletin de la S.F.R.M.P.*, 8 (1924), 38-66 and pl. XIV illus. fol. 1, pls XXI, XXX, XXXII-XXXIV illus fols 1, 11^v, 41, 45^v, 46, 48, pls XVIa, XVIIIa, XIXa-b, XXIIa-c, XXVa, XXVIa-b, XXVIIIa-b illus. mins fols 4, 5, 5^v, 6, 12, 12^v, 13, 17, 25, 27, 30, 31; James, pp. 331-36; Exh., *Age of Chivalry*, no. 438; Morgan, *Early Gothic MSS*, no. 126 and colour pl. p. 17 illus. fol. 48, illus. 131-41 illus. mins fols 1, 1^v, 15^v, 21, 11^v, 41^v, 46, 51^v, 53 (reduced); S. Lewis, *Reading Images: Narrative Discourse and Reception in the Thirteenth-Century Illuminated Apocalypse* (1995), no. 6 in her census of MSS, pp. 340-44, and figs 14, 33, 46, 47, 86, 90, 187, 188, 212-19, 227-9 illus. 47,v, 2, 5v, 6, 15, 15v, ii^v, 1, 19, 49, 220^v, 45^v, 46^v, 47, 48^v, 49, 50^v, 51, 51^v, 52, 53 (all reduced).

Pl. 26

64   **Lambeth Palace 222, fols 1-218**   *1356*
                                                              Crich, England

Jacobus de Voragine, Legenda aurea

Parch. 218 fols. 265 × 175 mm. 2 cols, 203 × 130 mm. 42-55 lines. Col. inits, rubrics.

Fol. 218, col. 1: 'Explicit legenda sanctorum que dicitur passionarium. Scriptus per manus Willelmi de Weston perpetui vicarii de Cruch' [Crich, Derbyshire] et terminatur in festo sancte Lucie virginis Anno domini Millesimo CCC^{mo} quinqua-gesimo sexto'. Weston also wrote fols 218, col. 2-222^v. He became vicar of Crich in 1356 (cf. J.C. Cox, *Notes on the Churches of Derbyshire*, 4 vols (1875-79), IV: 33-63, and for further information see *The Cartulary of the Wakebridge Chantries at Crich*, ed. A. Saltman, Derbyshire Archaeological Soc., Record Series, 6 (1976), *passim*).

Fol. 1: 'I Richarde Bankys vicar of Cryche [*BRUO 1501-40*, 23] doe geve & bequethe this booke to my parisshe Crurche [*sic*] of Crych per me Ricardum Bankys vicarium de cruche'. At foot of page: 'Sub: de: Re: Le: J.H' (s. xvi). For other MSS with this inscription, see James, p. 144; it is apparently that of John Hunt,

gentleman, of Leicester or Derbyshire (*ex info.* Dr A.I. Doyle). James, pp. 360-61.

Pl. 54

65   **Lambeth Palace 224, fols ii, 1-174**
          [betw. 1120 and c.1143] [Malmesbury, England]

Anselmus, Opera

Parch. 175 fols, foliated ii, 1-174. 275 × 180 mm. 2 cols, 210 × 135 mm. 40-43 lines. Col. inits, rubrics.

Fol. ii: 'Disputat anselmus presul cantorberiensis.
      Scribit Willelmus monachus malmesberiensis.
      Ambos gratifice complectere lector amice'
followed by a list of contents in the same hand which also wrote fols 125-34^v, 155^v-74^v, and part of fol. 86^v. The hand is that of Oxford, Magdalen College, Lat. 172, the autograph MS of William of Malmesbury's *Gesta pontificum* (*DMO*, no. 832); for other MSS by him, see R.M. Thomson in *William of Malmesbury Gesta Regum Anglorum. The History of the English Kings*, ed. R.A.B. Mynors, R.M. Thomson and M. Winterbottom, 2 vols (1998-99), II: xlvii. The present volume includes a collection of Anselm's letters compiled by William at Canterbury in 1120-22 (for William's part in the letters' transmission, see R.W. Southern, *Saint Anselm: A Portrait in a Landscape* (1990), pp. 459-81). As only the first 12 items (fols 1-174) are given in William's list of contents, only they must have been copied before his death, c.1143. Two scribes who collaborated with him in other volumes have been identified in the present MS by Thomson ('The 'scriptorium' of William of Malmesbury', *Medieval Scribes, MSS and Libraries*, pp. 130-37, and his 'More manuscripts from the 'scriptorium' of William of Malmesbury', *Scriptorium*, 35 (1981), 49-52). They are Thomson's scribe A who assisted William in Oxford, Lincoln College, lat. 100 (*DMO*, no. 818) and Bodleian Library, Rawlinson G. 139; and Richard who signed his stint in Cambridge, Trinity College 0.5.20 (*DMC*, no. 379). Another contemporary hand began item 13, *De processione spiritus sancti* (fol. 174), but broke off abruptly (fol. 175^v). The text was completed in s. xiv by a scribe who added further Anselm works to the collection.

From Malmesbury (fol. 1: pressmark '.xxvj.'). In Oxford by 1453; see the monogram of John Godsond, University Stationer 1439-53, on fol. 211 (endleaf): 'IG xiijs iiijd Cista Vniuersitatis' (I owe this information to Professor M.B. Parkes). Beneath this the erased pledge: '<... exposita in c>ista antiqua vniuersitatis anno domini millesimo cccc° <lx .. xv die> mensis Februarij et jacet pro vijs iiijd' (two further pledge notes are so erased they are impossible to read. For other instances of monastic books pledged for loans, see M.B. Parkes, 'The provision of books', in *The History of the University of Oxford*, II, *Late Medieval Oxford*, ed. J.I. Catto and R. Evans (1992), pp. 451-52). Fol. i^v (flyleaf): 'Liber Magistri T. Stevynson [*BRUO* 1775]. Ex dono Magistri J. Mersh<*all*> [*BRUO* 1229] Cuius anime deus propicietur'. Marshall was keeper of the Ancient University chest in 1463. 'Liber Magistri rowlandi Philipps vicarii de croydon [*BRUO* 1477]', to which a later hand (s. xvi) has added 'the vicar wch vsed moche to preache at poulys cross in ye dayes of henry the vijth 7 henry ye viijth'. Fol. ii: 'Tho. Heatly' (s. xvi); 'Ti.2'. Acquired by Matthew Parker, archbp of Canterbury, from whom it passed to his son John (S. Strongman, 'John Parker's manuscripts: an edition of the lists in Lambeth Palace MS 737',

TCBS, 7 (1977-80), 1-27, in whose list this is no. 3).

N.E.S.A. Hamilton, *Gesta pontificum*, RS (1870), pp. xi-xii; W. Stubbs, *Gesta regum*, 2 vols (RS 1887-89), I: cxxxi; PS, 2nd ser., II, pl. 192 illus. fol. 1; James, pp. 364-68; F.S. Schmitt, 'Zur Entstehungsgeschichte der handschriftlichen Sammlungen der Briefe des hl. Anselm von Canterbury', *Revue Bénédictine*, 48 (1936), 312-17; *Anselmi Opera Omnia*, ed. F.S. Schmitt, 6 vols (1938-61), I, pl. facing p. 282 illus. fol. 122; Ker, 'William of Malmesbury's hand-writing', *Books, Collectors and Libraries*, pp. 61-66, and pl. 5(b) illus. part of fol. ii; Thomson, 'The "scriptorium"', pl. 34 illus. part of fol. 1; R.M. Thomson, *William of Malmesbury* (1987), pls 4, 9-10 illus. pressmark fol. 1, part of fols 1, 12ᵛ.

Pl. 8

66 Lambeth Palace 236   *[betw. 1215 and 1223]*
[Lincoln? England]

Giraldus Cambrensis, Gemma ecclesiastica, etc.

Parch. 167 fols, foliated i, 1-110, 112-68. 265 × 180 mm. 2 cols, 174-80 × 100-115 mm. 33-34 lines. Col. inits, headings in blue, rubrics.

This, the only extant copy of the *Gemma* (fols 2-157ᵛ), contains marginal additions made to the text by the copyist. It is followed by the *Epistola ad Stephanum Langton* (fols 157ᵛ-60), the *Epistola ad capitulum Herefordense* (fols 160-64), and poems of Gerald's, less neatly copied by the scribe than the rest of the book. James, p. 383, suggests the present MS was prepared under Gerald's supervision. Other MSS of Gerald's writings (Vatican City, Bibl. Apostolica Vaticana, Reginenses latini 470 (the *Speculum Duorum*), Dublin, National Library of Ireland 700 (the *Expugnatio Hibernica*), and Cambridge, Corpus Christi College 425, vol. I (*Vitae SS Remigii et Hugonis*; *DMC*, no. 166) suggest he had working copies prepared, and continually revised and altered, by a team of scribes in his employ, presumably at Lincoln where he spent his latter years (see further Y. Lefèvre and R.B.C. Huyghens, *Giraldus Cambrensis, Speculum Duorum* (1974), pp. lvii-lxvi and figs 1-5; A.B. Scott, *Expugnatio Hibernica, The Conquest of Ireland by Giraldus Cambrensis* (1978), pp. xliv-lvi and frontispiece). R.M. Loomis ('Giraldus de Barri's homage to Hugh of Avalon', *De Cella in Seculum: Religious and Secular Life and Devotion in Late Medieval England*, ed. M.G. Sargent (1989), pp. 32-33) detects a similarity between one of the revising hands of the Vatican MS and the hand of Corpus (cf. Lefèvre and Huyghens, fig. 3, with Loomis, *Gerald of Wales, The Life of St Hugh of Avalon 1186-1200* (1985), frontispiece and pl. opp. p. xiii; also *DMC*, pl. 102) and suggests that it may be Gerald's. The hand of the present MS is not illustrated elsewhere. Loomis (*St Hugh*, p. xxiii) argues that the letter to Hereford's chapter cannot be dated before 1220, since it lists amongst Gerald's writings the *Speculum ecclesiae*. The latter 'confidently alludes' to the miracles and sainthood of Hugh of Avalon canonized in that year. However, saints may be accepted as such before their official canonization (cf. M.C. Garand, 'Observations sur quelques critères liturgiques, computisques et historiques de datation des manuscrits médiévaux', *Scrittura e Civiltà*, 12 (1988), 213-24). Loomis ('Giraldus de Barri', p. 39) further suggests the present MS could have been a presentation volume for Langton. J.J. Hagen's suggestion (*Gerald of Wales, The*

Jewel of the Church; a translation of Gemma ecclesiastica by Giraldus Cambrensis, Davis Medieval Texts and Studies, II (1979), pp. xv-xvi) that it might have been the copy of the *Gemma* Gerald gave to Pope Innocent III on his visit to Rome, 1199, is improbable since the letter to Langton was written to dissuade the archbishop from resigning his see in 1215 (for this date see F.M. Powicke, *Stephen Langton* (1928), pp. 132-33). Gerald died in 1223.

A MS entitled 'Gemma sacerdot(alem)', the alternative title of the *Gemma ecclesiastica*, was among MSS of his works left by Gerald to Lincoln Cathedral (cf. R.M. Thomson, *Catalogue of the Manuscripts of Lincoln Cathedral Chapter Library* (1989), pl. 3).

James, pp. 381-83.

Pl. 22

67 Lambeth Palace 239   *[before 1174]*
[Lanthony Secunda, England]

Clemens Lanthoniensis, In Epistolas canonicas

Parch. 288 fols, foliated i, 1-246, 247-51, 252-82, + leaves omitted in foliation betw. 246 and 247 and betw. 251 and 252, + 3 inserted slips. 260 × 180 mm. 1 col., 198 × 135 mm. 35 lines. Col. inits, rubrics.

Since this is the only known MS of Clement's commentary, contains several alterations and additions to text by the scribe, and belonged to Lanthony Secunda in s. xii ex (fol. i: 'lant'), it is likely to have been the author's own copy (cf. James, p. 391). Clement was elected 5th prior of Lanthony Prima (Monmouthshire) and 3rd prior of Lanthony Secunda (Gloucester) from *c*.1150 and is last recorded in 1169. His successor as prior of both houses, Roger of Norwich, is first recorded in 1174.

Item 111 in the library catalogue of *c*.1355-60 (*Augustinian Libraries*, p. 49, described as 'liber mediocris').

James, pp. 391-93

Pl. 16

68 Lambeth Palace 241   *1372 Dover, England*

Cartularium Dovoriensi

Parch. 263 fols, foliated iii, 1-262. 352 × 235 mm. 1 col., 268 × 155 mm. Up to 45 lines. Col. inits, rubrics.

Fol. iiiᵛ (preface): 'Cum dudum in prioratu Douoriensi .... Tandem Anno domini Millesimo .CCCᵒ .lxxij. nos fratres Robertus de Well et Johannes hwytefeld' ipsius prioratus expresse professi per consensum et expensas dompni Johannis Newenam prioris nostri [1371-93] de gremio eiusdem prioratus assumpti. succurente nobis in parte fratre Thoma de Cantuariensis …'. The hand of the preface (pr. C.R. Haines, *Dover Priory* (1930), pp. 490-91) is that of John Whytefelde, precentor and librarian, who compiled Dover's 1389 library catalogue (Oxford, Bodleian, Bodley 920: *DMO*, no. 122) as well as copying Canterbury Cathedral 71, dated 1380 (*ex info.* Dr M. Barber; on Whytefelde, see W.P. Stoneman, *Dover Priory*, Corpus of British Medieval Library Catalogues (1999), pp. 3-13). The cartulary itself is copied by another scribe who also copied the 1373 cartulary of St Bartholomew's Hospital, Buckland by Dover (Oxford, Bodleian, Rawlinson B. 335: *DMO*, no. 664), again drawn up by Robert de Welle and John Whytefelde with Thomas of Canterbury's assistance. Several

48

contemporary and later additions have been made to the present volume.

Fol. i^v: 'Henry Dyneley writ this xxth of August anno domini 1570 12th year' of the rayne of *her* sou*e*rayne Lady Elizabeth by the grac' of God etc betwe one & ij off ye Clocke'. Fol. iii: 3 notes now crossed out witnessed by 'George Tosts' (s. xvi). Fol. 262^v: 'Georgius Byngham de <*Canterbury*> [farmer of the Priory lands, 1592; cf. Haines, *Dover Priory*, p. 135] deliberauit librum istum'. Three paper leaves unfoliated, the third blank, are bound in at the front of the MS; leaves one and two record the production of the MS as evidence in the Elizabethan Court of Wards. Leaf 2 is a letter from John Parker, 1598, to Archbp Whitgift (d. 1604) about a law suit between Mr Thomas Moninges and Mr William Hanington concerning tithes in the parish of Hougham and the boundaries of the said parish. '… The old ligeer boke somtyme belongyng to the sayd pryorye wold do muche good in this matter & manye others, The obteynyng of wch boke more then xx^{ti} yeres past, was chardges [*sic*] to me xxiij^{li} vj^s viij^d (besyde thassystaunce of yowre graces then *pre*decessor), and wch boke aboutt thre yeres past, Mr [Edward] Darcye of her maj*es*tyes Pryvye Chamber, borowed of me to shewe for evydence in a matter of his, in the courte of Wardes, where the late *Lord* Treasorer steyed the boke to her highenes vse, (supposyng that somwhatt in itt myght belonge to her maj*es*tie, where in truthe, there is nothyng therein conc*er*nyng anye thyng, butt that wch belonged to the sayd Pryorye, & so to yowre Grace), wherefore I humblye beseache yowre graces favor & ayde in obteynyng agayne the sayd boke /:' Leaf 1 contains a memorandum dated Michaelmas Term, 44 and 45 Elizabeth (1602) recording that, as a result of Whitgift's petition and upon the Court's studying the volume, it has been decreed that '… except vij leaves therof tochinge Customes & such matters supposed to apperteine vnto the *Queen's* Maj*es*tie so as ther is no cause for this Courte to reteyne the same whole booke but only to haue a copie taken of the said leaues to remaine here for her Maj*es*tie It is therfore this *pre*sent xxvjth daie of Aprill in the xliiijth yere of her Maj*es*ties raigne ordered & decreed by the M*aster* & Counsell of this Courte that a copie shalbe fourthw*ith* taken & Remaine in this *C*ourt of the said vij leaues and then the same Leigeer booke shalbe diliu*er*ed out of this Courte to the said Archbisshoppe of Cant*er*bury'; then a different hand notes 'the said vij leaues that were written out were folys 28 29 30 31 32 31c 32 [*sic*]. The note wherto my *Lord* Grace sett his hand is this that followeth'. The first hand resumes 'Received of Mr [John] Hare Clerke of the Courte of Wards a Leygeere booke of the Priory of Dover being *p*arcell of the possessions of my Archbishopricke of Canterbury In wittnesse wherof I have herevnto sett my hand' This second day of D<ecem>ber in the xlvth yere of the Raigne of *our* Gracious Sou*e*raigne lady Elizabeth Queene of England etc.'

James, pp. 393-97; Davis, *MC*, no. 312; *IMEP*, XIII: 16.
Pl. 60 a, b

69 **Lambeth Palace 264, fols 143-68^v**   *1510 [England]*
The Prose Brut

Paper. 24 fols, foliated 143-68. 290 × 210 mm. 1 col., *c*.237 × 165 mm. 25-27 lines. Space left for inits. Gold-tooled leather bdg, clasps gone.

Fol. 168^v: 'Thus endeth yis *pre*sent booke of Cronicles of Englond wryten by me Thomas Rydyng ye iiij day of Nouembre ye yere of our lord M ccccc x'. A copy of the Brut by three scribes (fols 1-142), to which Rydyng has appended part of the 1419-61 continuation (cf. Lister M. Matheson, 'Printer and scribe: Caxton, the *Polychronicon*, and the *Brut*', *Speculum*, 60 (1985), 595-96).

Fols 169^v-70: five title deeds, from 49 Edw III to 38 Henry VI, relating to land in Cookham, Bray, and Winkfield, Berkshire, added by a single hand (s. xv^{ex}); the latest property owner is Richard Coterelle. Fol. 170^v: 'Iste liber constat Johanni Willeys'. Arms on the binding are those of George Carew, earl of Totnes (d. 1629); see further M.R. James, 'The Carew manuscripts', *EHR*, 42 (1927), 261-67. No. 6 in the list of MSS found in Archbp Sheldon's closet (Oxford, Bodleian, Tanner 275).

James, pp. 410-11; *IMEP*, XIII: 17.
Pl. 241

70 **Lambeth Palace 265**   *1477 Westminster, England*
Earl Rivers, Dictes and Sayings of the Philosophers

Parch. 109 fols, foliated iii, iv, 1-106 + endleaf unfoliated. 283 × 200 mm. 1 col., 157 × 103 mm. 24 lines. Illum. min. (fol. vi^v), illum. vine-stem inits.

Fols 105^v-106: 'Thus endeth the boke of the dictes and notable wise sayenges of Philosophers. late translated out of Frenssh into Englissh. by my forsaide lorde. Therle of [erasure] / and by his comaundment sette in fourme 7 enprinted in right substanciale maner And this boke was Finisshed the xxiiij. day of Decembr*e*. the xvijth . yere of our liege lord. King Edwarde þe iiijth', then in the bottom right hand corner of fol. 106: 'Apud sanctum Jacobum in campis [the hospital of St James in the Fields, Westminster] per haywarde'. Produced from a copy of Caxton's first edition of the *Dictes*, 1477 (see L. Hellinga, *Caxton in Focus* (1982), pp. 77-83; N.F. Blake, 'Manuscript to Print', *Book Production and Publishing*, pp. 413-14). Since the issue of this edition in John Rylands Library, Manchester (*STC* 6827), is dated 18 November 1477, V.M. O'Mara ('"Perauenture the wynde had blowe ouer the leef": Caxton, *The Dicts and Sayings of the Philosophers*, and the Woman Question', *Poetica: An International Journal of Linguistic-Literary Studies*, 49 (1998), 27-47) doubts whether the scribe of the present MS could have copied the text by 24 December. However, this is to discount Hellinga's view that the colophon in Rylands was added. None of the other extant issues (*STC* 6826) of the same edition have it. The miniature (fol. vi^v) depicts Rivers, watched by a cleric in a cape, presenting the work to Edward IV (d. 1483) for whom this copy was probably made. The cleric is perhaps the scribe Haywarde. The artist also illustrated BL, Harley 326 (Scott, *Later Gothic MSS*, Cat. no. 125; C. Meale, 'Patrons, buyers and owners: book production and social status', *Book Production and Publishing*, p. 212).

An erased signature on the endleaf is not that of Richard III (as suggested by James, p. 414 n. 1); see further A.F. Sutton and L. Visser-Fuchs, 'Richard III's books: mistaken attributions', *The Ricardian*, 9, no. 118 (Sept. 1992) 303-7. Fol. 106, verse conclusion to text supplied by a hand of s. xvi¹ with the initials 'TNER' at end (pr. C. Bühler, 'The verses in Lambeth Manuscript 265', *MLN*, 72 (1957), 5-6). Later belonged to George Carew, earl of Totnes (d. 1629): no. 8 (not no. 7, as stated by James, according to Scott) in the list of MSS found in Archbp Sheldon's closet (Oxford, Bodleian, Tanner 275).

James, pp. 412-14; R. Strong, *Tudor and Jacobean Portraits* (1969), II, pl. 162 illus. presentation min.; M. Kekewich, 'Edward IV, William Caxton, and literary patronage in Yorkist England', *MLR*, 66 (1971), 486-87; P. Tudor-Craig, *Richard III*, Catalogue of an Exhibition held at the National Portrait Gallery 27 June-7 October 1973 (2nd edn, 1977), no. 66; *Caxton in Focus*, colour pls III, V illus. fol. 17ᵛ (reduced) and detail presentation min., fig. 41 illus. colophon (reduced); Meale, 'Patrons, buyers', pl. 18 illus. presentation min. (reduced); Scott, *Later Gothic MSS*, Cat. no. 125 and ills 471-72 illus. fols viᵛ and 63ᵛ (reduced); A.F. Sutton and L. Visser-Fuchs, *Richard III's Books* (1997), p. 297 no. XXI; *IMEP*, XIII: 17-18.
Pl. 199

71 Lambeth Palace 324   *1589 [England]*
Richard Cosin, Ecclesie Anglicanae Politeia in Tabulas digesta

Paper. 63 fols. 420 × 283 mm. Tables drawn across inside of each bifolium. Up to 56 lines.

Fol. 2 (title page): 'Prima lineamenta praesentis politeiae Ecclesiasticae Angliae Anno Domini 1589'. One of a number of works on ecclesiastical law by Cosin (1549?-97), published 1604, 1634.
Pl. 295

72 Lambeth Palace 329, fols 8-172   *1417 [England]*
Nicholas de Aquavilla, Sermones

Parch. 168 fols, foliated 8-62, 63-65, 66-172, + leaves unfoliated betw. 62 and 63 and betw. 65 and 66. 268 × 190 mm. 1 col., 182 × 120 mm. 32-36 lines. Col. inits, rubrics.

Fol. 172ᵛ: 'Expliciunt sermones magistri Nicholai de aque villa vniuersitatis Paris' sacre pagine confessore. Scriptus per manus Willelmi Marchall' licet inmerito magistri in artibus decimo die mensis Augusti Anno domini Millesimo quadringentesimo decimo septimo'. Fols 174-245, also by Marshall, were presumably copied about the same time. Fols i-iii, 1-7 form an added quire containing the beginning of an index to the sermons, supplied by a later hand (s. xv²).
Fol. 7ᵛ: 'liber sermonum ex dono Reuerendi in christo dampni [*sic*] Johannis danyell' prioris [of Lewes, Sussex, 1445-64; *BRUC* 177] tali condicione vt ex eo vsum habeat quamdiu vixerit'.
James, pp. 434-35.
Pl. 92

73 Lambeth Palace 332   *1556 [Scotland]*
Sir David Lindsay, The Monarche or Ane dialog betuix experience and ane courteoure

Paper. 133 fols, foliated i, 1-132. 262 × 185 mm. 1 col., 190 × c.100 mm. 22-25 lines. Flourished inits.

Fol. iᵛ: 'Heir begynnis ane litill dialog betuix experience and ane courteoure of the miserabill estait of ye warld compilit be Schir dauid Lindesay of the mont knicht Lioun king of armis [1542-55; d. 1555] Quhilk is diuidit in foure partis as eftir followis begun on thursday ye /ii/ of Junij 1556'. An almost contemporary copy of the poem, composed 1554.
The Works of Sir David Lindsay of the Mount 1490-1555,

ed. D. Hamer, IV, Scottish Text Soc., 3rd ser., 8 (1936), 5-8.
James, p. 437.
Pl. 261

74 Lambeth Palace 354   *1470 [England]*
Piero del Monte, De virtutum et vitiorum inter se differentia; etc.

Parch. 119 fols, foliated i-iii, 1-116. 257 × 175 mm. 1 col., 147 × 85 mm. 32-35 lines. Col. inits, rubrics. Red leather bdg over boards, clasps gone (s. xvᵉˣ).

Fol. 115 (note scribbled by a contemporary hand): 'Scriptus expensis Roberti Ayscogh' legum doctoris Anno domini Millesimo CCCC° lxx'. Robert Ayscogh may be the Fellow of Peterhouse, D.Cn.L. by 1441, d. 1471 (*BRUC* 26) or, more probably, the commoner of King's Hall, D.C.L. by 1454, d. 1482 (*BRUC* 27). Ayscogh also owned London, BL, Add. 11983, s. xii Seneca (*ex info*. Professor A.C. de la Mare).
A hand very like that of the scribe has written 'John Gale' in the top right hand corner of fol. 4ᵛ. Fol. ii: 'Thys ys master gale hys boke Recorde of master denes'; also on back pastedown: 'Gilberte gale est possessor huius librum' (s. xvi). Fol. iiᵛ: 'Noverint Vniuersi per presentes me Edwardum Tayler de london' generosum posuit seipsum ad scienciam', and monogram 'RF'.
James, pp. 472-73.
Pl. 175

75 Lambeth Palace 370   *[c.1418] [Oxford, England]*
Robert de Cowton, Questiones super Sententias, abbrev. Richard Snetisham

Parch. 186 fols, foliated i-ii, 1-184. 245 × 165 mm. 1 col., 166 × 105 mm. 41 lines. Col. border (fol. 19), col. inits. Whittawed leather bdg over boards, clasps gone (s. xv).

Fol. 16ᵛ: 'liber monasterij siue prioratus lanthonie iuxta gloucestriam emptus per fratrem Ricardum Calne [*BRUO* 340] eiusdem loci canonicum et scolarem. anno domini Millesimo cccc. xviij. et qui eum a predicta domo absque licencia prioris uel conuentus eiusdem alienauerit anathema sit. fiat fiat. amen'. The date of purchase accords with the appearance of the script. The scribe gives his name fol. 181 (at end of text): 'Amen. Thomas et sic est finis Kom'. James (p. 503) reads the scribe's name as Korn. The text is preceded by a tabula (fols 1-16, fols 17-18 blank) in Thomas's hand. For other books purchased by Calne at Oxford, see no. 77 below.
James, pp. 502-3.
Pl. 96

76 Lambeth Palace 393   *[betw. 1412 and 1421]*
                                     [Oxford, England]
William Penbegyll, Universalia; etc.

Parch. 278 fols, foliated i-ii, 1-276. 230 × 145 mm. 1 col., 157 × 90-100 mm. 33-43 lines. Col. inits, diagr. (fol. 30).

Fol. 274ᵛ: 'liber monasterij siue prioratus lanthonie iuxta Gloucestriam quem partim scripsit et partim scribi fecit Frater Ricardus Calne [*BRUO* 340] eiusdem loci canonicus tempore quo fuit scolaris Oxonie [betw. 1412 and 1421] et qui eum a predicta domo absque licencia prioris et conuentus eiusdem alienauerit Anathema sit fiat fiat Amen'. The MS consists of three booklets, fols 1-68, 69-214, 215-74, written by several hands (fols 275-76 are blank endleaves). Calne himself wrote fols 33-68; the same hand occurs in no. 77 below, mainly written by him.

In addition to the present volume, Calne acquired other books at Oxford (including nos 52, 57, 75 and see especially no. 77) which he took back to Lanthony.

James, pp. 542-43.

Pls 84, 85 a, b

77   Lambeth Palace 396   *[betw. 1412 and 1421]*
[Oxford, England]

Questiones

Parch. 276 fols. 223 × 150 mm. 1 col., 152-57 × 98 mm. 34-39 lines. Col. border (fol. 16), col. inits.

The MS consists of three booklets of questiones, fols 16-135, 136-79 and 180-276, preceded by a tabula, fols 1-15. Text in fols 16-135 ends fol. 130^v: '... et in hoc finiuntur questiones alique super libros phisicorum superficialiter collecte modo quo in scolis philosophicis oxonie disputari consueuerant. ¶Frater Ricardus Calne [*BRUO* 340] canonicus lanthonie iuxta Gloucestriam'; fols 131-34 contain a tabula by another hand, fols 134^v-35^v blank. The following booklet, fols 136-79, written by another scribe, has the *ex libris*, fol. 179: 'liber monasterij siue prioratus lanthonie iuxta Gloucestriam quem partim scripsit et partim scribi fecit Frater Ricardus Calne eiusdem loci canonicus tempore quo fuit scolaris Oxonie [betw. 1412 and 1421]. Et qui eum a predicta domo absque licencia prioris et conuentus eiusdem alienauerit anathema sit fiat fiat. Amen'. Calne began the third booklet (fols 180-99^v, line 20) which was completed (fols 199^v, line 21-276^v) by the hand of fols 136-79. On fol. 276^v an almost identical *ex libris* to that on fol. 179 reads: 'liber monasterij siue prioratus lanthonie iuxta Gloucestriam quem partim scripsit et partim scribi fecit frater Ricardus Calne eiusdem loci canonicus et scolaris. et qui eum a predicta domo absque licencia prioris et conuentus eiusdem alienauerit. anathema sit fiat. fiat. amen'. Calne also wrote the tabula, fols 1-15. His hand occurs in no. 76 above. For other MSS he acquired at Oxford and took back to Lanthony, see nos 52, 57, and 75, and see further M.B. Parkes, 'The provision of books', *The History of the University of Oxford*, 8 vols, gen. ed. T.H. Aston, II, *Late Medieval Oxford*, ed. J.I. Catto and R. Evans (1992), pp. 423-24.

James, pp. 546-47.

Pls 86 a, b

78   Lambeth Palace 412   *1458 Corkatenny, Ireland*

Speculum sacerdotum, etc.

Parch. 118 fols, foliated 1-18, 20-118, + leaf unfoliated between 30 and 31. 225 × 155 mm. 1 col., 160 × 105 mm. 29 lines. Full-page border in red and black, col. inits, rubrics, explicits with letters picked out in red.

Fol. 118: 'Finit Amen Finit qui scripsit ne mala morte peribit. Scriptus et finitus est liber iste per edmundum Ochomayn' [Ó' Comáin]. Domino Donaldo Okahvyll [Ó' Cearbhaill, the canon of Cloyne and of Cork (?), for whom see *Calendar of entries in the Papal Registers relating to Great Britain and Ireland: Papal Letters*, ed. W.H. Bliss *et al*. (1893-) XI: 374-75]

in ecclesia Korcoteny [Corkatenny, identified with the present parish of Templemore, Co. Tipperary] Anno domini M^o C^o C^o C^o C^o .l. viij^o Mense decembri in die veneris proximo post festum sancti thome Appostoli Quorum animabus propicietur deus'. Fol. 118^v is blank. Fols 119-120, a bifolium, were added by a later (s. xv) hand. The leaf foliated 19 is a blank insert.

James, pp. 56-67.

Pl. 150

79   Lambeth Palace 413
[c.1417]; annual entries 1417-1481 [England]

Cartae capituli generalis ordinis Cartusie, 1417-1481

Parch. and paper. 522 fols. From 175 × 110 mm to 225 × 145 mm. 1 col., from 140 × 85 mm to 182 × 110 mm. 22-39 lines.

A collection of the annual *cartae* (ordinances) of the General Chapter of the Carthusian order between 1417 and 1481 made for the use of an unknown English Charterhouse, preceded (fols 1-6) by *ordinationes* of the order 1411-16. Fols 1-6 were copied by a uniform English hand. Thereafter *cartae* 1417-81 were copied into separate quires for each year, and, apart from fols 55-59^v, 89-93, 240-52^v, and 301-26 (*cartae* for 1425, 1431, 1456, 1461-62 and papal bulls) by foreign hands, by many different English hands with, from 1449 onwards, as many as five alternating in each *carta*. 'Altogether the incidence of hands and the occurrence of marginal markings and liturgical notes are most compatible with annual copying of the current cartae, either in one house (apart from the foreign imports) or in more than one over the whole span ...' (A.I. Doyle, 'Comments on the palaeography and diplomatic of Lambeth 413', *The Chartae of the Carthusian General Chapter: London, Lambeth Palace MS 413, part 4, 1475-1481*, ed. J. Clark, *Analecta Cartusiana*, 100/12/2 (1992), 98-99). The *carta* for 1417 (fols 7-13) is signed fol. 13^v: 'Johannes prior ⎰ manu propria
Cartusie ⎱ anno cccc xvij'
M.G. Sargent, 'Die Handschriften der Cartae des General-kapitels: Ein analytischer Überblick', *Kartäuserregel und Kartäuserleben: Internationaler Kongress vom 30. Mai bis 3. Juni 1984, Analecta Cartusiana*, 113/3 (1985), 15, took this to be the signature of Johannes von Griffenberg, prior of the Grande Chartreuse, but the hand is English. The present text is probably a contemporary copy of the original sent to another English charterhouse (cf. Doyle).

Fol. 522 (in red): 'Orate specialiter pro bono statu domini Willelmi et pro animabus Thadei et <de> Filorcie id est derwayll parentum eius' (s. xv^{ex}).

James, pp. 567-69; *The Chartae of the Carthusian General Chapter: London, Lambeth Palace MS 413, part 1*, ed. J. Hogg and M. Sargent, *Analecta Cartusiana*, 100/10 (1988), p. vi; J.P.H. Clark, 'The Acta of the Carthusian General Chapter in the Paris and Lambeth Manuscripts', *Die Geschichte des Kartäuserordens*, 2 vols, *Analecta Cartusiana*, 32 (1991), I: 242-56; A.I. Doyle, 'English Carthusian books not yet linked with a charterhouse', *'A Miracle of Learning': Studies in Manuscripts and Irish Learning. Essays in honour of William O'Sullivan*, ed. T. Bernard, D. Ó Cróinín, and K. Simms (1998), p. 123.

Pls 93, 100, 111, 129, 149, 165, 180, 208

80 Lambeth Palace 415 *[betw. 1201 and 1205?]*
[Canterbury, England]

Epistolae Cantuarienses

Parch. 143 fols, foliated i-iii, 1-140. 229 × 162 mm. 2 cols,
174 × 120 mm. 46 lines. Col. inits, rubrics.

Fol. i (in caps): 'Epistole Reginaldi de tempore Bald< >'. A
collection of letters concerning the dispute between the monks
of Christ Church, Canterbury, and Archbishops Baldwin (1184-
90) and Hubert Walter (1193-1205) arising from archiepiscopal
attempts to found a church and college of secular canons. The
collection has been dated between 1201 (when the dispute was
finally settled) and 1205 (when a new dispute arose over the
election of Stephen Langton as archbishop; cf. *Chronicles and
Memorials of the reign of Richard I*, ed. W. Stubbs, 2 vols, (RS
1864-55), II: xi-xiii). Reginald was elected subprior by the
monks of Christ Church not later than October 1205; his election was quashed by the Pope before 20 December 1206 (see
further C.R. Cheney, 'A neglected record of the Canterbury
election of 1205-6', *BIHR*, 21 (1948), 233-38).
Fol. i: 'D. iijᵃ .G. xiij '(s. xiii), then in a later hand 'De secunda
[crossed out and 'prima' substituted] demonstracione'. Fol. 1:
'De claustro christi cant' (s. xv). Fol. iii: 'Thomas Draper'
(s. xviᵉˣ). Fol. 1: 'Tho. Allen' of Oxford (1540-1632), on whom
see A.G. Watson, 'Thomas Allen of Oxford and his manuscripts', *Medieval Scribes, MSS and Libraries*, pp. 279-314.
Fol. i: 'Aeton' or 'Eaton' written several times, which led James
(p. 577) to suggest Allen was the Fellow of Eton, 1604; also
fol. i 'Eliott' and 'Beaufey' (s. xvii).
James, pp. 576-77.
Pl. 20

81 Lambeth Palace 444, fols 25-46 *1451*
Oxford, England

Bernardus Pictaviensis, De crisi et creticis diebus; etc.

Parch. and paper, mixed. 22 fols. 210 × 140 mm. 2 cols,
142 × 97 mm. 47 lines. Space left for inits.

Fol. 37: 'Anno domini .M.CCCC.lj. vicesimo quinto die mensis
octobris in Catstreth \in/ opido .Oxon'. per hermannum de
Gripesswaldis. alias Zureke'; fol. 46ᵛ: 'Explicit liber Microtegni
Galieni de .12. portis Anno domini .1451. 3⁰ die mensis
Nouembris Oxon' in vico muriligorum [Catte Street] in
parrochia sancte marie feria 4. hora quasi 5ᵃ post prandium Per
hermannum zurekem alias de Gripessualdis'. Zurke also wrote
the following booklet, fols 47-68. For other MSS by him, see
DMO, nos 80, 81, 610, 843, and *DMC*, no. 60; and L.E. Voigts,
'Hermann Zurke: a fifteenth-century medical scribe in England'
(forthcoming). Fols 1-24, 128-75, 176-83 were also written in
s. xv; fols 69-127 in s. xiii.
James, pp. 617-19.
Pl. 137

82 Lambeth Palace 448, fols 117-49
[betw. c.1462 and 1470] [Ely, England]

Memoranda Eliensia

Paper. 33 fols. 210 × 150 mm. 1 col., 166 × 110 mm. 34-37
lines.

Notes and annals mainly by one scribe, jotted down hap-

hazardly, in a composite volume produced at Ely. After various
miscellaneous items (fols 117-35), a series of annals (fols 136-
38ᵛ + fols 142-46) runs to 1462, with an addition for the year
1464 by the same hand (fol. 146). The annals are intercalated
(fols 139-41) by various items including an account of a vision
in 1462, and a list of English kings running to Edward IV (1461-
83), with the number of years he reigned altered from the original 'ij' (1462-3) to 'xxij' (1482-83). Events for 1462 (fols
146-47ᵛ) are recorded in the present tense and appear to have
been written down as the news reached Ely (cf. *Three fifteenth-
century Chronicles*, ed. J. Gairdner, Camden Soc., 28 (1880),
p. xvi). The scribe also added a list of popes to Calixtus III, 1470
(*sic*, fols 148-49). Fols 117-49 were not formerly foliated (in
ink) whereas the first part of the MS, written by various hands,
was. Thus the present fols 1-32 + 39-77, containing a chronicle
of Ely's abbots and bishops to Simon Langham (1362-66), were
formerly fols 1-70 (s. xv²); fols 92-99 (first quarter s. xv) and
fols 100-6 (s. xv med), containing several regulations and
customs of the priory, were formerly fols 71-78 and 79-86;
while fols 106-16, annals to 1450, were formerly fols 87-93.
Fols 106-16 form a quire into which two leaves (fols 108-9),
containing the genealogy of Robert Steward (alias Wells), last
prior (1522-39) and first dean of Ely (d. 1557), were inserted
in s. xvi. The same hand, presumably Steward's, also supplied
the present fols 33-38 (not included in the ink foliation) with
text missing from the chronicle (fols 1-32 + 39-77). Two later
supplements, fols 78-88 and 89-91 (also without ink foliation),
continued it, first to John Morton, bishop 1478-86 (fols 78-88),
and then to the succession of Thomas Thirlby in 1554. Finally,
fols 150-54 contain further notes on the history of Ely (s. xvi).
Fol. 99ᵛ: 'Iste liber pertinet domino Johanni de Burktone [fl.
1379-1420]', for whom, see J. Greatrex, *Biographical Register
of the English Cathedral Priories of the Province of Canterbury,
c.1066-1540* (1997), p. 394. Also fol. 99ᵛ: 'Iste liber pertinet
ecclesie alien'. Fol. 107ᵛ: 'Robert Steward Elien' 1550', responsible for many of s.xvi additions to the volume. For Steward, see
Greatrex, p. 457, s.n. Wells.

> Gairdner, pp. xv-xx and 148-63; F.R. Chapman, *Sacrist
> Rolls of Ely*, 2 vols (1907), I: x; James, pp. 619-23;
> C. Ross, 'Rumour, propaganda and popular opinion during
> the Wars of the roses', *Patronage, the crown and the
> provinces*, ed. R.A. Griffiths (1981), p. 17; D. Sherlock,
> *Signs for Silence: the sign language of the monks of Ely in
> the Middle Ages* (1992); *IMEP*, XIII: 35-36.
> *Pl. 163*

83 Lambeth Palace 450 *1485 London, England*

Lorenzo Guglielmo Traversagni di Savona, Triumphus amoris domini nostri Jesu Christi

Parch. 54 fols, foliated i, 1-53. 213 × 140 mm. 1 col., 132
× 72 mm. 30 lines. Col. inits., rubrics. Bld-stamped bdg
over boards, with clasps (s. xvᵉˣ).

Dedicated and intended for presentation to William Waynflete,
bishop of Winchester (d. 1486). The dedicatory epistle concludes (fol. 6): 'Per fratrem Laurentium Guilelmum de Sauona
[*BRUC* 593] ordinis minorum sacre theologie doctorem R.d.v.
oratorem ac seruulum .1485. 18 aprilis In almo conuentu sancti
francisci londonijs. Laudes itaque sint summo et inmortali deo
totique curie triumphanti. Amen'. Although this epistle is in a
separate quire, the date probably applies to the whole MS

52

since it is autograph, cf. J. Ruysschaert, 'Lorenzo Guglielmo Traversagni de Savone (1425-1503): un humaniste oublié', *Archivum Franciscanum Historicum*, 46 (1953), 195-210; and for another specimen of Traversagni's hand, his 'Les manuscrits autographes de deux œuvres de Lorenzo Guglielmo Traversagni imprimées chez Caxton', *BJRL*, 36 (1953-4), 191-97, pls I-II illus. Vatican City, Biblioteca Apostolica Vaticana, Vat.lat. 11441. Traversagni left Waynflete's name blank in the address 'Ad reuerendissimum in christo patrem et dominum d. [blank] Vintoniensem episcopum' (fol. 1, in red) and it was only later supplied in the margin by Sancroft. The arms of Magdalen College, Oxford (founded by Waynflete) in pen and ink appear to have been added within the initial on fol. 1.

Thought to have been left with the London Franciscans on Traversagni's return to Italy (*MLGB*), but Professor R. Hanna informs me that a note added on fol. 53ᵛ is the incipit of Gerard of Zutphen's Spiritual Ascents and was 'almost certainly copied' from Oxford, Magdalen College Lat. 93, fol. 245, the only copy of Gerard's work made in England. The binding also suggests Magdalen provenance. Fol. i: 'Alani Copei iste liber R.S.' (s. xvi ex). For Alan Cope, Fellow of Magdalen, see H. Frowde, *A Register of the Members of St Mary Magdalen College, Oxford*, n.s. ii (1897), pp. 97-99; R.S. may be Richard Slithurst, his successor as rector of Tubney, Berkshire (Frowde, p. 80).

> James, pp. 624-25; R. Weiss, *Humanism in England during the fifteenth century* (2nd edn, 1957), 162-63; V. Davis, *William Waynflete: bishop and educationist* (1993), pp. 97-98.
> *Pl. 213*

84 **Lambeth Palace 454, fols 1-27**   *[c.1460] [England]*
Almanac
Parch. 28 fols, foliated i, 1-27. 193 × 134 mm. 1 col., 127 × 87 mm. 23 lines. Gold inits, rubrics, diagrms in red and black. Volvelle (fol. 26) in blue, gold, and red. Kal. in red and black.

Fol. 3 (preface): '... which is ȝoure pask dai in þⁱ ȝeer þⁱ ȝe were ynne þo whanne þis kalender was writen þⁱ is to wite in þe ȝeer of oure lord 1460 ...'; the date is written in red. The accompanying kalendar has a page facing each month giving the 5th, 6th and 7th 19-year cycles, respectively headed 1463, 1482, 1501. Tables of solar and lunar eclipses are provided for 1460-81, but only eclipses for 1460-62 have been painted in.

Fol. 27ᵛ: 'Thomas Thomsonus vendicat 1577⁰'. Now bound with two copies of Geoffrey of Monmouth, one of s. xiv (fols 28-123), and another composite copy of s. xiiᵉˣ (fols 124-88) and s. xiiiⁱⁿ date (fols 189-204). Table of contents supplied by Archbp Sancroft.

> James, pp. 628-29; *IMEP*, XIII: 36.
> *Pl. 153*

85 **Lambeth Palace 466, fols 1-43**   *1526*
[Oxford or London? England]
Musicae compendium
Paper. 43 fols. 200 × 145 mm. 1 col., 132 × 95 mm. Up to 19 lines a page. Col. inits, diagrs. Bl.-stamped leather bdg, clasps gone (s. xviⁱ).

Fol. 30ᵛ: 'Scriptum per me dominum Willelmum Chelle Musice bachalaurium 19. die Julij Anno domini .1526.'; also fol. 43:

'Scriptum guilhelmum Chelle . in Musica bacalaurium Anno domini 1526 Cuius anime propicietur deus. Amen'. For Chell, BMus of Oxford 1524 and later precentor of Hereford cathedral, see *BRUO 1501-40*; p. 115. The same collection of musical treatises, in the same order, is found in BL Add. 10336 (*DMBL*, no. 25), copied by John Tucke, the Fellow of New College, Oxford (for whom see F. Ll. Harrison, 'Music at Oxford before 1500', *The History of the University of Oxford*, 8 vols, gen. ed. T.H. Aston, II, *Late Medieval Oxford*, ed. J.I. Catto and R. Evans (1992), pp. 357-58). Chell is said to have copied Tucke's MS (Harrison, loc. cit.; G. Reaney, *Johannes Hothby Opera Omnia de Musica Mensurabili*, Corpus Scriptorum de Musica, 31 (1983), p. 49), but with some abridgement of text. Fols 43ᵛ-48, 49-70, 71-72ʳ of the present MS have been left blank, apart from a table of metrical feet and equivalents in musical notes (fol. 48ᵛ) copied by Chell, and two inventories scribbled by later hands on fols 70ᵛ, 72ᵛ. Bound by 'H.N.' who (unusually for a London binder) used MSS as pastedowns, here from s. xv commentary on Pauline Epistles; see J.B. Oldham, *Blind Panels of English Binders* (1958), p. 35, Ro. 20 and HE 28.

Fol. 48ᵛ: 'Thys ys John Parkar [not the hand of Matthew Parker's son] hys boke the gyft of my master Master wylyam chell Bauchelar of musik'.

> Frere, *BML*, no. 18; James, pp. 644-45.
> *Pl. 249*

86 **Lambeth Palace 474, fols 181-3**
[betw. 1483 and 1485] [England]
Devotiones
Parch. 3 fols. 193 × 140 mm. 1 col., 115 × 87 mm. 18 lines. Gold-tooled leather bdg with clasps (s. xvi).

Devotions added for Richard III when king (1483-85) to an earlier Sarum book of Hours; see fols 182, 183: '... me famulum tuum Regem Ricardum ...' (in both instances 'Ricardum' has been erased but is still visible). The same hand also added (fol. 1, flyleaf) a collect for St Ninian to whom Richard had a special devotion; see further A.F. Sutton and L. Visser-Fuchs, *The Hours of Richard III* (1990), pp. 61-66. Another hand has supplied another devotion, presumably also for Richard, on fol. 184. He himself added his date of birth to the preliminary kalendar, fol. 7ᵛ: 'Hac die natus erat Ricardus Rex anglie iijᵘˢ apud Foderingay Anno domini M CCCC lij'. Bound in s. xviᵐᵉᵈ, in the workshop of the King Edward and Queen Mary Binder (*Hours of Richard*, p. 4).

After Richard's death passed into the possession of Margaret Beaufort (erased inscription on endleaf read by James, p. 653, as 'In the honour of god and Sainte Edmonde Pray for Margaret Richmonde'). For Margaret's acquisition of Richard's goods, see M.K. Jones and M.G. Underwood, *The King's Mother: Lady Margaret Beaufort, Countess of Richmond and Derby* (1992), p. 68; and for her books, S. Powell, 'Lady Margaret Beaufort and her books', *The Library*, 6th ser., 20 (1998), 197-240. Fol. 4: 'Iste die obijt Thomas Harward anno domini 1543.'

> James, pp. 650-54; *Hours of Richard*, fig. 29 illus. fol. 181; A.F. Sutton and L.Visser-Fuchs, *Richard III's Books: Ideals and Reality in the Life and Library of a Medieval Prince* (1997), pp. 50-57, 294-95 no. XV and figs 11, 28 illus. fols 7ᵛ (part), 181; Scott, *Later Gothic MSS*, Cat. no. 52.
> *Pl. 211*

87   Lambeth Palace 489   *[betw. 1050 and 1072]*
[Exeter, England]

Sermons, in Old English

Parch. 58 fols, 192 × 113 mm. 1 col., 167 × 80-85 mm.
Fols 1-21 19 lines, fols 21ᵛ-58 25 lines. Col. inits, rubrics.

Two booklets (fols 1-24, 25-58) copied by scribes who participated in the production of a group of MSS written at Exeter during the episcopate of Bishop Leofric, 1050-72 (see E.M. Drage, 'Bishop Leofric and Exeter Cathedral Chapter (1050-1072): a reassessment of the manuscript evidence', Unpublished D.Phil. thesis, Oxford, 1978). The hand of fols 20ᵛ-24ᵛ is Drage's scribe 6 (other work by him includes *DMC*, nos 55, 164, 334) while that of fols 25-31, l. 2 is her scribe 2 (see *DMC*, nos 48, 138, 139, 144, 164). Probably intended as part of a single collection with BL, Cotton Cleopatra B. XIII, but separated from it by the time a table of contents was supplied for the latter volume by one of Matthew Parker's scribes (cf. Drage, pp. 377-78; and also *DMBL*, no. 524).

James, pp. 678-81; Ker, *Anglo-Saxon MSS*, no. 283; P.W. Conner, *Anglo-Saxon Exeter: A Tenth-Century Cultural History* (1993), p. 6 and no. 29 in his list of MSS; B. Ebersperger, *Die angelsächsischen Handschriften in den Pariser Bibliotheken mit einer Edition von Aelfrics Kirchweihhomilie aus der Handschrift Paris, BN, lat. 943*, Anglistische Forschungen, 261 (Heidelberg, 1999), pp. 224-61.
Pls 2, 3

88   Lambeth Palace 499   *[betw. 1273 and 1284]*
[Stanlaw, England]

Collectiones

Parch. 302 fols. 235 × 168 mm. 1 col., 190 × 125 mm. 48-54 lines. Col. inits, rubrics. Whittawed leather bdg over boards, with 4 bosses on front cover and label (presumably with title) on back cover, now gone.

The MS, written throughout by a single scribe, is in four parts (fols 1-131, 132-63, 164-216, and 217-302), each with its own table of contents. Part III (quires 20-25) contains tables of 19-year cycles 1140-1653; the year 1273, start of the 8th cycle, is written in red (fol. 208ᵛ). Part IV (quires 26-35) contains documents relating to the Cistercian order in general and to Stanlaw Abbey, Cheshire in particular. Its original list of contents runs as far as the end of quire 30 (fol. 262) in which the latest document is dated 1274; thereafter the scribe continued for a further five quires. The latest additional document he copied is dated 1284 (fols 301-302ᵛ). The rest of the volume (2 parts but not 2 booklets: quires 1-19) is most probably contemporary. See further J. Goering and F.A.C. Mantello, 'Notus in Iudea Deus: Robert Grosseteste's Confessional Formula in Lambeth Palace MS 499', *Viator*, 18 (1987), 253-73; and O.S. Pickering, 'Newly discovered secular lyrics from later thirteenth-century Cheshire', *RES*, n.s., 43 (1992), 157-61. On back pastedown: 'Anno domini mᵒ cccxlix obiit Henricus Banaff Whalley' (the monks of Stanlaw moved to Whalley, Lancs, in 1296); 'Johannes Ston' monachus in W\h/all' (s. xv).

James, pp. 691-701; O.S. Pickering, 'An early Middle English verse inscription from Shrewsbury', *Anglia*, 106 (1988), 411-14.
Pl. 28

89   Lambeth Palace 505   *1430 Salle, England*
Michael de Massa, Vita Christi

Parch. 90 fols. 255 × 165 mm. 1 col., 172 × 100 mm. 28 lines. Illum. init. (fol. 1), col. inits, rubrics. Leather chemise over boards, with clasps (s. xv).

Fol. 86ᵛ (in red): 'Explicit compilacio cuiusdam Michaelis de Massa fratris Heremitarum Ordinis sancti Augustini super tota passione. Hunc libellum fecit fieri Magister Willelmus Wode Rector de Salle [Norfolk, 1428-41] quem Edmundus Sowthwelle scripsit in rectoria de Salle. Anno domini Millesimo CCCC xxx Quorum animabus propicietur deus. Amen'. See further R. Beadle, 'Prolegomena to a literary geography of later medieval Norfolk', *Regionalism in late medieval manuscripts and texts: Essays celebrating the publication of 'A Linguistic Atlas of Late Mediaeval English'*, ed. F. Riddy, Proceedings of the 1989 York Manuscripts Conference (1991), pp. 89-108, in whose list of MSS this is no. 71. A pencil note on fol. 86 records 'lumining iijd'.

James, pp. 710.
Pl. 104

90   Lambeth Palace 506   *[betw. 1451 and 1475 and*
betw. 1483 and 1485]
[England]

William Worcester, Collection of documents on the war in Normandy

Parch. 64 fols, foliated 2-7,8-62 + 2 blank leaves unfoliated between 7 and 8 (earlier foliation in ink of 8-62 as fols 1-55). *c.*260 × 150 mm. 1 col. 175 × 102 mm, 27 lines fols 2-7; 175-80 × 92-5 mm, 32-8 lines fols 8-62. Col. inits. Gold-tooled leather bdg, clasps gone.

Fols 8-62 (quires 2-9) contain a collection of documents, compiled by William Worcester (for whom see K.B. McFarlane, 'William Worcester: a preliminary survey', *Studies presented to Sir Hilary Jenkinson*, ed. J. Conway Davies (1957), pp. 196-221), and copied by three different scribes, with various additions by Worcester himself. For other MSS written or annotated by him, see *DMC*, nos 145, 185, and *DMO*, no. 625. The present MS was made to accompany Worcester's *Boke of Noblesse*, a work originally written between 1451 and 1461, but later adapted for Edward IV and presented to him before his departure to France in 1475 (for these dates see McFarlane, pp. 210-13; A.F. Sutton and L. Visser-Fuchs, 'Richard III's books: XII. William Worcester's *Boke of Noblesse* and his collection of documents on the war in Normandy', *The Ricardian*, 9, no. 115 (Dec, 1991), 154-65. The *Boke* is extant only in BL, Royal 18 B. xxii, possibly the presentation copy to Edward). The accompanying documents copied here were presumably copied when the *Boke* was first composed. Fols 2-7 (quire 1) are later and contain a preface written by Worcester's son, also called William. The preface was originally addressed to Richard III, 1483-85, to whom this MS was presented. After Richard's death someone erased the first four letters of his name and rewrote 'Edw' over them, thus making it appear as if the preface had been addressed to Edward IV; however, the number following the king's name was only corrected to 'fourth' in s. xvii. Other references are also more appropriate to Richard than Edward. Fols 7ʳ⁻ᵛ: table of contents by Sir Robert Cotton. Arms tooled on the binding are those of George Carew, earl of Totnes (d. 1629).

James, pp. 710-14; P. Tudor-Craig, *Richard III*, catalogue of an Exhibition held at the National Portrait Gallery 27 June-7 October 1973 (2nd edn, 1977), no.168; A.F. Sutton and L. Visser-Fuchs, *Richard III's Books: Ideals and Reality in the Life and Library of a Medieval Prince* (1997), pp. 292-3 no. XIIB; *IMEP*, XIII: 45-46.
Pls 140, 212

91 Lambeth Palace 529, fols 83-91   *1479*
Scarperia, Italy

Thomas Aquinas, De articulis fidei et ecclesiasticis sacramentis

Parch. 9 fols. 195 × 115 mm. 2 cols, 133 × 72 mm. 38-39 lines. Border (fol. 83), illum. dec. inits, col. inits, rubrics. Bld-stamped leather bdg over boards, clasps gone (s. xv ex).

Fol. 91ᵛ (in red): 'Explicit summa sancti thome librata per fratrem Andream de Manzinis de florentia .M.ccccLxxix⁰ . viij⁰ kalendas decembris: dum in loco Nemoris [the Franciscan convent of Scarperia, near Florence] moram traxisset'. The last item in the second (fols 83-91) of two booklets written by the same scribe. The first booklet (fols 1-24) ends with a near-contemporary copy of Francisco Filelfo's *De sacerdotio Jesu Christi*, addressed to Pope Sixtus IV, 1 March 1476.

James, pp. 729-30.
Pl. 205

92 Lambeth Palace 554, fols 1-89   *1577 Rome, Italy*

'Tractatus de virtutibus, donis et beatitudinibus et fructibus spiritus sancti'

Paper. 89 fols. 128 × 103 mm. 1 col., 112 × 80 mm. 24 lines.

Fol. 89: 'finis Tractatus de Virtutibus Donis et Beatitudinibus et fructibus spiritus sancti Rome 1577 4⁰ Decembris'. Fols 89ᵛ-138ᵛ are by the same hand but undated; fols 139-40 blank. Fols 141-204 and fols 205ᵛ-277 (both containing quaestiones) were written by two other contemporary scribes, the latter signing fol. 277ᵛ: 'Robertus Barret Anglus scripsit'.

James, p. 757.
Pl. 281

93 Lambeth Palace 566   *1572 London, England*

John Leslie, Piae afflicti animi meditationes

Paper. 67 fols, foliated i-iii, 1-64. 163 × 110 mm. 1 col., 125 × 70 mm. 28 lines. Gold-tooled limp vellum bdg, with crowned inits 'M R' (s. xvi ex).

Fol. 1 (title page): 'Piae Afflicti animi meditationes, Diuinaque Remedia. Ad Illustrissimam Principem, Mariam, Scotorum Reginam. Cum placuerint Domino viae hominis, inimicos eius conuertet ad pacem. proverb. 16. 1572'. Again dated at the end of the dedicatory epistle, fol. 6: 'Ex ergastulo nostro in turri Londinensi septimo Die Maij 1572' (the author, John Leslie, bishop of Ross (d. 1596), was imprisoned in the Tower of London for his part in the Ridolfi Plot of 1570-72). A companion volume with BL, Add. 48180, containing Leslie's 'Tranquilitatis animi praeseruatio et munimentum', also addressed to Mary but dated 1573. The two books were printed, with substantial alterations, as *Libri Duo: Quorum vno, Piae Afflicti*

Animi Consolationes, diuinaque remedia: Altero, Animi Tranqvilli Mvnimentum et conservatio, continentur in Paris, 1574. The hand of both MSS is autograph, being that of Leslie's diary (BL, Cotton Caligula C.III, fols 4-40, 11 April-16 October 1571) and various of his letters, as well as authorial emendations to the draft of his 'Historie' (see no. 41 above).

As the dedicatory epistle and crowned initials on the binding suggest, the MS was probably the presentation copy to Mary Queen of Scots (d. 1587); see further P.R. Robinson, 'John Leslie's 'Libri duo': manuscripts belonging to Mary Queen of Scots?', *Order and Connexion: Studies in Bibliography and Book History*, ed. R. Alston (1997), pp. 63-75.

James, p. 777; Robinson, 'Libri duo', pl. illus. fol. 7.
Pl. 276

94 Lambeth Palace 878, pp. 1-158   *[c.1468]*
[London, England]

Chronicon parvum Londinense usque ad annum 1468; etc.

Parch. 79 fols, paginated 1-158. 105 × 75 mm. 1 col., 63 × 45 mm. Up to 18 lines. Diagrm. in red and black (p. 41), rubrics.

An historical miscellany written with strong Yorkist sympathies. A chronicle of England (pp. 93-117) ends with an account of the capture of Harlech castle in 1468, while an accompanying list of the mayors and sheriffs of London also runs to that year (pp. 121-51). Thereafter the list of city officials is continued by the same hand, but with several changes of ink, to 1476; other hands then kept up the list to 1530. The rest of the MS (pp. 159-83, Lydgate's Calendar, and pp. 184-91, paschal rota) is by the same hand.

James, pp. 815-17.
Pl. 172

95 Lambeth Palace 1106, fols 1-110
[c.1308; betw. 1308 and 1320; c.1325;
betw. 1325 and 1326; betw. 1327 and 1329;
betw. 1330 and 1341]
[London, England]

Flores Historiarum

Parch. 95 fols. 275 × 195 mm. 2 cols, 217 × 136 mm. 54 lines. Col. inits., rubrics. Bld-tooled leather bdg (s. xvi).

An abridgement of the *Flores Historiarum* (fols 1-93) copied by three different scribes: the first wrote fols 1-20, the second fols 20-50, and the third fols 50-93. The last also began (fols 93-95) the continuation known as the *Annales Paulini* which follows (for which see H.G. Richardson, 'The *Annales Paulini*', *Speculum*, 23 (1948), 630-40) but ceased copying towards the end of the entry for 1308. Thereafter, from fols 95-110, there are frequent changes of hand and ink in the subsequent annals to 1341. Entries appear to be by at least seven different scribes, presumably writing shortly after the events they record (cf. Gransden, *Hist. Writing*, II: 26 n. 138). Thus entries from the end of 1308 to 1320 (fols 95-98) seem mainly by one hand but with frequent changes of ink and short interventions by other hands; entries from the end of 1320 to mid 1325 (fols 98-102ᵛ) are by a single hand without any perceptible break in the handwriting; entries mid 1325 to 1326 (fols 102ᵛ-104) possibly by three different hands; entries 1327 to 1329 (fols 104ᵛ-106ᵛ) by a single hand but with changes of ink; and entries 1330 to 1341 (fols 106ᵛ-110ᵛ) again by a single hand but with changes of ink. A space several lines long has been left at the end of several entries for any additions to be made. The annals show particular interest in matters concerning the sacristy of St Paul's, London. Fol. 110ᵛ: 'N. Brigami liber est perlege, claude, vale'; Nicholas Brigham, General Receiver of Subsidies, who built Chaucer's tomb in Westminster Abbey, c.1555 (d. 1558). Item 26 in the list of books John Bale (1495-1563), bishop of Ossory, was forced to leave behind in Ireland, according to his letter to Archbp Parker, 1560 (cf. H. McCusker, 'Books and Manuscripts formerly in the possession of John Bale', *The Library*, 4th ser., 16 (1935-6), 145-65). Bound up with fols 111-20, containing *Annales ad annum 1268* (a MS given by Elias de Trikyngham (*BRUO* 1905) to Oriel College, Oxford), also owned by Bale (item 60 in his list). Referred to by John Joscelyn (1529-1603), Parker's Latin Secretary (cf. T. Graham and A.G. Watson, *The recovery of the past in early Elizabethan England: documents by John Bale and John Joscelyn from the circle of Matthew Parker*, Cambridge Bibliographical Soc. Monographs, No. 13 (1998), item J2.79 in Joscelyn's pre-1567 list of writings on English history). Fol. iiᵛ (flyleaf): 'M.W. Darell liber', William Darrell, prebendary of Canterbury (1553-80).

W. Stubbs, *Chronicles of the reigns of Edward I, and Edward II*, 2 vols (RS 1882-83), I: xlii-lviii; W. Sparrow Simpson, 'A short chronicle of St Paul's Cathedral from 1140 to 1341, transcribed from a manuscript in the library of the Archbishop of Canterbury at Lambeth Palace', *Trans. of the London and Middlesex Archaeological Soc.*, 5 (1881), 311-12; James, pp. 818-24; Gransden, *Hist. Writing*, II, pl. I illus. fol. 96ᵛ (reduced); W. O'Sullivan, 'The Irish "remnaunt" of John Bale's manuscripts', *New Science out of old Books; Studies in manuscripts and early printed books in honour of A.I. Doyle*, ed. R. Beadle and A.J. Piper (1995), p. 375.
Pl. 42 a, b

96 **Lambeth Palace 1112**   *1598 London, England*

Robert Tofte, 'A Discourse of the five laste Popes of Rome, and of the firste Originall and begininge of that famous Pilgrimage of our Ladie of Loreto whereunto is added a Draught of the Liues of all suche Romane Cardinalls, as are Liuinge nowe at this Daye'

Paper. 101 fols. 228 × 155 mm. 1 col., 165 × 115 mm. 28-30 lines. 5 large engravings of popes tipped in, with 60 small engraved pasted-in ports of cardinals, crudely coloured. Gold-tooled leather bdg (s. xvi).

The preface, addressed to Richard Bancroft, bishop of London (1597-1604), ends '... and so I humblie take my leave From my Lodginge in Holbourne this first of Januarie 1598 your Lordships most devoted Robert Tofte'. For Tofte, 1562-1620, see F.B. Williams, Jr, 'Robert Tofte', *RES*, 13 (1937), 282-96, 405-23. The engravings were either part of a series or were cut from an unidentified book, that depicting Pope Sixtus V (inserted before fol. 6) bears the signature 'Battista parmense fontis Romae 1589'. Tofte had visited Rome in 1593 where Parmense worked 1586-92 (cf. R.C. Melzi, *Robert Tofte's Discourse to the Bishop of London*, Biblioteca del Viaggio in

Italia, 33 (1989), p. xxiii and n. 29).
Williams, 'Robert Tofte', 411-13; Melzi, *Discourse*, pp. xxiii-xxviii, and p. xiv illus. p. 29.
Pl. 305

97 **Lambeth Palace 1370**   *[c.888 or 891?]*
                                      [Armagh, Ireland]

Evangelia (the 'MacDurnan Gospels')

Parch. 213 fols, foliated 1-3, 5-70, 72-115, 117-70, 172-216 + leaf unfoliated between 3 and 5. 160 × 110 mm. 1 col., c.90 × 50 mm. 20-26 lines. Evang. ports, col. inits. Gold-tooled leather bdg with clasps (s. xvi).

Fol. 3ᵛ (in display capitals): 'MÆIELBRIÐVS. MACDVRNANI. ISTVM. TEXTVM. PER. TRIQVADRVM. DEO. DIGNE. DOGMATIZAT. AST. AETHELSTANVS. ANGLOSÆXANA. REX. ET. RECTOR. DORVERNENSI. METROPOLI. DAT. PER ÆVVM'. 'Mæielbriðus mac Durnani' has been identified as Máel-Brigte mac Tornáin or Dornáin, died 927 (see J.F. Kenney, *The Sources for the Early History of Ireland: Ecclesiastical*, rev. L. Bieler (1966), p. 645). If this inscription can be taken to mean that the present MS was made for him, dates of either c.888 (when he became *comarba* of Patrick) or 891 (when he became *comarba* of all the Columban churches) seem plausible (see further F. Henry, *Irish Art during the Viking Invasions (800-1020 A.D.)*, (1967), pp. 102-5). However, L. Bieler ('Insular palaeography: present state and problems', *Scriptorium*, 3 (1949), 276) argues that the script is earlier s. ix. Textual variants are shared with the Book of Armagh (Trinity College Dublin 52, datable to 807) and two twelfth-century gospel books, BL, Harley 1802 (*DMBL* 644) and Harley 1023, all associated with Armagh; see M. MacNamara, 'The Echternach Gospels and the MacDurnan Gospels: some common readings and their significance', *Peritia*, 6-7 (1987-88), 214-22.

Given by King Athelstan (924-939) to Christ Church, Canterbury, where documents relating to the house have been added (s. xi¹) by various hands on originally blank leaves at the ends of the Gospels of Matthew (fols 69ᵛ-70) and Mark (fols 114-15), and on fol. 87ʳᵛ (Ker, *Anglo-Saxon MSS*, no. 284). Fol. i: 'Matthaeus Parker', for whom the MS was bound (cf. H.M. Nixon, 'Elizabethan Gold-tooled bindings', *Essays in honour of Victor Scholderer*, ed. D.E. Rhodes (1970), p. 254). It was probably Parker who inserted four full-page mins (fols 4, 71, 116, 171), since pictures from the same French psalter (s. xiii) are inserted in two other MSS of his, Cambridge, Corpus Christi College, 419 and 452.

E.G. Millar, 'Les principaux manuscrits à peintures du Lambeth Palace à Londres', *Bulletin de la S.F.R.M.P.*, 8 (1924), 7-15 and pl. I a-d illus. fols 4ᵛ, 5, 70ᵛ, 72; James, pp. 843-45; P. McGurk, 'The Irish pocket Gospel Book', *Sacris Erudiri*, 8 (1956), 249-70; Henry, *Irish Art.*, pls 36, 42-44 and I, K, L illus. fols 170ᵛ, 70ᵛ, 72, 4ᵛ, 5, 1ᵛ, 115ᵛ (enlarged); J.J.G. Alexander, *Insular MSS: 6th to the 9th century* (1978), no. 70 and ills 321-28, 354 illus. fols 2, 5, 117, 172, 1ᵛ, 4, 115ᵛ, 170ᵛ, 70ᵛ; S. Keynes, 'King Athelstan's books', *Learning and Literature in Anglo-Saxon England; studies presented to Peter Clemoes on the occasion of his sixty-fifth birthday*, ed. M. Lapidge and H. Gneuss (1985), pp. 153-59 and pl. V illus. fol. 3ᵛ; G. Henderson, *From Durrow to Kells: the Insular Gospel*

Books 650-800 (1987), pl. 50 illus. fol. 1ᵛ (reduced); R. Gameson, 'The decoration of the Tanner Bede', *Anglo-Saxon England*, 21 (1992), 140-42.
Pl. 1

98 Lambeth Palace 1506   *1531*
[diocese of Freising, Germany]

Kalendarium

Parch. 7 fols, foliated i, 1-6. 240 × 172 mm. 1 col., 220 × 136 mm. Up to 26 lines. Entries in red and black.

Fol. i: 'Hoc missale exarauit leonnardus de wulp<.> frising' dioc' die sancte anne Anno 1531 Et est proprium eius'. The kalendar (formerly prefixed to the missal) includes 'Dedicacio ecclesie frisingen' (2 May), 'Corbiniani episcopi' (8 September), 'Translacio sancti corbiniani episcopi' (20 November), 'Rudberti episcopi' (27 March) and 'Udalrici episcopi' (4 July), all in red.
Fol. i: a St Andrew's cross with the initials W G W M in its four arms (reading clockwise from left), with the date 1531 above and initials F.V.T. below.
MMBL, I: 103.
Pl. 252

99 Lambeth Palace 2018   *[betw. 1429 and 1432]*
[London, England]

Statuta Cantarie Thome More Ecclesie Cathedralis Sancti Pauli

Parch. 11 fols. 315 × 235 mm. 1 col., 227 × 150 mm. 40 lines, fols 1-5, 9-11; 29 lines fols 6-8. Col. inits. Vellum wrapper.

A booklet originally consisting of a quire of 8 leaves (fols 1-5, 9-11) containing copies of the 1424 and 1429 statutes of the chantry of Thomas More, Dean of St Paul's (d. 1421), copied by a single scribe. Three leaves (fols 6-8) inserted by a second scribe after fol. 5 contain further statutes dated 1432, fol. 7: 'sub anno domini millesimo quadringentesimo tricesimo secundo [then partly erased: Indiccione vndecima pontificatus sanctissimi in christo patris et domini domini Eugenij diuina prouidencia pape quarti] anno secundo mense Octobris die decima septima. In ecclesia cath' sancti Pauli London' presentibus discretis viris Magistro Jacobo Cole Juniore [*BRUO* 460] Notario publico et domino Johanne Hecham capellano Norwicen' dioc' testibus ad premissa vocatis specialiter et rogatis', followed by Cole's subscription and notarial sign 'sub anno Indictione pontificatu Mense die et loco in fine. presencium superius ante hanc presentem meam subscripcionem ...'. Added prayers (s. xvi), fol. 10ᵛ, for the souls of Henry VII and his queen, Elizabeth. Fols 7ᵛ-8ᵛ and 11ʳ⁻ᵛ blank.
Fol. 1: 'Iste liber constat Cantarie Thome More' (s. xv²).
E.G.W. Bill, *A Catalogue of Manuscripts in Lambeth Palace Library MSS. 1907-2340* (1976), pp. 65-66.
Pls 103, 108

100 Lambeth Palace 2078   *[betw. 1366 and 1379]*
[Bury St Edmunds, England]

The Ingham Roll, in Latin

Parch. 2 membranes. 1070 × 460 mm.

An account of the foundation and privileges of the Priory of the Holy Trinity at Ingham, Norfolk, written for John de Brinkley, abbot of Bury St Edmunds 1361-79, consisting principally of a bull of Pope Urban V, dated Avignon, 8 November 1366, addressed to Brinkley (as well as the bishops of London and Ely) which confirms the rights and privileges of Bury.
E.G.W. Bill, *Catalogue of Manuscripts in Lambeth Palace Library, MSS 1907-2340* (1976), pp. 86-87.
Damaged at the edges and too faded to photograph

101 Law Society 9007451, part b
[betw. 1479 and 1486] [England]

Registrum brevium

Paper. 48 fols. 312 × 220 mm. 1 col., 220 × *c*.145 mm. 30 lines.

A register of writs in six parts, each individually foliated by letter and numbers; thus the second part consists of four quires of twelve foliated b1-b48. In a writ on fol. b38 the name of the Master of the Rolls was given by the original scribe as Robert Morton (Master 1479-83, 1485-86, and later bishop of Worcester 1486-97); Morton's name has subsequently been crossed out and that of Thomas Hanybal (Master 1523-27) substituted by another hand. The scribe of part b also copied part c, fols c1-c12 (fols c13-c20 contain later additions). Parts a, d, and e, by other scribes, were probably all copied about the same time as b.
Fol. e34: 'Eeste (*sic*) liber est meus possum producere testis qui scripsit scripta dextra sua sit benedicta nomen scriptoris Barlowus plene amoris nvnc finem feci sit mecum gracia christi' (s. xvi). Possibly George Barlow of Mynwere, Pembroke, admitted to the Inner Temple in November 1583, since the MS later belonged to two members; cf. bookplates of Francis Williamson (d. January 1667/8), and Alexander Gerrard, proposed as Reader at Clement's Inn, May 1789.
MMBL, I: 121, catalogued as Law Society MS 7 (105.g).
Pl. 207

102 Lincoln's Inn Hale 12, fols 449-51
[betw. 1279 and c.1300] [England]

Annales Angliae

Parch. 3 fols. 250 × 170 mm. 1 col., 200 × 145 mm. Up to 35 lines.

Annals from 1067-1279 were written by a single scribe; thereafter entries for the years 1280-1300 are by another hand. Ker (*MMBL*, I: 126) suggests that entries added for 1288 ('Obitus dompni J. de Vesci ... Obitus Agn' de Mora in xlᵃ') and 1291 ('Dedicata est capella beati Edmundi confessoris apud Abendon') were perhaps of local interest.
Three single leaves taken from a larger volume and bound by John Selden (1584-1654) with a collection of other extracts, documents and copies. For Selden, see G. Parry, *The Trophies of Time, English Antiquarians of the Seventeenth Century* (1995), pp. 95-129. His papers probably passed to Sir Matthew Hale (d. 1676) as Selden's executor (see also D.M. Barrett, 'The library of John Selden and its later history', *Bodleian Library Record*, 3 (1950-51), 128-42). For another MS owned by Selden, see no. 106 below.
Hunter, p. 21; *MMBL*, I: 126.
Pl. 30

103 Lincoln's Inn Hale 71   *[betw. 1488 and 1504]*
                                        [London or Westminster, England]

Nova Statuta Angliae, in Latin and French

Parch. 403 fols. 345 × 240 mm. 1 col., *c*.220 × 140 mm. Up
to 41 lines. Illum. inits with full-page borders (fols 64, 67,
353), illum. dec. inits with border, col. inits. Blind-stamped
bdg over boards, with clasps (rebacked).

Statutes of the Realm (fols 64-373), ending 3 Henry VII, 22
August 1487-21 August 1488. The MS was copied by at least
six different scribes, two of whom seem to have worked later
than the others since their stints are undecorated. One of these
later scribes was first identified by Mr J.J. Griffiths as the hand
of a number of Statuta manuscripts including fols 3-92 of no.
132 below. Here Griffiths' 'Statuta scribe' copied statutes 12
Edward IV to 3 Henry VII (fols 373ᵛ-403), and completed or
supplied earlier statutes on fols 174-76 (176ᵛ blank), 207-12
(212ᵛ-14ᵛ blank), 233-35 (235ᵛ blank), and fols 337-50 (fols
350ᵛ-52ᵛ blank). Whereas the other scribes wrote a Secretary
or Secretary-influenced hand, 'Statuta' alone wrote a legal
Anglicana. Arms, probably added to the initials on fols 64 and
67, have been identified (by J.H. Baker) as those of Gregory
Adgore, Serjeant at Law 1503, for whom see Baker's *The Order
of Serjeants at Law*, Selden Soc., Suppl. Ser. 5 (1984), p. 495.
Adgore died 1504.

End pastedown: 'Ricardus Fulbroke' (s. xvᵉˣ).

> Hunter, pp. 47-48; *MMBL*, I: 126.
> *Pls 219, 220*

104 Lincoln's Inn Hale 94   *1493 [France]*

Bernhard von Breidenbach, Peregrinatio in Terram Sanctam

Paper. 164 fols. 299 × 210 mm. 1 col., 210 × 125 mm
32 lines. Col. inits. Original boards of bdg, clasps gone.

The invocation 'ihesu + maria 13 die nouembris 1493' at the top
of fol. 1 probably indicates the date when the scribe began to
write. Breidenbach's account of his journey in 1483-84 to the
Holy Land was first printed by Erhard Reuwich in Mainz 1486
(see *Deutsche Buchdrucker des Fünfzehnten Jahrhunderts*
(1971), nos 65-66). For Breidenbach, see H.W. Davies,
*Bernhard von Breydenbach and his journey to the Holy Land
1483-84, A Bibliography* (1911, repr. 1968), and *Die Reise nach
Jerusalem, Bernhard von Breydenbachs Wallfahrt ins Heilige
Land*, ed. C. Schneider, Catalogue of an Exhibition held 5 May-
30 September 1992 at the Gutenberg-Museum, Mainz (1992).
Fol. 1: 'Johannes Smythus me suum vendicat'. Fol. ii: 'Liber
Wilhelmi Cholmeley Ex Georgii Thwaits 1577'.

> Hunter, p. 71; *MMBL*, I: 129-30.
> *Pl. 223*

105 Lincoln's Inn Hale 95   *[betw. 1303 and 1314]*
                                                        [England]

Legal miscellany, in Latin and French

Parch. 151 fols. 230 × 150 mm. 1 col., 180-203 × 110-20
mm. Up to 61 lines. Blank spaces left for inits. Rebound,
but s. xvi panels used on bdg.

An untidy legal collection written by a number of early fourteenth-century hands. Medieval quire signatures establish that
quire 10 (after fol. 75) is missing and that the present fols 139-

44, numbered quire 16, originally followed fol. 117. The present
quires 16 (fols 118-21), 18 (fols 130-37), and 20 (fols 145-51)
were unnumbered. Frequent changes of ink and the way text has
often been squashed onto a leaf suggest that many items were
jotted down soon after the proceedings they record. The earliest
date cited occurs in a register of writs (fols 16-51) which begins
with a writ of right of 32 Edward I (1303-4). An original writ
of 21 Edward I (1292-93), folded in half, has been inserted
into this register (fols 34 and 38). The latest date is that of a plea
7 Edward II (1313-14) which was added to a series of scribbled
notes of pleadings in Latin and French (fols 85-138 and 145-51)
which begins 33 Edward I (1304-5), and includes one dated
1307 (fol. 106) naming John de Waneting, Warden of Merton
College, Oxford (d. 1329). The scribe of the added plea began it
on fol. 134ᵛ, continued on the next page, and fitted the conclusion onto a piece of parchment sewn to the foot of fol. 135.
The added plea and many of the others may have been written
by the same hand. Fols 2-8 contain a shortened form of the
coronation *ordo* of Edward II (1307) written by a hand not
unlike that of fols 134ᵛ-35. Fols 76 and 108 are inserted slips
with contemporary (undated) additions. Fols 1 and 152 were
pastedowns. For the panel used on the binding, see J.B. Oldham,
Blind Panels of English Binders (1958), ST 7.

Copies of documents added in s. xv on fols 129ᵛ, 149ᵛ contain
the name Richard Foristall and the Irish place names Kilmagh,
Kilferath, Newgrange, and Carraman. Fol. 2: 'Math. Hale'.

> Hunter, pp. 77-78; *MMBL*, I: 130.
> *Pl. 41 a, b*

106 Lincoln's Inn Hale 135   *[betw. 1285 and 1290]*
                                                        [England]

Gilbert de Thornton, Summa de legibus

Parch. 197 fols. 348 × 225 mm. 1 col., 280 × 165 mm. 59
lines. Col. inits, rubrics.

A 'rigorously practical' abridgement of Bracton's Summa by
Gilbert de Thornton, chief justice of the King's Bench 1290-95,
d. 1295 (cf. J.H. Baker, *Biographical Dictionary of the Common
Law*, ed. A.W.B. Simpson (1984), p. 504). S.E. Thorne, 'Gilbert
de Thornton's Summa de legibus', *University of Toronto Law
Journal*, 7 (1947), 1-26, has established that Thornton must
have produced the text after 1285 (the date of the second Statute
of Westminster, to which the text refers several times) but before
1290 (the date of the statute *Quia emptores terrarum*). Financial
transactions recorded on the flyleaf (fol. iᵛ) are dated 1297.
Since these financial memoranda refer to Alan de Thornton,
who in 1310 held land at Cabourne, Lincolnshire, that had been
granted to Gilbert in 1289, it is probable Alan was Gilbert's son
and that the present MS was formerly Gilbert's own copy.

Fol. 5: Greek motto of John Selden (1584-1654). Acquired by
Sir Matthew Hale (d. 1676), one of Selden's executors. For
another MS owned by Selden, see no. 102 above.

> Hunter, p. 91; G.E. Woodbine, 'The Summa of Gilbert
> de Thornton', *Law Quarterly Review*, 25 (1909), 44-52;
> *MMBL*, I: 132-33.
> *Pl. 32*

107 Lincoln's Inn Hale 194 *[betw. 1461 and 1471]*
[London or Westminster, England]

Nova Statuta Angliae, in Latin and French

Parch. 225 fols, foliated 2-130, 130*, 131-225. 332 × 230 mm. 1 col., 200 × 125 mm. 42-44 lines. Hist. inits with full-page borders (fols 34, 131, 153ᵛ, 168ᵛ), gold inits.

The latest Statute copied is dated 'en le fest de seint leonard' lan de son reigne xxix [Henry VI]', 6 November 1450. Arms within the initial on fol. 2 and in the borders of fols 34, 131, 153ᵛ, 168ᵛ, are those of John Neville, Lord Montagu, 1461, earl of Northumberland, 1464, and Marquess Montagu, 1470. He died 1471. By one hand which, *pace* K. Scott, *The Mirroure of the Worlde*, Roxburghe Club 241 (1980), p. 67, is not that of the scribe of London, Inner Temple 505.
Fol. 190: 'THOME LUCAS'. Fol. 2: the monogram 'ASRYDTOL' (?); 'Liber Haywardi Towneshend Hospit. Lin: Æt 20. et 2 dies. Junij 19. 1597. Eliz. 39°', on whom see *The Records of the Honorable Society of Lincoln's Inn, The Black Books*, 5 vols (1897-1977), II: 31, 68.

> Hunter, pp. 150-51; *MMBL*, I: 140; Scott, *Later Gothic MSS*, II: 300.
> *Pl. 156*

108 Lincoln's Inn Maynard 45 *1597 [England]*

A collection of copies of documents relating to the town and manor of Crediton, Devon

Paper. 143 fols, foliated 1-84, 84*-142. 312 × 205 mm. 1 col., 255 × 150 mm. Up to 40 lines. Limp vellum bdg.

Fol. 141ᵛ: 'Finis Deo Gracias per Ricardum Sutton 1 Januar 1597'. A Richard Sutton, member of Lincoln's Inn and MP for Newport, Isle of Wight, died 1634 (see *A History of Parliament: The House of Commons 1558-1603*, ed. P.W. Hasler, 3 vols (1981) III: 465).
Belonged to John Maynard, d. 1690, who also owned no. 125 below.

> Hunter, p. 110.
> *Pl. 302*

109 Lincoln's Inn Misc. 1 *[betw. 1285 and 1292]*
[London or Westminster, England]

Statuta Angliae, etc., in Latin and French.

Parch. 190 fols. 214 × 145 mm. 1 col., 170 × 108 mm. 33 lines. Blank spaces for inits except col. init., fol. 1. Leather bdg over boards, strap- and pin-fastening.

A handbook containing various legal texts, statutes, and formularies. The MS consists of three booklets, fols 1-56, 61-132, 133-90, written by a single scribe. Fols 57-60 were inserted by a later scribe who also added items at the end of the first booklet (on fols 54ᵛ-56ᵛ) and the third (on fol. 190ᵛ). The latest datable item in the second booklet is a copy of Parva Hengham (fols 112-18ᵛ), composed between 1285 and 1290 (cf. W.H. Dunham, Jr, *Radulphi de Hengham Summae* (1932), p. lxi; the present copy is not among the MSS listed pp. lxxiii-lxxviii), the third booklet (fols 133-90) contains a register of writs beginning 1 May 16 Edward I (1288), while the latest dated item copied by the scribe is a copy of the Novum Statutum de Moneta, copied near the end of the first booklet and dated to 1292 (fol. 48ᵛ). Additions made by the later scribe include a note of probate, fol.

190v, recording that the will of Joan La Spicer, who had left a tenement in London to John de St Maur, was proved and enrolled in the court of common pleas, 1314 (cf. *Calendar of Wills proved and enrolled in the Court of Husting, London, AD 1258-AD 1688*, ed. R.R. Sharpe (1889), p. 249). He also added, in the inserted quire, a statute dated 12 Edward II, 1318-19 (fols 59ᵛ-60ᵛ). Fols ii-iii include a table of contents. Pastedowns and endleaves (fols i, 191; *not* 194, as stated in *MMBL*) are bifolia from an English service book, s. xiv.

> Hunter, pp. 153-54; *MMBL*, I: 140-41.
> *Pl. 33*

110 Mercers' Company *[betw. 1442 and 1443]*
[London, England]

Ordinances for Richard Whittington's Almshouse, in English

Parch. 20 fols, medieval foliation by scribe. 205 × 150 mm. 1 col., 122 × c.75 mm. 28 lines. Pen and ink drawing (fol. i). Limp vellum bdg.

Fol. xv: 'Go litel boke go litel tregedie
      The lowly submitting' to al correccioun
      Of theym beyng maistres now of the Mercery
      Olney. Feldyng. Boleyne / and of Burton
      Hertily theym besekyng wᵗ humble salutacion
      The to accepte and thus to take in gre
      For euer to be a seruant wᵗ In þeire cominalte'.

John Olney, Geoffrey Feldyng, Geoffrey Boleyn, and John Burton were Wardens of the Mercers' Company from Midsummer 1442 to Midsummer 1443 (see J. Imray, *The Charity of Richard Whittington: A History of the Trust administered by the Mercers' Company 1424-1966* (1968), p. 38 n. 2). English version of the Latin ordinances for Whittington's Almshouse founded in 1424. For Whittington, d. 1423, see C.M. Barron, 'Richard Whittington: the Man behind the Myth', *Studies in London History presented to P.E. Jones*, ed. A.E.J. Hollaender and W. Kellaway (1969), pp. 197-248. The drawing (fol. i) depicting him on his deathbed, is ascribed to William Abell (J. Alexander, 'William Abell "lymnour" and 15th century English illumination', *Kunsthistorische Forschungen Otto Pächt zu seinem 70. Geburtstag*, ed. A. Rosenauer and G. Weber (1972), pp. 166-72). Abell was also the artist of no. 154 below. The first four leaves and the last, all blank, are unfoliated by the scribe.

> Imray, *Charity*, pl. 1 illus. fol. i; Alexander, 'William Abell', pl. I illus. fol. i; Christianson, *Directory*, pp. 59-60.
> *Pl. 119*

111 Merchant Taylors' Co., Ancient MS Books No. 1
1491 London, England

Book of Oaths

Parch. 8 fols. 395 × 272 mm. 1 col., 270 × 184 mm. Up to 35 lines. Rubrics.

A list of obits at the end of the book (fols 7ʳ⁻ᵛ) is headed: 'To the pleasir of god our lady saynt Marye the Virgyn and saint John Baptist Patrone of the Fraternytie of Taillours and lynge armorers in London by the commaundement of William Hert maister Henry Clough Nicholas Nynes [Master, 1496] Henry Bellowe and Rauf Bukberd Warden<s> of the same Fraternyte this table was compiled and made by me William Duryvale

Clerk of the same Fraternytie In the yere of our Lorde M¹ CCCC lxxxxj for a *per*petuell remembraunce and knoweleche of kepyng of all such obyts as ben accustumed to be kept by this Crafte as herafter foloweth'. Duryvale also copied the preceding forms of oaths to be taken by the Master, officers and members of the Fraternity respectively (fols 1-6); fol. 8 left blank. He subscribed the Scriveners' Company 'Common Paper' in 1487 (see no. 38 above, and pl. 214).

Now deposited at the Guildhall Library as MS 34007.

> H.L. Hopkinson, *Report on the Ancient Records in the possession of the Guild of Merchant Taylors of the Fraternity of St. John Baptist* (1915), 6-7.
> *Pl. 221*

112 Middle Temple Anc. 5
1387, 1390, 1393, 1400, 1414, 1415 [Germany]

Astrologica, etc., in Latin and German

Paper. 230 fols. 288 × 200 mm. 1 col., 220 × 135 mm. 29-30 lines. Col. inits, rubrics, tables and diagrms.

A miscellany or notebook containing various astrological, astronomical, and other texts, copied, in no particular order, by a single hand at various dates between 1387 and 1400, to which a later scribe/owner has made additions in 1414 and 1415. The first scribe copied fols 36-75 containing astronomical tables from 1387-1462 and tables of radices, 1387-1444, headed 'Anno domini 1387 F est littera dominicalis I est aureus numerus viij Ebdomade 7 dies'. He also dated the colophon of another text in the same year on fol. 215ᵛ: 'Completum Egidij anno domini 1387'. Later dates given in colophons are 1390 (fol. 26: 'Finiui in vigilia pasche anno domini M⁰ ccc⁰ lxxxx⁰'), 1393 (fol. 19 (in red): 'Hic est Finis Incepi et compleui ipsa die Luce Ewangeliste anno domini 1393'; fol. 34: 'Completus in vigilia Michahelis Anno domini M⁰ CCC⁰ lxxxx tercio'; fol. 94ᵛ 'Compleui in vigilia Symonis et Jude Apostolorum Anno domini 1393'), and 1400 (fol. 209ᵛ: 'Anno domini Millesimo Quadragesimo'). On fol. 77ᵛ he started to date a diagram showing solar cycles, etc., to the 1380s and had to correct the date to an earlier year 'Anno domini Millesimo CCCᵐᵒ [lxxx] lij⁰'. The second scribe made various additions throughout the MS. Some of his colophons are dated 1414 (fol. 112ᵛ: 'Scriptum vigilia georgij martyris anno 1414⁰ hora 8ᵃ ante meridie argentine [Strasburg]'; fol. 195: 'Finiui v⁰ kalendas decembris anno millesimo M⁰ cccc⁰ xiiij⁰'; fol. 197: 'Finiui in vigilia nycolay episcopi anno 1414 hora fere 4ᵃ post meridie') and others 1415 (fol. 111ᵛ: 'hec sciencia hic posita et superior ante sexternum scripta fuerat reportata Avinione in festo Sancti Georgij Anno domini 1360 hora vesperarum set scripta huc pridye nonas [*altered to* ydus] aprilis hora completorii argentine anno domini 1415'; fol. 225ᵛ: '… finitus octaua assumpcionis gloriose virginis et symphoriani et thymothey festo die mercurii anno 1415 post septimam horam ante medium noctis').

> *MMBL*, I: 158-62; Kramer, I: 750.
> *Pls 70, 89*

113 National Maritime Museum NVT 19, fols 3-14
1470 Venice, Italy

On the art of the sea and the building of ships, in Italian

Paper. 12 fols. 405 × 290 mm. 2 cols, 300 × 195 mm. 57 lines. Blank spaces left for inits.

Fol. 3 (at the top of the page): 'Jesus Maria 1470 a di 27 Dezcenbrio Veniexia [sic]'. The date is probably that on which the scribe began copying. The text ends fol. 14 'Deo gratias Amen' and is followed, fols 14-15, by other items in the same hand. The rest of the MS, fols 16-67, is written by various s. xvi hands. A title 'Ragioni Antique Spettanti all'Arte Del Mare Et Fabriche De Vasselli 1470 a di 27 Dec⁰' has been supplied (fol. 1) by a later hand.

> *Guide to the Manuscripts in the National Maritime Museum*, ed. R.J.B. Knight, 2 vols (1977-80), II: 130 § 123.
> *Pl. 176*

114 National Maritime Museum NVT 25
1567 [Italy]

Agostino Cesareo, 'L'Arte della Navigatione con il Regimento della Tramontana, e del sole …'

Paper. 72 fols. 205 × 138 mm. 1 col., 150 × 95 mm. 19 lines. Col. and pen and ink diagrms, tables fols 26-33. Limp parch bdg with green silk ties.

The dedicatory preface (fols iiⁱ⁻ᵛ), addressed to 'ALLO ILLVSTRISSIMO Signore Donno EMANVEL de LVNA Gouernatore di Cremona. AGOSTINO CESAREO', concludes '… ogni felicità humilmente me le raccomando. M.D. lxvij'. Fols 61-63 contain an index by the scribe. Fols i, iii-iv, 59ᵛ-60ᵛ and 64-68 are blank.

> *Pl. 269*

115 Oratory 12544
1469 [England]

Officium mortuorum ad usum Sarum

Parch. 86 fols. 147 × 105 mm. 1 col., 95 × 68 mm. 12-15 lines text or 4 staves music. Col. inits, rubrics.

Fol. 86ᵛ: 'Scriptum est anno domini 1469'.

> *MMBL*, I: 165.
> *Pl. 173*

116 Oratory 12744, fols 21-83
[betw. 1365 and 1367]
[Germany? Netherlands?]

Decisiones rotae romanae

Paper. 63 fols. 270 × 200 mm. 1 col., c.200 × 140 mm. 29 lines.

The text, the so-called Decisiones antiquiores by Bernard du Bosquet (Bisgneto), auditor 1355-65 (d. 1371), begins imperfectly: '… sidens in cancellaria iusticie et dominus G bragose ['G' for 'Guilelmus' corrected from ?E] tunc referendarius domini pape …'. The corrector, whose hand is contemporary with that of the text, has added in the margin that Bragose was 'nunc Cardinalis sancti Georgij [1361-67] et summus Penitenciarius de anno lxj sub domino Innoc' papa vj in ultimo anno pontificatus de mense septembris'. The rest of the volume, fols 1-20 and fols 84-211, is written by other scribes of s. xiv². The binding (s. xviii), with the erased arms of the Praemonstratensian abbey of Parc, near Louvain, bears on the inside cover Parc's characteristic pressmark 'K Theca, 11'; see E.van Balberghe, 'Deux manuscrits de Parc retrouvés', *Analecta Praemonstratensia*, 46 (1970), 345-46 and cf. *Monasticon Belge*, 16 vols (1890-1993), IV, 3: 784.

MMBL, I: 176-78; G. Dolezalek, 'Die handschriftliche Verbreitung von Rechtsprechungssammlungen der Rota', *Zeitschrift der Savigny-Stiftung für Rechtsgeschichte, Kanonistiche Abteilung*, 58 (1972), 46.
Pl. 57

117 PRO C47/34/12 no. 9; C47/34/13, fols 1-34; E163/22/2/54; and SP 46/123, fols 171-79

[c.1416?] [England]

Grammatica, in Latin and English

Paper. 61 fols. Up to 218 × 150 mm. 1 col., *c*.170 × 135 mm. 30 lines.

Fragments of a schoolboy's exercise book, the leaves badly damaged by damp and much of the text illegible. E163/22/2/54, fol. 1 contains two model letters, in English, of letters to one's parents. Three Latin exercises, C47/34/13, fols 13ᵛ, 15, 17, refer to the siege of Harfleur by the French and one (fol. 28ᵛ) to the expected arrival of the emperor (Sigismund) at Dover in 1416. Fol. 15ᵛ: 'Stephanus Bukherst xvj' (the name Bukherst also occurs fols 11ᵛ, 28ᵛ); to judge from the reference to Dover and the use of Kentish spellings in the English texts, he may have been at school in Kent (see D. Thomson, *A Descriptive Catalogue of Middle English Grammatical Texts* (1979), pp. 258-61). Both Thomson and Ker, *MMBL*, I: 180, knew only of C47/34/13. Fols 35-36 of the latter, containing verse copied by another, earlier, hand, probably formed the parchment wrappers of the original collection.

Too badly damaged to photograph

118 PRO C115/80   *1408 [Ireland?]*

Registrum terrarum domus Lanthonie Prime in Hibernia

Parch. 71 fols, foliated i, 1-61, 61bis-69. 300 × 195 mm. 1 col., 215 × 140 mm. 42 lines. Col. inits, rubrics. Leather bdg over boards, strap and pin fastening gone (s. xv).

Fol. 2 (in red): 'Incipiunt capitula cartarum cirographorum conuencionum composicionum et Instrumentorum de omnibus ecclesijs beneficij redditubus terris possessionibus et rebus alijs que domus lanthonie prime in Wallia possidet in Hibernia tam in Dublinensi diocesi quam armachansi eciam et Midensi [Meath] Scriptarum per adam Elmeley et Willelmum Temset procuratores dicte domus in Hibernia Anno domini Millesimo Quadragentesimo Octauo titulatarum per quaternos'; the MS is again dated fol. 62 (the letters picked out in red): 'Extenta omnium possessionum Prioris et Conuentus Lanthonie prime in Wallia tam spiritualium quam temporalium in Hibernia existencium facta per Willelmum Temset canonicum domus predicte ad tunc procuratorem eorundem in hibernia mensis Millesimo CCCCᵐᵒ viij et regni Regis henrici'. Fols 2-60 are by Elmeley, fols 62-68 by Temset. Fols 61ᵛ-61bisʳ contain a short account, added by a third, contemporary, hand, of Hugh de Lacy, founder of Lanthony, and his descendants, beginning '<.>e ʒere from þe incarna*cioune* offe oure lord a þowzand ⁊ lx. vj come into Englond Wylla*m* Bastard and was crowned Kyng off Englond at londyn apon a moneday …'. Fols 60ᵛ-61ʳ are blank as are fols i, 1.

Fol. 69: 'Domini Tomi' and monogram 'R T' (s. xvi).

E. St John Brooks, *The Irish Cartularies of Llanthony Prima and Secunda*, Irish MSS Commission (1953);

Davis, *MC*, no. 532.
Pls 78, 79

119 PRO C115/81 and 83   *1449*
Lanthony Secunda, England

Cartularium, in 2 vols

Parch. Vol. 1 215 fols, vol. 2 139 fols. 380 × 270 mm. 1 col., 230 × 160 mm. 30 lines. Illum. hist. inits and borders (vol. 1, fols 1, 15), col. inits, rubrics. Leather bdg over boards, strap and pin fastenings gone (both vols).

A 2-volume cartulary written throughout by the same scribe. Vol. 1 (C115/83) begins with a table of contents headed fol. 1 (in red): 'Presentis tabula voluminis quod Dominus Johannes Garlond Prior [1436-1457] ibidem fieri fecit de Cartis et Scriptis suis subsequentibus Adhibita inde Curia confratris magistri Ricardi Steymo*ur* Anno domini Millesimo .CCCCᵐᵒ. xlixº. Et anno Regni Regis Henrici sexti xxviij° facit …'; the placename 'lanthon' iuxta Glouc' is given in the border. (Steymour's name has been expanded in the literature as 'Steymour' and 'Steymous', but in no. 120 below the abbreviation for 'ur' is clearly used.) Fol. 139 contains copies of two letters in English concerning the threatened distraint by Richard, Duke of York (d. 1460), of priory land at Colesborne, Gloucs, 9 July 25 Henry VI (1447). Throughout both volumes Steymour left leaves (fully ruled in purple ink) blank; on these a few late fifteenth- and early sixteenth-century additions have been made.

Davis, *MC*, no. 534; R.I. Jack, 'An archival case history: the cartularies and registers of Llanthony Priory in Gloucestershire', *Journal of the Society of Archivists*, 4 (1972), 370-83.
Pl. 130

120 PRO C115/84   *1440*
Lanthony Secunda, England

Tabula sive kalendarium de cartis

Parch. 212 fols. 277 × 190 mm. 1 col., 180-214 × 115-30 mm. 28-36 lines. Col. inits, rubrics. Leather bdg over boards, strap and pin fastenings gone (s. xv).

Fol. 1 (in red): 'Presens tabula siue kalendarium de cartis … in hoc sequenti Registro scriptis et compilatis pro litteras alphabeti et numeros subscriptos seriatim requirendis et inueniendis tangentibus tantummodo teras tenementa redditus et seruicia Priori et Conuentui Lanthon' iuxta Gloucestr' et suburbijs et locis contiguis eiusdem pertinencia Facta fuit per Fratrem Ricardum Steymo*ur* de Aure post festum Annunciacionis beate Marie anno domini Millesimo CCCCᵐᵒ quadragesimo. Et anno regni Regis henrici sexti post conquestum decimo nono. Tempore Dompni Johannis Garlande Prioris [1436-57] Que postea scripta sunt per Fratres Robertum Cole Rentarium et Johannem Machyn coquinarium'. The table of contents, fols 1-27, is by one hand, fols 28-139 by another (with interruptions by other hands fols 72-74 and 101-103ᵛ), and fols 140-95 by a third. For another cartulary compiled by Steymour, see no. 119 above. Fr Robert Cole also made another cartulary (Davis, *MC*, no. 535), apparently based on vol. 1 of no. 119 above, and 'compiled and wrote' a rental, with a chronicle (in English) of the kings of England to Henry VI on its dorse (Gloucestershire Record Office, Gloucester Borough Records (GBR) J5, for which see *Rental of All the Houses in Gloucester A.D. 1455*, ed.

W.H. Stevenson (1890), and cf. 'Transactions at Gloucester', *Trans.of the Bristol and Gloucestershire Archaeological Soc.*, 13 (1888-89), 60-61).

Davis, *MC*, no. 533; R.I. Jack, 'An archival case history: the cartularies and registers of Llanthony Priory in Gloucestershire', *Journal of the Society of Archivists*, 4 (1972), 370-83.

Pls 114, 115 a, b

121 **PRO C150/1, fols 10-14, 18-257, 260-331**

[betw. 1285 and 1306] Gloucester, England

Cartularium

Parch. 317 fols. 300 × 200 mm. 1 col., except fols 10-14 2 cols, 200 × 125 mm. 34 lines. Hist. init. (fol. 18), col. inits, rubrics. In limp vellum bdg.

Fol. 10 (in red): 'Incipit tabula cartarum ecclesie Sancti Petri Glouc' que sic incipit', and again on fol. 246 (in red) 'Transcripta priuilegiorum Ecclesie sancti Petri Gloucestr', followed by 'In nomine domini Amen Anno eiusdem M⁰ CC⁰ Octagesimo quinto Indictione quartadecima et pontificatus domini Honorij pape quarti Anno primo. Die septimo. Mense Februarij …', a passage subsequently marked 'vacat'. No document is included later than the abbacy of John de Gamages, 1284-1306, and H.R. Hart (*Historia et Cartularium Monasterii Sancti Petri Gloucestriae*, 3 vols (RS 1863-67), III: xi) was probably right to identify the present MS with the 'Transcripta Cartarum' recorded in the *Historia* as the second of three volumes given by Gamages (ibid., I: 40). Fols 26ᵛ-28 contain a short treatise describing the financial arrangements on Gloucester's estates, dated by D. Oschinsky (*Walter of Henley and other Treatises on Estate Management and Accounting* (1971), p. 23) to between 1301-7. Fols 7-9 include early s. xiv additions, the latest dated 9 Edward II, 1315-16. Other additions, fols 14ᵛ-17ᵛ, 258-59, and fols 332-37, are s. xv. Fols 1-6 are endleaves.

Davis, *MC*, no. 454; Oschinsky, pp. 254-57.

Pl. 35

122 **PRO DL 42/1 and 2**

[betw. 1402 and 1407]
[London, England]

Duo Magna Registra Hereditatis Ducatus Lancastrie ('The Great Cowcher')

Parch. Vol. 1 453 fols. 402 × 265 mm. Vol. 2 511 fols foliated 1-175, 175bis, 176-214, three fols blank, 215-506, one leaf blank. 415 × 270 mm. 1 col., 250 × 160 mm. 40 lines. Illum. hist. inits and full-page borders, illum. dec. inits and borders, gold and col. inits. Vol. 2, fols 4-21, 16 banners of lordships held by the Duchy emblazoned.

Compiled by John Leventhorpe, receiver general of the duchy of Lancaster 1399-1423, who arranged that Richard Frampton, clerk, should copy the volume at 13*s* 4*d* a quire, including the cost of 'parchemyn et lymyner de voz lettres' (PRO, DL, 42/15, fol. 174; for Leventhorpe, see R. Somerville, *History of the Duchy of Lancaster*, I (1953), pp. 397-98). Payments to Frampton are recorded in Leventhorpe's accounts for the years 1402-7, final payment being made before 2 February, 8 Henry IV (DL 28/4/5, fol. 12ᵛ; cf. R. Somerville, 'The cowcher books of the duchy of Lancaster', *EHR*, 51 (1936), 598-615). Frampton later made a transcript of the present cartulary, for

which see no. 125 below. He also copied Glasgow, University Library, Hunterian T.4.1 (84), which he signed; for other MSS by him, see Christianson, *Directory*, pp. 106-7. Two historiated initials in vol. I (fols 1, 51) are 'close in figure style to the later work of the 'Carmelite-Lapworth Master' (Scott, *Later Gothic MSS*, II: 85) whose work is to be seen in San Marino, Huntington Lib., HM 19920, copied by Frampton. This artist also appears in the Chichele Breviary, no. 51 above (see Scott, *Later Gothic MSS*, II: 28 for a list of his work). S. Wright ('The author portraits in the Bedford-Psalter Hours: Gower, Chaucer and Hoccleve', *British Library Journal*, 18 (1992), p. 192), on the other hand, calls the artist the 'Master of the Great Cowchers' and, besides work in BL Royal 1.E. ix (with which Scott agrees), detects his hand in the portrait initials of BL, Add. 42131.

Somerville, *History*, I, pls II, VII (reduced); Davis, *MC*, nos 1268-69; A.I. Doyle, 'The manuscripts', *Middle English Alliterative Poetry and its Literary Background*, ed. D. Lawton (1982), pp. 93-94 and n. 19; Scott, *Later Gothic MSS*, II: 84-85; J.A. Goodall, 'Heraldry in the decoration of English medieval manuscripts', *Antiquaries' Journal*, 77 (1997), 190-92 and 214-15.

Pl. 74

123 **PRO DL 42/3**

1412 Furness Abbey, England

Registrum abbatiae de Furnesia, pars i

Parch. 256 fols, with medieval foliation in red. *c*.405 × 270 mm. 1-2 cols, 265 × 177 mm. 36-42 lines. Illum. hist. inits and borders, illum. dec. inits (some with coats of arms), gold and col. inits, rubrics.

Fol. 6v: 'Huius cenobii nomine Furnesii
   Cartas terrarum tenet in se quod variarum …
   Willelmus Dalton abbas hunc condere librum
   Fecit eo cribrum sathane terat et petat altum
   Sicque liber plenum finem sortitur amenum
   Anno milleno centum quater ac duodeno
   Quem John Stell digitis monachus scripsit siue penna'
part of an introductory metrical account of the abbey (for which see S.B. Gaythorpe, 'Richard Esk's metrical account of Furness Abbey', *Trans. of the Cumberland and Westmorland Antiquarian Soc.*, n.s. 53 (1954), 98-109). Pars ii, also copied by Stell and with an abridged version of Esk's introduction, is BL, Add 33244 (*DMBL*, no. 357 and pl. 333). The medieval foliation of the present MS shows leaves are missing; they are replaced by modern parchment leaves included in the PRO's foliation. Other folios are badly damaged.
Fol. 55: 'George Willot' (s. xvi). Became the property of the duchy of Lancaster on the crown's annexation of the abbey's lands. Fol. 70, previously lost and only restored to the MS in 1930, was formerly owned by the antiquary, Henry Oldfield (d. 1791): 'Richardus Julius mihi donabat decembro [*sic*] Anno 1786 Henry George Oldfield' (see C.T. Flower, 'The Cowcher Book of Furness Abbey', *Chetham Miscellanies*, 6, Chetham Soc., n.s. 94 (1935), iii-4).

J.C. Atkinson and J. Brownbill, *The Coucher Book of Furness Abbey*, Chetham Soc., n.s. 9 (1836), 11 (1887), 14 (1888), 74 (1915), 76 (1916), 78 (1919); Gaythorpe, fig. 1 illus. init. fol. 7; Davis, *MC*, no. 428; A.I. Doyle, Appx to R. Morris and E. Cambridge, 'Beverley Minster before the early thirteenth century', *Medieval Art and Architecture*

in the East Riding of Yorkshire, ed. C. Wilson, British Archaeological Association Conference Transactions, IX (1989), p. 21; Scott, *Later Gothic MSS*, Cat. no. 34 and ills 146, 149 illus. inits fols 94, 234ᵛ (reduced).
Pl. 82

124 PRO DL 42/9 *[betw. 1376 and 1377]*
Daventry, England

Cartularium, in Latin and French

Parch. 33 fols, foliated i, 1-8, 11-20, 20bis, 21-33. 336 × 210 mm. 1 col., 255 × 155 mm. Up to 43 lines.

Fol. 1: 'Copia Cartarum <Manerii de Dauentre> et manerii de Tyngrith et Skyrwyth Copia composita Anno Regni Regis Edwardi tercii post conquestum quinquagesimo [1376-77]'. The majority of deeds copied are in the name of Thomas, son of Walter, of Daventry, Northamptonshire. Fols 3ᵛ-4 contain 'Exposicio vocabulorum qui vocabuli continentur in carta Huntyndonie', a popular legal glossary, this copy is not among those listed either by J.H. Baker, *Catalogue of English Legal Manuscripts in Cambridge University Library* (1996), pp. 62, 100, or D.C. Skemer, 'Exposicio vocabulorum: a medieval English glossary as an archival aid', *Journal of the Society of Archivists*, 19 (1998), 63-75. A leaf added by Thomas between fols 20 and 21 (my fol. 20bis) is not included in the PRO's foliation; fols 9-10 contain a transcript made in s. xviii of a deed on fol. 8ᵛ.

Davis, *MC*, no. 1233.
Pl. 63

125 PRO DL42/192 and 193 *[betw. 1413 and 1416]*
[London, England]

A transcript of 'the Great Cowcher', in 2 vols

Parch. Vol. I 281 fols. 392 × 260 mm. Vol. II 339 fols. 390 × 260 mm. 1 col., 260 × 173 mm. 42-43 lines. Col. inits, full-page col. borders (vol. I only), col. borders. Kals in red and black.

Payments to Richard Frampton, 'clericus', for making 'vn transcript' of no. 122 above, are recorded in the accounts of the receiver general of the duchy of Lancaster, John Leventhorpe, for the years 1413-16 (PRO, DL 28/4/8; cf. R. Somerville, 'The cowcher books of the duchy of Lancaster', *EHR*, 51 (1936), 612-14). Whereas the total cost of no. 122 was £115 12s 1d, the present transcript cost only £35 12s 9d. The kalendar preceding both volumes of the transcript does not include the new liturgical feasts of David or Chad (introduced 1415), or John of Beverley (1416). The feast of St Anne (established in England after 1383) is given in red.
DL42/192, fol. iii: 'Liber Johannis Maynard'; fol. iiᵛ: 'Liberatur in Curia secundo die Junij anno Regni Regis Caroli secundi xxvjᵗᵒ [1674] per manum Johannis Maynard militis senioris seruientis eiusdem domini Regis ad legem'. Maynard (d. 1690) also owned no. 108 above.
Christianson, *Directory*, pp. 106-7.
Pl. 87

126 PRO E 31/1 *[betw.1086 and 1088?]*
[England]

'Little Domesday'

Parch. 451 fols. 270 × 170 mm. 1 col., 205 × 115 mm. 22-

28 lines. Inits (fols 118ᵛ, 125ᵛ, 128, 131), rubrics.

Fol. 450 (in red capitals): 'Anno millesimo octogesimo sexto. ab incarnatione domini. Vigesimo vero regni Willelmi facta est ista descriptio. Non solvm per hos tres comitatvs. Sed etiam per alios'. This colophon, added by the rubricator, refers to the date when the 'descriptio' (or survey, initiated Christmas 1085) was carried out, and not to the date of the present MS (see A.R. Rumble, 'The Domesday manuscripts: scribes and scriptoria', *Domesday Studies*, ed. J.C. Holt (1986), pp. 79-99). Since the MS contains the circuit returns for Essex, fols 1-108, Norfolk, fols 109-280, and Suffolk, fols 281-45 (now bound as three separate volumes), which have not been incorporated in 'Great Domesday' (no. 127 below), they presumably arrived too late for their inclusion in that volume. Work on 'Great Domesday' ceased in 1087 or 1088. Rumble identifies six scribes in the present MS (for their stints see 'The Domesday manuscripts', pp. 98-99), though one, his scribe 4, only wrote a short addition. See also his 'The palaeography of the Domesday manuscripts', *Domesday Book: A reassessment*, ed. P.H. Sawyer (1985), pp. 28-49).

In 1320 payment of 3s 4d was made to William le Bokbynder of London for the repair and rebinding of the MS (PRO E 403/193, m. 10). For other work commissioned from this man, see Christianson, *Directory*, p. 71.

Fol. 450ᵛ (scratched in hard point): 'Henri D'Oilli', possibly the sheriff of Oxfordshire 1150-60, and 'Samson'. For the later history of the volume, see no. 127 below.

V.H. Galbraith, 'The making of Domesday Book', *EHR*, 57 (1942), 161-77; R. Welldon Finn, *Domesday Studies: The Eastern Counties* (1967), pp. 64-87; Rumble, 'The palaeography', pl. 3.3 illus. fols 228ᵛ-29 (reduced); H. Forde, *Domesday Preserved* (1986), figs 9, 17, 23, 29, 30 illus. fols 195 (reduced), 450 (detail), 437ᵛ-442 (detail), 36 (detail), 387 (detail) and colour pl. B illus. colophon; E. Hallam, *Domesday Book through Nine Centuries* (1986), pl. 8 illus. fols 127ᵛ-28 (reduced); *Domesday Studies*, ed. Holt, pl. Vb (colophon) and pls VI a-c, VII a-c illus. part of fols 49, 288ᵛ, 105, 110ᵛ, 410, and 240 (the hand of each scribe); M. Gullick, 'The Great and Little Domesday Manuscripts', *Domesday Book Studies*, ed. A. Williams (1987), pp. 93-112 and figs 17a-d and 18 illus. part of fols 19ᵛ, 109, 338ᵛ, 387, 450.
Pls 4, 5, 6

127 PRO E31/2 *[betw. 1086 and 1088?] [England]*

'Great Domesday'

Parch. 382 fols. 370 × 250 mm. 2 cols, 280-90 × 200-5 mm. 44-53 lines. Rubrics.

Presumed to be intended as the final edited version of the Domesday survey, the MS (now bound as two volumes) has traditionally been dated between 1086 (the date of the survey itself, see no. 126 above) and 1087 (assuming that work stopped when William the Conqueror unexpectedly died). However, P. Chaplais ('William of Saint-Calais and the Domesday Survey', *Domesday Studies*, ed. J.C. Holt (1986), pp. 65-77) has suggested that work on 'Great Domesday' was supervised by William of St Calais, bishop of Durham 1081-96, since the hand of the main scribe occurs in three MSS of possible Durham origin: BL, Harley 12; Oxford, Trinity College 28; and Hereford Cathedral P.I.10. It has also recently been identified in a fourth possible Durham book: Oxford, Bodleian Library, Lat. d. th. 34 (I owe my knowledge of this MS to Mr M. Gullick). Given the bishop's involvement, work may not have ceased until his exile in 1088 rather than upon the king's death. The main scribe also made two additions to the 'Exon Domesday' (Exeter Cathedral 3500, fols 153ᵛ, 436ᵛ). A second hand has corrected text (see M. Gullick and C. Thorn, 'The scribes of Great Domesday Book: a preliminary account', *Journal of the Society of Archivists*, 8 (1986), 78-81; A.R. Rumble, 'The Domesday manuscripts: scribes and scriptoria', *Domesday Studies*, ed. Holt, pp. 79-99). In addition to the main and correcting scribes (whom he calls A and B), Michael Gullick informs me he has identified the work of five other hands, scribes C-F (who only made minor interventions) and G (who supplied quire signatures for the last 10 quires). An addition by a twelfth-century hand, H, on fols 332ᵛ-33 is discussed by P. King, 'The return of the fee of Robert de Brus in Domesday', *Yorkshire Archaeological Journal*, 60 (1988), 25-9, and A.R. Rumble, 'A Domesday postscript and the earliest surviving Pipe Roll', *People and Places in Northern Europe 500-1600*, ed. I. Wood and N. Lund (1991), pp. 123-30.

Kept in the royal treasury and already known as 'Domesday' in the 1170s (cf. Richard FitzNigel's *Dialogus de Scaccario*, ed. C. Johnson, rev. F.E.L. Carter and D.E. Greenway (1983), pp. 62-64). For medieval, and later, use of the survey, see E. Hallam, *Domesday Book through Nine Centuries* (1986), and her 'Arthur Agarde and Domesday Book', *Sir Robert Cotton as Collector: Essays on an Early Stuart Courtier and his Legacy*, ed. C.J. Wright (1997), pp. 253-61.

Domesday Book, or the Great Survey of England of William the Conqueror, A.D. MLXXXVI (1861-65), facsim; V.H. Galbraith, 'The making of Domesday Book', *EHR*, 57 (1942), 161-77; *Domesday Re-bound* (1954), pl. I illus. fol. 36, pls III-VI illus. brief entries from various counties; A.R. Rumble, 'The palaeography of the Domesday manuscripts', *Domesday Book: A reassessment*, ed. P.H. Sawyer (1985), 28-49 and pls 3.1, 3.2 illus. fols 87ᵛ, 299 (both reduced) and pl. 3.4 illus. part of fol. 87ᵛ (actual size); H. Forde, *Domesday Preserved* (1986), figs 5, 8, 14-16, 26 illus. fols 92 (part), 76 (reduced), 146-49ᵛ (reduced), 313 (part), 63ᵛ, 9ᵛ-14 (reduced); Hallam, *Domesday Book*, pls 9,10, 43, 55 illus. fols 299, 166ᵛ, 272, 128 (all reduced); *Domesday Studies*, ed. Holt, pls III c-h, IV b, V a illus. parts of fols 87ᵛ, 120, 167, 64ᵛ, 333, 32, 294 (all reduced); Alecto Facsimile Edition, *Great Domesday* (1986); M. Gullick, 'The Great and Little Domesday Manuscripts', *Domesday Book Studies*, ed. A. Williams (1987), pp. 93-112 and figs 8a-e, 11b-d, 12-14, illus. part of fols 299, 87ᵛ, 252, 44ᵛ, 63ᵛ, 191ᵛ, 83ᵛ, 332ᵛ, 250, 39ᵛ, and fig. 9 illus. fol. 64ᵛ; E. Hallam, 'Annotations in Domesday Book since 1100', *Domesday Book Studies*, ed. Williams, pp. 136-49.

Pl. 7

128 PRO E 36/57   *[betw. 1300 and 1307] [England]*
Cartularium
Parch. 74 fols. 300 × 215 mm. 1 col., 225-32 × 145-48 mm. 30-39 lines. Blanks for inits.

P. A: 'In isto libro continentur omnes carte .... que fuerunt domino Ed<mundo> quondam Comiti Cornub' nunc in manibus domini Regis existentes'. Edmund, earl of Cornwall died without issue in 1300. After his death the lands were in the king's hands until 1307, when the earldom was granted to Piers Gaveston. According to marginal notes made by the scribe five original deeds could not be found, see fols 7ᵛ, 28, 43 (cf. pl.), 47ᵛ, 67. Another secular cartulary covering land in Cornwall (particularly the lands of the Courtenay family, earls of Devon) is the late s.xiv London, Duchy of Cornwall Office S/b/6, not recorded by Davis, *MC*.

Davis, *MC*, no. 1236.

Pl. 40

129 PRO E 36/268   *1323 [London, England]*
Kalendarium de bullis papalibus etc ('Bishop Stapeldon's Calendar')
Parch. 150 fols, paginated 1-286 (the first 3 and last 3 leaves, blank, are unpaginated). 292 × 195 mm. 1 col., c.234 × 130 mm. Up to 32 lines. Pen and ink drawings.

A preface pp. 1-2 explaining the purpose of this register of diplomatic documents, papal bulls, and other documents stored in the Treasury, drawn up as part of a major reorganisation of that office, conducted when Walter Stapeldon, Bishop of Exeter (*BRUO* 1764) was Lord Treasurer 1320-25, states that '... ad excitacionem venerabilis in christo patris domini .W. Exon' Episcopi dicti domini Regis [Edward II] Thesaurarij ... Quod actum fuit. Anno Incarnacionis domini Millesimo. Trescentesimo vicesimo tercio . et regni dicti domini Regis Edwardi decimo septimo ...'. A mandate to Master Henry of Canterbury, king's clerk, to make such a register with the help of Masters Elias de Joneston and Roger of Sheffield, king's clerks, was issued 28 July 1321 (*CPR, Edward II, A.D. 1321-24* (1904), p. 7). However, only the two latter, assisted by three other clerks, transcribed the volume. Payments on the Issue Rolls reflect the progress of the work, completed by late 1323 (PRO, E 403/197, passim, and cf. V.H. Galbraith, 'The Tower as an Exchequer Record Office in the Reign of Edward II', *Essays in Medieval History presented to T.F. Tout*, ed. A.G. Little and F.M. Powicke (1925), pp. 231-47; M.Buck, *Politics, Finance and the Church in the reign of Edward II: Walter Stapeldon, Treasurer of England* (1983), pp. 167-68). The clerks copied the documents quire by quire, leaving many leaves blank for future additions. Marginal drawings serve as pictograms to help identify the location of documents; for the use of such signs, see E. Hallam, 'Nine centuries of keeping the public records', *The Records of the Nation*, ed. G.H. Martin and P. Spufford (1990), pp. 32-33.

A list of books kept in the Treasury, p. 180 (see pl. 46), includes a volume of Welsh religious verse; see A. Breeze, 'A manuscript of Welsh poetry in Edward II's library', *The National Library of Wales Journal*, 30.2 (1997), 129-31.

The Antient Kalendars and Inventories of the Treasury of His Majesty's Exchequer, ed. F. Palgrave, 3 vols (1836), I: 1-155.

Pls 45, 46

130 PRO E164/9, fols 32-34, 44-94, 180-220   *[c.1291] [England]*
Statuta Angliae; Registrum brevium ('Liber Scac. X')

Parch. 180 fols. 325 × 230 mm. 2 cols, fols 32-34, 44-94 245 × 168 mm, 36 lines; fols 180-220 240 × 165 mm. 44 lines. Col. inits, rubrics. Leather bdg over boards with chemise, strap and pin fastening (s. xv).

Two booklets, written by two different scribes. In the first (fols 32-34 + 44-94) the latest legislation referred to is the 1290 proceedings of Quo warranto (fols 54, 77), while the latest writ in the register of writs in the second booklet (fols 180-220) is dated 1291. Further writs added at the latter's end, fols 219ᵛ-20, some by the scribe of the main text, are dated 1292-94. Several of these additions mention Hugh de Cressingham, d. 1297 (also mentioned in added writs fol. 30), for whose use H.G. Richardson and G. Sayles ('The early Statutes', *Law Quarterly Review*, 50 (1934), 209, 217-23) suggest the present MS was compiled, on Hugh's appointment in 1296 as Edward I's treasurer of Scotland. The core of the MS (fols 32-34 + 44-94 and 180-220) was added to, from s. xiii ex to s. xv (fols 5-31 35-43, 95-179). Fols 1-4 are blank.
In the exchequer by 1354 if, as Richardson and Sayles suggest (p. 218), this is to be identified with 'libro de quibusdam statutis in scaccario residente', cf. writ pr. *Statutes of the Realm*, 11 vols (1810-28), I: 68.
MMBL, I: 185-90.
Pl. 38 a, b

131 PRO E164/10, fols 2-313   *[betw. 1445 and 1461]*
[London or Westminster, England]

Nova statuta Angliae, in Latin and French

Parch. 312 fols. 274 × 190 mm. 1 col., 180 × 110 mm. 38 lines. Illum. dec. init. and full-page border (fol. 44), illum. dec. inits with borders (fols 124ᵛ, 183, 217ᵛ) gold and col. inits. Tawed leather bdg over boards, with chemise, 5 bosses on upper and lower cover, 2 strap- and pin-fastenings, brass clasps engraved with letter 'm', pins lost. Green tassels at top corners of chemise.

Statutes from 1 Edward III to 23 Henry VI (1444-45), copied by a single scribe; they are preceded by an index, fols 2-43 (quires 1-6). According to Ker (*MMBL*, I: 190), the statutes begin on fol. 47 but in the PRO's foliation they begin on fol. 44 (the latter does not include the four blank leaves between the end of the index (fol. 43) and the start of the statutes). Supplementary quires (Ker fols 319-41, PRO fols 313-36) copied by a second scribe contain further statutes from 25 Henry VI-39 Henry VI (1446-61).
Pl. 122

132 PRO E164/11, fols 3-92   *[c.1495-96]*
[London or Westminster, England]

Nova Statuta Angliae

Parch. 90 fols. 370 × 245 m. 1 col., *c.*240 × 165 mm. 40 lines. Hist. dec. inits with full-page borders (fols 3, 41, 48), gold inits and borders. Leather bdg over boards with chemise and 4 metal bosses on both covers, clasps gone (s. xvi).

Statutes of the Realm for Edward IV (fols 3-40) and Richard III (fols 41-47) in French, and in English from 1 Henry VII (fols 48-92) until 11 Henry VII, 1495-96. Ker's foliation (*MMBL*, I: 190-91) is not that of the PRO, which is followed here. The scribe is the 'Statuta scribe' of no. 103 above; he also wrote

London, Inner Temple 505 (for other manuscripts attributed to him, see K. Scott, *The Mirroure of the Worlde*, Roxburghe Club 241 (1980), pp. 46-48). At a later date two different scribes supplied further statutes, 19 Henry VII, 1503-04 (fols 93-113) and 1-7 Henry VIII, 1509-16 (fols 114-89) respectively. Both later scribes wrote Secretary rather than the legal Anglicana of fols 3-92. The artist of the original volume (fols 3-92) has been identified as the 'Placentius Master'; for other manuscripts painted by this 'court artist', who appears in MSS made for Henry VII or his family, see Scott, *Later Gothic MSS*, Cat. no. 133.

G.R. Elton, 'The sessional printing of statutes, 1484-1547', *Wealth and Power in Tudor England: Essays presented to S.T. Bindoff*, ed. E.W. Ives, R.J. Knecht and J.J. Scarisbrick (1978), p. 74 n. 21; K.L. Scott, 'A late fifteenth-century group of *Nova Statuta* Manuscripts', *Manuscripts at Oxford: R.W. Hunt memorial exhibition*, ed. A.C. de la Mare and B.C. Barker-Benfield (1980), p. 105.
Pls 226, 227

133 PRO E164/20, fols 5-193   *[betw. 1403 and 1404]*
[Godstow, England]

Cartularium

Parch. 188 fols. 336 × 225 mm. 1 col., 255 × 158 mm. 51 lines. Pen drawn inits, rubrics. Leather bdg rebound, but original chemise.

Fol. 5: 'Compositus autem est liber iste tempore domine Margarete Mounteneye venerabilis abbatisse [1387-1414] anno Regni Regis henrici quarti post conquestum quinto. Sumptibus et labore Alicie de Eatoun commonialis \tunc temporis priorisse/ de Godestowe quibus omnibus propricius sit deus qui regnat et imperat vivis in trinitate perfecta per infinita secula seculorum Amen'. The cartulary of Godstow Abbey ending abruptly fol. 193; fols 1-4 and five endleaves contain various later additions, dating from 5 Henry VI (1426-27); fol. 25 is an insert (s. xvi) concerning tithes in Little Barford. An English abstract (Oxford, Bodleian Library, Rawlinson B.408) of the present volume was made between 1467 and 1470 for the then prioress, Dame Alice Henley (cf. D.N. Bell, *What Nuns Read: Books and Libraries in Medieval English Nunneries* (1995), p. 139).
On original pastedown 'Monasterium de Godstowe'; 'liberatur in Curia Scaccarij vndecimo die Februarij anno xxvij per manus Ricardi Browne gen' pro commodo Regine [Elizabeth, thus 1585]'. Fol. 198: 'Edward Smyth' (s. xvi).

A. Clark, *The English Register of Godstow Nunnery, near Oxford*, EETS OS 142 (1911), p. xviii; Davis, *MC*, no. 462 (who says wrongly that this MS was also made for Alice Henley).
Pl. 75

134 PRO E315/330   *[betw. c.1431 and 1443] [England]*

William Kyngesmyll, De forma et compositione cartarum; etc.

Paper. 58 fols. 300 × 210 mm. 1 col., *c.*200 × 140 mm. 35 lines.

Kyngesmyll's formulary was produced in 1415-16 (see M.D. Legge, 'William of Kingsmill. A fifteenth-century teacher of French in Oxford', *Studies in French Language and Medieval*

Literature presented to Professor M.K. Pope (1939), pp. 241-46). Most of the deeds in this version (fols 20-57) are dated 1430; however, on fol. 35ᵛ the date 1431 has been crossed out 'primo die mensis Julij anno <domini Millesimo cccc^mo xxxj°>'. A later hand has substituted in the margin the formula 'regni Regis Henrici sexti post conquestum vicesimo primo' [1442-43]. Fols 2-19 contain a series of indentures relating mainly to places in Bedfordshire and Hertfordshire, most of them in the same hand as the formulary, the latest dated 21 Henry VI. The same hand has added (fol. 1) a note about a court at Wymondley, Herts, 11 Henry VI (1432-33), and (fol. 58ᵛ) an undated letter to John Marchall, vicar of Wymondley.
Fol. 1ᵛ (added): 'Obitus W. Aualle iiij^to die Junij Anno domini M^l CCCC^mo lxiiij^to et anno regni regis E iiij^ti quarto'. Added formulae contain the names 'Johannes Dogat de Dunstaple [Dunstable, Beds]' (fols 7, 58) and 'William Dogat' (fol. 1).
MMBL, I: 191.
Pl. 107

135 Royal Astronomical Society Add. 1 vol. 2, fols 65-127
[betw. 1348 and 1365] [Stonehouse? England]

Tabulae astronomicae
Parch. 63 fols. 260 × 180 mm. 1 col., 210 × 124 mm. 32 lines. Rubrics. Accompanying tables and kal. in red and black. Leather bdg over boards, 2 strap- and pin-fastenings gone (s. xiv).

Three booklets, fols 65-95, 96-123, 124-27, written by the same scribe. The heading of a table of mean motions (fol. 124), 'anno christi 1348 imperfecto. Radix in die sancte lucie aggregatum', and the marginal note, 'anno christi 1349 imperfecto' (fol. 65ᵛ) at the beginning of a set of such tables for the years 1349-1408, suggest that the scribe was working 1348-49. An addition by another hand at the end of the volume, fol. 125ᵛ, speaks of 1365 as in the future: 'Hec coniunccio erit anno christi 1365 ...'. Fols 1-64 are by another hand.
Fol. 76ᵛ (added to kalendar): '1348 obitus sibille at stonhous [Devon]'.

R. Harris, 'An account of some astronomical tables in the library of the Rev. C. Turnor', *Memoirs of the Royal Astronomical Soc.*, 15 (1846), 183-91; *MMBL*, I: 194-96 (under former shelfmark,QB. 7/1022).
Pl. 52

136 Royal College of Physicians 45
1451
Bologna, Italy

Celsus, De medicina
Parch. 236 fols. 275 × 180 mm. 1 col., 171 × 98 mm. 30 lines. Gold vine-stem inits, col. inits, rubrics.

Fol. 233 (in red): 'Aurelij cornelij celsi liber octauus explicit feliciter .iii° . nonas. Septembris. Mcccc .Li. Bononię vale qui legis'. Fols 234-35 are blank; fol. 236 contains a few medical notes in a hand of s. xv ex. The hand is probably that of Valerius Sanvenantiis, scribe of BL, Add. 31842 (*DMBL*, no. 350), though the initials appear to be later than 1451 and Veronese in style (*ex info.* Professor A.C. de la Mare). Now bound as 2 volumes.
At the foot of fol. 1 a gold roundel bears a defaced shield. Fol. 233: 'Mei Gasparis Zacchij Volaterranj Episcopi Auximanj [bishop of Osimo, 1460-74] et fratrum suorum'. For Zacchi's

library see F. di Benedetto, 'Il curioso inventario dei libri di Gaspare Zacchi da Volterra (1425-1474)', *Miscellanea di studi in memoria di Anna Saitta Revignas*, Biblioteca di Bibliografia Italiana, 86 (1978), pp. 181-206. According to a note (s. xix) on the pastedown of the present vol. 1, the MS formerly belonged to Alessandro Padovani (historian and philosopher, of Forli, fl. s. xvii), owner of nos 209, 259, and 272 below.
MMBL, I: 197-98.
Pl. 138

137 Royal College of Physicians 161
1597 London, England

William   Bedwell,   'Specimen   Arabici Dictionarij hoc est vocum Arabicarum collectio et interpretatio nimis accurata, qualis nempe haberi potuit ...'.
Paper. 530 fols. Fols alternate in size: 300 × 190 mm or 203 × 150 mm. Small fols: 1 col., 176 × c.120 mm. Up to 31 lines. Interleaved with large fols: 2 cols, 253 × 146 mm. Up to 43 lines. Gold-tooled leather bdg (s. xvi ex).

P. 1 (after the title): 'Exscriptum per Lancelotum Brunium medicum Londiniensem horis succisivis spatio ferme trium mensium, et finitum 11 maij 1597', followed by Lancelot Browne el tebis, written in Arabic. For Bedwell and Browne (FRCP, d. 1605), see A. Hamilton, *William Bedwell, the Arabist, 1563-1632* (1985). Bedwell's name is given as the headline on each of the smaller leaves, while the larger interleaved folios contain a lexicon which refers frequently to 'Av'. For Browne's interest in Avicenna, see G.J. Toomer, *Easterne Wisedome and Learning. The Study of Arabic in Seventeenth-Century England* (1996), p. 55. The present lexicon may be Browne's 'lost dictionary' to which Toomer refers.
Pl. 303

138 Royal College of Physicians 408, fols 1-103
1474
Cologne, Germany

Medica
Paper. 104 fols, foliated 1-11, 11*, 12-103. 285 × 200 mm. 2 cols, c.210 × 145 mm. 48 lines. Col. inits. Bld-tooled leather bdg over boards, with clasps.

Fol. 103: 'Finitum et completum per me Wilhelmum straben Rectorem scolarium in Volingen [Pfullingen, near Tübingen] Sub anno domini Millesimo quadringentesimo lxquinto In profesto Decollacionis Iohannis Baptiste hora quasi xii etc; Finitum et completum per me gerhardum Flanderback rectorem scholarium ad Colonie ad gradus [..................................] Sub incarnacione domini Millesimo quadringentesimo lxxiiij die vero Iouis 3ᵃ mensis Octobri hora quasi xᵃ ante prandium etc. Et sic est finis fit laus et gloria trinis'. Gerhard, who presumably copied the 1465 date from his exemplar, is not listed in R.C. Schwinges, *Rektorwahlen. Ein Beitrag zur Verfassungs-, Sozial- und Universitätsgeschichte des altes Reiches im 15. Jahrhundert mit Rektoren- und Wahlmanner verzeichnissen der Universitäten Koln und Erfurt aus dem zweiten Halfte des 15 Jahrhunderts* (1992), pp. 67-120. The remainder of the MS, fols 103ᵛ-39ᵛ, is undated and copied by a different but contemporary hand.
From St Maria ad Gradus, Cologne.
MMBL, I: 223-25; Kramer, I: 444.
Pl. 193

139 Royal College of Physicians 409

[betw. 1224 and 1246?] [Salisbury, England]

Psalterium ('The Wilton Psalter')

Parch. 223 fols. 290 × 205 mm. 1 col., 197 × 120 mm. 18 lines. Mins., hist., dec., and col. inits, rubrics fols 209ᵛ-20ᵛ only. Kal. in red and black. Orig. parch bdg preserved within modern cover.

Since Franciscan friars are depicted in some of the initials, the MS must have been produced after 1224 when the Franciscans first came to England. Francis himself, canonised 1228, is an addition to the kalendar. Edmund of Abingdon, canonised 1246, is also added (fol. 6). The MS is judged to be 'probably the earliest work' of the Sarum Master and 'certainly before' his Bible of William of Hales, dated 1254 (BL, Royal 1.B.xii (*DMBL*, no. 855) and see Morgan, *Early Gothic MSS*, no. 99). The kalendar here and that in Manchester, John Rylands Library, lat. 24, by the same artist (Morgan, no. 100), both omit the octave of the Nativity of the BVM, instituted 1252, although the feast had been widespread in England before that date. However, the Rylands kalendar includes St Edmund among the original entries. The present volume has traditionally been assigned to the Benedictine nunnery of Wilton, since prayers (fol. 206) refer to the 'congregationem sancte marie sancteque edithe', to whom the abbey was jointly dedicated; St Edith is also prominent among virgins in the Litany. However, Morgan argues the kalendar is not a Wilton one and suggests that, while the psalter may have been copied from a Wilton book, the presence in some of the initials of lay figures associated with nuns could indicate that this MS was produced for a lay patron. Fols 220ᵛ, 221: 'R. Lepton [*BRUC* 364]'; and given by him in 1523 to his great-niece, a nun of Romsey, fols. 144ʳ⁻ᵛ: 'The xᵗʰ day of Octobre yn the yere of our lord God oon Thousand fyve hundreth and xxiij. The xvᵗʰ yere of kyng henry the viijᵗʰ . and the xxiijᵗʰ yere of the Translacion of my lord. Rychard Foxe Bysshop of Wynchestre. Maister Raufe Lepton parson of alresford and kyngs worthy. servaunt and Chapelayne to my sayde lord Rychard . gaue thys boke to Elizabeth Langrege whos Granfader John Warner gentylman was vncle to my lady dame Anne Westbroke abbes of Romsey [1515-23] to the saide Elizabeth mynchynne of Romsey the said Maister Raufe was grete vncle vnto aboue that the seide Maister Raufe gaue first at the vellyng of the saide Elizabeth. In money. Fyue pounds delyuered to John Raye Bayllyff of Romsey aboue that the saide Maister Raufe gaue to saide Elizabeth oon goblet of syluer all gylted couered with thre lyons ouer the fote and two sponys the oon crystalle garnysshed with syluer gyltede with an Image ouer the ende. The oder all whyte'. Given or left by Elizabeth to John Lepton of Yorks, great-great-grandfather of Nicholas Saunders, MP, fol. iᵛ: 'This was my great grandmothers fathers booke, and therefore for the antiquityes sake I keepe it Nich. Saunder [1563-1649]', and cf. fol.ᵛ: 'Protestat sit omnibus visuris quod ego Willelmus Saunder [Nicholas's grandfather, d. 1570, also an MP, and son of Joan Lepton] denego et abranuncio nomine papisti extra totum istum librum'. Probably bequeathed to the College by Henry Pierrepont, 1st Marquess of Dorchester, 1606-80.

BFAC, *Exhibition of Illuminated MSS*, pl. 40 illus. fol. 66ᵛ; E.G. Millar, 'Les manuscrits à peintures des bibliothèques de Londres', *Bulletin de la S.F.R.M.P*, 4 (1914-20), pp. 128-49 and pls LIII-LV illus. fols 33, 66ᵛ and inits fols 72, 76, 90ᵛ, 161, 164ᵛ, 182, 212; A. Hollaender, 'The Sarum illuminator and his school', *Wiltshire Archaeological and Natural History Magazine*, 50 (1944), 230-62 and pls XIV, XVI illus. inits fols 66ᵛ, 212, 39 (enlarged); *VCH*, Wilts, iii, pl. facing p. 234 illus. fol. 207; Exh., *English Illum. MSS 700-1500*, no. 52; *MMBL*, I: 226; Morgan, *Gothic MSS*, no. 99 and ills 18, 19 illus. inits fols 33, 66ᵛ; D.N. Bell, *What Nuns Read: Books and Libraries in Medieval English Nunneries* (1995), pp. 161-62, 214; *The Royal College of Physicians and its Collections: An illustrated history*, ed. G. Davenport, I. McDonald and C. Moss-Gibbons (2001), p. 89 illus. inits on fols 33, 66ᵛ, 8, and fols 156ᵛ-57 (reduced).
Pl. 24

140 St Paul's Cathedral 5, fols 3-4 and 57-88

[c.1501] [Syon, England]

Rules for Syon Abbey, etc.

Parch. 34 fols. 305 × 220 mm. 2 cols, c.210 × 145 mm. 36-41 lines. Col. inits (engravings pasted within those on fols 57, 69, 69ᵛ, 84), rubrics.

Fol. 72: 'Deo Gracias. Prey for your thomas betson'. Betson, who probably entered Syon c.1481, became the abbey's librarian and drew up its surviving catalogue; he died in 1516 (see further A.I. Doyle, 'Thomas Betson of Syon Abbey', *The Library*, 5th ser., 11 (1956), 115-18; M.C. Erler, 'Syon Abbey's care for books: its sacristan's account rolls 1506/7-1535/6', *Scriptorium*, 39 (1985), 293-307; and V. Gillespie, 'The Book and the Brotherhood: reflections on the lost library of Syon Abbey', *The English Medieval Book: Studies in memory of Jeremy Griffiths*, ed. A.S.G. Edwards, V. Gillespie and R. Hanna (2000), pp. 185-208). An outline of a table of years, 1501-30, on fol. 72ᵛ, suggests that Betson's work in this MS is datable to c.1501. Fols 1-2ᵛ and 6-55ᵛ are by another, contemporary, hand. Fols 5, 56 blank. The pasted-in engravings, by an unknown continental artist, were cut from a broadsheet comprising devotional verses composed by Betson; see M.C. Erler, 'Pasted-in embellishments in English manuscripts and printed books', *The Library*, 6th ser., 14 (1992), 185-206.

Fols ivᵛ (original pastedown), 1, 6: 'Roberti Hare', d. 1611 (for whose library, see A.G. Watson, 'Robert Hare's books', *The English Medieval Book*, pp. 209-32; no. 37 in his list of Hare's MSS). Now deposited at the Guildhall Library as MS 25524.

MMBL, I: 243-44; J. Hogg, *The Rewyll of Seynt Sauiour*, III, *The Syon Additions for the Brethren and the Boke of Sygnes from the St. Paul's Cathedral Library MS*, Salzburger Studien zur Anglistik und Amerikanistik, 6 (1980); Erler, 'Pasted-in embellishments', fig. 4 illus fol. 84 (detail); C. de Hamel, *Syon Abbey: The Library of the Bridgettine Nuns and their Peregrinations after the Reformation*, Roxburghe Club (1991), pp. 71, 100, 116 and no. 17 in his list of MSS; Gillespie, 'The Book and the Brotherhood', *The English Medieval Book*, pp. 195-96.
Pl. 232

141 St Paul's Cathedral 18

1497 [Germany]

Processionale cum exequiale defunctorum (Dominican use)

Parch. 72 fols, foliated i-ii, 1-70. 170 × 130 mm. 1 col., 115

× 80 mm. 18-20 lines or 5 staves music. Col. inits, rubrics. Blind-stamped leather bdg over wooden boards, clasps gone (s. xvi in.).

Fol. 67 (in red): 'Anno domini .1.4.97'. Fols 67ᵛ-69ᵛ are blank, fol. 70 pasted down.

Inside the front cover of the binding a pastedown (fragment of a noted service book, s. xiv) bears the name 'margrett didlerm' (?), s. xvi.

Frere, *BML*, no. 561; *MMBL*, I: 259-60.

Pl. 229

142 Sion College Arc.L.40.2/L.15, fols 1-164

1447 Swine, England

Johannes de Mirfield, Florarium Bartholomei (abridged)

Parch. and paper, mixed. 165 fols, foliated 1-48, 48*-164. 212 × 140 mm. 1 col. (except 2 cols fols 163-64ᵛ), 31-33 lines. *c*.175 × 120 mm. 31-33 lines. Col. init. (fol. 1), other inits left blank.

Fol. 164ᵛ: 'M. cum quater .C. anno domini simul .x. et. Primo namque die Mensis Julij sibi cesset. Anno domini. Millesimo CCCCᵐᵒ . xl° vij° . Amen quod Johannes hebyn' Diaconus'. Mirfield died 1407, so could not have completed the *Florarium* in 1410 as the scribe thought (see P. H-S. Hartley and H.R. Aldridge, *Johannes de Mirfeld of St Bartholomew's of Smithfield: his Life and Works* (1936), pp. 102-3, who suggest Hebyn may have miscopied an Arabic '4' as the Roman numeral 'x'). The remainder of the volume, fols 165-95, undated, is by the same hand; cf. fol. 193:

'Nunc finem feci penitet me si male scripci ⎫
Amen quod Johannes hebynum [*sic*] de   ⎬
  Swynum clericus   ⎭ Explicit liber'

Swine is near Kingston upon Hull, Humberside (formerly East Riding of Yorkshire).

Pastedown (front cover): 'The gift of the Rev. John Bradshaw Rector of St. George's, Botolph-Lane. 1664'. Now at Lambeth Palace Library.

MMBL, I: 276-78.

Pl. 125

143 Sion College Arc.L.40.2/L.25, fols 1-225

1442 Basel, Switzerland

Egidius Romanus, De regimine principum

Paper. 225 fols. 286 × 210 mm. 1 col., 196 × 120 mm. 43 lines. Some col. inits, most left blank, rubrics. Armorial shield (fol. 1). Gold-tooled leather bdg (s. xvii¹).

Fol. 225ᵛ (in red): 'Explicit liber de regimine \regum et/ principum editus a fratre Egidio Romano ordinis fratrum heremitarum sancti Augustini', then in black ink: 'quem scribi fecit Reuerendissimus in Christo pater et dominus dominus ludouicus miseratione diuina titulo sancte Susanne sacrosancte Romane ecclesie presbiter Cardinalis de Varambone vulgaritus nuncupatus [Cardinal Louis de Palude, bishop of Maurienne 1441-51; from Varambon, Savoy] Basilee Anno a natiuitate domini Millesimo quadringentesimo quadragesimo secundo. die vero veneris xxv mensis octobris completus extitit. sacro generali Concilio residen' similiter et sanctissimo domino felice papa vᵗᵒ '. Fols 226-56 contain tabulae copied by the same scribe, fols 256ᵛ-59ᵛ blank. Fols i-viii and ix-x are medieval

endleaves. The arms at the foot of fol. 1 are those of the Cardinal.

A label pasted inside the cover of the binding records the MS's purchase in 1632 from £50 donated by Robert Parkhurst, citizen and alderman of London. Arms of the Parkhurst family on binding. Now at Lambeth Palace Library.

MMBL, I: 282.

Pl. 117

144 Sir John Soane's Museum 2, fols 1-280

1482 [France]

Missale secundum usum Romanum

Parch. 280 fols, medieval foliation in red. 346 × 257 mm. 2 cols, 207 × 165 mm. 29 lines. Mins (both in text and margins), full-page borders, gold and dec. inits, rubrics. Kal. in red and black.

Fol. 280ᵛ: 'Explicit missale secundum vsum romanum anno domini 1482⁰ die 12 mensis februarii'. Fols 281-90, by the same scribe as the rest of the MS, are undated. Written for Louis, Bastard of Bourbon and Admiral of France (d. 1488), whose arms appear in initials and borders; cf. E.G. Millar, 'Les manuscrits à peintures de bibliothèques de Londres', *Bulletin de la S. F. R. M. P.*, 4 (1914-20), 108-9. For other books owned by him, see L.V. Delisle, *Le Cabinet des manuscrits de la Bibliothèque impériale*, 4 vols (1868-81), I: 170; III: 351.

Fol. 1: 'Joan. Dupuy lib. MSS inscript.' ? Jacques Dupuy, French royal librarian and son of the bibliophile, Claude Dupuy, for whose library see J. Delatour, *Une bibliothèque humaniste au temps des guerres de religion: les livres de Claude Dupuy* (1998), and for the family's collections, *Cabinet des mss*, I: 263.

MMBL, I: 291.

Pl. 209

145 Skinners' Company, s.n., fols 2-19

[c.1441] [London, England]

Book of the Fraternity of the Assumption of Our Lady

Parch. 18 fols. 415 × 280 mm. 1-2 cols, *c*.290 × 180 mm. Up to 39 lines. Col. inits, rubrics.

The volume, which contains the ordinances and annual lists of Wardens and members of the Fraternity, was copied by a single scribe from 21 Richard II to 19 Henry VI (1441), fols 2-19. There is no obvious change in the handwriting between fols 17ᵛ and 18ᵛ-19 although fol. 18ʳ is blank. An inventory of the Fraternity's possessions drawn up in 1441 (fol. 19) includes the present MS, 'Also the seid Wardeynes han ordeyned and do make this registr*e* boke in p*ar*cell of her entres the valewre to .xxx. s', as well as 'ij masbokes'. Thereafter the volume was enlarged and continued by a series of scribes (fols 19ᵛ-94). Entries from 1442-1689 were presumably made annually. The decoration becomes more elaborate from fol. 30v onwards (for miniatures on fols 32ᵛ, 34ᵛ and 41, see Scott, *Later Gothic MSS*, Cat. no. 130). On fol. 52 the scribe of the entry for 1528 concludes 'Made in Pater Noster Rowe at the syne of the Bedes by me Thomas Wygge'. From 1557 the date is expressed by the year of grace as well as the regnal year.

Now deposited at the Guildhall Library as MS 31692.

J.F. Wadmore, *Some Account of the Worshipful Company of Skinners of London* (1902), pp. 33-42; J.J. Lambert,

Records of the Skinners of London (1933), pp. 74-103; E.M. Veale, *The English Fur Trade in the Later Middle Ages* (1966), pp. 105-15.
Pl. 116

146 Society of Antiquaries 38, fols 10-220

[betw. 1358 and 1361] [Peterborough, England]

Cartularium (the 'Great Book of John of Achurch')

Paper. 202 fols. 202 × 140 mm. 1 col., 160 × 110 mm. 33 lines. Pen and ink drawings (fols 159ᵛ-70), col. inits, rubrics. Bld-tooled leather bdg, clasps gone (s. xvi med).

A document copied on fol. 152ᵛ is dated 32 Edward III, 1358-59. Notes added by the scribe on fol. 80ᵛ concern transcripts 'extracta de Rotulis de scaccario', one of which is dated 34 Edward III, 1360-61. The MS, mainly in one hand, was cited by Henry of Pytchley in his *Liber feodum* or Book of Fees of Peterborough, datable 1391-1405 (Peterborough, Dean and Chapter Lib., MS 7, ed. W.T. Mellors, *Henry of Pytchley's Book of Fees*, Northants Record Soc., 2 (1927)). Pytchley refers to a fine 'inter nos et Philippum Marmiune ut in libro maiori Fratris Johannis achirche, fo. cxxix' which is found on the present fol. 40ᵛ of the Antiquaries MS (fol. cxxix in its medieval foliation). John of Achurch was keeper of the abbey's manors during the abbacy of Henry of Morcot, 1338-53 (cf. memorandum dated 21 Edward III, fol. 62). He also compiled Peterborough's 'Red Book' (Peterborough, Dean and Chapter Lib., MS 6) and its *Carte Nativorum* (Peterborough, Dean and Chapter Lib., MS 39); see J.D. Martin, *The Cartularies and Registers of Peterborough Abbey*, Northants Record Soc., 28 (1978), p. xiii. Willetts (p. 18) notes the presence of portrait heads said to be similar to those drawn on fols 159ᵛ-70 in BL, Add. 47170, a roll-chronicle from Peterborough. They appear dissimilar to me. The binder can be identified as 'F.D.', whose work dates mainly from 1554-80 (see J.B. Oldham, *English Blind-Stamped Bindings* (1952), p. 32 and pl. xxix), and who has (as the medieval foliation establishes) misbound the present volume. Fols 1-9, 106-13 are later s. xiv additions while fols 221-36 date from s. xv.

Fol. 2: 'Presented by the Rᵗ Honorable [Brownlow] the [9ᵗʰ] Earl of Exter to the Society of Antiquaries of London, 25ᵗʰ June, 1778'. He also gave no. 149 below.

> Davis, *MC*, no. 759; *MMBL*, I: 300; Martin, *Cartularies and Registers*, pp. 19-22 and pl. 3 illus. part of fols 72ᵛ, 74v; Willetts, p. 18.
> *Pl. 55*

147 Society of Antiquaries 46   *1592 [Siena, Italy]*

Orazio Lombardelli, De' Fonti della Lingua Toscana

Paper. 81 fols. 222 × *c*.160 mm. 1 col., 160 × 113 mm. 18-21 lines.

Fol. 80ᵛ: 'Di casa il giorno dedicaco alla memoria della Purificazion di Nostra Donna dell' anno, dall' Incarnazion di suo Figliuolo, e Nostro Signore, Mille cinquecento nouanta due;'. The text, addressed to Sir Henry Wotton (1568-1639), was published as *I Fonti Toscani* in Florence, 1598. Fol. 1 is an autograph letter from Sir Henry, dated '19 of Aprile 1597', in which he presents the MS to his friend Sir Maurice Barkley, MP for

Somerset 1597-1614, and relates how it had been written for him in Siena. See further L. Pearsall Smith, *The Life and Letters of Sir Henry Wotton* (1907), I: 22 n.3; II: 484; R. Weiss, 'Henry Wotton and Orazio Lombardelli', *RES*, 19 (1943), 284-89.
Willetts, p. 22.
Pl. 297

148 Society of Antiquaries 59, fols 25-236

[betw. 1214 and 1222] [England]

Psalterium

Parch. 212 fols. 240 × 157 mm. 1 col., 145 × 85 mm. 20 lines. 3 full-page tinted drawings, 2 full-page mins (fols 33-38), illum. dec. inits, col. inits, rubrics. Kal. in red, blue and black. Leather bdg (repaired), marks of 2 straps visible on upper cover.

Fol. iii: 'Psalterium Roberti de Lindeseye abbatis [abbot of Peterborough, 1214-22]', by whom it was bequeathed to Peterborough (cf. M.R. James, *Lists of Manuscripts formerly in Peterborough Abbey Library*, Transactions of the Bibliographical Soc. Suppl. 5 (1926), p. 22 no. 60). A contemporary hand has added to the kalendar (of Peterborough, see L.F. Sandler, *The Peterborough Psalter in Brussels and other Fenland Manuscripts* (1974), pp. 154-61), the translation of Becket, 1220 (fol. 29). Obits of the abbots of Peterborough, ending with Geoffrey of Crowland, d. 1321, were added in s. xiv to the margins of the kalendar (fols 26-31ᵛ), as were prayers, etc., on fols 1-24 and 237-56.

Fol. i: the erased signature of Smart Lethieuiller, FSA (d. 1760). Bookplate of the Revd Charles Lyttleton, PSA, bishop of Carlisle 1762-8.

> NPS, 2nd ser., pl. 128 illus. fols 38ᵛ, 132ᵛ; BFAC, *Exhibition of Illuminated MSS*, pl. 36 illus. fols 35ᵛ-36; *MMBL*, I: 302-3; Exh., *Engl. Illum. MSS 700-1500*, no. 44 and pl. 24 illus. fol. 35ᵛ (reduced); *The Benedictines in Britain* [Catalogue of an exhibition held at the British Library, 11 July-30 November, 1980], p. 31 and pl. 14 illus. fol. 35ᵛ (reduced); R. Marks and N. Morgan, *The Golden Age of English Manuscript Painting, 1200-1500* (1981), pls 3-4 illus. fols 35ᵛ, 36 (reduced); Morgan, *Early Gothic MSS*, no. 47 and ills 151, 156-59 and fig. 7 illus. hist. init. fol. 32ᵛ, and fols 36, 35ᵛ, 34, 33ᵛ, 33 (all reduced); Exh., *Age of Chivalry*, no. 254; Willetts, pp. 28-29 and pl. 2 illus. fol. 36 (reduced).
> *Pl. 21*

149 Society of Antiquaries 60, fols 6-73

[after 1125] [Peterborough, England]

Cartularium ('Liber niger monasterii S. Petri de Burgo')

Parch. 66 fols, foliated i-lxvi. 253 × 170 mm. 1 col., 194 × 107 mm. 24 lines. Col. inits, rubrics.

Fol. 6: 'Hec est descriptio maneriorum de abbatie de Burhc desicut Vualterius archidiaconus [of Oxford, d. 1151] eam recepit. et saisiuit in manu regis'. Walter was King's Justice by 1118 (*BRUO* 1971). The abbey's lands were in the king's hands after the death of Abbot John de Séez in 1125 until the appointment of Henry of Poitou in 1127. The hand has been identified by T.A.M. Bishop ('Notes on Cambridge manuscripts, part I', *TCBS*, 1 (1949-53), 440) as that of the second hand of the

Peterborough Chronicle, datable 1155 (Oxford, Bodleian Library, Laud Misc. 636: *DMO*, no. 620), and of corrections, if not text, in Cambridge, Corpus Christi College 134. Bound up in the Middle Ages (cf. medieval foliation of MS) with fols 209-19 (see no. 150 below). Fols 75-80ᵛ + 85-136ᵛ contain a Peterborough chronicle, 1122-1295, probably compiled by the sacrist William of Woodford, abbot 1296-99 (cf. Gransden, *Hist. Writing*, I: 452); fols 74, 81-84, 137-208, 220-61, 220-63 contain charters and other documents in many different s. xiii and s.xiv hands, with some s.xv additions. Fols 1-5 and 262-63 are endleaves.

Fol. 2ᵛ: 'Iste Liber vocatur Niger Liber anglice The black bowke' (s. xvi). Fol. 263: 'Iste liber constat abati de burgo sancti Petri liberatur Ricardo Goodehynde per Wilelmum est \ Et Robert Eston Junij/', 'Frater Rogerus Byrde monachus de burgo sancti Petri in comunit', 'Robertus London monachus < >', and 'Johannes Bocher Flyngtoken' (s. xvi). Fol. 263ᵛ: '[Sir] Robert Wingfield [of Upton, d. 1636]', descended from Robert Wingfield, auditor to the commissioners valuing monastic property in Leicestershire in 1535 (cf. J.D. Martin, *The Cartularies and Registers of Peterborough Abbey*, Northants Record Soc., 28 (1978), p. 37). Wingfield also owned two Peterborough registers, London, BL, Cotton Vespasian E. XXI, fols 45-106 and Vespasian E. XXII. Presented in 1778 by Brownlow, 9th Earl of Exeter, who also gave no. 146 above.

T. Stapleton, *Chronicon Petroburgense*, Camden Soc., 47 (1849), pp. 157-83; W.T. Mellors, *Henry of Pytchley's Book of Fees*, Northants Record Soc., 2 (1927), pp. xxvi and xxxviii; Davis, *MC*, no. 754; *MMBL*, I: 303; Martin, *Cartularies of Peterborough*, pp. 1-7; D. Roffe, 'The Descriptio Terrarum of Peterborough Abbey', *Historical Research*, 65 (1992), 1-16; Willetts, p. 29.
Pl. 11

150 **Society of Antiquaries 60, fols 209-19**
[betw. 1275 and 1290] [Peterborough, England]
'Les estabilissemenz le Roy Edward'
Parch. 11 fols. 253 × 170 mm. 1 col., 190 × 125 mm. 28-29 lines. Col. inits.

Fol. 209: 'Ces sunt les estabilissemenz le Roy Edward fiz le Roy Henri fez a sun *primur* parlement gen*eral* a Wemos*tre* apres sun coronement lendemeyn de la chise Pasch lan de sun Regne t*er*ce', a copy of the First Statute of Westminster of 1275. Added on fols 219ᵛ-20 is a summary of the Statute of Quo Warranto of 1290. C. Clark (*The Peterborough Chronicle*, EEMF, 4 (1954), Appx., p. 39) notes that the hand of fols 209-19 closely resembles that which added the Anglo-Norman chronicle, *Le Livere de Reis de Brittanie*, running to the accession of Edward I (1272), in the margins of the Peterborough Chronicle (Oxford, Bodleian Library, Laud Misc. 636, fols 89ᵛ-90ᵛ).
For the MS's history, see no. 149 above.
Pl. 29

151 **Society of Antiquaries 94**   *1563 [England]*
Richard Wright, A Treatise on Gunnery
Paper. 37 fols. 310 × 205 mm. 1 col., *c*.230-40 × 145 mm. Up to 26 lines. Pen and ink drawings.

The date '1563' is incorporated in a full-page drawing on fol. 3ᵛ. Fol. 1: 'S*a*muell Thomas' (s. xvi ex).

Willetts, pp. 43-44.
Pl. 266

152 **Society of Antiquaries 154**   *[c.1148]*
[Winchester, England]
'Winton Domesday'
Parch. 33 fols. 251 × 174 mm. 2 cols, 185 × 125 mm. 29 lines. Col. inits., rubrics. Bld-tooled leather bdg (s. xii, rebound s. xx).

Two twelfth-century surveys of Winchester, both copied by the same scribe. The first was carried out *c*.1110, the second in 1148; see fol. 13ᵛ (rubric): 'Hec est Inquisitio De terris Winton' quisquis tenet et quantum tenet et de quocumque tenet et quantum quisque inde capit precepto Episcopi Henrici [of Blois, 1129-71] Anno ab incarnatione domini M.c.xl viij'. 13 bifolia (from a sacramentary of s. xᵛ), pasted together, originally formed the 'boards' of the English romanesque binding. They have been removed and are now bound separately as MS 154* (for descr. of which see R.W. Pfaff, 'Massbooks', *The Liturgical Books of Anglo-Saxon England*, Old English Newsletter Subsidia 2 (1995), pp. 26-28). For a detailed discussion of Winton Domesday itself and its binding, see *Winchester in the Early Middle Ages: An Edition and Discussion of the Winton Domesday*, ed. M. Biddle (1976), esp. Appx II, pp. 520-49.
Owned by John Young (1585-1655), Dean of Westminster Abbey.

NPS, 1st ser., pl. 212 illus. fols 1, 13ᵛ; *VCH* Hampshire, I, 527-37 and pls illus. bdg and fol. 1; G.D. Hobson, *English Binding before 1500*, Sandars Lectures 1927 (1929), pp. 3-4 and pls 4-5 illus. bdg; *MMBL*, I: 307; *Winton Domesday*, pls 1-5 illus. fols 3ᵛ, 13ᵛ, 22ᵛ and bdg, frontispiece illus. fol. 1; Willetts, pp. 72-73 and pl. I illus. bdg.
Pl. 13

153 **Society of Antiquaries 335, fols 51-266**   *1473 [Italy]*
Antoninus, Confessionale; etc.
Parch. and paper, mixed. 216 fols. 206 × 150 mm. 2 cols, 125 × 95 mm. 30 lines. Col. inits, rubrics. Vellum bdg, title in German hand (s. xvi).

Fol. 266ᵛ: 'finis Die xᵒ aprilis 1473'.
MMBL, I: 311-12; Willetts, pp. 168-69.
Pl. 189

154 **Society of Antiquaries 501**   *[betw. 1447 and 1455]*
[London, England]
Genealogical roll chronicle of kings of England, popes, and kings of France
Parch. 16 membranes. *c*.13000 × 600 mm. Text of varying length. 6 tinted drawings, col. roundels, figures, crowns, rubrics.

The chronicle ends imperfectly at 1264 but from the introduction at the head of the roll it appears that it was compiled during the papacy of Nicholas V, 1447-55, and when Henry VI and Charles VII were respectively king of England and king of France, 1422-61. Thus (in red): '... Regnum Brutannie [*sic*] que nunc Anglia dicitur ... usque ad illustrissimum principem regem nostrum Henrici post conquestum sextum ... Et sic descendendo in lynea genealogie regum Francorum usque ad Karolum septimum … (in black) Et sic a beato Petro per successores suos Romanorum Pontifices in linea sua descendendo usque ad Nicholaum quintum sicut inferius intuenti patet'. The tinted drawings are by William Abell (Scott, *Later Gothic MSS*, Cat. no. 95), who also illustrated no. 110 above. A separate roll, in a hand of s.xvii, continues the chronicle down to 1665.

> Scott, ills 369, 370 illus. part of membr. 3, 6 (reduced); Willetts, p. 240 and pl. III illus. part of membr. 3 (reduced).
> *Pl. 126*

155 Society of Antiquaries 503 *[between 1399 and 1413]* *[England]*

Genealogical chronicle roll, in Latin

Parch. 3 membranes. *c*.2500 × 550 mm. 1 col. of text at foot of roll, 270 × 110 mm. 44 lines. Col. roundels surmounted by crowns.

A genealogical table running from the foot of the roll to the top and showing the descent of Henry IV of England (1399-1413) and Charles VI of France (1380-1422). The short text concludes '… de cuius prosapia ad huc reges regnant in francia et nostris temporibus in Anglia'. On the dorse there are apparently unfinished Anglo-Saxon genealogies added in s. xv². At head of roll: 'Henrici Spelmannj', for whom see H.A. Cronne, 'The study and use of charters by English scholars in the seventeenth century: Sir Henry Spelman and Sir William Dugdale', *English Historical Scholarship in the Sixteenth and Seventeenth Centuries*, ed. L. Fox (1956), pp. 73-91; and for MSS owned by him, F.M. Powicke, 'Sir Henry Spelman and the "Concilia"', *Proceedings of the British Academy*, 16 (1930), 373-74. At foot: 'Henrici St George Militis [1581-1644, Garter King of Arms] ex dono Henrici Spelmannj 1632'.

> *MMBL*, I: 313; Willetts, pp. 240-41.
> *Pl. 73*

156 Southwark, Roman Catholic Metropolitan See, 1, fols 14-367

[c.1415?][Lichfield? England]

Breviarium ad usum Sarum

Parch. 353 fols. 162 × 120 mm. 2 cols, 108 × *c*.85 mm. 31 lines. Col. inits, rubrics. Kal. in red, blue, and black.

David and Chad are included in both kalendar (the latter in blue, fol. 195) and sanctorale (fols 250, 251). Their feasts were accepted by the Convocation of Canterbury in 1415. However, John of Beverley, whose feast was accepted in 1416, is a later addition. Fols 1-13 contain s. xv ex additions. Chad's prominence in the kalendar points to use in the diocese of Lichfield. Fol. 196: 'Dedicacio sancti martini ecclesie de desforde [Leics]'; the same hand of s. xv² also adds 'Obitus Anne Shirley' (fol. 199ᵛ).

> *MMBL*, I: 320-21.
> *Pl. 91*

157 Southwark, Roman Catholic Metropolitan See, 4

[c.1390?] [Paris, France]

Horae ad usum Parisiensem

Parch. 232 fols. 184 × 128 mm. 1 col., 95 × 57 mm. 14 lines. Mins, hist. and dec. inits with full-page borders, gold inits, rubrics. Kal. in blue, red, gold and black.

A prayer, headed 'Pro unitate ecclesie', copied by the scribe at the end of the MS (fols 231-31ᵛ), is addressed to 'beate petre' of Luxembourg. He died 2 July 1387, and, although not beatified until 1527, the French argued the case for his canonization at Avignon, 1390 (see *Acta Sanctorum*, July, I: 610). A memoria of St Frambald, abbot and confessor (fols 227ᵛ-28ᵛ), points to use at Senlis, near Paris, where there was a local cult. A shield in the bottom margin of fol. 215ᵛ is rubbed and partly cut away; it may have been that of the woman depicted kneeling in the miniature of the Entombment in the upper part of the page. Now deposited as BL, Loan MS 85/4.

> *MMBL*, I: 323-24.
> *Pl. 67*

158 Southwark, Roman Catholic Metropolitan See, 10

1520 [Netherlands]

Reynier Snoy, Dialogus de gratia divina

Paper. 128 fols. 130 × 95 mm. 1 col., 82 × 60 mm. 22 lines. Col. inits. Limp vellum bdg.

Fol. 38ᵛ: 'Vale anno sesquimillesimo et vigesimo kalendis Martij bisextilibus'; the MS is again dated fol. 93ᵛ: 'Vale ab orbe redempto sesquimillesimo xx⁰ Ipso die parasceues'. Unlisted by B. and M.E. de Graaf, *Doctor Reynerius Snoygoudanus ca.1477-1st August 1537* (1968).

> *Pl. 247*

159 United Grand Lodge of England, Grand Lodge 1

1583 [England]

'The Old Charges of Masonry'

Parch. 7 membranes. *c*.2610 × 121 mm. 1 col.

At end: 'Amen So be it Scriptum Anno domini 1583⁰ die decembris 25⁰'. The earliest surviving copy of the revised version of the medieval text; cf. W. McLeod, 'The Old Charges; with an appendix reconstituting the "Standard Original" version', *Prestonian Lecture*, 1986.

According to A.C.F. Jackson ('Our predecessors: Scottish masons of about 1660', *Ars Quatuor Coronatorum* [The Transactions of Quatuor Coronati Lodge 2076, the masonic lodge of research], 91 (1978), 18), the MS belonged in 1665 to the Lodge of Edinburgh (Mary Chapel), where a copy was made for the use of Lodge Kilwinning, but he gives no evidence for this. McLeod's study of the text's transmission has established that the Kilwinning MS was not copied from Grand Lodge 1 (cf. 'The Old Charges', p. 14).

> Facsim. ed. G.W. Speth, *Quatuor Coronatorum Antigrapha*, IV (1892); D. Knoop and G.P. Jones, *A Handlist of Masonic Documents* (1942), pp. 30-31.
> *Pl. 288*

160 UCL Angl. 2, fols 1-144 *1600 [Scotland]*

Robert Lindsay of Pitscottie, The Historie and Cronicles of Scotland

Paper. 144 fols, original foliation in ink. 300 × 198 mm. 1 col., 250 × 135 mm. 43-47 lines. Pen flourished inits. Bld-tooled leather bdg, with inits 'I S' in gold in centre of upper and lower covers.

Fol. 144ᵛ: 'liber hic Inceptus a me scriptore 23 mensis aprilis ac finitus penultimo die Julij anno salutis humanj 1600'. Fols 145-

9 contain an 'addition' by the same hand. Fols 149ᵛ, 149bis-153 blank.

Fol. 149ᵛ has the opening lines of the will of 'Jon Wilisone somtym ... of glasgoue and at the present tym of his departour [in] seruing Mr serint of the estats of scotland an signet to colonel John Junes 1650 ...', subsequently crossed out.

> Æ.J.G. Mackay, *The Historie and Cronicles of Scotland ... written and collected by Robert Lindesay of Pitscottie*, Scottish Text Soc., 42 (1899), pp. lxxxiv-lxxxv; Coveney, pp. 20-21.
> *Pl. 306*

161 UCL Angl. 3   *[betw. 1461 and 1464?]* *[London? England]*

Genealogical roll chronicle of the kings of England, in Latin

Parch. 8 membranes. 5955 × 308 mm. 2 cols. Col. roundels surmounted by gold crowns, col inits, rubrics.

Although the text ends on the seventh membrane with the birth of Edward, Prince of Wales, son of Henry VI, in October 1453 (d. 1471), the scribe continued the line of succession with roundels on the final (eighth) membrane for the six children of Richard, Duke of York (d. 1460), including Edward IV, who is said to be (in red) 'verus heres et rex istius britannie. francie. et hispanie'; he was king 1461-83. As Edward's marriage is not given, this roll was presumably produced before 1464 when he married Elizabeth Woodville. One of a group of chronicle rolls or roll-codices copied by the so-called 'Considerans' scribe; work by him includes no. 4 above, *DMO*, nos 637, 654, 758 and 777, and Copenhagen, Kongelige Bibliothek, Ny kgl. S. 1858 2⁰ (*Living words & Luminous Pictures: Medieval Book Culture in Denmark*, ed. E. Petersen, Catalogue of an Exhibition held at the Royal Library, Copenhagen, 1999, no. 147). For his other work, see Scott, *Later Gothic MSS*, II: 315-16. Alongside the final set of roundels in the present copy are the initials 'T N' in blue, possibly those of the scribe. Because of the variety of artists who worked with 'Considerans' and the provincial decorative styles of some of them, Scott suggests that he either worked in London where undecorated copies were sold and taken away to be illustrated elsewhere, or that he was an itinerant copyist and provincial buyers employed local artists.

> Coveney, p. 21; *MMBL*, I: 332; A.C. de la Mare, *Catalogue of the Collection of Medieval Manuscripts bequeathed to the Bodleian Library Oxford by James P.R. Lyell* (1971), p. 85.
> *Pl. 155*

162 UCL Germ. 1   *1471 Bolzano, Italy*

Volkskalender, in German

Paper. 188 fols. 212 × 150 mm. 1 col., 140 × 100 mm. 24-26 lines. Col. drawings and inits fols 1-44, thereafter blank spaces. Rubrics. Kals and tabulae in red and black. Red leather bdg over boards with central and corner bosses on upper and lower covers, two clasps replaced.

Fol. 106ᵛ (in red): 'Finitum est per nicolaum Pfaldarff*er* de Ingolstat [Bavaria] tunc temporis astans in Bozano [Bozen (now Bolzano), S. Tyrol, ceded to Italy 1919] sub anno domini etc 1471 Jare In die veneris et quinta die Julij In hora saturni'. The scribe also dated fols 12ᵛ (in red: 'Deo gracias 1471), 128ᵛ ('Deo

gracias 1471 per nicolaum'), and 186ᵛ ('Deo gracias 1471'). Fols 107-9, 130ᵛ, 159ᵛ, and 187 are blank. Fol. 188, a parchment endleaf, contains added prayers by a later hand.

> Coveney, pp. 29-33; *MMBL*, I: 332; F.B. Brévart, 'The German *Volkskalender* of the fifteenth century', *Speculum*, 63 (1988), 312-42.
> *Pl. 182*

163 UCL Germ. 10, fols 1-46   *1456 [Germany]*

Gerard van Vliederhoven, Cordiale de IV novissimis, in German

Paper. 46 fols. 272 × 202 mm. 2 cols, 191 × 140 mm. 27 lines. Col. inits, rubrics. Vellum bdg with clasp.

Fol. 46ᵛ (in red): 'Expliciunt quatuor nouissima. Anno domini Millesimo Quadringentesimo Quinquagesimo Sexto mensis Augustus die vltimi'. Other items were copied by the scribe on fol. 47; fol. 48 blank. He also copied the other two booklets in the MS, fols 49-60 and 61-104, concluding fol. 104 (in red): 'Qui rapit hunc librum. Demon frangit sibi collum. Explicit hic totum De vino da michi potum. etc'. Prayers, fol. 104ᵛ, were added later.

> Priebsch, *Deutsche HSS*, no. 56; Coveney, pp. 45-49; *MMBL*, I: 333; R.F.M. Byrn, 'The Cordiale-Auszug. A Study of Gerard van Vliederhoven's Cordiale de IV novissimis with particular reference to the High German Versions', Unpubl. PhD thesis, Leeds University, 1976, p. 177; R.F.M. Byrn, 'Johannes Bämlers Cordiale-Auszug vom Jahre 1473', *Poesie und Gebrauchsliteratur im deutschen Mittelalter*, ed. V. Honemann *et al.* (1979), pp. 95-106.
> *Pl. 145*

164. UCL Germ. 15, fols 3-196   *1592 [Germany]*

Gebetbuch, in Latin and German

Paper. 194 fols. 138 × 90 mm. 1 col., 95 × c.70 mm. 13-17 lines. Col. inits, rubrics.

Fol. 196ᵛ: 'volendet an dem 8 dag yanuarrij ano domini 1592'. Fols 1, 2 were added later.

> Coveney, pp. 58-60.
> *Pl. 298*

165 UCL Germ. 16, fols 13-17   *[betw. 1145 and 1153] [Germany]*

Series pontificum romanorum

Parch. 5 fols. 190 × 123 mm. 2 cols, 163 × 97 mm. 20 lines. Col. inits, rubric.

A quire (fols 13-18) containing a list of popes down to Eugenius III, 1145-53. Fols 17ᵛ-18ᵛ contain collects and an antiphon added by another hand. The rest of Germ. 16, fols 1-4 + 7-12, 19-33, and 34-43, by other hands, is probably contemporary, the hand of fols 17ᵛ-18ᵛ being like that of fols 1-4 + 7-12 and an addition on fol. 25ᵛ. An inserted bifolium, fols 5-6, is of later s. xii date. Formerly bound with UCL MSS Lat. 1-3 containing a number of quires from different s. xiii MSS, although it is not possible to determine when all parts were first put together (see further *MMBL*, I: 335-38).

> Priebsch, *Deutsche HSS*, no. 129; Coveney, pp. 60-62; E. Hellgardt, 'Die deutschsprachigen Handschriften im 11.

und 12. Jahrhundert. Bestand und Charakteristik im chronologischen Aufriss', *Deutsche Handschriften 1100-1400; Oxforder Kolloquium 1985*, ed. V. Honemann and N.F. Palmer (1988), p. 62 no. 107.
Pl. 12

166 **UCL Germ. 17** *1462 [Cologne, Germany]*
Heiligenlegenden
Paper. 265 fols, foliated 1-12, 12*, 13-264. 207 × 140 mm. 1–2 cols, *c*.140-55 × 100-10 mm. Up to 40 lines. Col. inits, rubrics. Bld-tooled leather bdg over boards, with clasp; spine repaired.

Fol. 261 (underlined in red): 'biddet om gotz willen vůr die onnůtze schriuerse [*sic*] eyn Aue maria etc in dem iair M CCCC lxij op sante Jacobs auent'. Some contemporary corrections to text. Fol. 262 contains a table of contents, fols 262ᵛ-63ᵛ blank. Fol. 264 is a pastedown from a liturgical MS (Sanctorale?) of s. xiii. Three rubrics (fols 25, 46ᵛ, 180) referring to 'Collen' and the scribe's orthography suggest the MS was written in Cologne (*ex info*. Professor J. Flood).
Priebsch, *Deutsche HSS*, no. 58; Coveney, pp. 62-63; *MMBL*, I: 333.
Pl. 160

167 **UCL Germ. 18, fols 1-68** *1488 Ewig, Germany*
Mystische Traktate
Parch. 68 fols. 143 × 105 mm. 1 col., 90 × 60 mm. 20 lines. Col. inits, rubrics. Bld-tooled leather bdg over boards, with clasp.

Fol. 68ᵛ (underlined in red): 'In den iaren do men schreif dusent veirhundert ind achte ind achtich vp sent six*tus* des hilge*n* \pays [*sic*]/ daich wert [*sic*] dyt bokelin geschreue*n* ind geendiget ym dem cloister to Ewich reguleirs orde*ns* [Augustinian canons of Ewig, Westphalia] va*n* frater iohannes herte*n* supp*ri*or [d. 1491] aldair den geistliken sust*er*en to Ruden [Rüthen] der nyer v*er*gaderi*n*ge'. Fols 66-99, the remainder of the MS, are by the same scribe but undated.
Priebsch, *Deutsche HSS*, no. 46; Coveney, pp. 64-65; *MMBL*, I: 333; G. Rehm, 'Rüthen', *Westfälisches Klosterbuch. Lexikon der vor 1815 errichteten Stifte und Klöster von ihrer Gründung bis zur Aufhebung*, ed. K. Hengst, 2 vols (1992-94), II: 307, § 3.4.2; Kramer, I: 241.
Pl. 217

168 **UCL Germ. 23, fols 1-32, 98-154** *1534, 1536, 1539 [Germany]*
Gebetbuch
Paper. 88 fols. 142 × 95 mm. 1 col., 105 × 60 mm. 21-23 lines. Col. inits, rubrics. Bld-tooled leather bdg over boards with letters 'AMVDH' in gold on upper cover, clasps gone.

A booklet, fols 1-32, dated fol. 32ᵛ (in red): '1534'. The scribe also wrote fols 98-154, dating fol. 126ᵛ (in red) 'Amen deo gracias 1536', and fol. 154 (in red) '1539' preceded by 'Amen' in black. Fols 33-93 by the same hand are undated. The rest of the MS, fols 154-71, by a different scribe, is also undated. Additions on fols 93ᵛ-97 and 171-73 are later.
Coveney, pp. 71-72.
Pl. 254

169 **UCL Germ. 24, fols 11-42, 91-95, 146-209** *1491, 1493, 1496 [Switzerland]*
Carthusian miscellany, in German
Parch. fols 11-42, 91-5; paper fols 146-209. 101 fols. 196 × 144 mm. 1 col., 147 × 112 mm fols 11-42, 140 × 85 mm fols 91-95, 158 × 105 mm. 24-25 lines. Col. inits, rubrics. Bld-tooled leather bdg over boards, with clasps.

A miscellany of nine booklets, of which only three are dated. The earliest, fols 91-95 (headed 'hie hebet sich an der Bruder gebet Cartheuser ordenns'), is dated fol. 95 (in red): '149.1'. This is preceded by fols 10-90 (sermons and prayers), written by four scribes, only the first of whom dated his stint, cf. fol. 42ᵛ (in red): '1.4.9⁰.3'. The third of the dated booklets, fols 146-211 (containing 'die heilgen ewangelia durch die gantzen fasten'), is dated fol. 209ᵛ (in red): 'Brudern … yn der Carthausen ist das buch .1.4.9.6. Tercia post dionysij'. The scribe of fols 146-211 also wrote fols 100-45 and 296-331. Fols 1-9 (a Carthusian kalendar, in red and black, with St Bruno in large red letters) and fols 96-99 are also in late fifteenth-century hands. The layout of text in these seven booklets, apart from the kalendar, is the same. Fols 212-59 and 260-95 were added in s. xvi. On leaves originally left blank by the fifteenth-century scribes (fols 10ʳ, 95ᵛ, 99, 210-11) a single sixteenth-century hand has made additions.

In the colophon on fol. 209ᵛ a later hand has inserted in the gap left blank between the words 'Brudern' and 'yn' the words (in purple) 'zu yttinge*n*', the Charterhouse of Ittingen, Thurgau, Switzerland.
Coveney, pp. 72-79; *MMBL*, I: 334.
Pls 222 a, b, 228

170 **UCL Germ. 26** *1466 [Germany]*
Preces, with German rubrics
Parch. 55 fols. 157 × 100 mm. 1 col., 98 × 65 mm. 18 lines. Col. inits, rubrics. Leather bdg over boards with strap and pin fastening.

Fol. 55ᵛ: 'Anno etc. lx sexto'. The MS is written throughout by the same s. xv hand. Prayers to Sts Dominic, Peter Martyr, Thomas (Aquinas) and Vincent (Ferrer) on fols 45-46 and the presence of Dominic doubled in litanies on fols 6ᵛ, 43 and 48 establish it was intended for Dominican use. The rubrics are addressed to a 'swester'. Preceded by fols 1*-17*, paper, containing additions in a later s. xv hand.
Coveney, pp. 81-82; *MMBL*, I: 334.
Pl. 168

171 **UCL Lat. 4, fols 110-29** *1405 Ulm, Germany*
Petrus de Pulka, 'Exerciciorum Primi tractatus Petri Hispani'
Paper. 20 fols. 217 × 155 mm. 2 cols, 172 × 118 mm. 47-48 lines. Col. inits, rubrics. Leather bdg over boards with 5 links of chain attached to top of lower cover, clasp gone.

A compilation consisting of fols 1-133 written by Johannes Sintram, OFM, d. 1450; fols 134-248, 259-59, written by various other hands in s. xiv/xv; and fols 250-53 (parchment) written s. xii/xiii; fols 260-65 are blank. Sintram's stint consists of three booklets: fols 1-49, 50-109, 110-33, the last of which contains exercises on the Summulae logicorum of Petrus

Hispanus by Petrus de Pulka and is dated fol. 129ᵛ (colophon underlined in red and enclosed in red box): 'Et sic est finis exerciciorum Primi tractatus Petri Hispani habite a petro pulka wienne finita Anno domini 1405⁰ dominica 3ᵃ post octauas pasce scripta per me fratrem Johannem sintram \de erbipoli/ et pro tunc fui studens vlme solus et magister studencium h. a*m*stler et futurum erat capitulum generale celebraturum super festum pentecostes in monacho Et habui pro tunc defectum in auribus quod vix potui audire alta voce loqui'. Fols 129ᵛ-32 contain further notes in Sintram's hand, fols 132ᵛ-33ᵛ blank. Fols 1-49 and 50-109 (the latter signed, fol. 109ᵛ in red, 'hec scripta sunt per fratrem Johannem Sintra*m*') contain a commentary on the Summulae logicorum and other lectures and exercises in logic by Pulka and were probably copied by Sintram about the same time as fols 110-33. For him see *BRUO* 1703; also, and for other MSS by him, N.F. Palmer, 'Sintram, Johannes OFM', in *Die deutsche Literatur des Mittelalters. Verfasserlexikon*, 2nd edn, 8 (1992), cols 1284-87. The list includes BL, Add. 44055, for which see *DMBL*, no. 412. Presumably one of the 60 books deposited by Sintram in the library of the Franciscan convent of Würzburg, February 1444; cf. *ex dono* (fol. 96ᵛ) of London, BL, Add. 30049.

Coveney, pp. 4-6 and pl. II illus. colophon; D.K. Coveney, 'Johannes Sintram de Herbipoli', *Speculum*, 16 (1941), 336-39; T.C. Petersen, 'Johs. Sintram de Herbipoli in two of his MSS', *Speculum*, 20 (1945), 77-83; L. Meier, 'Aufzeichnungen aus vernichteten Handschriften des Würzburger Minoritenklosters', *Archivum Franciscanum Historicum*, 44 (1951), 205-6; *MMBL*, I: 38-39; Kramer, I: 858; R.H. Rouse and M.A. Rouse, *Manuscripts and their makers: commercial book production in medieval Paris 1200-1500*, 2 vols (2000), II: 87.
Pl. 77

172 UCL Lat. 15, fols 25-28　　　*1327 Montegiorgio, Italy*
Compotus manualis
Parch. 4 fols. 215 × 160 mm. 1 col., 150 × 100 mm. 28 lines. Col. inits, rubrics.

Fol. 28ᵛ (numbers underlined in red): 'In dei nomine amen. anni sunt .13027. [*sic*] indiccione .10. die .5. exunte [*sic*] febr' tempore domini iohannis pape .22. Completus fuit iste liber in monte sancte marie in Georgio [Montegiorgio, near Fermo]'. The scribe also wrote fols 1-24, though fols 29-33 are by a different hand. Fols 11-24 (quires 2-3) are palimpsest.
Fol. 1 (originally blank): 'Iste liber est iacobi Vannis de Cam' Et ego iacobus Vannis scripsi sub anno M ccc⁰ lxxxiij⁰ Indictione vj⁰ [......] Vrbanj pape vj'.
Coveney, pp. 14-15; *MMBL*, I: 344-45.
Pl. 48

173 UCL Lat. 16, fols 43-72, 103-16　　*1467, 1468 [Italy]*
Arithmeticae et astronomie
Paper. 44 fols. 330 × 230 mm. 2 cols, fols 43-72 215 × 148 mm. 48 lines; fols 103-16 220 × 140 mm. 50 lines. Col. inits fols 103-16, blanks for inits fols 43-72, rubrics, pen and ink diagrm fol. 47. Wooden boards, a third covered with bld-stamped bdg, with clasps.

A compilation of six booklets (fols 3-42, 43-72, 73-102, 103-16, 117-26, 127-34) by various hands. Only the second and fourth booklets are dated. The earlier (fourth) booklet, fols 103-16, ends fol. 116: 'Et est finitus per me paulum de Iulc*r*imonte anno natiuitatis domini m⁰ cccc 67', fol. 116ᵛ blank. Paul also wrote the third booklet, fols 73-102, concluding fol. 100: 'Explicit exposicio theorice planetarum secundum tadeum de parma. transcripta per me paulum de olomuncz [Olomouc, Moravia, Czech Republic]'; fols 100ᵛ-102 blank. The later (second) booklet, fols 43-72, is dated by its scribe, fol. 69ᵛ: 'Scriptus per me hainricum langenbach anno etc 68', fols 70-72ᵛ blank. Heinrich was also responsible for an addition, fol. 39, to the first booklet, fols 3-42; fols 40-42 blank. Fols 3-42, 117-26 and 127-34 are probably contemporary with Paul's and Heinrich's work; apart from the last (in long lines), text throughout is laid out the same way and the scribes write University hands. The only visible watermarks, a demi-stag and demi-griffon, are exclusively Italian (cf. C.M. Briquet, *Les filigranes*, facsim. of 1907 edn with supplementary material, ed. A. Stevenson, 4 vols (1968), I: 219, 407).
Fol. 134 (medieval pressmark): 'XIII . a. I'. The upper cover of the binding bears the pressmark 'N. 18' in ink.
Coveney, pp. 15-16; *MMBL*, I: 345-46.
Pls 170 a, b

174 UCL Lat. 17, fols 85-89 + 91-99　　　　　　*1507*
　　　　　　　　　　　　　　　's Hertogenbosch, Netherlands
Preces
Paper. 14 fols. 138 × 100 mm. 1 col., 100 × 70 mm. 21 lines. Col. inits, rubrics.

Fol. 99ᵛ: 'Scripte sunt he in boscoducis ['s Hertogenbosch] per me A.D. Anno domini 1507 in octaua sancti lamberti'. A quire (fol. 90 inserted by a different scribe) within a compilation of prayers and computistica written by various contemporary hands in early s. xvi. Ker (*MMBL*, I: 346) suggests the scribe's initials 'may stand for Antonius de Meer, to judge from a torn inscription on fol. 183ᵛ: 'obitum charissimi Aui mej .d. Ant.[....] van der meer hunc librum a se [.......] reseruauit sibi et suis [.....] Eerssellentis (?)'. Fols 1-8 contain a kalendar with added obits for the de Meer family.
Coveney, pp. 16-17; *MMBL*, I: 346-51.
Pl. 238

175 UCL Lat. 23　　　　　　　　　*1532 [Germany]*
Bonaventura, Vita S. Francisci
Parch. 81 fols. 278 × 192 mm. 2 cols, 200 × 140 mm. 30 lines. Col. inits, rubrics. Bld-stamped leather bdg over boards, with metal corners and remains of label on upper cover, clasps gone; chain staple mark top of lower cover.

Fol. 81: 'Infra octauam corporis Christi .1532. ferias. Finit legenda beatissimi patris nostri Francisci.' Fol. 81ᵛ blank.
Fol. 1: 'Pro Conuento Franciscorum Tabern*s*ium [Zabern, near Strasbourg, Alsace]' (s. xvii).
MMBL, I: 355; Kramer, I: 863.
Pl. 253

176 UCL Ogden 3　　　　*1453, 1454 Zerbst, Germany*
Logica
Paper. 272 fols. 157 × 108 mm. 1 col., 127 × 80 mm. 32-33 lines, fols 1-197; *c*.120 × 80 mm. 10-11 lines, fols 198-

250; 128 × 80 22-25 lines, fols 251-72. Col. inits, fols 198-252. Parch. bdg over boards, with clasp.

Three booklets, fols 1-197, 198-250 and 251-72, all written by the same hand. The earliest (fols 251-72) is dated 1453, fol. 269^v: 'Finito libro sit laus deo Sub annis domini etc 1 3^0 In die agate hora 5ta post meridiem etc'. Fols 1-197 and 198-250 are both dated 1454. Thus fol. 197^v: 'Et est finitus huius paruuli loyce per me Iulianum osuelt scriptum in zerbst tunc temporis scolatizantem ibidem Sub annis domini 1454^0 Heu male finiui scripsi sine manibus ipsum'; fol. 250: 'Finito libro sit laus deo Sub annis domini .1.4.5.4'. Fol. 250^v contains added recipes by another hand, fols 198 and 270-71 are blank, and fol. 272 is a pastedown.
Possibly from the Franciscan convent of Zerbst.

> *MMBL*, I: 361-62; Kramer, I: 864.
> *Pl. 143*

177 UCL Ogden 11, pp. 1-104   *1574 Paris, France*
Chronique d'Angleterre, 1569-74

Paper. 52 fols. 330 × 217 mm. 1 col., 235 × 148 mm. 19-23 lines. Illum. init., p. 77, dates, proper names, etc written in red. Gold-tooled limp vellum bdg, with stubs of silk ties.

P. 102: 'A st Germain des prez de Paris le [blank] jour et [blank] .1574.' A chronicle of contemporary affairs in England, addressed to Henri III, king of France 1574-89, followed by a consideration of whether Elizabeth I would wish to break the treaty (of Blois, 1572) between the two countries. Pp. 103-4 blank, pp. 105-16 contain a table of contents.

> *Pl. 277*

178 UCL Ogden 12   *1538 Rovigo, Italy*
Encyclopaedia

Paper. 264 fols. 310 × 210 mm. 2 cols, 230 × c.150 mm. Up to 33 lines. Col. inits, diagrms fols 39, 67^v, 68. Bld-tooled leather bdg, ties gone.

Fol. 264^v (in capitals): 'Villae Dvcis Agri [Doge Andrea Gritti, d. 28 Dec 1538] Rh\o/digini in aedibus .M.D. Nicolai Lion Veneti mense Maii .M.D. XXXVIII'. Immediately before the colophon the scribe has listed the sequence of quire signatures A-Z, a-d (27 quires) and noted 'omnes quinterniones, excepta d [fols 261-64] duernione'. Fol. 264^v is otherwise blank. The text is preceded by nine unfoliated leaves of which the first two are blank, the third is a title page with 'Encyclopaedia' (in capitals), and the fifth to ninth leaves contain an index written by the scribe; three blank leaves at end.

> *Pl. 255*

179 UCL Ogden 18   *1577 [England]*
William Lambarde, Nomina Saxonica

Paper. 10 fols. 297 × 200 mm. 1-4 cols, c.243 × 155 mm. Up to 39 lines. Limp vellum bdg.

Fol. 5 (title): 'Angliae tetraphonia siue de propijs vrbium oppidorum fluuiorum montium [locorum] aliorumque locorum Angliae nominibus commentarius ex optimis quibusque scriptoribus collectus Guilielmo Lambardo Authore 1577'. The text, unfoliated, is in Lambarde's hand. For him, see R.M. Warnicke, *William Lambarde, Elizabethan Antiquary, 1536-1601* (1973). His notes are preceded by 4 leaves and followed by 14 more, all

containing notes and memoranda in various other hands up to at least 1602.
Bound in a discarded indenture, dated 26 October 14 Elizabeth (1571-2), between Walter [Devereux], Earl of Essex, d. 1576, and his servant, William Barrett, concerning property at Barr Park, Staffordshire.

> *Pl. 282*

180 UCL Ogden 27, pp. 63-122   *1462 [Italy]*
Cicero, De senectute

Paper. 30 fols. 210 × 145 mm. 1 col., 125 × 75 mm. 21 lines.

P. 122 (in capitals): 'Marci: Tulii: Ciceronis: De Senectute: Liber: Explicit: Deo gratias: Amen', then the scribe writes 'manus scriptoris Benedicas uirtus saluatoris [erasure] Adi 16 de set*embre* 1462'. A volume of Cicero's philosophical works all copied by the same scribe, probably in North East Italy [*ex info*. Professor A.C. de la Mare]. *De senectute,* beginning abruptly, is preceded by *De amicitia* which begins and ends imperfectly. The following item, *Paradoxa Stoicorum*, pp. 123-54, concludes p. 154: 'Marci tuli ciceronis liber paradoxorum explicit deo patri gracias amen. Jo Ego sum \martir etiam (?)/ me scripsit'. The words 'martir etiam', written over an erasure, are blotched and difficult to read.

> *MMBL*, I: 364-65.
> *Pl. 161*

181 UCL Phillipps 1   *1594, 1597*
    Bremen and Hildesheim, Germany
Baltzasar Clammern, 'Extract vnd auszug der Vornehmestenn Lehnrechte'; 'Newe Ordnung vnd Erclerung der Statuten der Stadt Bremen'

Paper. 143 fols. 310 × 190 mm. 1 col., 222 × 105 mm. Up to 31 lines. Gold inits, rubrics. Bld-tooled vellum bdg, with name 'Hinrich Bredelo' and date '1598' on upper cover, ties gone.

Two booklets, the earlier of which (fols 89-141) is dated 1594, the later (fols i-ii, 1-88) 1597. Thus, fol. 90 (title page of second booklet): 'Extract vnd auszug der Vornehmestenn Lehnrechte vnd anderer Gemeiner sachen auss den Vortreflichesten Scribenten vnd Rechteslehrern Weilandt durch den Erntuesten vnd hochgelarten Baltzasar Clammern In diese Ordnung zusamen gebracht Itzo uber mundirt vnd Insz Reine Geschreiben durch Johan Neuen vonn Bremen Im Jhar MD XCIIII'; fol. ii (title page of first booklet): 'Dispositio et Commentatio Statvtorvm Reipublicae Bremensis Das ist Newe Ordnung vnd Erclerung der Statuten der Stadt Bremen Zu Ehren vnd Wolgefallenn des Erbarn vnd Wolweise*n* Herrn Heinrich Bredeloen Rhatsuerwa*n*ten deroselben stadt Schreib Johan Neuen S. Erb. W. vnwurdiger Vetter selbige*n* zur gedechtnus Im Jar des Herrn MD XCVII'. Heinrich Bredeloe's name is written in gold letters. The scribe again dated this booklet, fol. 85 (in red): 'Completus an sûlta prope Hildesiam [Hildesheim] per Joannem Naeuium Bremensem Anno Salvtis MD XCVII', fols 85^v-88^v blank.

> Coveney, p. 97.
> *Pl. 299*

182 UCL Phillipps 81 *1512 [Freiburg, Switzerland]*

Berner Chronik – Zürcher Chronik

Paper. 78 fols, foliated 2-79. *c*.318 × 217 mm. 1 col., 224-40 × 145 mm. Up to 49 lines. Limp vellum bdg with coat of arms and crest drawn in pen and ink on upper cover, now bound separately at front of MS.

Fol. 79ᵛ: 'Die abgeschribne matery han Ich Petter Falck [of Freiburg, 1468-1519] abgeschriben vss E*iner* vast alten geschrifft die mir meyster Hans Velder geluchen [*sic*] hatt geendet vff zinstag morndes nach sant apolonyen der heilgen Jungfrowen vnnd martrerin tag als man zalt Tusent funff hundert vnd zwolff Jar'. The roughly drawn coat of arms and crest on the cover are Falck's. A. Wagner, *Peter Falcks Bibliothek und humanistiche Bildung*, Bibliothek der Schweizer Bibliophilen, ser. II, 2 (1926), pp. 109-10, mistakenly reports that this MS (formerly Phillipps 3583) is in Berlin (the word order of the colophon he cites differs slightly from here). The Staatsbibliothek's only chronicles of Bern, MSS Germ. Fol. 1262 (dated 1575) and Germ. Fol. 1263 (s. xviii), both formerly owned by Phillipps (his MSS 1218 and 1261), are too late to have been Falck's.

> Coveney, p. 109; R. Gamper, *Die Zürcher Stadtchroniken und ihre Ausbreitung in die Ostschweiz*, Mitteilungen der Antiquarischen Gesellschaft in Zürich, Bd 52, Hft 2 (1984), pp. 169-70; his MS A.1.3.
> *Pl. 242*

183 ULL 278, fol. iiᵛ *1516 [England]*

'A Spesiall Glasse to loke in daily'

Parch. 1 fol. 242 × 170 mm. 1 col., 198 × 38-130 mm. 35 lines.

Fol. iiᵛ: 'wrete*n* þᵉ viijᵗʰ yer' of ky(ng) hary the viijᵗʰ on holy rod day in haruyste', 14 September 1516, the scribe William H signing his name in cipher (see J.H.P. Pafford, 'A cipher signature of about 1500', *Journal of the Society of Archivists*, 1 (1959), 288-89). Precepts ending in '-ly' added on the flyleaf of an early fifteenth-century copy of Robert of Gloucester's metrical chronicle. Pafford's suggestion ('University of London Library MS 278, Robert of Gloucester's Chronicle', *Studies presented to Sir Hilary Jenkinson*, ed. J.C. Davies (1957), p. 315) that Richard Whitford was their author can no longer be accepted. Although they were printed in shortened form several times in the sixteenth century as an appendix to a translation believed to be by Whitford of the *Imitatio Christi*, his authorship of the translation has been called into question. See further G. Williams, 'Two neglected London-Welsh clerics: Richard Whitford and Richard Gwent', *Trans. of the Honourable Society of the Cymmrodorion*, Session 1961, Part I (1961), 30-32; and J. Hogg, *Richard Whytford's The Pype or Tonne of the Lyfe of Perfection with an Introductory Study of Whytford's Works*, I: *Introductory Study, Part 2*, Salzburg Studies in English Literature, Elizabethan and Renaissance Studies, 89 (1989), iii and 79-99.

Fol. i (conjoint with fol. ii): 'Noverint per presentes me Johannes Cope Bladesmyth de london' tener'', sworn as Joint Master of the Mistery of Bladesmiths of London, 3 September 1488. Fol. ii: 'Marget Steven' (s. xvᵉˣ/xvi). Later belonged to William Cecil, Lord Burghley (1520-98); cf. Sale Catalogue of the 'main part of [his] library' in *Bibliotheca illustrissima sive catalogus variorum librorum ... viri cujusdam praenobilis ac honoratissimi olim defuncti* (London: T. Bentley and B. Walford, at the Bear, Ave Mary Lane, November 21, 1687), p. 89, item 33.

> Pafford, *Studies ... Jenkinson*, pl. III illus. fols ii r-v (reduced); *MMBL*, I: 366.
> *Pl. 245*

184 ULL 889, fols 1-71 *1428 Lipnice, Czech Republic*

Diurnale, pars

Parch. 71 fols. 110 × 87 mm. 1 col., 80 × 60 mm. 19-21 lines. Rubrics. Leather bdg over boards, 4 corner bosses on upper and lower covers gone.

Fol. 70ᵛ (in red): 'Explicit diurnale partis yemalis in vigilia sancte Barbare sub anno domini Mᵒ ccccᵒ xxviijᵒ per manus Tedrici kaczschicz capellani in lypenicz [Lipnitz, Bohemia, now Lipnice, Czech Republic]'; fol. 71 contains added prayers by a later hand. As well as fols 1-70 (Temporale, from 1st Sunday in Advent to Easter Saturday), Theodericus also wrote fols 72-109 (Sanctorale from Andrew to Ambrose, concluding (in red): 'Et sic est finis huius partis Deo gracias Et hic etc Orate pro scriptore vnum Aue maria'), and fols 110-18 (Commune Sanctorum); fols 117ᵛ-18ᵛ, originally blank, contain added prayers. Fols 119-77 and 178-97 contain hymns and psalms copied by a contemporary hand. An added paper quire (fols 197bis-207, containing psalm 4) includes further prayers in the hand which made additions elsewhere.

> *Pl. 101*

185 ULL Sterling Library SLV.17 *[betw. 1403 and 1419?]*
[London? England]

William Langland, Piers Plowman (C text); etc.

Parch. 114 fols. 365 × 240 mm. 1 col. fols 1-97, 2 cols fols 97ᵛ-114ᵛ, 258 × 177 mm. 37 lines. Illum. init. and border (fol. 1), col. inits, rubrics. Blank spaces left for mins, fols 97ᵛ-111ᵛ.

Originally part of a larger volume broken up and sold as three separate MSS between 1927 and 1942. The other two parts are Washington D.C., Folger Shakespeare Library, V.b.236, and Princeton, N.J., University Library, Taylor Medieval 10 (*olim* Boies Penrose, Barbados Hill, Devon, Pa., Penrose 20). Although Ker (*MMBL*, I: 376-77) doubted the identification, the central shield of three in the bottom margin of fol. 1 of the Folger MS (illus. J. Preston and L. Yeandle, *English Handwriting 1400-1650* (1992), pl. 1) is probably that of Sir William Clopton of Quinton, Gloucestershire, and Joan Besford, his wife (cf. A.I. Doyle, 'Remarks on surviving manuscripts of *Piers Plowman*', *Medieval English Religious and Ethical Literature: Essays in Honour of George Russell*, ed. G. Kratzmann and J. Simpson (1986), p. 44; T. Turville-Petre, 'The relationship of the Vernon and Clopton manuscripts', *Studies in the Vernon Manuscript*, ed. D. Pearsall (1990), pp. 36-38. If this is so, the volume was presumably made for them between 1403, by which date they had married (VCH, *Worcestershire*, IV: 21) and 1419, when William died (*Inquisitions post mortem*, 7 Henry V, no. 46).

Fol. 4: 'Richard hodyson' (s. xvi). Fol. 107: 'thys ys george langgam ys rytenge Thys ys george langam ys rytynge Iste liber pertenett ad' (s. xvi).

William H. Robinson Ltd, *Catalogue 62, Rare Books and Manuscripts* (1937), no. 1 and pl. illus. fol. 1 (reduced); *The Sterling Library. A Catalogue of the Printed Books and Literary Manuscripts collected by Sir Louis Sterling and presented by him to the University of London* (1954), pp. 544-45 and pl. VI illus. fol. 1 (reduced).
Pl. 76

186 V & A Reid 23, pp. 21-292, 297-560   *1450, 1453*
      Diepenveen, Netherlands

Biblia, pars

Parch. 269 fols. *c*.305 × 215 mm. 2 cols, *c*.215 × 145 mm. 42-43 lines. Hist. and dec. inits (though many cut out), col. inits, rubrics.

A bible, with prologues, copied by one of the regular canonesses of the Augustinian house of Diepenveen, near Deventer. The first surviving part (pp. 21-292, 18 quires, containing I Kings to II Ezra), concludes p. 289 (in red): 'finitus in profesto sancti michaelis archangeli Anno domini millesimo quadringentesimo quinquagesimo cum multo corporis labore sed non paruo cordis affectu per quandam monialem in diepenveen ancillarum christi ultimam cuius nomen scriptum sit in libro vite'; pp. 290-92 left blank. At the end of the second surviving part (pp. 297-560, 18 quires, containing Isaiah – Malachi), the unnamed *scriptrix* used the same formula, p. 558 (again in red): 'finitus in octaua visitacionis beate virginis marie Anno domini Millesimo quadringentesimo quinquagesimo tercio cum multo corporis labore sed non paruo cordis affectu per quandam monialem in dyepenveen ancillarum christi ultimam cuius nomen scriptum sit in libro vite'; pp. 559-60 left blank. Pp. 1-20 and 293-6 contain indexes to each part supplied by a later hand (pp. 18-20 and 296 blank).

The sisters of Diepenveen were well-known as scribes (see W. Scheepsma, *Deemoed en devotie: De koorvrouwen van Windesheim en hun geschriften* (1997), pp. 62-65; L. Wierda, *Middeleeuwse Handschriften uit het Klooster Diepenveen*, Catalogue of an Exhibition held at the Athenaeum Library, Deventer (2000), *passim*. I owe these references to Dr Thérèse de Hemptinne). For two examples copied by contemporaries of our scribe, cf. J.P. Gumbert, *Manuscrits datés conservés dans les Pays-Bas: Les manuscrits d'origine néerlandaise (XIVᵉ-XVIᵉ siècles)*, (1988), nos 348, 356.

A.W. Byvanck and G.J. Hoogewerff, *La miniature hollandais dans les manuscrits des 14ᵉ, 15ᵉ et 16ᵉ siècles* (1922-26), no. 78 and pls 49, 50 and 71 illus p. 21 and part of pp. 61, 243, 256, 432; *MMBL*, I: 380; *Monasticon Windeshemense*, ed. W. Kohl, E. Perssons, and A.G. Weiler, 4 vols (1976-84), III: 602; Exh., *Universal Penman*, no. 30; Whalley, *Pen's Excellencie*, pp. 10, 15, 70, 71 illus. inits pp. 1, 431 (both enlarged) and pp. 1, 112 (not fol. 112ᵛ as stated, both pp reduced).
Pl. 134

187 V and A Reid 60, fols 13-266   *1446 [Italy]*

Horae ad usum romanum

Parch. 254 fols. 133 × 90 mm. 1 col., 70 × 45-50 mm. 16 lines. Illum. dec. inits and full-page borders, gold and col. inits, rubrics. Gold-tooled leather bdg (s. xvi).

Fol. 266 (in red): 'Frater paulus de mediolano ordinis sancti

bartholomei de hermineis. scripsit .M.CCCC.46'. Although Paul's hand is Italian, that of the kalendar (fols 1-12, quire 1) is Northern French or Flemish, as is the decoration. Leaves (fols 46ʳ⁻ᵛ, 52ᵛ, 58ʳ⁻ᵛ, 64ʳ⁻ᵛ, 70ʳ⁻ᵛ, 79ᵛ-80ᵛ, 103ᵛ-104ᵛ, 151ᵛ-52ᵛ, 161ᵛ-62ᵛ, 213ʳ⁻ᵛ, 219ᵛ, 222ᵛ-23, 235ᵛ-36ᵛ, 241ʳ⁻ᵛ, 253ʳ) have been left blank between the different offices but the MS is not in booklets. Fols 266ᵛ-72ᵛ contain the Hours of the Holy Spirit and a collect to St Antony of Padua added by another hand.

E.F.S., 'The Reid Gift', *The Burlington Magazine*, 2 (1903), 75; F. Winkler, *Die flämische Buchmalerei des XV. und XVI Jahrhunderts* (1925), p. 180; *MMBL*, I: 383; Whalley, *Pen's Excellencie*, p. 101 illus. fol. 71 (enlarged).
Pl. 123

188 V & A L. 251-1861   *[1368?] [Italy]*

'Epistole et prophetie totius anni'

Parch. 103 fols. 330 × *c*.267 mm. 2 cols, 205 × 140 mm. 21 lines. Illum. init. and full-page border (fol. 1), hist., dec., and col. inits, rubrics. Leather bdg over boards, with bosses; straps gone (s.xiv).

The date 'M⁰.ccc⁰.lxviii die mercurii primo februarij' is written in a tiny hand across the initial 'F' of 'Fratres' on fol. 1. Dr R. Watson informs me that in his opinion the page layout of this lectionary is more typical of earlier MSS and suggests that the date might have been added to record the volume's presentation to some unknown institution.

MMBL, I: 385; Exh., *Universal Penman*, no. 19; Whalley, *Pen's Excellencie*, p. 99 illus. fol. 8ᵛ (reduced).
Pl. 58

189 V & A L. 1888-1879   *1597 Cremona, Italy*

Hieronimo Morescho, 'Varie sorte di lettere'

Paper. 121 fols. 147 × 100m. 1 col., up to 90 × 70 mm. Up to 13 lines. Pen-flourished inits.

Fol. 120ᵛ: 'Mentre io Hieronimo Morescho era nel seminario di Cremona scrissi queste lettere nel anno 1597'. This calligraphic specimen book is also dated 1597 on fol. 1 (title page, in capitals): 'Libro nel qvale si contiene varie sorte di lettere fatte per mano di me Hieronimo Moreschi 1597', and throughout.
Pl. 304

190 V & A L. 1346-1891   *[c.1350] [Paris? France]*

Missale secundum usum ecclesie Sancti Dionisii

Parch. 439 fols, fols 16-439 with medieval foliation i – iiijᶜ xxvj. 234 × 170 mm. 2 cols, 156 × 103 mm. Up to 33 lines text or 11 lines music. Mins in grisaille, hist. inits and full-page borders, dec. inits and borders, gold and col. inits, rubrics. Kal. in gold, red, blue and black.

From the royal abbey of St Denis, and containing Offices for the Dedication of the Church and for the Relics of St Denis. The kalendar, in a preliminary quire unfoliated by the scribe (fols 4-15), contains obits of the abbots, the latest of whom (and the only one whose name is written in gold) is Guy de Castres, d. 22 Feb 1350 (fol. 10ᵛ); his successor, Gilles Rigaud, died 1351 or 1352. Among the royal obits the latest of the French kings is Charles IV (le Bel), d. 1 February 1328; his successor, Philip VI, d. 22 August 1350. See further A. Wilmart, 'Les anniversaires célébrés á Saint-Denis au milieu du XIVe siècle', *Revue Mabillon*, 14 (1924), 22-31. Identical obits are found in a companion volume, the St Denis Breviary, now Oxford, Bodl., Canon. liturg. 192. The missal was illustrated by the Maître du Remède de Fortune (for this artist and his work, see F. Avril, 'Les manuscrits enluminés de Guillaume de Machaut', *Guillaume de Machaut: Colloque-Table Ronde organisé par l'Université de Reims, 19-22 Avril 1978*, Actes et Colloques, 23 (1982), pp. 117-33).

Fols 400-8, added at the end of the MS, contain 'Ordo ad cathechuminum faciendum' (s. xv^{ex}), with the arms of Cardinal Ferry de Clugny in the full-page border, fol. 400. For the Cardinal's library, see J. Ruysschaert, 'La bibliothèque de Ferry de Clugny, évêque de Tournai (1473-1483). Imprimés et manuscrits', *Le Pontifical de Ferry de Clugny, Cardinal et Évéque de Tournai*, ed. A. de Schryver, M. Dykmans and J. Ruysschaert (1989), pp. 241-51, in whose list of MSS this is no. 24. Fol. 396, a faint inscription reads: 'Ad molto mio dilecto filio Jean Baptist Antonius de Collaxino a Antonius m de Castiliane'.

> J.W. Bradley, *Historical Introduction to the Collection of Illuminated Letters and Borders in the National Art Library, Victoria and Albert Museum* (1901), pl. 3 illus. fol. 284^v; A. de Laborde, *Les manuscrits à peintures de la Cité de Dieu* (1909), I: 232 n. 5 and III: pl. X illus. fols 256^v, 261 (reduced); *MMBL*, I: 387; F. Avril, 'Un chef-d'œuvre de l'enluminure sous la règne de Jean le Bon: la Bible moralisée, manuscrit français 167 de la Bibliothèque nationale', *Monuments et mémoires de la Fondation Eugène Piot*, 58 (1972), 91-125, fig. 21 illus. init. fol. 296; F. Avril, *Manuscript Painting at the Court of France, the Fourteenth Century (1310-1380)*, (1978), p. 26 and pls 21-22 illus. fols 256^v, 261 (enlarged); Exh., *Universal Penman*, no. 12; Whalley, *Pen's Excellencie*, p. 58 illus. fol. 242; Avril, 'Guillaume de Machaut', figs 5, 6 illus. fols 256^v, 261; D. Nebbiai-Dalla Guarda, *La bibliothèque de l'Abbaye de Saint-Denis en France du ixe au xviiie siècle* (1985), pp. 313, 319; C. Sterling, *La peinture médiévale à Paris* (1987), I: 156-59 and figs. 81-82 illus. init. fol. 261 (enlarged), 256^v; A.W. Robertson, *The Service-Books of the Royal Abbey of Saint-Denis. Images of Ritual and Music in the Middle Ages* (1991), pp. 406-7 and pl. 20 illus. fol. 419 (reduced).
> *Pl. 53*

191 **V & A L. 318-1894**   *1477 [Florence? Italy]*

Horatius, Carmina

Parch. 80 fols. 182 × 118 mm. 1 col., 118 × 55 mm. Up to 25 lines. Illum. init. and border (fol. 1), gold and col. inits, rubrics.

Fol. 80^v: 'Finis. M⁰ cccc <l>xxvii⁰ kalendis Iulii'. The date has been tampered with; thus the 'l' has been erased and another 'i' appears to have been added after 'xxvii' to read 1428. Perhaps decorated by a follower of Francesco d'Antonio del Cherico, see J.J.G. Alexander and A.C. de la Mare, *The Italian Manuscripts in the Library of Major J.R. Abbey* (1969), pp. 61-62.

> *MMBL*, I: 388; Exh., *Universal Penman*, no. 47.
> *Pl. 200*

192 **V & A L. 404-1916**   *[betw. c.1197? and 1220]*
                                    [Lesnes, England]

Missale de Lesnes

Parch. 196 fols. c.320 × 225 mm. 1 col., 245 × 150 mm. 22 lines or 12 lines music. 2 cols, 260 × 177 mm. 34-38 lines. Mins, illum. hist. and dec. inits, col. inits, rubrics. Kal. in red, blue and black.

From the Augustinian abbey of Lesnes (or Westwood), Kent, founded by Richard de Lucy in 1178 in expiation for his part in the murder of St Thomas Becket. Since Lesnes was dedicated to Becket, the absence from both sanctorale and kalendar of the Feast of his translation suggests the MS was produced before 1220. It contains two sanctorales, the second of which (fols 181-96) is based on the calendar of Arrouaise, to which congregation Lesnes had affiliated by 1208, when Fulk, 2nd abbot, who appears in the Necrology of Arrouaise, died. He first occurs in a Kent Fine of 1197; see further P. Jebb, *Missale de Lesnes*, HBS 95 (1964), pp. xv-xvii. The MS is in fascicules and Jebb suggests the first sanctorale (fols 113-49) was probably the earliest portion of the MS to be written and the kalendar (fols 2-7), which includes all the saints found in both sanctorales, the last. Collects for the Translation of Becket were soon added in s. xiii on an originally blank leaf (fol. 179), by a hand which writes below top line. In s. xv someone noted in the first sanctorale (fol. 130 margin) where these added collects were to be found: 'Require collectas de t<rans>lacione beate Thome martyris post Ev<an>gellia. que scripta sunt post offic<ium> pro defunctis'. In the Canon of the Mass different hands have inserted (fol. 82 margin), beside the *Memento* for the Dead, the names of the abbey's benefactors, including those of members of the Lucy family.

S. xvi annotations include fol. 68^v: 'Rycharde Hoglay'; fol. 86: 'Gill Wa< >', with fol. 116^v a pen and ink drawing of a man in Elizabethan costume labelled 'Gill'; fol. 117: 'Aspicis vt venerint ad candida tecta columbae accipi et nullas sordida et nigris suas Stephen Bremall', and 'John Raye'.

> M.R. James, *A Descriptive Catalogue of Fifty Manuscripts from the Collection of Henry Yates Thompson* (1898), no. 7; A.W. Clapham, 'The Lesnes Abbey Missal', *Woolwich District Antiquarian Soc.*, Occasional Papers, n.s. 1 (1920), 9-12 and frontispiece illus. fols 113^v and 76 (both reduced); W.H. Mandy, 'Matters of local interest in the Lesnes Missal', *Woolwich District Antiquarian Society*, Occasional Papers, n.s. 1 (1920), 13; Jebb, *Missale de Lesnes*, frontispiece and pl. opp. p. 60 illus. fols 76 and 68 (both reduced); *MMBL*, I: 389; Whalley, *Pen's Excellencie*, p. 53 illus. fol. 113^v (reduced); S. Lewis, *Reading Images: Narrative Discourse and Reception in the Thirteenth-Century Illuminated Apocalypse* (1995), fig. 207 illus. fol. 76 (reduced).
> *Pl. 18*

193 **V & A L. 2607-1936, fols 1-12**   *1561 Germany*

Johann Neudörffer the Elder, Ein gute Ordnung und kurzer Unterricht

Parch. 12 fols. 290 × 165 mm. 1-2 cols, 52 × 170 mm. 7-16 lines. Pen-flourished inits. Gold-tooled leather bdg, dated '1569'.

Fol. 2 (title page): 'Ein gutte ordnung vnnd kurtze vnterricht der furnembsten grunde aus denen die Jungen zierlichs schreibens begirlich mit besonderer khunst vnnd behendigkheyt vnterricht vnnd geubet mogen werden. Durch Johann Newdorffer Burger vnnd Rechenmaister zu Nurmberg seinen schuelern zu mererm verstanndt geordnet Im Jar der geburt Jhesu Christi vnsers Herrn vnnd seligmachers Funfftzehenhundert vnd Im Ainundsechtzigsten'. For Neudörffer (1497-1563), see W. Doede, *Schön schreiben, eine Kunst: Johann Neudörffer und seine Schule* (1957), also Doede's 'Johann Neudörffers Hauptwerk "Ein gute Ordnung" von 1538', *Philobiblon*, 1 (1957), 20-29 and his *Bibliographie deutscher Screibmeisterbücher von Neudörffer bis 1800* (1958), pp. 13-25 and 38-39; and *2,000 Years of Calligraphy: A Three-Part Exhibition organized by the Baltimore Museum of Art, Peabody Institute Library, Walters Art Gallery, June 6 – July 18 ~ 1965*, ed D.E. Miner, V.I. Carlson, and P.W. Filby (1965), no. 83. Originally produced in 1538, this copy of his writing manual, possibly made by Neudörffer himself (Whalley, *Pen's Excellencie*, p. 172), or by his pupil Adam Lempt (Exh., *Universal Penman*, no. 72), is followed by 14 blank unfoliated paper leaves and 8 paper leaves (foliated as 1-8) with woodcut initials.

Fol. 1 (flyleaf): 'Sebastian Zollikoffer von Sanct Gallen Anno 1570', followed by (according to the typescript catalogue) the initials 'AL' (in gold; for Adam Lempt?); but only the initial 'A' is visible. Whalley, *Pen's Excellencie*, p. 173 illus. fols 3ᵛ, 6ᵛ (reduced).
Pl. 265

194 V & A L. 2158-1947   1558 [Venice, Italy]
Laws and regulations for the government of the procurators of St Mark's, Venice, in Latin and Italian

Parch. 95 fols, fols 17-95 with original foliation in red 2–80. 250 × 185 mm. 1 col., 170 × 112 mm. Up to 22 lines. Gold inits, rubrics.

Fol. 95: 'Presbyter Joannes de Vitalibus Brixiae scripsit, et literis aureis celestinisque ornauit hunc librum Anno Domini .M.D.L VIII'. The laws and regulations, fols 17-95, are preceded by indexes, fols 1-16. The beginning of the text, fol. 1 in the MS's original foliation, is wanting; the present fols 16ᵛ and 95ᵛ are blank.

A. Fairbank and B. Wolpe, *Renaissance Handwriting: An Anthology of Italic Scripts* (1960), pl. 41 illus. fol. 91 (reduced); Exh., *Universal Penman*, no. 63; Whalley, *Pen's Excellencie*, pp. 132-33 illus. fols 70, 95 (reduced).
Pl. 262

195 V & A L. 2879-1947   1580 [Florence, Italy]
Salvadore Gagliardelli, 'Il Gagliardelli'

Paper. 29 fols. 200 × 272 mm. 1 col., 36 × 130 mm. 4 lines. Engraved borders. Limp parch. bdg.

Fol. 1 (title-page, in red): 'Per Il Signor Girolamo Sommaj', then in a smaller script 'Il Gagliardelli scriueua. 1580'. Gagliardelli was a famous Florentine writing master; the present manual consists of passages from Dante's Inferno, each passage being written within the same engraved border.

A.F. Johnson, 'A Catalogue of Italian Writing-Books of the Sixteenth Century', *Signature: A Quadrimestrial of Typography and Graphic Arts*, n.s., 10 (1950), p. 43;

C. Bonacini, *Bibliografia delle arti scrittorie e della calligrafia* (1953), no. 652; A.S. Osley, *Luminario. An Introduction to the Italian Writing-Books of the Sixteenth and Seventeenth Centuries* (1972), p. 99 n. 1; Exh., *Universal Penman*, no. 83; Whalley, *Pen's Excellencie*, p. 165 illus. fol. 25 (reduced).
Pl. 284

196 V & A L. 2740-1950   1566 Ulm, Germany
Jonathan Sautter, 'Kurtze Ordnung Kunstlicher vnnd Artlicher wol geproportionerter Teutscher vnnd Latinischer schrifften'

Parch and paper. 33 fols. 115 × 170 mm. 1 col, 40 × 85 mm. 6-12 lines. Col. and pen-flourished inits. Gold-tooled bdg, ties gone.

Fol. 1: 'Kurtze Ordnung Kunstlicher vnnd Artlicher wol geproportionerter Teutscher vnnd Latinischer schrifften Grundtlich zusamen getragen vnnd gemacht Durch mich Jonathan Sautter [1546-1612] in Vlm Im Jar Nach Christi vnnsers Herrn vnd seligmachers geburt MDLXVI', followed by the motto (in capitals): 'Nil penna sedvsvs'. Fol. 10ᵛ is written in gold, fols 15ᵛ-33ᵛ blank.

W. Doede, *Bibliographie deutscher Schreibmeisterbücher von Neudörffer von 1800* (1958), p. 31 n. 43; Exh., *Universal Penman*, no. 71; Whalley, *Pen's Excellencie*, p. 175 illus. fol. 1 (enlarged).
Pl. 268

197 V & A L. 1769-1952   1465 Rome, Italy
Macrobius, Saturnalia

Parch. 150 fols. 301 × 205 mm. 1 col., up to 198 × 115 mm. 31 lines. Illum. init. and border, fol. 1, illum. and col. inits.

Fol. 150: 'Completus diem xiiij augusti Rome 1465'. Fol. 150ᵛ blank. 111 folios earlier, at the foot of fol. 39v, the scribe noted 'In ven' sancto' (i.e. Good Friday) which in 1465 fell on 12 April. Part of a larger volume, of which 34 fols are now Cambridge, Mass., Harvard University, Houghton Library Typ 496, for which see R.S. Wieck, *Late Medieval and Renaissance Illuminated Manuscripts 1350-1520 in the Houghton Library* (1983), p. 135 (I owe this information to Professor A.C. de la Mare). Our scribe also wrote Biblioteca Apostolica Vaticana, Val. lat. 3232 and 3283, the latter dated 'xx decembris 1463'.

MMBL, I: 391; Exh., *Universal Penman*, no. 46; Whalley, *Pen's Excellencie*, p. 124 illus. fol. 113 (reduced); S. Knight, *Historical Scripts from Classical Times to the Renaissance* (1998), F11 and pls illus fols 113 (reduced), 5 (part, enlarged).
Pl. 167

198 V & A L. 1792-1953   1540 Florence, Italy
Horae ad usum romanum

Parch. 138 fols. 130 × 85 mm. 1 col., c.87 × 50 mm. 15 lines. Full-page mins, illum. inits and full-page borders, gold inits, rubrics. Kal. in gold, blue and black.

Fol. 1ᵛ (in a cartouche in gold letters): 'Aloysius scribebat Floren' Die .x. Februarij M.D.XXXX'. Written for Eleanora da Toledo, Duchess of Tuscany (d. 1562), who married Cosimo de

Medici, 1st Duke, 1539. Her arms, impaled with those of the Medici, appear in the border, fol. 2ᵛ; the laurel tree, a Medici emblem, occurs fol. 27; and Capricorn, Cosimo's *impresa*, fol. 3 passim. Fols 138ʳ⁻ᵛ blank.

In Spain by 1576 when the content was approved by the Holy Office, fol. 137ᵛ: 'Vistas y aprobadas, pero aduiertese, *que* quien tiene oblig*acion* de Rezar el off*icio* de N*uestra Senora* no cumple Rezando lo por estas sino por el off*icio* q*ue* mando imprimir el papa pio s*egund*o En madrid set*iembre*. 22. 1576. C.L.D. Heredia'.

Exh., *Universal Penman*, no. 62; Whalley, *Pen's Excellencie*, pp.118-19 illus. fols 90ᵛ-91, 5ᵛ-6, and 136ᵛ-37 (the latter two openings reduced).
Pl. 256

199 V & A L. 1609-1954   *1495 Rome, Italy*
Cicero, De officiis

Parch. 122 fols. 168 × 110 mm. 1 col., 100 × 50 mm. 25 lines. Full-page border with arms (fol. 1), title in capitals in lines of gold alternating with blue, red, green and purple, col. inits, rubrics. Gold-tooled leather bdg, with clasps gone.

Fol. 121 (capitals, in 3 lines of blue, red and green): 'M.T.C. Officiorum Lib. finit Romae die lunae .II. Novembris MCCC-CLXXXXV', followed by the initials 'B.S.' in gold and blue. Fols 121ᵛ-22ᵛ blank. Marginal annotations in red throughout. The scribe, Bartolomeo Sanvito of Padua, made five other copies of *De officiis* in Rome in the 1490s (see J.J.G. Alexander in Alexander and A.C. de la Mare, *The Italian Manuscripts in the Library of Major J.R. Abbey* (1969), p. 105 n. 2). They include BL MSS, Add 6051, dated 1494 (*DMBL*, no. 5) and Harley 2692, dated 1498 (*DMBL*, no. 691). A virtually identical series of annotations by him is to be found in all of them and probably derived from Sanvito's exemplar (I owe this information to Professor de la Mare). For Sanvito and his work, see A. Fairbank, 'Bartolomeo San Vito', *Bulletin of the Society for Italic Handwriting*, 28 (1961), 12-13, and *Journal of the Society for Italic Handwriting*, 37 (1963), 14-19; Fairbank, 'More of San Vito', *Journal of the Society for Italic Handwriting*, 42 (1965), 6-12; J. Wardrop, *The Script of Humanism. Some Aspects of Humanistic Script 1450-1560* (1963), pp. 19-35; Alexander and de la Mare, pp. 105-9; *The Painted Page: Italian Renaissance Book Illumination 1450-1550* [Catalogue of an Exhibition held at The Royal Academy of Arts, London, and the Pierpont Morgan Library, New York, 27 October 1994 – 7 May 1995], ed. J.J.G. Alexander (1994), nos 7, 26, 38-39, 41, 43, 71-75, and 77; and A. de la Mare, 'Bartolomeo Sanvito da Padova, copista e miniatore', *La miniatura a Padova dal medioevo al Settecento* [Catalogue of an Exhibition held at the Palazzo della Ragione, Padua and the Palazzo del Monte, Accademia dei Concordi, 21 March – 27 June 1999], ed. G. Baldassin Molli, G. Canova Mariani, and F. Toniolo (1999), pp. 495-511. Bound by the 'Sanvito binder', on whom see A. Hobson, *Humanists and Bookbinders. The Origins and Diffusion of the Humanistic Bookbinding, 1459-1559* (1989), pp. 79-86; the present MS is no. 5 in his list of the binder's work.

Arms of Cardinal Raffaello Riario (cr. 1477, d. 1521) in the lower border of fol. 1. Sanvito produced another volume of Cicero's works for the Cardinal, now New York, Pierpont

Morgan Library, M. 882. Written on the pastedown of the lower cover of the binding of the present MS is:
'P
TV
Mi dai tormento'
MMBL, I: 391; Exh., *Universal Penman*, no. 60; Whalley, *Pen's Excellencie*, pp. 126-27 illus. fols 72, 121 (enlarged).
Pl. 225

200 V & A L. 366-1956   *1471 [Mantua, Italy]*
Lucanus, Pharsalia

Parch. 106 fols. 232 × 115 mm. 1 col., 162 × 58 mm. 38 lines. 3 painted medallions, the central one with shield (fol. 1), illum. inits, rubrics. Bld-tooled leather bdg with 4 bosses on each cover and clasps with red velvet thongs, and gilt-edge leaves.

Fol. 106: 'Finitus est per me Magistrum Johannem franciscum genuesium artium doctorem die 20 octobris 1471 \Niuiolarii/'. Elsewhere the scribe signs and dates the MS in red, establishing that fols 51ᵛ-106 were written in four months. Thus fol. 51 (end of Book V): 'Finis per me Johannem Franciscum genuesium de Mantua die 19 Junii 1471'; fol. 62: 'Septimus liber Lucani Incipit die 27 Augusti 1471'; fol. 85: 'M. Anei Lucani pharsaliae liber nonus incipit 1471 15 octobris'; and fol. 99: 'Decimus liber Pharsalie lucanj incipit die 18 octobris 1471'. The MS is in a faded brown ink. The initials are probably by one of a team of illuminators focused on the Gonzaga court (cf. A.C. de la Mare and C. Reynolds, 'Illustrated Boccaccio manuscripts in Oxford libraries', *Studi sul Boccaccio*, 20 (1991), p. 55). The binding provides one of the earliest extant examples of edge-gilding, for which technique see J.A. Szirmai, *The Archaelogy of Medieval Bookbinding* (1999), p. 202.

Unidentified coat of arms on fol. 1. The flyleaf bears an erased *ex libris*: '<Cornelij pignei a …>' (s. xvi).
MMBL, I: 392; Exh., *Universal Penman*, no. 59; Whalley, *Pen's Excellencie*, p. 114 illus. fol. 42ᵛ and colophon fol. 106 (reduced).
Pl. 186

201 V & A L. 1964-1957   *1550 Rome, Italy*
Victor Brodeau, Traicté à la louenge à Dieu

Parch. 31 fols. 194 × 134 mm. 1 col., 130 × c.90 mm. 14 lines. Decorated title page (fol. 2ᵛ), hist. inits and full-page border (fol. 3), gold inits. Gold-tooled leather bdg, ties gone (s. xvi).

Fol. 2ᵛ (in a cartouche): 'Ce present traicté à la louenge de Dieu, fut faict & compose par M. Victor Brodeau, Conseillier et Secretaire de madame Marguerite de France, soeur vnicque du roy Francoys premier de ce nom, et royne de Nauarre. Escript à Rome, l'an Iubilé du .1550.', surmounted by the arms of Claude d'Urfé. Another cartouche, fol. 30, encloses the colophon: 'Escript pour Monseigneur Claude d'Vrfé, cheualier de l'ordre, et gouuerneur de Mo*n*seigneur le Daulphin, Conseillier du roy & son Ambassadeur au s*aint* siege apostol*ique*'. Fols 30ᵛ-31ᵛ blank. The scribe also wrote San Marino, Henry E. Huntington Library, HM 1102 for Claude d'Urfé, which he dated Rome 1549, and signed 'Franc. Wydon'; other MSS by him are Chantilly, Musée Condé 102 (1398), signed and dated 1544 (*MSS datés*, I: 9) and (unsigned) Paris, BN n.a. lat. 1506, datable

1556 (*MSS datés*, IV: 187). In the Chantilly MS he calls himself 'britannus' which L. Dorez, *Le psautier de Paul III* (1909), p. 24 n. 2, interprets as 'Breton'. The typescript catalogue suggests the present volume was probably bound by the so-called 'Canevari bindery', but on this bindery see now A.R.A Hobson, *Apollo and Pegasus. An Enquiry into the Formation and Dispersal of a Renaissance Library* (1975).

Item 39 in A. Vernet's catalogue of 'La bibliothèque de Claude d'Urfé', *Claude d'Urfé et la bâtie: l'univers d'un gentilhomme de la Renaissance*, Catalogue of an Exhibition held at the Musée d'Allard, Montbrison, 1990, pp. 198-92, 198-208 (previously unlisted in Vernet's 'Les manuscrits de Claude d'Urfé (1501-1558) au Château de la Bastie', *Académie des Inscriptions et Belles-Lettres: Comptes Rendus* (1976), 81-97).

> Exh., *Universal Penman*, no. 56; Whalley, *Pen's Excellencie*, pp. 136-37 illus. fols 25 (enlarged), 30.
> *Pl. 260*

202 Wellcome 5, fols 3-119   *1580 [Vercelli, Italy]*

Petrus Advocatus a Quinto, 'Super genituram Francisci Mariae Advocati a Quinto'

Paper. 118 fols, foliated 3-74 [74bis], 75-119. 260 × 175 mm. 1 col., 165 × c.100 mm. 20-22 lines. Pen and ink horoscopes. Limp vellum bdg. from fragment of s. xiii MS.

The future life of the writer's son is foretold, ending fol. 119: 'Anno 1580 expletum amnio tamen reuidendi et emendand' si quid erratum [deletion] offendero Cuius rei gratia computationes et etiam causas aliquando iudicijs inserui Compendia autem et conclusiones eorum que dicta sunt ad cuiusius [*sic*] intelligentiam Deo dante non differam Finis'. The writer describes himself as of 'Vercelli'. Fol. 119ᵛ contains brief notes on the births of 4 other children, added 1581, 1582, 1583 and 1586; fols 1-2 and 120-29ᵛ blank. Fols 130-37 contain further astrological items by the same hand. Fol. 3: 'Ex Bibliotheca Conuentus Sancti Francisci Vercellarum'.

> Moorat, p. 5.
> *Pl. 285*

203 Wellcome 6, fols 1-12   *1471 [Low Countries]*

Adalbertus, Liber de vita et de gestis sancti Heinrici imperatoris et confessoris

Paper. 12 fols. 200 × 145 mm. 1 col., 149 × 93 mm. 32 lines. Col. inits, rubrics.

Fol. 12ᵛ (in the same hand as the text and underlined in red): '¶egidij abbatis 1473'. Fols 13-22 (containing Gerson, De pollutionibus diurnis, ending abruptly) by a different scribe are undated.

> Moorat, p. 5; *MMBL*, I: 394.
> *Pl. 185*

204 Wellcome 11   *1374 [Germany]*

Commentarius in librum Alberti Magni de secretis mulierum

Paper. 56 fols. 290 × 210 mm. 1 col.,197 × c.125 mm. 38-40 lines. Col. inits (fols, 1, 2ᵛ only), rubric.

Fol. 55: 'amen et sic est finis huius operis anno Mⁿ cccⁿ lxxiiijᵗᵒ'. Fols 55ᵛ-56ᵛ blank.

> Moorat, pp. 7-8.
> *Pl. 62*

205 Wellcome 12, fols 34-98   *1450 [Germany]*

Albertus Magnus, De causis et processu universitatis

Paper. 65 fols. 288 × 208 mm. 2 cols, 210 × 135 mm. 55-58 lines. Col. inits, rubrics. Bld-stamped leather bdg over boards, clasps gone (s. xv ex).

Fol. 98ᵛ (underlined in red): 'Et sic finitur liber de causis et processu vniuersitatis a prima causa Per fratrum albertum de ordine predicatorum editus scriptus et completus Anno domini .M.CCCC. et .lⁿ.', then in red 'Deo Gracias'. The rest of the volume, fols 1-33, 99-197, 198-257 and 258-93, all by the same scribe, was probably written about the same time. He foliated fols 99-293 as fols 1-198 (fol. 100, probably blank, wanting). Fol. 293ᵛ (largely erased): 'Dit boech hoert to meyster march (?) braegel [...] to Colne wonende to dem dorne op der brugghen'. O 53 in s.xvii shelf list of the Charterhouse of St Barbara, Cologne (see R.B. Marks, *The Medieval Manuscript Library of the Charterhouse of St Barbara in Cologne*, Analecta Cartusiana, 21 (1974), p. 405).

> Moorat, pp. 8-9; *MMBL*, I: 394; Kramer, I: 431.
> *Pl. 135*

206 Wellcome 15   *1408 Montpellier, France*

Questiones in octo libros physicorum Aristotelis

Paper. 130 fols. 287 × 216 mm. 2 cols, 227 × c.155 mm. 46-48 lines. Col. inits. Wooden boards, part covered with bld-tooled leather bdg.

Fol. 130: '¶ Expliciunt questiones phisicorum operis maioris alberti ¶ qui scripsit scribat semper cum domino viuat ¶ Johannes vocatur qui scripsit benedicatur ¶ questiones has frater Johannes de manga ordinis beate virginis marie de monte carmeli st<uden>te in phisica. scripssit in conventu montespesulanj propria manu . conventus tholeti prouincie yspanie .25. die Marcij Anno domini Mⁱ CCCC viij'. Fol. 130ᵛ (at foot of page): 'Iste liber est ad vsum fratris francisci domini de bagulio'; above 'Iste liber est ad usum Fratris Johannij baudi conuentus pinerolii [Pinerolo, Italy]' (s. xv ex). A third inscription at the top of the page has been erased.

> Moorat, p 11; *MMBL*, I: 394.
> *Pl. 80*

207 Wellcome 16   *1437 [Bubeneč, Czech Republic]*

Siegmund Albich, Regimen sanitatis; etc.

Paper. 69 fols. 205 × 145 mm. 2 cols, 145 × 105 mm. 30-31 lines. Col. inits, rubrics. Bld-tooled red leather bdg over boards, 2 strap- and pin-fastenings gone, 2 bosses only remaining (on lower cover).

Fol. 66: 'Reuerendissime pater et domine gratiose hunc libellum paruum licet compendiosum paternitati vestre offero tamque patri in domino meo carissimo. Hinricus de geismaria Prior canonicus in buben [Bubeneč, near Prague, Czech Republic] Cappellanus paternitatis vestre deuotissimus Anno domini mⁿ ccccⁿ xxxvijⁿ'. The colophon at the end of the Regimen sanitatis (fol. 15ᵛ, in red) reads: 'Anno domini mⁿ ccccxxijⁿ hec collegit reuerendissimus dominus Albicus [archbishop of Prague 1411-

12, d. 1427] in wrat'. Moorat, pp. 11-12, took this to mean the MS was dated 1422-1437 but the 1422 date is also found in Munich, Bayerische Staatsbibliothek, Clm 14526 (cf. H.J. Weitz, 'Albich von Prag: eine Untersuchung seiner Schriften', Inaug.-Diss., Univ of Heidelberg, 1970, p. 96). A copy of Albich's text nearly contemporary with that in the present MS was produced at 'Wratislauie' in 1436 (Vienna, Österreich-ischen Nationalbibliothek, Cod. 5512, for which see *Die datierten Handschriften der Österreichischen National-ibliothek*, 5 vols (1969-81), II: 147-48). 'Wratislauie' is gener-ally taken to be Breslau (now Wrocław, Poland) but Professor Flood has suggested Bratislava, Slovak Republic, is more prob-able (and cf. Weitz, p. 75). Fols 66ᵛ-69ᵛ blank. Fols i and 70, originally pastedowns, are s. xii.

Fol. 2: 'Inscriptus Catalogo Fratrum de Oliua [the Cistercian abbey of Oliva, now Oliwa, near Gdańsk]'.

E. Schultheiss, 'Über die Werke des Albicus. Ein Beitrag zur spätmittelalterlichen medizinischen Handschriften-kunde', *Janus*, 49 (1960), 228; Weitz, 'Albich von Prag', p. 76; Kramer, I: 639.

Pl. 112

208 **Wellcome 17 + 781**   *1462, 1463 Padua and Asolo, Italy*

Petrus de Tussignano, Ordinatione receptarum; Albucasis, Liber servitoris, in the translation of Abraham Judaeus Tortuosienis

Paper. 40 and 51 fols respectively. 300 × 205 mm. 2 cols, 202 × 139 mm. 36-37 lines. Col. inits, rubrics.

Two booklets, now bound separately, but originally part of the same volume. Wellcome 781 is the earlier, cf. fol. 51ᵛ: 'Finis receptarum magistri petri de tusignano. quas ego karolus guarnarinus patauus scripsi die .7°. mensis aprilis .1462. in ciuitate Pad'. Wellcome 17 concludes fol. 38: 'Explicit liber seruitoris quem ego karlus de Guarnarinis scripsi et expleui die .iij°. mensis nouembris .1463. asillo [Asolo, north of Padua]'; fols 38ᵛ-40b blank. The scribe also wrote Udine, Bibl. Arcivescovile 83, in Padua in 1458 (for which see *Manoscritti in Scrittura Latina in Biblioteche Friulane Datati o Databili*, ed. G.M. del Basso (1986), p. 103 and pl. [68]).

Moorat, pp. 12 and 576.

Pl. 164

209 **Wellcome 19**   *1332, 1335 Vicenza, Italy*

Albumasar, Opera; etc.

Parch. 100 fols. 290 × 210 mm. 2 cols, 227 × 140 mm. 46-48 lines. Gold and col. inits, rubrics. Tables and diagrms.

Three booklets, all written by the same scribe. The earliest is bound as fols 95-108 dated fol. 107ᵛ: 'Finitus .1332. Indictione .15. die .18. Jullij in ciuitate .vincencie.'; fol. 108 blank. Next was the present fols 79-94, dated fol. 94ᵛ: 'Explectus .in .1332. Indictione .15. die .20. Jullij'. The third (fols 5-20 + 29-78, fols 21-28 being supply leaves) is dated fol. 78ᵛ (in red): 'Hic est finis libri Introductorij maioris in magisterio sciencie iudicio-rum Astrorum e dictione Albumasar et interpretacione Johannis yspalensis ex arabico in latinum. Amen. Guidotus cyrugicus de ciuitate Vincencie hoc scripsit Et expleueit Anno a natiuitate christi currente 1335 die mercurij .18. octubris'. Many of the leaves have been repaired with parchment strips cut from

another MS.

Supply leaves (fols 1-4 and 21-28) are in the hand of 'Allesandro Padoani' whose *ex libris* is on fol. 5 and who anno-tates the MS throughout (s. xvii). He also owned no. 136 above and nos 259, 272 below.

Moorat, pp. 13-14.

Pl. 51

210 **Wellcome 31**   *1390 Paris, France*

Aldobrandino da Siena, Le régime du corps

Parch. 91 fols. 220 × 160 mm. 1 col., 148 × 105 mm. 29-30 lines. Illum. hist. inits and full-page borders (fols 1, 2ᵛ), gold inits, rubrics.

Fol. 89ᵛ: 'Pour messire Hugues de Saluces Escript a Paris lan de grace Mil CCC iiijˣˣ et dix le lundi xxᵉ Jour de mars *par* la main a Jehan Quatredens escouli*er* a paris'. Fols 90-91ᵛ by the same hand contain added receipts.

Moorat, pp. 19-20; L. MacKinney, *Medical Illustrations in Medieval Manuscripts* (1965), p. 144, no. 94.2; R.H. Rouse and M.A. Rouse, *Manuscripts and their makers: commercial book producers in medieval Paris 1200-1500*, 2 vols (2000), II: 84.

Pl. 66

211 **Wellcome 40**   *[betw. 1463 & 1481] [England]*

Kalendarium, etc.

Parch. 7 fols. 270 × 175 mm (135 × 45 mm when folded). 1 col., 110 × 28 mm. Up to 32 lines. Col. drawings, col. inits, rubrics.

Folded into parch. cover with tab for suspending from a girdle. The date 1463, which Moorat gives (p. 26), appears on the cover in faded modern Arabic numbers. However, a table of lunar and solar eclipses on fol. 6 runs from 1463 to 1481; the first of four 19-year cycles (unmarked) also begins 1463. Text is written on the recto of a leaf only; each leaf is then folded in half and again into three, with the verso outside. After it was folded, each leaf's content was noted on the uppermost fold of its verso so that a brief title could be read when the book was suspended from the owner's girdle. For a description of such a MS, see C.H. Talbot, 'A mediaeval physician's vade-mecum', *Jnl of the History of Medicine*, 16 (1961), 213-33. F. Wallis, 'Medicine in medieval calendar manuscripts', *Manuscript Sources of Medieval Medicine: A Book of Essays*, ed. M.R. Schleissner (1995), p. 139 n. 41, adds the present MS to Talbot's example.

Moorat, p. 40; L. MacKinney, *Medical Illustrations in Medieval Manuscripts* (1965), p. 144 no. 94. 4.

Pl. 166

212 **Wellcome 55**   *1472, 1473, 1474 Leipzig, Germany*

Aristoteles, Analytica posteriora; etc

Paper. 203 fols. 305 × c.210 mm. 1 col, 205 × 110 mm. 28 lines. Pen and ink drawing, fol. 93; col. inits, rubrics. Half bld-stamped leather bdg over boards, with remains of engraved metal catches. Paper label 'Scolastica<lia>' on upper cover, 'Scolas' written across fore-edge.

A collection of eight booklets written by Johann Lindner (c.1450-c.1530) while he was a student at Leipzig. Two are dated 1472, two 1473, and one 1474. Thus fols 49-83, ending fol. 83ᵛ: 'Deo gracias .1.4.7.2. in lipczk'; fols 101-48, ending fol. 148ᵛ (in a red scroll): 'Anno mᵒ ccccᵒ lxxijᵒ in lipczk'; fols 18-48, ending fol. 48ᵛ: 'Finit 2ᵘˢ posteriorum .1473. in lipczk . per Johannem lintner' de münchperg [Münchberg]'; fols 84-92, ending fol. 91ᵛ (in red and blue scroll): 'Finitus .1.4.7.3. in lipczk'; fols 199-203, ending fol. 203v (in red): '1474'. A sixth booklet (fols 148-98) was also partly written in 1473, cf. fol. 175v (in red): 'Anno .1.4.7.3. in lipczk'. Of the remaining two booklets, fols 1-17 ends imperfectly and fols 93-100 contains an added index to the 'Ethica' dated '.1.4.7.3ᵒ. in lipckz'.

Moorat, pp. 39-41; L. MacKinney, *Medical Illustrations in Medieval Manuscripts* (1965), p. 144 no. 94.6; *MMBL*, I: 395; P.M. Jones, *Medical Illustrations in Illuminated Manuscripts* (rev. edn, 1998), pp. 38-39 and fig. 27 illus. fol. 93 (reduced).
Pl. 190

213 **Wellcome 56, fols 335-361**   *1478 Meissen, Germany*

Questiones circa Analytica posteriora

Parch. 27 fols. 313 × 210 mm. 2 cols, 262 × c.145 mm. 60 lines. Space for init.

Fol. 361ᵛ: 'Anno domini 1478 die vero lune post oculi loco habitacionis sue burse myssnensis'. The volume is mainly in the hand of one scribe, apart from fols 197ᵛ-213 where a second hand has taken over for two and a half quires.
Rebound since the descriptions of Moorat, pp. 41-42, and Ker, *MMBL*, I: 395.
Pl. 203

214 **Wellcome 57**   *1526*

Disputationes in libros Aristotelis

Paper. 379 fols. 223 × 165 mm. 1 col., c.160 × 108 mm. Up to 48 lines. Limp vellum bdg formed from s. xv service book, ties gone.

Fol. 376ᵛ: 'Laus Deo .op. maximo 1526 17 Decembris'. The contemporary foliation shows the MS has been misbound as fols 1-60, 73-88, 61-72, 89-131 where the foliation ceases.
Moorat, p. 42.
Pl. 250

215 **Wellcome 71**   *1569 [England]*

Jenkyn Gwynne, Tyrocaesar, etc.

Paper. 40 fols. 270 × 208 mm. 1 col., 208 × 142 mm. 25-27 lines. Gold-tooled leather bdg, with remains of green silk ties.

Fol. 4ᵛ (end of the dedicatory epistle): 'Your honors most humbly at commaundement 1569 Jenkyn Gwynne'. The epistle, contained in a preliminary quire, is addressed 'To the Right honorable Syr Wa[lter] Myldmay Knight Chauncellor of the Quenes maiesties highe Courte of Escheaquer [1559-89], and Threasurour of the same, one of her highnes most honorable pryueye Counsaill, your humble orator Jenkin Gwynne, one of the particuler Surueyours of the same Courte, and seruante to the right honorable Earle of penbroke ...'. Among Gwynne's prophecies (fols 22-40) is one (fol. 39) foretelling the conversion of the Jews in 1926 with the sidenote 'yet to come 356 yeres'.

Moorat, p. 48; M.A. Manzalaoui, *Tyrocaesar: a manual

for Sir Walter Mildmay', *Manuscripta*, 19 (1975), 27-35; *Secretum Secretorum: Nine English Versions*, ed. M.A. Manzalaoui, EETS OS 276 (1977), pp.xliii-xliv.
Pl. 271

216 **Wellcome 93, fols 102-20**   *1524 [Germany]*

'Von den verdeülichen artzneien aller seücte'

Paper. 19 fols, foliated in red 41-57. 155 × 95 mm. 1 col, up to 125 × 60 mm. Up to 28 lines. Headings in red and blue.

Fol. 120ᵛ: 'Amen 1524'. This physician's handbook, rebound since the description by Moorat (p. 64), is too tightly bound to determine the collation. However, the core of the MS is evidently fols 60-360, written by a single scribe and foliated by him in red 'i' to 'CC79' (fols 102-20 were thus originally fols 41-57; leaf omitted between fols 48 and 49). Coloured drawings of urine flasks occur on fols 67ᵛ-87ᵛ. Fols 1-56 are by other hands; fols 57-59 blank.

L. MacKinney, *Medical Illustrations in Medieval Manuscripts* (1965), p. 144, no. 94.8; P.M. Jones, *Medical Illustrations in Illuminated Manuscripts* (rev. edn, 1998), pp. 96-97 and fig. 88. illus. fol. 48ᵛ.
Pl. 248

217 **Wellcome 106**   *1494 [Germany]*

Avicenna, Liber medicinalis

Paper. 132 fols. 210 × 150 mm. 1 col., 160-67 × c.100 mm. 32-35 lines. Col. inits and rubrics fols 1-35, 79-87 and 110ʳˉᵛ only, otherwise spaces left blank. Limp vellum cover with leather spine; title 'Liber Medicinalis' on upper cover.

Fol. 129: 'Amen anno 94ᵒ'. Although the '14' has been omitted, it is evident from the appearance of the handwriting that the intended date was 1494. Fols 129ᵛ-32 contain added recipes. An index has been supplied by a later hand on the inside of the lower cover.
The centre of each quire has been reinforced by a parchment strip; these strips were cut from two different MSS, one with German text.
Moorat, pp. 70-71.
Pl. 224

218 **Wellcome 111, fols 1-274**   *1583-1585 [Perugia, Italy]*

Giovanni Battista Baffi, In Avicennae Fen primam libri quarti

Paper. 278 fols, foliated [i], 1-161 [161 bis], 162-231 [231 bis], 232-33, [233 bis], 234-74. 285 × 210 mm. 1 col., 210 × c.145 mm. 30 lines.

Fol. 274: 'Completum opus Die iiij Augusti siue iij Nonas Augustas 1585 quo die Beati Dominici confessoris festum celebratur, et occeptum fuerat anno 1583. Martis mense. Curinalti', fol. 274ᵛ blank. Baffi, a professor at Perugia, was born at Corinaldo. The MS, which is heavily corrected, is clearly his holograph. Fols 279-306ᵛ contain an index, and fols 307-10 an address to the reader; fols 307-14 left blank. A loose bifolium contains a poem in praise of Baffi's work by Sebastiano Macci (d. 1615).
Wellcome 112, also in Baffi's hand, is datable from a passing reference in the text to 1595; he died 1596.

Moorat, pp. 74-74.
Pl. 290

219 Wellcome 117, pp. 1-207   *1462 [Florence, Italy]*

Bartolomeus de Ripa Romea, De lapidus; etc.

Parch. 104 fols, paginated 1-207. 160 × 105 mm. 1 col., 148 × 64 mm. 39 lines. Pen and ink drawings, rubrics.

Pp. 206-7 (in red): 'Et ego Bartolomeus Marcellus Abiat cirra furtim hoc exemplum ex bisticij corrosis ac fumo tinctis codicibus excerpsi et diebus 8 octo transscripsi currenti admodum calamo quare quicumque leges si emendosum Inuenies non me sed temporis angustiam et exemplar ab aurifice scriptum culpabis nihil tamen deficere scito quod te quicumque sis sicut bisticium medicum ex aurifice [Jacopo da Bisticci, *c.*1413-68] facere possit VALE 1462 septembris xxvii'. For Jacopo, physician, goldsmith, and elder brother of Vespasiano, see G.M. Cagni, *Vespasiano da Bisticci e il suo epistolario* (1969), pp. 11-46. The rest of the volume is contemporary but further colophons, pp. 240 and 274, are restorations by a hand of s. xvi
Moorat, pp. 79-82.
Pl. 162

220 Wellcome 119, fols 9-49   *1429 [Germany]*

Tract on herbal remedies, in German

Parch. 41 fols. 278 × *c.*175 mm. 1 col., *c.*210 × 130 mm. 38-43 lines. Col. inits, rubrics.

Fol. 49ᵛ (in red): 'Anno domini 1429 sabato proximo ante festum natiuitatis gloriose virginis marie. Finis adest fere scriptor vult precium habere [1st of 6 lines of macaronic rhymes] Si melius scripssissem nomen meum imposuissem Vero male scribo nomen meum imponere nolo Deo gracias Amen'. Fols 1-8 and 50-59 are by other hands.
A mutilated legal document (in German), dated 1547, bound in at the end of the volume probably once formed the parchment wrapper.
Moorat, pp. 82-83.
Pl. 102

221 Wellcome 120, fols 5-168 and 171-238   *1442*
[S. Germany or Austria]

Liber medicinalis primus, in German; etc.

Paper. 232 fols. 282 × 198 mm. 1 col., *c.*210 × 120-30 mm. 25-29 lines. Col. inits, rubrics.

Fol. 168ᵛ (in red): 'Das puech hat ein ende Got vns zu den ewign freyden nemen vnd das [pue] edel erciney puech hat schreibn lazzen der Edel vnd vest Ritter herre hans der hofkircher vnd ist vollendt warn des Samstag vor dem heilign weinachtag als man zalt anno domini mᵒ cccc vnd in dem xlij jar iorg schreiber hat es geschribn ...'; fols 169-71 are by a different hand, then the main scribe resumes fol. 171ᵛ (in red): 'Hie hebt sich an ein anders edell Erczney puech vnd hat Gedicht Ein maister der hies partholomeus vnd ist das erczney puech angehebt warn an dem heiligen weinacht aben vnd sagt uns Von manigerlay als man Zahzt [*sic*] nach Kristy Gepurd mᵒ c.c.c.c. xlij iare', and copies up to fol. 238. Fols 1-3 and 239-50 contain indexes by another hand, while fol. 4 was inserted later. The orthography shows the MS was written by a scribe from Southern Germany (Bavaria) or Austria (*ex info.* Professor J. Flood).

The limp parchment binding bears on the upper cover the initials 'C S D D K' and below the date '1650'.
Moorat, pp. 83-84.
Pl. 118

222 Wellcome 125   *1516 [Germany]*

Heinrich Bebel, Historia horarum canonicorum de S. Hieronymo.

Paper. 18 fols. 196 × 143 mm. 1 col., 155 × *c.*100 mm. Up to 29 lines. Col. inits, rubrics. Unbound.

Fol. 18: '... Mentem ad sublimia deumque pro viribus erigito. 1516.' For Bebel, see K. Graf, 'Heinrich Bebel (1472-1518). Wider ein barbarisches Latein', *Humanismus im deutschen Südwesten. Biographische Profile*, ed. P.G. Schmidt (1993), pp. 179-94. The MS was perhaps copied from the edition printed by Erhard Ratdolt, 1512 (for which see *Verzeichnis der im deutschen Sprachbereich erschienenen Drucke des XVI. Jahrhunderts: VD 16*, ed. I. Bezzel (1983-), II: B. 1184; IV C. 4071, and cf. J.G.T. Graesse, *Trésor de libres rare et précieux ou nouveau dictionnaire bibliographique*, 7 vols (1922), I: 319).
Moorat, pp. 86-87.
Pl. 246

223 Wellcome 128   *1487 Ferrara, Italy*

Astrologica

Paper. 25 fols. 205 × 150 mm. 1 col., *c.*135 × 85 mm. 26-29 lines. Space left for inits, rubrics fols 1-13 only. Pen and ink diagrms fols 14-25.

Two booklets both written by the same scribe. The first (fols 1-13) concludes fol. 11ᵛ: 'Anno .1487. die 28 mensis Julij conscriptus est liber iste per me Ro. bo. scriptorem ferrariensem'; fols 12-13 are blank. The second (fols 14-25) is dated two days later, fol. 17, 'Expliciunt imagines signorum contra infirmitates corporis hominis secundum picatricis libro .2°. et hoc die .30. mensis Julij 1487', and again fol. 23ᵛ: 'Explectus est libellus iste die .30. Julij 1487. ferrariae. per me Ro. bo. scriptus'; fols 24-25 blank. Annotations are by two later hands.
Moorat, pp. 88-89.
Pl. 215

224 Wellcome 130   *[1330?] [France]*

Bernardus de Gordonio, Lilium medicinae

Parch. 145 fols. *c.*335 × 260 mm. 2 cols, 260 × 183 mm. 58-62 lines. Dec. init. and border fol. 1, col. inits, rubrics.

Fol. 1, col. 1, lines 36-39: 'Incohatus est liber iste cum auxilio dei magni in preclaro studio montispesulani post annum .20. lecture nostro anno domini m. ccc. 30 in mense iulij'. The scribe has apparently adapted the wording of Bernard's prologue so that the date reads 1330 rather than 1303, the date of the text's composition (for which see L. Demaitre, *Doctor Bernard de Gordon: Professor and Practitioner* (1980), pp. 31 n. 164, 51-59). Y. O'Neill ('Dates in the Printed Editions of the Lilium Medicinae', *Sudhoffs Archiv*, 49 (1965), 87) has suggested that '30' was a mistake for '3°'. The MS has been heavily annotated throughout in s. xv, including references to patients; among such annotations are fol. 67ᵛ 'Hac passus est Petrus Martinus de Monticulo [Monchel, Pas de Calais]' and 'Hec uidi in vxore iacobi Mocioni de Belesio [Bilzen, Low Countries]'. The parchment is very yellow and heavily stained by damp.

Moorat, pp. 90-91; Demaitre, p. 186.

Pl. 50

225 Wellcome 157   *1579, 1580 Nuremberg, Germany*

Sigismund Bröll, 'Ein Künstliches vnnd bewerthes Artzneybüch'

Paper. 209 fols. *c.*330 × 205 mm. 1 col., *c.*300 × 170 mm. 36-40 lines. Cut-leather bdg, with ties.

Five booklets (pp. 1-72, 73-136, 137-232, 233-328, 329-418) each of them dated at its head. Thus p.1: 'Laus Deo Anno Christj 1579 denn 30 Nouember Sigmundtus Broll in Nuremberg'; p. 73: 'Anno Dominij 1579 ... 9 December In Nurinberg Sigismundtws Bröll'; p. 137: 'Anno domini 1579 ... 25 December In Nurinberg Sigmundtws Broll'; p. 233: 'Anno Domininij [sic] 1580 ... Primo Februarij ... Beschriben durch Mich Sigmundtws Bröll'; p. 329: 'Anno Dominj 1580 ... 18 Februarij'. The book passed to Sigismund's son who added his signature on pp.1 and 73 ('Johannes Bröll eius filius'), supplied a title page 'Ein künstliches vnnd bewerthes Artzneybüch allen güthertzigen frombenn Christen beschriben durch Sigmundum Bröllen', which he dated 'Anno christi .1601. Septimo Idus Novembris', and provided an index now imperfect (from F to Z only, pp. 419-26).

Moorat, p. 157.

Pl. 286

226 Wellcome 158   *1548 Rottweil, Germany*

Arzneibuch

Paper. 118 fols. 205 × 163 mm. 1 col., 130-35 × 102-10 mm. 20-21 lines. Bound in s. xv document.

Fol. 1 (title page): 'Item diss Büch Ist Hanns Brümmers von Rotwil vnd ist geschriben worden Im Jar 1548', then lined through but written by the same hand (*pace* Moorat, p. 194):

> 'Vrin dem schriber dreck dem lesser
> Von Mier Wolffgang wippler
> O wie fro ich was
> Do ich schrib deo gracias'.

The MS is again dated fol. 118: 'Laus Deo Hon Ich Wolffgang Wippler nit gut geschriben So hon ich aber die wyl vertriben 1548'. Wippler has also signed fol. 24ᵛ. Fol. 118ᵛ blank. The document used as a binding is dated 1470 and mentions 'Jorigen von Bundelsingen freyherre'.

In the colophon on fol. 118ᵛ Wippler's name has been crossed out and a later hand has written in the margin 'daniel berckibel von Swikau [Zwickau]'. Title page: 'Jorgen Fechtens von görlitz' (s. xvi). A coat of arms, gules a cross argent, is blazoned on the title page.

Moorat, pp. 104-5.

Pl. 259

227 Wellcome 164   *[1416, 1417, 1419]*
[Constance, Germany]

Frater Ulmannus, Das Buch der heiligen Dreifaltigkeit

Paper. 208 fols. *c.*160 × 112 mm. 1 col., up to 150 × 90 mm. Up to 54 lines. Col. drawings fols 30, 82ᵛ, 99ᵛ, 141, diagrm fol. 67ᵛ, col. inits, rubrics. Bound in soiled parch. leaf (text indecipherable).

The MS, written by a single hand, is haphazardly put together, with many additions (some on inserted slips) and revisions to text by the scribe, with large parts crossed out. H. Buntz ('Das "Buch der heiligen Dreifaltigkeit": Sein Autor und seine Überlieferung', *Zeitschrift für deutsches Altertum und deutsches Literatur*, 101 (1972), 150-60) seems overly cautious in characterizing as a fascinating hypothesis Moorat's suggestion (p. 108) that this is an author's holograph. Numerous changes of ink suggest the MS was written over a period of time, and dates occur throughout ranging from 1 August 1416 (fol. 59ᵛ, an inserted slip: 'Anno domini mᵒ ccccᵒ decimo 6ᵗᵒ In die saturni In die sancti petri vinculi geendet ist der heyligen driualtigkeit') to 11 June 1419 (fol. 183ᵛ, squashed lengthwise into the margin: 'Geendet ist die exsposicion der gab des heiligen geistes clarificacionis gegeben vff dem sontag sancte trinitatis geendet in die veneris in hora solis Anno etc x[v]iiij 19ᵒ'). Twice the author indicates he was writing in Constance; thus fol. 68: 'In die Solis Sancti Anthonij in hora saturni finitus est In vnser lieben frawen kyrchen zu Costenz des andern Sonntages nach der heilig dreyer konigtag Anno domini Mᵒ ccccᵒ decimo 7ᵒ', and fol. 173 (in red, written over an erasure): 'Datum in constancia in ecclesia sancte marie Anno domini m cccc decimo septimo'). He also informs us a copy was made for the Emperor Sigismund, who took a key role in the Council of Constance (1414-18), see fol. 39 (squashed onto the bottom of the page): 'Disses buchs ein aussgeschrifft hat der majestät konig von vngern Keyser Sigmund [king of Hungary, 1387-1437, and emperor, 1410-37] entpfangen zu Constancie in den heiligen consilio in sein haus von dem S' Junckffrawen ort'. A second version of the work was produced in 1433 (ed. U. Junker, *Das 'Buch der heiligen Dreifaltigkeit' in seiner zweiten, alchemistischen Fassung (Kadolzburg 1433)*, Kölner medizinhistorische Beiträge, 40 (1986)).

Moorat, pp. 106-9; H. Frühmorgen-Voss and N.H. Ott, *Katalog der deutschsprachigen illustrierten Handschriften des Mittelalters*, I (1986-91), no. 2.1.5 and pl. 6 illus. drawing fol. 99ᵛ; M. Pereira, 'Alchemy and the use of vernacular languages in the late Middle Ages', *Speculum*, 74 (1999), 346.

Pl. 94

228 Wellcome 166   *1565 Augsburg, Germany*

Johann Bürtzel, 'Ein schönes vnd bewertes Artzneybuch'

Paper. 202 fols. 293 × 195 mm. 1 col., 170-87 × 100-5 mm. Up to 28 lines. Rubrics.

Title page (heading in red and black): 'Ein schönes vnd bewertes Artzneybuch Darinnen Allerlay Leibs gebrechen . so an dem gantzen Leib seindt von dem haüpt Bisz Auff die Solen Innerlich vnnd Aüsserlich zugebrauchen zusamen getragenn durch Johann Bürtzeln Teutschen Schulmaistern zu Orinngew vnd Bürgern zu Augspurg. Anno .1563. vnnd geschriben Anno .1565.'

Moorat, p. 109.

Pl. 267

229 Wellcome 167, fols 1-111 and 164-253

*1464 Padua, Italy and
and 1470, 1472, 1473, 1474 Strasbourg, France*

Avicenna, Fen sexta quarti Canonis; etc

Paper. 201 fols, with medieval foliation. 383 × 277 mm.
2 cols. Fols 1-111: 235 × 170 mm, 60 lines; fols 164-203:
240 × 170 mm, 60 lines; fols 204-53: 255 × 160 mm.
52 lines. Col. inits throughout, rubrics fols 164-253 only.
Bld-tooled leather bdg over boards, with 1 of 2 clasps
remaining.

A collection of three booklets all written by the same scribe,
Hermannus Benedictus de Bulach (for whom see *Acta Graduum
Academicorum Gymnasii Patavini*, II. 2, ed. G. Pengo (1992),
nos 344, 426, 595). The earliest, fols 202-53, dated 1464, was
written while Bulach was at Padua, thus fol. 247 (in red):
'Expletus est Quartus liber canonis libri principis Abohaly
auicenj filij alybesenhy padue per manum Magistri hermanni
benedicti de bulach Medicine Scolarem die 11ᵃ mensis nouembris Anno domini Millesimo quadringentesimo sexagesimo
quarto'; fols 247ᵛ-48ᵛ containing a list of chapter headings are
undated, fols 249-53ᵛ blank. The next in date, fols 164-203, was
mainly written in 1470 after Bulach had moved to Strasbourg,
thus fol. 188ᵛ: '¶ Explicit dietarium magistri Stephani Arlandj ¶
Finitum per Egregium artis et medicine doctorem Magistrum
Benedictum Hermannum de Bulach ¶ Anno dominj mᵒ ccccᵒ
Septuagesimo 2ᵒ die mensis Julij Argentine [Strasbourg]'. The
third booklet, fols 1-111, also written in Strasbourg, is thrice
dated 1472, thus fol. 99ᵛ: 'Expliciunt Synomina Simonis
Januensis. Ad laude in dei altissimi et tocius curie celestis
triumphantis Argentine scriptum Anno dominj Millesim-
quadringentesimo [*sic*] Septuagesimo secundo Vicesimatercia
februarij que fuit Dominica Reminiscere Per egregium artis et
medicine doctorem Magistrum Benedictum hermannum De
Bulach'; fol. 103ᵛ: 'Expliciunt synomina Mesue breviter
collecta et scripta Per egregium artis et medicine doctorem
Benedictum hermannum de Bulach. Anno domini mᵒ ccccᵒ lxxijᵒ
die uero quarta Marcij'; and fol. 106ᵛ: 'Scriptum Argentine
Anno domini Mᵒ ccccᵒ Septuagesimo secundo .12. mensis
marcij Per egregium Benedictum hermannum de Bulach artis et
medicine doctorem'; fols 107ᵛ-11ᵛ blank. A fourth booklet, fols
112-63, is undated. Finally Bulach made additions to fols 164-
203 dated 1473 and 1474 respectively, thus fol. 197ᵛ: '1473 14
Februarij .d.b.h.b' and fol. 201ᵛ: '1474ᵒ 17 mensis Marcij Per
.do. be. he. bulach', leaving fols 202-3ᵛ blank.

The pastedown inside the upper cover of the binding, part of a
notarial document dated 1400, relates to the election of Baptista
Panochiatis (Panoyiatis) as a beadle at the University of Padua
(for him see *Acta Graduum Academicorum Gymnasii Patavini*,
ed. G. Zonta and J. Brotto, 3 vols (1970) I: *passim*). Pastedowns
inside the lower cover, fragments of two documents, dated 1465
and 1473, relate to the collegiate church of St-Pierre-le-jeune,
Strasbourg.

Moorat, pp. 110-12; Kramer, I: 749.
Pl. 187

230 Wellcome 174 *1529 [Legnano, Italy]*

Gasparo di Cagali, Libro di ricette medicinali

Paper. 80 fols. 175 × 115 mm. 1 col., 140 × 85 mm. Up to
30 lines. Pen and ink drawings. Limp vellum bdg with ties,
coat of arms in pen and ink and inits 'G C' on upper cover.

Inside the upper cover is written: 'Questo libero sie di .mᵒ.
gasparo barbero e ceroicho che fu fioli de mᵒ antonjo ceroicho
da legnago di chagalij … e questo libro fo scrito adj 15. agosto
1529'. The date is also given on the front of the cover: 'Questo
libro sie de [me] gasbaro barbero et ciroicho filio che fu de mᵒ a.
di cagalij da lig[nago] ciroicho adi .15. agosto .1529.' The writer
jots down personal memoranda including the birth of his son,
Antonio, in 1530 (fol. 80ᵛ) and, on the inside of the front cover,
that of his daughter, 'Chatelina', in 1527, and the names of their
godparents. The marginal drawing of a dragon (see pl.) is
characteristic of MSS from the Veneto [*ex info.* Professor de la
Mare].

Moorat, p. 114.
Pl. 251

231 Wellcome 187 *1474 Verona, Italy*

'Opus naturae rerum compendiosum'

Parch. 102 fols. 195 × 130 mm. 1 col., 30 × 85 mm. 3-6
lines. Text written in red and black. Large blank spaces left
for illustrations.

Fol. 1ᵛ (at the top of the page in the hand of the scribe):
'M CCCC LXXIIII Codex Ludouici de [Cendratis] ciuis
Veronensis: qui nullum aliud nouit imperium: nisi Serenis-
simum uenetorum Dominium cum turba natorum numero
trigintaduorum ex vnico Matrimonio', fol. 1ʳ blank. The name
'Cendratis' has been tampered with. Most of each page is left
blank, presumably for illustrations of the plants, animals, etc.,
described in the text. An added index, fols 103-6, was supplied
in s. xvi.

Moorat, p. 120.
Pl. 194

232 Wellcome 202 *1443 [Germany]*

Computus

Paper. 22 fols. 202 × 142 mm. 1 col., 118-45 × 85-100 mm.
20-39 lines. Col. inits, rubrics. Diagrms.

Fol. 22ᵛ (enclosed in a red scroll): 'Explicit computus iudaicus
per manus Wilhellmi sub anno domini mᵒ cccc xljjj in die agathe
vigilii'.

According to a pencilled note (s. xix) on the flyleaf the MS
was bought from the Benedictine monastery of St Emmeram,
Regensburg, for which see M. Piendl, *Die Bibliotheken zu St.
Emmeram in Regensburg*, Thurn- und Taxis-Studien, 7 (1971).
Not listed among paper *quaterni* containing computus in the
late-medieval library catalogue (cf. *Mittelalterliche Bibliotheks-
kataloge Deutschlands und der Schweiz*, IV (1977), p. 139).

Moorat, p. 129; Kramer, I: 677.
Pl. 120

233 Wellcome 203, fols 93-152 *1459 [Pavia, Italy]*

Johannes de Concoregio, De curis febrium

Paper. 60 fols. 340 × 230 mm. 2 cols, c.225 × 150 mm. 49
lines. Col. inits, rubrics. Tawed leather bdg over boards,
clasps gone.

Fol. 152: 'Scripta per magistrum Bartolomeum de festorazijs
de belano et finita die primo maij 1459 2ᵒ anno Inceptionis mei
studij'. One of five booklets written by the same scribe but the
only one to be dated. The others are fols 1-90, 153-61, 162-71

and 172-78 (the latter imperfect). Fols 91-92 are a blank bifolium. On the bottom of the pastedown of the lower cover the scribe has noted 'Ego Magister Bartolomeus de festorazijs feci disputationem meam in medicinis die dominica octaua mensis Junij 1460 et fuit tercius annus mei studij et disputaui utrum pregnantes sint purgande et vtrum mulieres sint frigidiores viris et erat tunc rector papie dominus Magister Ant. Januensis etc'. This is presumably Antonio de Novis (elected rector 1432, according to *Memorie e documenti per la storia dell'Università di Pavia* (1878), I: *Serie dei Rettori e Professori con annotazioni*, p. 8). A further note records that in the following year '1461 feci quolibetum in medicina primo martij dubia fuerunt vtrum medicus aliquis debeat euacuare usque ad sincopim et vtrum in die crisis sit fienda euacuatio Factus fui doctor die 24 aprillis eodem anno ...'.

Moorat, pp. 129-31.
Pl. 151

234 **Wellcome 206, fols 1-61**   *1450 [Italy]*
Conselio de'poveri infirmi

Paper. 61 fols. 203 × 135 mm, medieval foliation 1-43 [43bis], 44-60. 1 col., 139 × 90 mm. 26 lines. Col. inits, rubrics. Incised leather bdg over boards, with clasps.

Fol. 1 (in red): '1450 die 7 octobris', in the hand of the scribe. The MS is written by the same hand to fol. 61. Thereafter, fols 62-73, originally blank, contain various additions, pen trials and jottings by other hands.
Fols 1 and 64: 'Ottauio Archt' and 'Ottauio Archiatro', Ottaviano Buccarini, physician to Pope Gregory XIV (1590-91), on whom see G. Marini, *Degli archiatri pontifici*, 2 vols (1784), I: 472. Fol. 72: 'Ego Jeronimus de Crispus' (s. xvi).

Moorat, pp. 132-33.
Pl. 136

235 **Wellcome 219**   *1575 Montargis, France*
'Les vertus de longuent'

Parch. 4 fols. 225 × 160 mm. 1 col., 170 × 110 mm. 20-23 lines. Sewn into parch. cover.

Fol. 3ᵛ: 'Escript a Argy [Montargis] le vingt neufieme jour de Janvier l'an 1575 Cotel'. The heading reads 'Sensuiuent les vertus de longuent qui a este faict et compose par Monsieur du son' and suggests this MS once formed part of a larger collection. A title 'Receptes de l'onguent de Boucart Aultrement dict Emplastre diuin' has been provided on the upper cover in s. xviii.

Moorat, pp. 138-39.
Pl. 278

236 **Wellcome 302**   *1559 Rome, Italy*
Ganimede Ispano, 'Opera quale se adimada secreta secretarum'

Paper. 74 fols. 215 × 142 mm. 1 col., c.180 × 120 mm. 19-21 lines. Limp parch bdg (from leaf of s. xiv MS).

Fol. 2: 'Adi :11: de avgusto ~ 1559 ~ Al nome del dio e della gloriosa vergin madre maria e di sancto pietro e di sancto pablo ... amen. questo libro eue [*sic*] di claudio Jouffroy borguinone in roma abuno prencipio et migliore fine dio le falcer Dio omnipotente eterne immense et immutabile el quale a la sato

le virtu nelle erbe nelle pietre nelle parole e di queste tre cose trattera la presente opera quale se adimada secreta secretarum magistri ganimedi ispani Recopiate per me Claudio Jouffroy borguinone'.
On fol. 1ᵛ a rough pen and ink drawing of a coat of arms (crown with 3 fleur de lis) does not, as suggested by Moorat, represent the arms of Jouffroy.

Moorat, p. 190.
Pl. 263

237 **Wellcome 309, pp. 191-93, 221-52, 322-28**
1572, 1575, 1576 Gottersdorff and Naumberg, Germany
Johann Gerlach, Libellus de creatione omnium rerum; etc, in German

Paper. 22 fols. 132 × 75 mm. 1 col., 98 × 49 mm. 25 lines.

The scribe has encoded most of the MS in a secret script (for the use of such scripts in alchemical writings, see F. Gettings, *Dictionary of Occult, Hermetic and Alchemical Sigils* (1981), pp. 231-34). However, some items in the present collection were written openly. Thus the 'Virtutes olei', pp. 191-93, is dated p. 193 (in red): 'Scriptum Gottersdorff in meo exilio apud pastorem Seuerinum Drescherum Anno Domini 1572 Die ♂ [Tuesday] 21 Octobris'. The 'Libellus de creatione omnium rerum', pp. 221-52 (16 fols), apparently took three days to write; thus it begins p. 221 'Libellus de creatione omnium rerum Anno 1575 Die 23 Augusti In der Naunburgk an der Sala', continues p. 238 'Anno 1575 24 Augusti', and ends p. 252 'Anno domini 1575 Die ♃ [Thursday] 25 Augusti'. At the head of each opening of the 'Libellus' is the running title 'Authore Johanne Girlachio'. Finally, the 'Lapis philosophorum', pp. 322-28, begins 'In Jhesu Christi nomine Amen Anno 1576 Die ♄ [Saturday] 25 Februarij'. Many leaves are left blank.
According to a note on the flyleaf the MS was originally bound in green velvet with a gold-stamped panel of the crucifixion and dated 1575 but the writer of the note (JB or JD, according to his monogram) has had it rebound in 1760.
P. 1: 'Daniel Crusius a k est in catalogo'(s. xvii); the words 'Crusius a k' have been rewritten.

Moorat, p. 196.
Pl. 279

238 **Wellcome 324-26**   *1505, 1508, 1510, 1514*
Nordhausen and Frankfurt an der Oder, Germany
Eberhard Guttenberger, Lectiones in primum librum primi canonis Avicennae; etc, in 3 vols.

Paper. MS 324 150 fols. c. 310 × 220 mm. 1 col., c. 255-60 × 145-60 mm. MS 325 186 fols, 350 × 220 mm. 1 col., c. 280 × 160 mm. MS 326 199 fols. 310 × 212 mm. 1 col., c. 245 × 130 mm. Up to 60 lines. All bound in bld-stamped half leather bdg over boards, with clasps. Titles on fore-edges: MS 324 'Prima primi de pulsu', MS 325 'Virtu et vrina', MS 326 '4ᵗᵃ primj'.

Three volumes of lectures written by Eberhard Guttenberger (first lecturer in the medical faculty of the University of Frankfurt an der Oder, founded 1502 and later physician of Joachim I, elector of Brandenburg 1484-1535), each volume being made up of three booklets: thus MS 324, fols 1-131, 132-72, and 173-91; MS 325, fols 1-70, 71-131, and 132-76; and MS 326, fols 1-190, 191-97, and 198-209. Although he left leaves blank, Guttenberger has made additions throughout on inserted slips (included in the foliation as fol. 2a, 6a, etc.). The earliest booklet to be dated (MS 324, fols 173-91) was written at Nordhausen, 1505; thus fol. 191ᵛ: 'Explicit commentariolum de peste … per Eberhardum Guttenberger de hallis: artium et vtriusque medicine doctorem tunc ipse phisicus Insignis et Imperialis ciuitatis Northausen: 1505'. By 1506 Guttenberger had moved to Frankfurt an der Oder (cf. *Aeltere Universitäts-Matrikeln. Universität Frankfurt a.O.*, 3 vols (1887-91) I: 2, 10) where subsequent booklets are all dated. MS 324, fols 1-131, MS 325, fols 71-131 and 132-76, were written in 1508. Thus MS 325, fols 132-76, was begun 4 September (fol. 132: 'Anno Incarnationis christi saluatoris 1508 : die sequenti post Gregorij pape festum …') and finished 10 October (fol. 174: '… Interpretata per me Eberhardum guttenbergensem de hallis sueuie [Schwäbisch Hall] in ordinarie : In achademia franck-afordiana finita 1508 die decima mensis octobris ante Gallj', where '1508' appears to have been added by Guttenberger); fols 174-75ᵛ are undated, fol. 176ʳ⁺ᵛ blank. MS 324, fols 1-131, is dated 16 October, fol. 131: 'Lecta ordinaria per me Eberhardum Guttenberger : decanum medicine : In gignasio almo franck-afordiano : finita : In vigilia Egidij 1508 xvi die mensis octobris'. MS 325, fols 71-131, was begun 24 November (fol. 71: 'Tractatus Eberhardi Guttenbergensis … ad vtilitatem academie franckafordiane … 1508 In vigilia sancte katharine') and finished 5 January (fol. 131ᵛ: '1508 In vigilia trium regum explicatum per Eberhardum vbi in presenti'). MS 325, fols 1-70, was written in 1510; fol. 70: 'In gignasio franckafordiana anno domini 1510. In vigilia Michaelis archangeli . per Eberhardum Guttenbergensem'. The latest dated booklet, MS 326, fols 1-190, was begun on 3 February 1514 (fol. 2: 'Anno domini 1541 [*sic*] die sequenti festum Purificacionis Immaculate et gloriosis-sime virginis marie … In vniuersitate franckafordiana …'), continued through 28 September (fol. 181: 'in vigilia michaelis archangeli 1514'), and finished on 18 October (fol. 190ᵛ: 'Ad laudem dei … per Eberhardum Guttenbergensem artium vtriusque medicine doctorem: decanum medice facultatis gignasij franckfordianj Ad lucem datus et declaratus Anno domini millesimo quingentesimo [corrected from "quadringen-tesimo"] decimo quarto In die Sancte Luce euangeliste 1514 In die luce'. MS 324, fols 132-72, and 326, fols 191-97 and 198-209, are undated.

After the colophon on MS 325, fol. 174, Guttenberger listed those who had attended his lectures in 1508: 'Weyman Ebel Kalwis Petrus de Cansteda Apoticarius continuj scholares'. On fol. 1, originally blank, he has also noted '1509 [corrected from "1508"] In vigilia palmarum doctrinam sextam primi canonis Auicennae Incepi colligere manu propria [Pentecostis] \Martini/ aggressus in vniuersitate franckafordiana ordinarie etc. fuit audiens ordinaria magister petrus Cansteda medicine decanus doctor magister kalb ["doctor" added] magister andreas doctor moralium Apoticarius baccalarius Socius aliquis magister Zimmermann ["doctor iuris" added]'. Later he added another list on fol. 174: '1517 Anno hanc summam raris legi [s] fuerunt audiens magister Ambrosius medicus magister minckel magis-ter Andreas antiquus socius magister funck magister blisigk magister winsz quidam prepositus [?] Wolffgangus apoticarius franciscus [ ] kuch magister Jeorius bauarius'.

MS 324, pastedown of lower cover by hand of s. xvi: 'Dem durchleuchsten hochgeborenen fursten vnd herrn zu her Joachim Marckgraff zu Brandenbergk dess heyligen romischen reychss erczkamerers vnd kurfurst Zu stettin Pommern Der Cassuben vnd wenden herzog burckgraff in Nuzburgk vnd furst zu ruyge vnserem gneydigsten herrn'.

Moorat, pp. 206-8.
Pl. 244

---

239 **Wellcome 349, fols 1-23**   *1488*
                                    [Germany or Low Countries]

Computus

Paper. 23 fols. 218 × 140 mm. 1 col., 155 × 100 mm. Up to 40 lines. Col. init. and border fol. 1, col. inits, diagrms.

Fol. 23ᵛ: 'Finitum anno domini mᵒ CCCCᵒ lxxxviii mense decembris iiii per me heymandum de veteri busco explicit feliciter'. Fols 23ᵛ-28ᵛ contain further computistica copied by the same scribe but undated.

Moorat, p. 223; L. MacKinney, *Medical Illustrations in Medieval Manuscripts* (1965), p. 145 no. 94.19.
Pl. 218

---

240 **Wellcome 350**   *1446 [Italy]*

William of Heytesbury, Regulae solvendi sophismata

Paper. 51 fols, foliated ii-50. 213 × 145 mm. 2 cols, 150 × 93 mm. 35-36 lines. Blanks for inits, ruled in red fols 17ʳ, 25ʳ, 27ʳ and 31ʳ only.

Fol. 48ᵛ: 'Expliciunt regule soluendi sophismata tam in loyca quamque in physica date a magistro guillielmo de entisberi [*BRUO* 927] boccanelle doctore in theologia edite in exonia [*sic*] de anglia Deo gratias Amen', then in the margin '1446 ad 28 otubris'.

According to the colophon in Erfurt, MS Amplon. 2ᵒ. 135, fol. 17, the 'rules' were written 1355. The handwriting of the present MS suggests a student's or master's personal copy.

Moorat, pp. 223-4; *MMBL*, I: 397.
Pl. 124

---

241 **Wellcome 375, pp. 75-201**   *1506 Pesaro, Italy*

Thomas Presbyter, Chirurgia

Paper. 64 fols, paginated 75-156 [2 pp. omitted] 157-201. 285 × 208 mm. 2 cols, 195 × 154 mm. 26-30 lines. Col. inits, rubrics. Bld-tooled leather bdg, ties gone.

P. 201 (in red): 'Explicit Cyrugia Omni Laude Dignissima Venerabilis Presbyteri Domini Thome: Scripta cum supra scripto quoddam opusculo per me Bartholomeum Cynthium scalam pisaurensem Omni diligentia et Cura Anno domini ["14 1560" crossed out] 1506 Die 16 Augusti'. The 'quoddam opus-culo' is presumably the item in the first booklet, pp. 1-74 (Jacobus de Prato's De operatione manuali), copied by the same scribe.

The text here attributed to Thomas is attributed to John de Tracia in Biblioteca Apostolica Vaticana, Pal.lat. 1319; cf. L. Thorndike, 'Another manuscript of Leonard of Bertipaglia and John de Tracia', *Bulletin of the Institute of the History of Medicine*, 4 (1936), 259-60. The scribe also wrote no. 259 below.

P. 201: 'Di me Francesco muscini' (s. xvi).

Moorat, pp. 239-40.
Pl. 236

242 Wellcome 425 *1504 Ferrara, Italy*

Johannes Lichtenberger, Pronosticazione in volgare

Paper. 33 fols. 285 × 225 mm. 1 col., 225-28 × 160 mm. 41 lines.

Fol. 33: 'Chopiato p*er* mano domino Raffaelo B*er*nardo Lorenzi cittadjno fiotenjno [*sic*] gl'anno 1504 in ferrara ottinuto chom grande difichulta dal chonte di foiano jn q*uel*lo tempo sotto Ilolustrjssimo signore ducha erchole secondo di ferrara [Ercole I, 2nd duke 1471-1505]'. The rest of the MS, fols 33ᵛ-143ᵛ, is by the same hand; fols 144ʳ-45ᵛ blank. Lichtenberger's prophecies, published (in Latin) 1488, were avidly read in s. xvi Italy (see D. Kurze, 'Prophecy and history: Lichtenburger's forecasts of events to come (from the fifteenth to the twentieth century); their reception and diffusion', *JWCI*, 21 (1958), 63-85). They were first printed in Italian translation by Petrus Maufer, Modena 1492.

Moorat, pp. 285-86.
Pl. 233

243 Wellcome 441, fols 11-61 *1454 Braunau, Germany*

Raymond Lull, Ars generalis

Paper. 51 fols. 217 × 145 mm. 1 col., 165-75 × 104 mm. 34-44 lines. Col. inits, rubrics.

Fol. 61ᵛ (in red): 'Scripta sunt hec per Stephanum lannkchamer de Patauia [Passau] Clericum eiusdem diocesis Anno Mᵒ ccccᵒ liiij In die Sanctissimi principis apostolorum beati Petri ad Vincula In opido Praunaw [Braunau] duce ludwico regnante per Bauoariam [Ludwig IX, 1450-79]'. Part of a compilation of Lull's works written by Stephen and by another, unnamed, scribe working in collaboration; thus fols 291-315, containing 'Aliqua puncta artis generalis', was begun by Stephen and concluded by the second hand. Elsewhere (fols 187-206, a gloss on the Ars generalis) Stephen corrected the second scribe's work; and in fols 231-290, 'Disputatio quinque sapientum', written by the second scribe, Stephen provided the rubrics. Fols 1-10, 72-119, 207-30 are by Stephen alone, the second scribe writing fols 131-86 and 187-206. Fols 62-71 and 120-30 are blank.

Moorat, pp. 293-95; *MMBL*, I: 397.
Pl. 144

244 Wellcome 442, fols 11-69 *1467 [Spain?]*

Raymond Lull, Ars generalis

Paper. 59 fols. 219 × 157 mm. 1 col., 150-57 × 100-105 mm. 33-35 lines. Col. inits, rubric. Half-stamped leather bdg over boards.

Fol. 69: 'Explicit generalis tabula artis generalis magistri Raymundi Lullij de cathelonia scripta Anno domini 1467 et finita die 4 octobris pyr' [?] Laudetur Jesus cristus amen'; fol. 69ᵛ blank. The scribe resumed copying on fol. 70 (end quire 7) with 'breuis et utilis declaratio artis generalis' and completed it on fol. 97. Fol. 98ʳᵛ blank. Fols 1-10 (quire 1) contain an imperfect epitome of 'De auditu Kabbalistico' and some diagrams.

Moorat, pp. 295-96. *MMBL*, I: 397.
Pl. 169

245 Wellcome 458, fols 61-74 *1478 [Italy]*

Johannes de Sancto Paulo, Flores dietarum

Paper. 14 fols. 203 × 143 mm. 1 col., *c*.138 × 90 mm. 28 lines. Col. inits.

Fol. 73ᵛ: 'Explicit: Laus deo .1478.'; fol. 74ʳᵛ blank. The preceding booklet, fols 1-60, is by the same scribe.

Moorat, p. 311.
Pl. 204

246 Wellcome 459, fols 1-37 *1504 Rocca di Mezzo, Italy*

Macer Floridus, De viribus herbarum

Paper. 37 fols. 190 × 145 mm. 1 col., *c*.170 × 80 mm. 35 lines.

Fol. 37: 'Liber Macri philosophi de virtutibus herbarum finit feliciter Scriptus per felicianum de Benis de Montone In Rocca de medio prouincie Aprutine [Rocca di Mezzo, Abruzzi] eiusdem Terre Capitaneum sub annis Domini .M.D.iiij Die uero iij mensis octobris'. Fols 37ᵛ-43ᵛ contain an index by the same hand.

Moorat, p. 311.
Pl. 234

247 Wellcome 491 *1418 Wasserburg, Germany*

Mesue, Liber grabadim medicinarum particularium

Parch. 131 fols. 291 × 210 mm. 1 col., 205 × 133 mm. 30 lines. Col. inits, rubrics.

Fol. 131ᵛ: 'Finitus feria quarta post Judica per me Johannem Lindner de wasserwurga [Wasserburg, Bavaria] Anno domini .1418.'

Moorat, p. 326.
Pl. 95

248 Wellcome 502, fols 1-16 *1459 Perugia, Italy*

Ars memoriae artificialis

Paper. 16 fols. 218 × 145 mm. 1 col., 135 × *c*.70 mm. 30 lines. Rubric, blanks for inits.

Fol. 16ᵛ: 'M .CCCC. LIX'. The scribe left fol. 16ᵛ blank, then continued on fols 17-20 with a further work on memory. He also wrote a second booklet, fols 21-30, undated but signed fol. 30ᵛ: 'PERVSIE [Perugia]' followed by (in red) 'Finis'. The hand is that of Nicolaus Antonii de Datis de Visso, scribe and compiler of Florence, Biblioteca Riccardiana 1177, written in Perugia, 1453 (for which see T. de Robertis and R. Miriello, *I manoscritti datata della Biblioteca riccardiana di Firenze*, 2 vols (1997-99), II, no. 29). The present booklets are now bound with unrelated texts written s. xvi/xvii.

Moorat, p. 334; *MMBL*, I: 398.
Pl. 152

249 Wellcome 505, fols 1-24 *1479 [Germany]*

Hermann Zoestius (von Marienfeld), De calendarii emendatione

Paper. 24 fols. 215 × 155 mm. 1 col., 145 × 110 mm. 30 lines. Col. inits, rubrics.

Fol. 22ᵛ (in red): 'Explicit phaselexis seu tractatus de correctione kalendarij editus a venerabili et religioso uiro domino hermanno zoest de monasterio [*sic*] ordinis cistersiensis 2ᵃ feria post festum sancti egidij confessoris anno domini .1479'; fols 22ᵛ-24ᵛ blank. The colophon's wording might suggest the date was that of the text, but it was composed 1437 (cf. W. Wattenbach, 'Über Hermann von Marienfeld aus Münster', *Sitzungsberichte der Königlich Preussischen Akademie der Wissenschaften zu Berlin*, 9 (1884), 93-109). Other copies include Basel, Universitäts-Bibliothek, A V 25, dated 1455 (see *Katalog der datierten Handschriften in der Schweiz in lateinischer Schrift vom Anfang des Mittelalters bis 1500*, I, ed. B.M. von Scarpatetti (1977), no. 116). Bound with fols 25-72 (for which see no. 250 below), and fols 73-82, 83-113, 114-31, 132-55, and 156-66, all written by different scribes, and forming a collection of astronomical and medical texts. The scribe of fols 156-66 signed fol. 166 'Johannes Reysner'.

Moorat, pp. 340-42; *MMBL*, I: 398.
Pl. 206

250 Wellcome 505, fols 25-72   *1487 [Germany]*

Johannes de Sacrobosco, Opusculum sphericum

Paper. 48 fols. 215 × 155 mm. 1 col., 162 × 100 mm. Up to 36 lines. Diagrms, blanks left for inits.

Fol. 72ᵛ (written on a green background): 'Scriptum est hoc opusculum laboribus ac diligencia michahelis suter de wurtzen [Wurzen, Saxony] anno salutifere incarnacionis 1.4.8.7'. Bound with no. 249 above.

Moorat, pp. 340-42; *MMBL*, I: 398.
Pl. 216

251 Wellcome 506   *1462, 1470 Verona, Italy*

Pseudo-Aristoteles, Secreta secretorum; etc

Parch. and paper, mixed. 170 fols. 153 × 105 mm. 1 col., 100 × 65 mm. 29-30 lines. Hist. init and border fol. 1, dec. init. fol. 121, col. inits, rubrics. Bld-stamped leather bdg over boards, with clasp (repaired).

Two booklets, fols 1-120 and 121-70, both written by the same scribe. The earlier, fols 121-70, is dated fol. 169ᵛ (in red): 'Amen: Deo gratias amen: finis: frater Sebastianus ordinis minorum fratrum .1462.'; fols 170ʳˑᵛ blank. The later, fols 1-120, is twice dated 1470. Thus, fol. 50 (in red): '¶ Actum et completum per fratrem Sebastianum de Verona ordinis minorum de obseruantia sub .1470. die .17. mensis Junij in loco Sancti Bernardini Verone' [St Bernardino (d. 1444, canonized 1450) had been vicar-general, 1437-43, of the Observant branch of Friars]; fol. 100 (in red): 'Frater Sebastianus de Verona finit die vij septembris .1470. in sancto Bernardino Verone'. Fols 100ᵛ-12 were presumably copied about the same time. Fols 112ᵛ-13ᵛ contain additions by Fr Sebastian, a prophecy on fol. 112ᵛ being headed with the date '1472'. Fols 114-20ᵛ blank. The same scribe also produced a Franciscan miscellany (Florence, Biblioteca Medicea Laurenziana, Ashburnham 69), partly dated 1470, 1471, and 1480.

Parchment bifolia serve as endleaves, fols i-ii and 171-72. On fol. ii there is an almost illegible list of contents. At the end, fol. 172, the hand of the contents has written: 'Hunc librum concessit mihi fratri Laurentio ab auricalino Reuerendus pater frater Ludouicus uicentinus uicarius prouincie sancti antonij In sancto

Joanne apud campum sancti petri commoranti Anno 1507 die 15 nouembris et pertinet ad locum Sancti Bernardinj Amen'.

Moorat, pp. 342-44; *MMBL*, I: 398.
Pl. 177

252 Wellcome 508, fols 1-33   *1471 [Germany]*

Computistica, in German

Paper. 33 fols. 204 × 152 mm. 1 col., 147 × 100 mm. Up to 27 lines. Col. inits, rubrics. Diagrms, tables and kal. in red and black. Red leather bdg over boards with 5 bosses on each of upper and lower covers, single clasp remaining.

Fol. 32ᵛ (in red): 'Explicit per Hainricum Hengler de ysnina [Isny, Baden-Württemberg] Anno domini 1471 in festo quirini hora vesperarum'. A table of years 1404-79, fol. 9, has the date '1470' marked with two black strokes; usually such a mark indicates the date of the Easter next following, see H.M. Bannister, 'Signs in kalendarial tables', *Mélanges offerts à M. Émile Chatelain* (1910), pp. 141-49. Fol. 33 contains an addition, fol. 33ᵛ blank. Bound up with fols 34-55, 56-63, and 64-181, each written by a different scribe. Six blank quires, fols 182-254, follow.

Pastedowns from a s. xiv missal.

Moorat, pp. 347-48; L. MacKinney, *Medical Miniatures in Medieval Manuscripts* (1965), p. 146 no. 94.26; *MMBL*, I: 398.
Pl. 183

253 Wellcome 514, fols 87-116   *1507 [Venice, Italy]*

Arnaldus de Villanova, Rosarius

Paper. 30 fols. 205 × 142 mm. 1 col., 155 × 100 mm. 24-26 lines. Col. init. fol. 87, blank spaces left for others, rubrics. Limp parch bdg.

Fol. 113 (in red): 'Finit liber Rosarij maioris feliciter quem ad laudem dei pare uirginis marie tibique Jacobo aromatario amundo perscripsi Ego. Ago. phi. ariminensis [Rimini] de aquilantibus .M. CCCCC vij die xvij septembris hora 3ᵃ noctis regnantibus Julio 2° pontifice maximo. [1503-13] et Leonardo lauredano principe serenissimo Venetiarum Venetijs [1501-21]'. Fols 113ʳ, 114ʳ-16ᵛ, originally blank, contain additions by a later hand. An addition made fol. 116ᵛ continues on the originally blank first leaf of fols 117-22. Part of a larger compilation copied by the same scribe and containing 4 other booklets: fols 1-24, 25-42, 43-86, and 117-22. Fols 131-44 (foliated 131, 136-44) were written in late s. xvi.

Moorat, pp. 354-56.
Pl. 239

254 Wellcome 516   *1584, 1588, 1589*
        [Puylaurens, France]

Alchemica, in Latin and French

Paper. 136 fols, foliated by scribe 1-42, 1-93. 148 × 100 mm. 1 col., c.100 × 64 mm. 22 lines. Col. inits, rubrics.

A volume of alchemical texts written by the scribe of no. 270 below, where he identifies himself as P. Sabatier of Puylaurens, Tarn. He foliated the present MS from its 2nd to 43rd leaf as fols 1-42, and then recommenced the foliation at the 44th leaf (in the middle of quire 6, at the beginning of John Dastin's Rosarius philosophorum), continuing until the last (136th) leaf as fols 1-93. As in no. 270, it was the scribe's habit to note alongside its rubric the date at which he began to copy a text and/or date a text at its end. Thus in the present MS 'La Fleur du Lys entre les Espines' was begun (fol. 2) '12 decembre 1584' and ends (fol. 18ᵛ) '19 *decembre* 1584'. When he copied the same text in no. 270 he dated it 29 October – 2 November 1585. Two other items here, Geber's Testamentum (fols 31-38, in the first part of the MS) and the 'Aureolae sapientium' (fols 56ᵛ-60ᵛ), were also copied in no. 270, again at different dates. The present copy of Geber was finished '1588 . 15 septembris' but that in no. 270 on 28 November 1586; the present copy of the 'Aureolae' was finished '1589 Finis Aureolarum .28. Januier' (in red) but that in no. 270 on 13 June 1578. Other items dated here are Dastin's Rosarius (fols 1-56) where he has noted alongside the rubric '17 Septembris 1588'; and 'La maniere d'ouurer' (fols 63ᵛ-67ᵛ) where he has noted alongside the rubric '1589 22 Sept*embre*' and 'Ex dono D. De La Chalade'.

Moorat, pp. 357-58.

Pl. 294

255 **Wellcome 518, fols 1-47**　　　　*1566, 1567*
Langenargen, Germany

Alchemica, in German

Paper. 47 fols. 315 × 207 mm. 1 col., 230-40 × 130 mm. Up to 28 lines.

Two booklets, fols 1-21 and 22-47, in a collection all written by the same scribe. The earlier, fols 22-47, is twice dated 1566. Thus, fol. 22 (title page): 'Processus lapidis philosophicj particularis et vniuersalis ex Mercurio corporis scilicet Solis aut Lune procedens cum Practica Bernhardj Comitis Taruisinj 1566', and at the end, fol. 45: 'Anno 1566 21 Octobris'. Fols 45ᵛ-47ᵛ blank. The first booklet is also dated both on its title page and at the end; fol. 1: 'De lapide Philosophorum Autore Isaaco Holando Argone [Langenargen, Württemberg] 1567 mense Aprili', and fol. 18ᵛ: 'Anno 1567 6 Junij Zwey Particularia Wilhelmi Theophrastj so er seinem sun gen Salzburg geschickt hat ausz seiner aignen handischrifft'. Fols 20ᵛ-21ᵛ blank. Two further booklets, fols 48-95 and 96-137, are undated.

Moorat, pp. 362-63; H. Frühmorgen-Voss and N.H. Ott, *Katalog der deutschsprachigen illustrierten Handschriften des Mittelalters*, I (1986-91), no. 2.4.21

Pl. 270

256 **Wellcome 520**　　　　*1453 [Ferrara, Italy]*

Alchemica

Paper. 66 fols. 312 × 210 mm. 1 col., 200 × 113 mm. Up to 39 lines. Col. init., fol. 1, otherwise blanks left for inits.

Fol. 64ᵛ: 'Nota lectore Como Io. M°. matio nominata dalla viola scrisi el dito libro de mia *propria* mano del 1453 adi .17. hotore Et Auj la copia da uno cangeliero del duca borxo [Borso d'Este, Marquis of Ferrara 1450, Duke of Modena and Reggio 1452, and 1st duke of Ferrara 1471, d. 1471] el qual ne faxena vno gra*n* co*n*to *per* ch*e* luj laue co*n* gra*n* fadiga dale mano del marchexe [nicole] lionelo [Leonello, Borso's elder brother, Marquis of Ferrara, 1441-50]'. On fol. 65ᵛ the same scribe notes 'Questo libro sie de mi Matio barbiero Nominato dala viola ed auj la copia de vno libro che fo de la Il*lustrissima* S*ignora* del marchexe lionelo .mª.de. Este [either Leonello's 1st wife, Margherita Gonzaga, or his 2nd, Maria d'Aragona, both of whom predeceased him]'. Fol. 66ʳ⁻ᵛ blank.

Moorat, pp. 365-66; M. Pereira, 'Alchemy and the use of vernacular languages in the late Middle Ages', *Speculum*, 74 (1999), 350.

Pl. 142

257 **Wellcome 524, fols 1-97**　　　　*1543 [Germany]*

Alchemica

Paper. 97 fols. 191 × 160 mm. 1 col., *c*.145 × 110 mm. Up to 18 lines. Col. drawings. Gold-tooled leather bdg, ties gone.

The preface written in red (fol. 1ʳᵛ) ends with the date '15 xliij'. Some alchemical receipts have been added fols 93ᵛ-94ᵛ, fols 95ʳ-97ᵛ blank. Fols 98-124, 125-32, and 133-36, by different scribes, are undated.

Moorat, pp. 368-70; H. Frühmorgen-Voss and N.H. Ott, *Katalog der deutschsprachigen illustrierten Handschriften des Mittelalters*, I (1986-91), no. 2.4.22 and pl. 34 illus. drawing fol. 2ᵛ.

Pl. 257

258 **Wellcome 537, fols 323-36**　　　　*1462 [England]*

Tables of changes of the Moon

Parch. 14 fols. *c*.140 × 105 mm fols 232 and 336, 127 × 92 mm fols 324-35. 1 col., 92 × 60 mm. 16 lines. Tables in red and black. Tawed leather bdg over boards, with strap and pin fastening gone.

Fol. 326: 'In this qwaier ben conteyned alle the chaunges of the moone for lvj wynt*er* nowe next folowinge. with the daies of þe monthe the houres and the mynutes 7 with the prymes 7 the ȝerys of oure lorde which was made 7 drawe*n* in þe ȝeer of our*e* lorde .14lxij. a thosande .cccclxij. 7 shal serve as it \is/ writen above for .lvj. ȝeres nowe folowi*nge*'. The outermost bifolium, fols 323 and 336, is larger (*c*.140 × 105 mm) than the others (fols 324-35 at 127 × 92 mm) in this 'qwaier' and perhaps originally formed a wrapper. Fols 324-25ᵛ and 333ᵛ-35ᵛ are blank. The rest of the volume consists of fols 5-14, 15-47, 48-310 (paper) and fols 311-22 (parchment), all written by different scribes, probably about the same date.

Fol. 337 (endleaf): '… dico quod galfrydum halle' (s. xv ex).

Pl. 159

259 **Wellcome 540, fols 1-120**　　　　*1505 Pesaro, Italy*

Marsilius de Sancta Sophia, De pulsibus

Paper. 120 fols. 334 × 230 mm. 2 cols, 243 × 160 mm. 32-35 lines. Gold init. fol. 1, blanks left for rest, rubrics. 'Marsilius' written on bottom edge.

Fol. 115ᵛ (in red): 'Explicit Libellus de pulsibus Febrium ẹditum per famosissimum Marsilium, Scriptumque omni diligentia et Cura per Bartholomeum Cynthium. scalam Pisaurensem M D .V. die 12ª octobris, hora xxjª . Deo favente'; fols 116-20ᵛ blank. The scribe also wrote the rest of the MS, fols 121-50 and 151-76. He also wrote no. 241 above.

Fol. 1: 'Di Alessandro Padoani' who also owned nos 136 and 209 above and no. 274 below.

Moorat, pp. 398-99.

Pl. 235

260 Wellcome 549, fols 92-211 and 220-29 *1471*
[Germany]

Johannitius, Isagoge; etc.

Paper. 130 fols. 207 × 155 mm. 2 cols, 146 × 92 mm fols 92-211, 156 × 96 mm fols 220-29. 36-41 lines. Col. inits, rubrics. Leather bdg over boards, clasp gone.

A compilation of five booklets all written by the same scribe of which two, fols 92-211 and 220-29, are dated 1471. Thus the first (fols 92-211) is dated fol. 203ᵛ: 'Explicit libellus de regimine sanitatis et de pestilentia Anno .1.4.7.1.'; it is also dated fol. 101: 'Explicit Johannicius .71.' where 1471 is clearly intended. Receipts in German and two short tracts, fols 204-11, are undated. The second booklet, fols 220-29, is dated fol. 225ᵛ: 'Explicit secretum secretorum Aristotelis Anno 1471', but the following short items, fols 226-29, are undated. The other three booklets, fols 2-91, 212-19 and 230-81, are undated but were presumably written all about the same date.

Moorat, pp. 414-17.
Pl. 184

261 Wellcome 553, fols 173-187 *1470*
Nuremberg? Germany

Lanfranc, Chirurgia parva

Paper. 15 fols. 307 × 205 mm. 1 col., 210 × c.148 mm. 39 lines. Col. inits, rubrics. Red leather bdg over boards, clasps gone.

Fol. 187ᵛ (in a red scroll): 'Explicit Langfrancus minor Per me Johannem Resche de Naw. Nor' [?Norimbergae, i.e. Nuremberg] .xx. die mensis Januarij Anno etc Septuagesimo', where it is evident from the handwriting that 1470 is intended. The last in a MS containing three medical treatises; the scribe has left leaves blank at the end of the first two, fols 149ʳ⁻ᵛ and 171ᵛ-72ᵛ, as if he had copied the texts from booklets.

Moorat, p. 422.
Pl. 179

262 Wellcome 556 *1430 Venice, Italy*

Miscellanea medica, in Italian

Paper. 85 fols. 295 × 220 mm. 2 cols, 225 × 150 mm. 50 lines. Col. inits, rubrics.

Fol. 83 (in red): 'Qui finisse il libro de la fisicha chel maestro aldobrandino sopra. scrito chompuosse in lingua francescha de la sanitade del corpo e di ziaschuno menbro per [e]sse translatado di francesscho in italian volgare negli ani domini M ccc x nel meze di magio ischrito a uolgarizato fue ~ ~', then squashed beneath this (but again in red): 'E ora pro me benedeto longo quondam [?] christofari rinouato et asenpiato fue nel ano domini M cccc xxx Venecijs'. Fols 83-84ᵛ, containing an extract from Pseudo-Aristotle's Secreta secretorum, copied by the same scribe, are undated; fols 85ʳ⁻ᵛ blank. Fol. iᵛ contains an index written in red.

Moorat, pp. 424-26.
Pl. 105

263 Wellcome 558, fols 1-48 *1449 [Italy]*

Cristoforo Barzizza, Introductorium sive ianua ad omne opus practicum medicine; etc

Paper. 48 fols. 298 × 235 mm. 2 cols, 215 × 155 mm. 49 lines. Col. inits, rubrics. Pen & lead drawings, fol. 28.

A booklet twice dated; thus fol. 34ᵛ: 'Explicit Introductorium siue Janua ad opus practicum medicine compillatum per Magistrum christoforum de barzizijs de pergamo doctorem excellentissimum [professor of medicine, Padua 1431-44, d. 1445] Ad laudem domini nostri yesu christi et gloriose eius matris virginis marie Amen. 1449 die Jouis .8 mensis madij hora iiiᵃ', and fol. 45: 'Tractatus Gentilij de crisi explicit quem die xvj Junij 1449 scripsi'. Two further booklets (fols 49-88 and 89-148) by the same scribe are undated. The present MS of Barzizza's 'Introductorium' is not among those listed in *Dizionario Biografico degli Italiani*, VII (1965), p. 34 (and for his library, see P. Sambin, 'Ricerche par la storia della cultura nel secolo XVᵒ: Cristoforo Barzizza e i suoi libri', *Bollettino del Museo Civico di Padova*, 44 (1955), 3-23).

Moorat, pp. 427-29.
Pl. 131

264 Wellcome 572 *1560 [Netherlands]*

Medical astrology and receipts, in Latin, French and Netherlandish

Paper. 89 fols. 295 × 200 mm. 1-3 cols, c.227 × 170 mm. 29 lines. Col. drawings. 2 woodcuts and volvelle, fol. 2. Original limp vellum bdg with ties, now kept separately.

Fol. 88: 'M.V.LX'. Additions on fols 75ᵛ-78ᵛ are by another hand.
Fol. 1 (flyleaf, by the hand of the scribe): 'Dominus blasyus de mulio'; fol. 4: 'Toussain regnault chirurgien seruente a lille', 'Franchoise Regenault seruiteur de son pere demeurant allille'.

Moorat, pp. 445-46; R. Jansen-Sieben, *De Pseudo-Hippokratische Iatromathematika in vier Middelnederlandse Versies*, Scripta, 11 (1983), pp. 46-63.
Pl. 264

265 Wellcome 591 *1469 [Florence, Italy]*

Matteo Palmieri, Liber de temporibus

Parch. 101 fols. 285 × 200 mm. 1 col., c.193-200 × 80-90 mm. Up to 30 lines. Gold inits, rubrics. Bld-stamped leather bdg over boards, clasps gone.

Fol. 99ᵛ (in red): 'Matthei palmerii florentini ad petrum medicem liber de temporibus explicit laus deo in eternum 1469'. The scribe is identifiable as the Florentine notary, Ser Giovanni di Piero da Stia, for whom see A.C. de la Mare, 'New research on humanistic scribes in Florence', *Miniatura fiorentina del Rinascimento 1440-1525*, ed. A. Garzelli, 2 vols, Inventari e cataloghi toscani, 18 (1985), I: 499-500 and 596. He made at least three other copies of the text: Florence, Bibl. Riccardiana 802, dated 1467; Glasgow University, Hunterian Library U.I.2 (98); and Biblioteca Apostolica Vaticana, Urb. lat. 455. Other MSS by him include *DMBL*, nos 110, 686; *DMO*, nos 138, 372; and Paris, BN lat. 7245 (*MSS datés*, II: 405). Fols 100-101ᵛ contain added notes, in Italian, relating to events in Florence 1512-16.

An erased *ex libris* on the flyleaf, partially visible under ultraviolet light, reads: 'Iste liber est me Thomasii l[.......] de m[....]irgris'.

Moorat, p. 462; *MMBL*, I: 399.
Pl. 174

266 **Wellcome 608** *1509 [Germany]*

Hippocrates, Secreta; Directorium juvenum in arte medicine nondum in practica exercitatorum

Paper. 32 fols. 201 × 144 mm. 1 col., 160 × 90 mm. 28-31 lines. Blank spaces for inits.

Fol. 29ᵛ: 'τελωσ In profesto diui Michaelis Anno 1509 Simon Pernstich'. Fol. 30 contains a short Latin-German glossary of herbs; fols 1, 30ᵛ-32ᵛ blank.

Moorat, p. 470.

Pl. 240

267 **Wellcome 616** *1470 [Friuli, Italy]*

Petrus de Abano, De venenis; etc

Paper. 93 fols, foliated 340 [340 bis] 341-431. 208 × 143 mm. 1 col., 140 × 90 mm. 20 lines. Blanks for inits, rubrics.

Fol. 431ᵛ (in red): 'Et hęc de praelaturis prouinciarum sufficiant. Completus sacrosancti Danielis Anno domini M cccc° lxx° die uero Martis Foeliciter'. The MS is also dated earlier, fol. 384ᵛ: 'Anno domini millesimo cccc° septuagesimo mensis decembris'. The scribe is Battista da Cingoli [*ex info.* Professor A.C. de la Mare] who wrote Paris, Bibliothèque nationale lat. 9325 and 8953-54 (*MSS datés*, III: 156 and 626) for a priest of San Danieli del Friuli. He also wrote San Danieli del Friuli, Biblioteca Guarneriana MS 80 and Vienna, Österreichische Nationalbibliothek, Cod. 39 (F. Unterkircher, *Katalog der datierten Handschriften in Lateinischer Schrift in Österreich* (1979-), III: 17-18), and collaborated on Guarneriana 161. Not listed among MSS of De venenis by E. Paschetto, *Pietro d'Abano Medico e Filosofo* (1984), pp. 334-35.

Moorat, pp. 474-75; *MMBL*, I: 399.

Pl. 178

268 **Wellcome 617** *1451 Venice, Italy*

Petrus Hispanus [Pope John XXI], Thesaurus pauperum, in Italian

Paper. 51 fols. 297 × 200 mm. 2 cols, 212 × c.155 mm. 34 lines. Col. inits.

Fol. 47ᵛ: 'DEO GRATIAS AMEN Finito libro Thesaurum pauperum sit laus et gloria christo fuit in ciuitate uenetiarum dio [*sic*] primo mensis septembris anno domini nostri yhesu christi .1451.' Fols 47ᵛ-51ᵛ contain a phlebotomy, copied by the same scribe.

C. Liguori ('Il tesoro dei poveri di Zuane di Luza', *Medicina nei secoli*, 16 (1979), 339-45) attributes the translation of the Thesaurus pauperum to Zuane di Luza (Johannes de Luxa, chancellor of Kotor, Serbia) through conflating the evidence of colophons in Naples, Bibl. Governativa dei Girolamini, MCF. CF. 1. 9, and Venice, Bibl. San Marco, It. II. 173. That in Naples reads 'Complito e questo libero[*sic*] chiamato thesauro di poveri scripto per mano de mi Zuane da luza ... MCCCCX' (cf. E. Mandarini, *Il codici manoscritti della Biblioteca Oratoriana di Napoli* (1897), pp. 73-74), while the colophon in Venice informs us Zuane translated text, 'Traslatato de gramadega in volgar per lo circumspecto homo ser Çuan da Lusa ...' (MS copied by Çorçi Vallaresso, 1431; cf. N. Zingarelli, 'I trattati di Albertano da Brescia in dialetto Veneziano', *Studi di Letteratura Italiana*, 3 (1901), 151-92, and see C. Frati and A. Segarizzi, *Catalogo*

dei codici Marciani Italiani, I (1909), pp. 302-3). However, Zuane (or Johannes) himself seems to have been meticulous in distinguishing between his translation work (*DMO*, no. 245) and his copying a text (*DMO*, no. 145, *DMC*, no. 203, Paris, BN, lat. 7626 (*MSS datés*, II: 419), and *Colophons de mss*, iii, nos 10372-3 and 11453). The present translation was included in a recommended reading list, printed by Antonio Miscomini, Florence, 1494; see L.J. Rosenwald, *The 19th Book. Tesoro de Poveri* (1961).

Moorat, p. 475.

Pl. 139

269 **Wellcome 708** *1443 [Germany]*

Johannes de Rupescissa, De consideratione quinte essentie; etc

Paper. 57 fols, foliated 1-11, 13-58. 210 × 145 mm. 1 col., 160 × c.100 mm. 33-36 lines. Col. drawing fol. 5ᵛ, col. inits.

Fol. 42ᵛ: 'Deo omnipotenti patrique filio et spiritui sancto sit laus per infinita secula seculorum. Amen .1.4.43°.' (other copies of the text are to be found in nos 219 and 256 above; and for other MSS, see R. Halleux, 'Les ouvrages alchimiques de Jean de Rupescissa', *Histoire Littéraire de la France. Ouvrage commencé par des religieux bénédictins de la Congregation de Saint Maur*, 41 (1981), pp. 278-82). The MS is again dated at the end of a Latin-German 'Vocabularius herbarum', fol. 58: 'Et sic est finis .1.4.43°. mtispoe' sancte francisce ora pro me', followed by 'et pro omnibus fidelibus defunctis' added by another hand. Moorat suggests that 'mtispoe' is possibly Münchberg, Germany. Fols 34ᵛ-35ʳ are blank, as if the scribe had turned over an opening by mistake. Fol. 58ᵛ, originally blank, contains added receipts by a later hand.

Moorat, p. 522.

Pl. 121

270 **Wellcome 719**
1578, 1580, 1583, 1584, 1585, 1586, 1592 and 1593 Puylaurens, France

Alchemica, in Latin and French

Paper. 308 fols. 192 × 134 mm. 1 col., 130-40 × 85 mm. Up to 30 lines. Col. inits, rubrics. In limp parch bdg formed from fragment of legal document.

A collection of nine booklets (fols 2-53, 54-65, 66-121, 122-71, 172-83, 184-217, 218-54, 257-60, 261-308; fols 255-56 form a bifolium containing a drawing and diagrams) written by the scribe of no. 254 above. He identifies himself here at the end of the fifth booklet, fol. 182: 'Acheue de escrire 1583. 16 Juin par moy P. Sabatier A Puylaurens'. On fol. 172 at the beginning of this text ('La composition de la Pierre des Philosophes') he has noted the date at which he started copying, '14 Juing', alongside the rubric. Fols 181ᵛ-83 contain an undated note headed 'Cecy a esté tiré d'vn liure escript a la main', fol. 183ᵛ blank. As in no. 254, it was the scribe's habit to note alongside the rubric the date at which he began to copy a text and/or date a text at its end. Three items here, 'La Fleur du Lys entre les Espines', Geber's Testamentum (both in the first booklet) and the 'Aureolae sapientium' (in the seventh booklet), were also copied in no. 254 but at different dates. Thus the present copy of 'La Fleur du Lys' was begun (fol. 15) 'le 29 octobre 1585' and ends (fol. 29) 'acheue le 2 Nouembre 1585' whereas in no. 254 it is dated 12-19 December 1584; the present copy of Geber was begun (fol. 38) '1586. 28 Nouembris' but in no. 254 finished on 15 September 1588; finally, the present copy of the 'Aureolae' was begun (fol. 218) '3 Juin 1578' and finished (fol. 246ᵛ) 'Finis τελοσ 1578 13 Juing', whereas in no. 254 it was finished on 28 January 1589. The 'Aureolae' is followed here by an undated item, fols 252ᵛ-54ᵛ blank. Other dates occur throughout the present MS. In the first booklet (fols 2-53), apart from the dates given above, the first item was begun (fol. 2) '20 Aoust 1584' and a later item (fol. 30) on '1585 30 octobris' (fols 45-53 contain an addition by another, later, hand). In the second booklet (fols 54-65) the text was begun (fol. 54) '1593 .17. Aoust' and ends (fol. 63) 'acheue le 23 Aoust 1593' (fols 63ᵛ-65ᵛ blank). In the third booklet (fols 66-121) the text was begun (fol. 66) '16 Juing 1578' and ends (fol. 119ᵛ) 'Finis 1578 .24 Junij τελοσ' (fols 120-21 contain an index). In the fourth booklet (fols 122-171) the first item (fol. 122) was begun '1580 27 Aoust', followed by a text begun (fol. 149ᵛ) 'le 19 Aoust 1592' which ends (fol. 153) 'acheué le 21 Aoust 1592', the following item ends (fol. 161) '26 Aoust 1592', while the final item was begun (fol. 161ᵛ) 'le 24 Aoust 1593' and ends (fol. 169v) 'Acheue le 26 Aoust 1593' (fols 170-71ᵛ blank). In the sixth booklet (fols 184-217) the text was begun (fol. 184) '1578. 26 Juin' and ends (fol. 216ᵛ) 'Fin τελοσ 1578 .2. Juillet' (fols 217ʳ·ᵛ contain an added note). Finally, in the ninth booklet (fols 261-308) the first item was begun (fol. 261) '7 Juillet 1578' and ends (fol. 269ᵛ)'Deo Gratias Amen τελοσ 1578 9 Julij', the final item ending (fol. 289ᵛ) 'Finis τελοσ 1578 28 Octobris' (fols 290-308 undated). Only the eighth booklet (fols 257-60) is undated. The final quire (fols 309-22) is blank. The sequence of dates establishes that the first booklet (fols 2-53) was written over three years, 1584-86, with leaves (fols 11ᵛ-12ᵛ, 29ᵛ, 48ᵛ-52ᵛ) left blank between items, while the fourth (fols 122-71) was begun in 1580 but then left abandoned until 1592-93. A short addition in the first booklet on fols 13-14ᵛ exceptionally refers to the date of a printed edition: 'Sensuyt La Table d'Hermes ti [sic] de la Fontaine des amoureux de la Science, Imprimée a Lyon par Benoist Rigaud 1590'.

Moorat, pp. 528-31.
Pl. 289

271 **Wellcome 723**   *1456 [Italy]*

Gulielmus de Saliceto, Chirurgia, in Italian

Paper. 86 fols. 335 × 232 mm. 2 cols, 220 × 160 mm. 43 lines fols 1-58, 36 lines fols 59-86. Col. inits, rubrics. Red half leather bdg over boards, clasp gone.

Fol. 1 (in red): 'Chi comenza lo libro chiamato Guielmo fato a di 5. auril 1456'. The MS is written by two scribes, the first of whom wrote the first six quires (fols 1-58) and the second the last three (fols 59-86). Fol. 86ᵛ, originally blank, and four added leaves, fols 87-90, contain later s. xv additions.

Moorat, p. 533.
Pl. 146

272 **Wellcome 726**   *1433 [Italy]*

Galeatius de Sancta Sophia, 'Liber simplicium'

Parch. 116 fols. 246 × 192 mm. 2 cols, 170 × 120 mm. 37 lines. Col. inits, rubrics.

Fol. 110: 'Expliciunt Recepta febrium et pulcerrima simplicia per famosissimum arcium et medicine doctorem galeam de sancta sophia edita et ex dictis sublimorum medicorum hinc inde collecta quo ad sinplicia [sic] maxime sub anno dominj Mᵒ cccc 33 scripta ad laudem et honorem dei omnipotente eiusque pie [fol. 110ᵛ] matris marie virginis et tocius curie celestis et commodum mei bartholomei etc Deo gracias'. The text is followed by an index, fols 110ᵛ-12ᵛ. Receipts have been added in a later hand (s. xv²) in Latin and Italian. Fols 113, 114ᵛ-16ᵛ blank. The MS is a palimpsest. Leaves (originally c.365 × 243 mm) of a MS (s. xiii, 2 cols, col. inits) have been turned round and folded in half to form the bifolios of the present volume.
Fol. 1: 'Di Alessandri Padoani', the owner of nos 136, 209 and 259 above.

Moorat, p. 536.
Pl. 110

273 **Wellcome 735**   *1595 [Germany]*

Arzneibuch

Paper. 831 fols, foliated [v] 1-397 [+ ii] 399 [400-1 wanting] 402-546 [+ iii] 547-629 [630-59 wanting] 660-855 [856 wanting] 857. 290 × 198 mm. 1 col., 205 × 150 mm. Up to 21 lines. Wooden boards with printed label on upper cover 'Andreas Schweigkofer'.

Fol. i (title page): 'Artzeney puech wie es der vnlangst In Gott verschidene Herzog Ludwig zu Würtemberg [III, 1568-93] etc selligelicher gedechtnus zu gebrauchen gephleget, hat auch als fasst khunsstreich lieb vnnd werth gehalten .1.5.95.' A note by a later owner on the same page records that 'diss buch ist geschriben worden vor 125 Jahren vnd von mir überschri[ben] Anno 1720. d' rome Augustinus Jos: v. wend[.] p' t' Regii Parth' Midteg[....]'. The first five preliminary leaves and leaves containing indexes to the different parts of the work (2 fols betw. fols 397ᵛ and 399, 3 fols betw. fols 546 and 547) were left unfoliated by the scribe.

Moorat, pp. 542-43.
Pl. 300

274 **Wellcome 755, 756**   *1595, 1596 Dillingen, Germany*

Johann Spech, 'Commentarius ... in octo libros physicorum', in 2 vols

Paper. Vol. I 393 fols. 205 × 165 mm. Vol. II 366 fols. 210 × 160 mm. 1 col., 160 × 105 mm. Vol. I 14-23 lines, vol. II 16-17 lines. Diagrm, vol. I, fol. 111ᵛ. Bld-tooled leather bdgs, clasps gone.

A commentary on Aristotle in 2 vols written by the same hand throughout. Vol I is MS 756, vol. II MS 755. The title page of vol I reads: 'Commentarivs Reuerendi Patris Joannis Specij Societatis Jesv in octo libros physicorum Aristotelis exceptus a Fratre Jacobo Peter Ottenpurano Dilingae Anno Domini C I I XCV [1595]'. The vol. is again dated fol. 137ᵛ, 'Anno 1596 11 Januarij', and fol. 280ᵛ, 'Et haec de ista questione vii Martj anno 1596'. The title page of vol. II is almost identical to that of vol. I: 'Commentarivs Reuerendi Patris Joannis Specij Societatis Jesu publicae Professoris ordinarij in Aristoteles de coelo quatuor libros Exceptus a Fratre Jacobo Peter Monacho Benedictino Ottenpurona [Ottobeuren] Dilingae Anno virginei partus M. D. CXVI'; the scribe has corrected the date by noting

'2' above the 'C' and '1' above the 'X'. He has similarly corrected himself, fol. 219: 'Dilingae Anno recuperatae Salutis MDCXVI'. Spech is not listed by P. de Ribadeneyra, P. Alegambe and N. Southwell, *Bibliotheca scriptorum Societatis Iesu* (1676) or C.H. Lohr, *Latin Aristotle Commentaries*, II, *Renaisssance Authors* (1988).

Moorat, pp. 555-56.

Pl. 301

275 **Wellcome 760, fols 1-144**   *1570 [Italy]*

Secreti vari

Paper. 142 fols, foliated 1-36 [37 wanting] 38-47 [48 wanting] 49-144. 165 × 120 mm. 1 col., 112 × 85 mm. Up to 17 lines.

Fol. 144: 'Anno 1570 allj .7. di Nouenbre'. Fol. 144ᵛ blank. Fols 146-68 contain an index by the same hand as the text. Fols 169-245 contain receipts in a hand of s. xvii, fols 247-79 blank.
Fol. 1: 'Mei Andreę Stabilis, hic est Liber', by the hand of fols 169-245.

Moorat, p. 559.

Pl. 273

276 **Wellcome 780, fols 1-62**   *1430 Padua, Italy*

Petrus de Tussignano, 'Super nonum almansoris'

Paper. 62 fols. 296 × 215 mm. 2 cols, 229 × 162 mm. 44 lines. Red vellum bdg, with remains of clasps stamped 'S' and 'yhs', bosses gone. Label on upper cover with inits 'H L' and '24' (medieval form) in red; '54' in modern Arabic numbers crossed through.

Fol. 62: 'Scriptus est hoc opus in Alma vniuersitate paduana Anno dominj Mᵒ ccccᵒ 30 et finitum est cum dei adiutorio prima die mensis Septembris etc'. The rest of the MS, fols 62-211, is by the same scribe. Pastedowns and endleaves come from a copy of Justinian (s. xiv). Leaves from an earlier MS, pasted together, form the 'boards' of the binding.
'P .... que michi ... (p)lacet' written on the upper cover of the binding. On the front pastedown (in red crayon): 'Ad domum ordinis pertinet Cartus' (s. xv). Fol. 1: 'Buxheim' (s. xvii), but not listed in Kramer, I: 134.

Moorat, pp. 575-76.

Pl. 106

277 **Wellcome 790**   *1415 Evreux, France*

'Introductore de medicine et cyrurgie'

Parch. 54 fols. 133 × 105 mm. 1 col., 80-85 × 68-70 mm. 20-21 lines. Col. inits, rubrics. Diagrm fol. 29.

Fol. 53: '¶ Cy fine ce traictie de la qualite des herbes et choses medicinales bon et vtile Compile a la requeste Estiennot de vernon translate et escript par la main de R. de B. le jour premier de Juyn [fol. 53ᵛ] En La cite dEureux Lan de grace M.CCCC. et XV. Chienx monsieur pierre de pontpierre Et estoit apesee la guerre Fors au faulx anglois dengleterre. Verse moy du vin en ce verre Si nen ya si en va querre'. The MS is also dated fol. 40: 'Pour la quele chose ge [sic] vueil que ce present liuret ayt a nom le Recollectore. Ricard de lanathomie Galien Le quel fu compile le lundj xvjᵉ Jour de feurier M cccc et x par R. de B Et escript ainssy le vendredj xxiijᵉ Jour de may Lan M. CCCC

et XV'. Fol. 1 begins (in red): 'Cy commence lintroductore de medicine et cyrurgie pour E. de V[ernon] [.]edecin bon operateur et tout cyrurgien', but he is not listed by E. Wickersheimer, *Dictionnaire biographique des medecins en France au moyen âge* (1936).
Fol. 54ᵛ: 'Jehan le Roy compaignon barbyer demourant a Rouen Jevgne' (s. xvi).

Moorat, pp. 582-83.

Pl. 90

278 **Wellcome 794**   *1590 Pfaffenhofen, Germany*

'Probierbuech'

Paper. 307 fols. 300 × 200 mm. 2 cols, 208 × 120 mm. Up to 22 lines. Col. drawings, diagrms and tables in red and black, rubrics. Bld-tooled leather bdg over boards, with clasps.

Title-page: 'Probierbuech darinnen Erstlich auslegunng etlicher Lateinischer vnnd Alchimistischer Wörtter. Alphabeth. vnnd Caractor. auch derselben Nattürlichenn würckhung vnd Craft Bernnharden Vischer er zeit Teütschen Schuelhalter zue Pfaffenhouen [an der Roth, W. Bavaria] zughörig 1590 Manu propria'. The date is written in green, 'Probierbuech', 'Bernnharden Vischer' and 'Manu propria' in red, with the initials P, B and V in green.
Title-page: 'Ex libris Guilhelmi Georgij Welseri de Mettinga [..]', presumably for Meitingen, W. Bavaria (s. xvii).

Moorat, p. 585.

Pl. 296

279 **Wellcome 797, fols 1-42**   *1587 Falkenstein, Switzerland*

'Artzny Buch uss einem allten wolbewärten Kunstbuchli zusamen gebracht'

Paper. 42 fols. 203 × 150 mm. 1 col., 155-65 × c.115 mm. Up to 24 lines. Rubrics. Limp parch. wrapper (frag. of s. xiv service book), with ties gone

Fol. 1ᵛ: 'Beschrijben durch mich Hanns Jacob Wallin vogt zu falckimstein [Falkenstein, St Gallen, B. Rorschach] Anno 1587'. Fols 42ᵛ-52 contain additions by a hand of s. xvii, fols 52ᵛ-69ᵛ blank, fols 70-77ᵛ are again in s. xvii hand, fols 78-85ᵛ blank, and fols 86-87 are again s. xvii. Fols 1 and 87 have been pasted down on the original parchment wrapper of the MS.

Moorat, p. 587.

Pl. 293

280 **Westminster Abbey 34/2**   *[betw. 1395 and 1414] [Westminster, or Oxford? England]*

'De scismate'

Paper. 6 fols. 300 × 223 mm. 1 col., 240 × 165 mm. Up to 45 lines.

A pamphlet arising from the controversy of the papal schism (1378-1418). The text was occasioned by an unknown theologian's comments on an encyclical letter from the University of Paris, 'almost certainly *Quoniam Fideles*', brought to England by French representatives in Autumn 1395 (see M. Harvey, *Solutions to the Schism: A Study of Some English Attitudes 1378 to 1409*, Kirchengeschichtliche Quellen und Studien, 12 (1983), pp. 55, 67-8, 70-73). The writer (presumably an University-educated monk) is likely to have been addressing a topical issue. The three separate bifolia of which the pamphlet consists have been sewn individually onto two parchment strips cut from an inventory of relics in which the name 'Bassyngburn monach< >' occurs. The only Westminster monk of that name was John Bassyngbourne, 1388-1414 (cf. E.H. Pearce, *The Monks of Westminster* (1916), p. 123).

Originally folded in two so that fol. 6ᵛ (blank apart from the title 'De scismate') formed the pamphlet's outer cover. Not one of the texts on the subject seen in the Abbey library by John Leland, *c*. 1536-40 (for which see *English Benedictine Libraries*, p. 632).

MMBL, I: 402.

Pl. 72

---

281 Westminster Abbey 37   *[betw. 1382 and 1386]*
                                     [Westminster, England]

Missale (the 'Litlyngton Missal')

Parch. 342 fols, foliated 2-156, 157*, 157-342. 525 × 360 mm. 2 cols, 368 × 240 mm. 32 lines. Full-page min. fol. 157*ᵛ (an inserted leaf), mins, illum. hist. inits and full-page borders, dec., gold, and blue inits, rubrics. Kal. in gold, blue, red and black.

The arms and monogram of Nicholas Litlyngton, abbot of Westminster 1362-86, occur frequently, either singly or together, throughout the MS. His Treasurer's roll for 1383-84 (Westminster Abbey Muniments 24265*) gives a detailed bill for 'noui missalis'; this includes payment of £4 for two years board and lodging by the scribe, Thomas Preston, £4 6*s* 8*d* for 13 dozen skins of vellum, £22 0*s* 3*d* for the illumination of 'large letters', 21*s* for binding and 8*s* 4*d* for the cover (cf. J.A. Robinson and M.R. James, *The Manuscripts of Westminster Abbey* (1909), pp. 7-8). Preston began work 1382-83 (W. A. M. 24264*) when the Infirmarer received 21*s* 8*d* for his lodging for 26 weeks. The amount of vellum paid for in 1383-84 would not have been enough for the complete missal (only 312 fols not the actual 342), but payments on the Infirmarer's roll of 1386-87 (W.A.M. 19370) for 'nouo missali' could not have been (as suggested *MMBL*, I: 410, n. 2) for the Abbot's missal, since the Treasurer and Infirmarer had distinct responsibilities and payments would not have been transferred from one account to another. More likely the later payments were for a new missal for the Infirmary chapel which was virtually rebuilt at this time (I owe this information, as Muniment references, to Mr D. East). No further payments are recorded to Preston as he became a monk (Robinson and James, p. 8, but see Christianson, *Directory*, p. 144); he sang his first mass in 1386-7 (W.A.M. 19370), and died before 29 September 1420 (W.A.M. 23996). The historiated initials on fols 208-17 of Litlyngton's missal (in the coronation service for a king) have been left unfinished, presumably on Litlyngton's death.

Recorded as item 1 in the 1388 inventory of service books kept in the vestry 'unum bonum Missale et grande ex dono quondam Nicholai Lytlington abbatis' (cf. J. Wickham Legg, 'On an inventory of the vestry in Westminster Abbey, taken in 1388', *Archaeologia*, 52 (1890), 233). Fol. 2 (originally blank) contains a copy of a public instrument drawn up by John Paynter, apostolic notary, attesting the oath of John Islip, abbot elect of Westminster, to observe all the laws, statutes and customs observed by his predecessors, dated 25 November 1500.

Described in an inventory of 1540 as 'a Masse Booke of Abbott Nicholas Lytlyngton giffte, ij folio 'ad te levavi' with claspys of copper and the booke ys covered with clothe of gold' (pr. M.E.C. Walcott, 'The inventories of Westminster Abbey at the Dissolution', *Transactions of the London and Middlesex Archaeological Soc.*, 4 (1873), 343). Apparently alienated, but returned to the Abbey by Dean Dolben in 1663 (Library Register, fol. 71; Robinson and James, p. 40, no. 71). Rebound as two volumes in 1806 (see H.M. Nixon, *Five Centuries of English Bookbinding* (1978), p. 186).

Missale ad usum Ecclesie Westmonasteriensis, ed. J. Wickham Legg, HBS, 1 (1891), pls 1-7 illus. hist. inits fols 9, 10, 21, 121, 141; HBS, 5 (1893), pls 9-10 illus. part of fols 224, 277ᵛ; and HBS, 12 (1897); NPS, 2nd ser., pls 196, 197 illus. fols 157*ᵛ, 314; *MMBL*, I: 410-11; *Exh.*, *Engl. Illum. MSS 700-1500*, no. 71; J. Brückmann, 'Latin Manuscript Pontificals and Benedictionals in England and Wales', *Traditio*, 29 (1973), 444-45; Sandler, *Gothic MSS*, no. 150, ills. 393, 402 illus. fols 106ᵛ, 157*ᵛ (both reduced), and ills 403-5 illus. hist. inits fols 26, 95ᵛ, 120; L.F. Sandler, *Omne Bonum: A Fourteenth-Century Encyclopedia of Universal Knowledge*, 2 vols (1996), I, ill. 58 illus. init. fol. 120; D. East, 'A late fourteenth-century service book: the historiated and inhabited initials of the Great Missal (1383-4) of Abbot Nicholas Litlyngton', Unpubl. M.Phil. thesis, University of Essex (1998).

Pl. 64

---

282 Westminster Abbey Muniments Book 1
             [betw. 1474 and 1498] [Westminster, England]

Cartularium ('Liber Niger Quaternus')

Parch. 158 fols (fols 9-158 with medieval foliation i-cl). 340 × 245 mm. 1 col., 237-45 × 167 mm. 37-45 lines. Col. inits (blank spaces often left), rubrics.

Fol. 9 (medieval fol. i): 'Liber quaternus niger ex antiquo denominatus quem Thomas Clifforde vir honorabilis ac huius monasterii beati Petri Westm' quondam monachus [d. 1485] ad suos sumptus expensasque fieri fecit de nouo in tempore Reuerendissimi in christo Patris ac domini domini Johannis Estney permissione diuina prefati monasterii abbatis [1474-98] prestantissimi in dei gloriam et perpetuam ecclesiastici iuris memoriam feliciter incipit'. Clifford was the monk-bailiff from 1483-84 (cf. E.H. Pearce, *The Monks of Westminster* (1916), pp. 159-60). The scribe can be identified as William Ebesham for whose other work, see A.I. Doyle,' The work of a late fifteenth-century English scribe, William Ebesham', *BJRL*, 39 (1956-57), 298-325, and L.E. Voigts, 'A handlist of Middle English in Harvard manuscripts', *Harvard Library Bulletin*, 33 (1985), 87-88. Fols 1-8 contain the table of contents.

J.A. Robinson and M.R. James, *The Manuscripts of Westminster Abbey* (1909), pp. 95-98; Davis, *MC*, no. 1015; B. Harvey, *Westminster Abbey and its Estates in the Middle Ages* (1977).

Pl. 196

---

283 Westminster Cathedral Treasury, 3 fols 1-69
                                  1510 Arnstein, Germany

Ordinarius Premonstratensis

Parch. 69 fols. 151 × 108 mm. 1 col., 115 × 68 mm. 32-36 lines. Col. inits.

Fol. 69ᵛ: 'Explicit Ordinarius ordinis premonstratensis ... Diligenter conscriptum per me fratrem Iohannem Anre. eiusdem ordinis professor. videlicet Cenobii Arnsteynens' [Premonstratensian abbey of Arnstein, Nassau]. Anno incarnationis domini. Millesimo. Quingentesimo. Decimo. Sit laus deo qui est benedictus in secula seculorum. Amen'

> MMBL, I: 417-18 (whence the above description derives); Kramer, I: 26.
> *MS unavailable to readers.*

284 Westminster Diocesan Archives, H.38, fols 83-155
[betw. c.1393 and 1406?] [London, England]

Carthusian miscellany, in Latin and English
Paper. 73 fols. 205 × 150 mm. 1 col., c.180 × 110-20 mm. Up to 42 lines. Leather bdg over boards, clasp gone (s. xv).

A booklet containing short theological texts and extracts, all in one hand, written by a Carthusian. The writer often refers to himself in the 1st person and on fol. 83 has noted 'Anno domini millesimo nonogesimo tercio in festo sancti michaelis suscepi \primo/ ordinis cart'. An added inscription, apparently by the same hand, at the foot of the same page reads 'Magister Iohannes shillyngford doctor in iure'. If this is taken to mean that John Shillyngford, DCL, of Oxford (*BRUO*, 1689), was the owner of the present booklet it must have been written before 1406 when he died. However, Shillyngford was not a Carthusian. S.M. Horrall ('Middle English texts in a Carthusian commonplace book: Westminster Cathedral, Diocesan Archives, MS H.38', *Medium Aevum*, 59 (1990), 214-27) argues that the 'textual traditions of the individual pieces point towards London or its immediate vicinity as the most probable location for the copying of the manuscript'. Fol. 82, a leaf containing lists of apostles, martyrs, confessors, etc, may once have served as part of a parchment wrapper for fols 83-155. Two other booklets, fols 1-81 and 156-221, with which fols 83-155 were bound in s. xv, contain items of interest to a parish priest. Fol. 82: 'vᵗᵒ Idus februarij obiit dominus Johannes Fowler'. On the pastedown of the lower cover of the bdg are named persons to be prayed for: 'for the sowle of annys Afflyn for mylys ʒ Phylys wylyam hastwell water violet Alexander kly John Rykynnsal' (s. xv ex).

> MMBL, I: 419-21.
> *Pl. 71*

285 Dr Williams's Library Anc. 6, fols 7-198
[betw. 1328 and 1340?] [England]

Psalterium
Parch. 192 fols. 102 × 70 mm. 1 col., 68 × 45 mm. 18 lines. Illum. hist. inits with full-page borders, dec. and gold inits. Kal. in gold, blue, red and purple. Bld-stamped leather bdg with clasp (s. xviⁱⁿ).

Arms in the border (fol. 20) are those of France, England and Hainault. The kalendar (fols 7-19), in the same English hand as the psalter, includes (in blue) the obit of Philip IV of France, d. 29 Nov. 1314, and (in blue and red) that of his queen, Jeanne of Navarre, d. 2 April 1305. The couple's grandchildren, Edward III of England and Philippa of Hainault, married in 1328. J.J.G. Alexander ('Painting and manuscript illumination for royal patrons in the later Middle Ages', *English Court Culture in the Later Middle Ages*, ed. V.J. Scattergood and J.W.

Sherborne (1983), p. 142) has thus suggested that the present MS was a wedding gift for Queen Philippa. The kalendar includes St Francis (4 Oct.), with octave (11 Oct.) and translation (25 May), all in gold; and Philippa's confessor, John Mablethorpe, was a Franciscan (cf. L. Dennison, 'An illuminator of the Queen Mary Psalter group: the Ancient 6 Master', *The Antiquaries Journal*, 6 (1986), 298 and n. 78). Since the English royal arms are not quartered with those of France, it is likely the MS was produced before Edward's assumption of the arms of France (ancient) in 1340. For the panels used on the binding, see J.B. Oldham, *Blind Panels of English Binders* (1958), ST 27 (on upper cover) and ST 4 (on lower cover).

Fol. 199: 'henr. amyes' (s. xviⁱⁿ).

> MMBL, I: 428-9; Exh., *Engl. Illum. MSS 700-1500*, no. 65; M.A. Michael, 'A manuscript wedding gift from Philippa of Hainault to Edward III', *The Burlington Magazine*, 127 (1985), 590; Sandler, *Gothic MSS*, no. 74 and ills. 183 illus. fol. 20; Dennison, 'The Ancient 6 Master', pls XL a-b, XLI a-b illus. fols 20, 43ᵛ, 105, 122ᵛ and pls illus. inits fols 105ᵛ, 87 (all enlarged).
> *Pl. 49*

REJECTED MANUSCRIPTS

The following list has been kept as short as possible and includes only manuscripts about which it seems necessary to make a positive statement. I have thought it necessary to contradict published statements that a manuscript is either dated or datable only when these are made in a catalogue or main source of reference to the manuscript or in a monograph or article devoted to it. Modern palaeographical practice is to express a date in calendar years only when a manuscript is precisely dated by its scribe, or is generally datable from internal evidence of the text or external evidence such as ownership. Therefore I have ignored statements of date in calendar years, e.g. *c*.1420-30 or even 1420, when it is evident such dates are presumed dates: that is, the expression of an informed opinion based on a study of the script or art of a manuscript.

Central St Martin's College of Art and Design, MIS. 119   Although the date 1578 suits the appearance of the handwriting, it is the date of the latest in a collection of statutes copied by the Venetian notary Gabriele Gabrieli.

College of Arms, Arundel 19   One of the London Chronicles discussed by M.R. McLaren, 'The Textual Transmission of the London Chronicles', *English Manuscript Studies 1100-1700*, 3 (1992), 38-72 at 42-45, 66. She observes changes of hand at 1433, 1438, and 1451, implying that the MS was written in stints at these different dates. However, in my opinion, the text was written by one hand to 1451 (fol. 33v). Subsequent additions were made in s. xvi.

College of Arms, M. 3   A miscellany, including accounts of ceremonies in which he had taken part, written for and probably largely written by William Ballard, March King of Arms. The MS has been dated between *c*.1465 (it includes an account of the coronation of Queen Elizabeth Woodville) and 1490 (assuming that Ballard died in that year), a span of 25 years. However, the precise date of his death is unknown. A note (fol. 1) records only that the MS was bought from his widow `Anno vj^{to} Regis henrici septimi' (21 August 1490 – 22 August 1491).

College of Arms, M. 9   An account of the wars with France, produced (according to its title) for Sir John Fastolf, for which see B.J.H. Rowe, 'A contemporary account of the Hundred Years' War with France from 1415 to 1429', *EHR*, 41 (1926), 504-13. Although the date of 1459 given in the title would suit the appearance of the handwriting, it is supplied by a hand other than that of the scribe in an inserted reference to Fastolf's death.

Dutch Church 13   Although the date 1584 suits the appearance of the handwriting, it occurs in a note added in the top left hand margin of the title page of this copy of Jan Engelram's 'Defensio doctrinae christianae … Aduersus quendem aduersarium [Gerardum Goosenium]'. On fol. 87^v the date '13 January 1585' also occurs. Now deposited at the Guildhall Library as MS 20185/13.

Goldsmiths' Company 2523   The date 1513 is that of the Ordinances copied, not necessarily that of the MS.

Guildhall 2207   Although a note on fol. 2 of the Ordinance Book of the Plumbers' Company records 'In the yere of oure lorde god .M. CCCCC. And .xx. and in the .xj. yere of the rayne of oure sou*er*ayne lorde kyng henry the .viij. … wreten the viij day of marche. the yere and rayne abouesayde', a date which would suit the appearance of the handwriting, it does not specifically state that the MS (as opposed to the note itself) was written in that year.

Guildhall 7114   An inscription, fol. 9^v, records 'Be hit had in mynde that Robert Chamburlayn Citezen and peuterer' of london. and Cecile his wife 3afe þis boke in to þe Crafte of peuterers in the worschep of god and þe assumpc*ion* of oure lady to be prayde fore euer p*er*petuall ¶ The xj. day of august in þe 3ere of oure lorde .M^0. CCCC lxiij. And in the þirde 3ere of the Reigne of Kyng' Edward the foureth'. However, since the hand of the inscription does not occur elsewhere in this Ordinance Book and since Robert and Cecily obviously gave a blank book (much of it is still blank), it is uncertain how much of the MS was actually written in 1463.

Guildhall 20845   Although the date 1554 suits the appearance of the handwriting of this copy of the 'Spirituall Exercises and ghostly meditacions' of William Peryn, prior of St Bartholomew's, Smithfield, 1553-58, it is that of the dedicatory epistle only (fols 2-4). The date '1597' at the top of fol. 5 is added.

Inner Temple, Petyt 511/7   The date 1338 (colophon, fol. 195^v) is that of the completion of the text and not that of this copy; see R. Stepsis, 'The manuscripts of Robert Mannyng of Brunne's *Chronicle of England*', *Manuscripta*, 13 (1969), 131-41.

Inner Temple, Misc. 13   A note that 'thys present boke' was made in 1505 is an addition to the so-called 'Old Grace Book' which contains calendrical tables and laws copied by a hand of s. xv med.

Inner Temple, Misc. 71   Although the date 1591 suits the appearance of the handwriting, it is that of the two deeds of sale (10 and 11 December) copied into this MS.

Lambeth Palace 78   The inscription (fol. ii) 'Liber compositus et perquisitus dompni Willelmi Chartham monachi huius ecclesie. Anno domini M⁰ .cccc⁰. xlviij⁰ ', written in a humanist hand, is probably posthumous. Chartham, a monk of Christ Church Canterbury, died 14 February 1448.

Lambeth Palace 177   Although it suits the appearance of the handwriting of fols 1-126 of this MS, the date 1493 is that of the publication of Vice-Chancellor Guillaume Caoursin's recodification of the statutes of the Order of St John of Jerusalem. An ordinance of 5 August in that year provided for their translation from Latin into various vernaculars (cf. E. Nasalli Rocca di Corneliano, 'Origine et évolution de la "Règle" Hiérosolymitain des Hospitaliers de St. Jean (dit de Rhodes, dit de Malte) II', *Annales de l'Ordre Souveraine Militaire de Malte*, 19 (1961), 119-25; A. Luttrell, 'The Hospitallers' historical activities: 1400-1530', *Latin Greece, The Hospitallers and the Crusades 1291-1440* (1982), Study II). Fols 127-44 contain supplementary statutes in French, s. xvi.

Lambeth Palace 326   James, p. 427, associated this copy of Jean Galopes' Latin prose translation of Deguileville's *Pèlerinage de l'âme* with the copy made for John, duke of Bedford, for which payment was recorded in 1427. However, the arms in the presentation miniature (fol. 1) are not Bedford's; see further J. Stratford, 'The manuscripts of John, Duke of Bedford: Library and Chapel', *England in the fifteenth century: Proceedings of the 1986 Harlaxton Symposium*, ed. D. Williams (1987), p. 348 and n. 67.

Lambeth Palace 1171   Listed (as Lambeth 1170) by Scott, *Later Gothic MSS*, II: 316, this genealogical roll chronicle by the 'Considerans' scribe is said to be probably datable *c*.1470-72. However, the text here ends (as in three other copies) with the birth of Henry VI's son, Edward, in 1453 (cf. *MMBL*, I: 94-5).

Law Society   The MS of Robert Persons's 'Memorial for the Reformation of England' listed by J. Nicholson, *Catalogue of the Mendham Collection* (1871), p. 229, cannot now be traced. However, it is unlikely that it was written in 1596 since that was the date of the composition of the text.

Lincoln's Inn, Hale 99   While the content of this volume catalogued as 'Registrum Magistri Willielmi Gonson Armigeri, vice-admiralli et commissarii admiralitatis in com' Norff' et Suff', de computo apud Lennam [King's Lynn] anno 1536' (Hunter, p. 79) relates to that year, there is no such date in the MS.

Lincoln's Inn, Maynard 20   Although the date 1596 suits the appearance of the handwriting, it is that of the composition of the text (Francis Bacon's *Maxims*) and appears in three other manuscripts (cf. *The Works of Francis Bacon*, ed. J. Spedding, R.L. Ellis and D.D. Heath, 14 vols (1858-74), VII: 309-87).

Lincoln's Inn, Misc. 99   While the date 1591 suits the appearance of the handwriting, it is that of the presentation of William Lambarde's *Archeion* to Sir Robert Cecil and not that of this particular copy.

Middle Temple, Anc. 1   Although the date 1406 would suit the appearance of the handwriting of this copy of John Lathbury's Commentary on Lamentations, the same date also occurs in Oxford, Merton College 189.

National Maritime Museum NVT 14   Although an appropriate date for the handwriting, the date 1557 said to occur in this copy of a treatise on mathematical rules for measuring height and length does not appear in the MS.

National Maritime Museum P 13   The date 1420 is that of the text, Cristoforo Buondelmonte's Liber Insularum Archipelagi, and not that of this copy.

National Maritime Museum P 20   The date 1422, added in this copy, is the date of Cristoforo Buondelmonte's redaction of his Liber Insularum Archipelagi, and not that of this copy.

Royal Astronomical Society QB. 7/1021   Although 1348, the radix date of several tables in this MS, would suit the appearance of the handwriting, the same date is to be found elsewhere.

Royal College of Physicians 131   According to the description of this MS (catalogued as MS 111 in the typescript catalogue of 1928), it was presented to Sir Walter Mildmay by the author George Etherege in 1528. There is no such date in this MS of 'In libros aliquot Pauli Aeginetae hypomnemata quedam, seu observationes medicamentorum'.

Royal College of Physicians 388   Cited in previous literature as Royal College of Physicians 13, this copy of *The Canterbury Tales* is by the well known 'Hammond scribe' (for other MSS by him, see L.R. Mooney, 'A new manuscript by the Hammond scribe discovered by Jeremy Griffiths', *The English Medieval Book: Studies in Memory of Jeremy Griffiths*, ed. A.S.G. Edwards, V. Gillespie and R. Hanna (2000), pp. 113-23). The scribe's career has generally been dated to the reign of Edward IV (1461-83). A suggestion that he may be identified with the London stationer, John Multon, d. 1475 (Christianson, *Directory*, pp. 136-37), would provide only a *terminus ante quem* for his work, were it accepted. The scribe's apparent signature, 'Quod Multon 1458', in Cambridge, Trinity College R. 14. 52, has been discounted by L.R. Mooney, 'More manuscripts by a Chaucer scribe', *Chaucer Review*, 30 (1995-96), 401-7. She argues that, as the name occurs only at the end of one text within Trinity, Multon was more probably the name of the particular text's author rather than that of the scribe of the volume.

St Bartholomew's Hospital HC 2/1   Generally known as 'Cok's cartulary' (after the compiler John Cok, renter of the hospital), the MS chiefly contains fifteenth-century copies, by different scribes, of thirteenth- and fourteenth-century deeds (for which see N.J.M. Kerling, *Cartulary of St Bartholomew's Hospital, founded 1132: a calendar* (1973)). Cok himself made only a few additions on leaves originally left blank. Some of these additions were dated by him, the dates spanning 50 years from 1418 to 1468. A rental preceding the cartulary and written by Cok is dated 1456.

Sion College Arc.L.40.2/L.26   Although the MS later belonged to Richard III (A.F. Sutton and L. Visser-Fuchs, *Richard III's Books: Ideals and Reality in the Life and Library of a Medieval Prince* (1997), pp. 118-19 and 283-85), it is unclear who commissioned it. Hence it cannot be dated to the 1430s, as suggested by C.F. Briggs, 'Manuscripts of Giles of Rome's *De Regimine Principum* in England, 1300-1500: A Handlist', *Scriptorium*, 47 (1993), 60-73, no. 35.

Skinners' Company, s.n.   Although a list of 'Founders and brethern and sustern of the fraternitee of Corpus Christi Founded by the worshipfull Felawship of Skynners of the Citee of London' (fols 12-15) in this 'Book of the Fraternity of Corpus Christi' includes Edward IV (1461-83), Queen Elizabeth Woodville (whom he married in 1464), and Richard Duke of Gloucester, the appearance of the handwriting suggests a date later in s. xv. The volume also contains annual lists of Masters and Wardens from 1485-1732.

UCL Germ. 25   Although a date of 1522 would suit the appearance of the script (cf. *MMBL*, I: 334), it does not occur in this Book of Hours. It is deduced from a marginal note, cropped in binding, '<t> iaer ons < >eren dusent', beside the date 1522 in an almanac for the years 1522-41 found in a preliminary quire containing calendrical tables (fols 1-4).

UCL Lat. 11   While a date of 1425 would suit the appearance of the script of this medical dictionary (cf. *MMBL*, I: 341), the wording of the colophon, 'Explicit Tabule Medicine incepta anno 1416 et terminata 1425', together with the fact there is no discernible break in the handwriting throughout the text, suggests that 1425 was the date of the text's completion and not that at which the MS was made.

UCL Ogden 7/40   While the date 1590 would suit the appearance of the handwriting, it occurs as part of the *ex libris*, 'Liber Willelmi Tothill Anno Domini 1590 Reg: Eliz. 32°', and need not refer to the production of this copy of a Yearbook of Richard II (as believed by S. Clark, 'Wisdom Literature of the seventeenth century: a guide to the contents of the 'Bacon-Tottel' commonplace books', *TCBS*, 6 (1976), 294, 297; *TCBS*, 7 (1977), 72).

UCL Ogden 13   The dates 1550, 1559 in this copy of 'Duello del [Sebastiano] Fausto da Longianio regolato a le leggi dell'Honore' have been copied from editions printed by Rutilio Borgominieri of Venice.

UCL Ogden 14   The dates 1584 and 1587 given in this English translation of L.G. Goslicki's *De optimo senatore* conflict. While it is possible that the scribe supplied the title page with the 1587 date later, there is no obvious break between the handwriting of it and the following text where Book I is dated 'Aprilis jx° Anno 1584', and book II, 'Finis Anno Domini Maij xxiij° 1584'. The present translation differs from that presented by Robert Chester to Thomas Meade, Puisne Judge of Common Pleas 1577-79 (in London, BL Add 18613), and from that of the first printed edition, 1598 (*STC* 12372).

UCL Ogden 15   The date 1562 is added in a note at the foot of p. 12 ('dedi x^mo februarij 1562') and does not date this tract (beginning 'Comes Westmorlandiae ducit in vxorem sororem vxoris demortuae …') by John Hales I, MP, d. 1571.

UCL Ogden 20   The date 1565 is supplied by William Lambarde to this MS undated by its scribe; for facsim. of Lambarde's note, detailing the circumstances of this MS's production, see *A Discourse of the common weal of this realm of England*, ed. W. Cunningham and E. Lamond (1893), fig. 4.

UCL Phillipps 39   The date 1575 is that of an inserted, printed, title page and not that of the MS (containing 'Handveste und Satzungen der Stadt Bern').

UCL Phillipps 59   The date 1529 is that of the First Peace of Kappel and not that of this copy of the articles of peace.

ULL 1   A date of 1385 is indicated for the text's composition (cf. D.B. Tyson, *La Vie du Prince Noir by Chandos Herald edited from the manuscript in the University of London Library, Beihefte zur Zeitschrift für Romanische Philologie*, 147 (1975), p. 4). J.J.G. Alexander has suggested ('Painting and manuscript illumination for royal patrons in the later middle ages', *English Court Culture in the Later Middle Ages*, ed. V.J. Scattergood and J.W. Sherborne (1983), p. 145) that this MS could have been the presentation copy for Richard II (1377-99). However, the presence of the royal arms (on fol. 4) need not imply this, and other possible owners have been suggested by M. Connolly, *John Shirley; Book Production and the Noble Household in Fifteenth-Century England* (1998), pp. 106-7.

V & A L.1601-1893   The date 1585 given in the colophons and also tooled on the bindings of this two-volume MS suits the appearance of the handwriting. However, it is clear from the wording of the colophon in vol II that it was the date when the text was completed (October 1585) and that the author, the Nuremberg goldsmith Wenzel Jamnitzer, had died in December of that year.

V & A L.2320-1947   Although the date 1501 suits the appearance of the handwriting (cf. *MMBL*, I: 390), it is the date of Leonardo Loredano's election as Doge of Venice, which the text (Antonio Vinciguerra's De principe libellus) was composed to celebrate, and not necessarily that of this copy.

Wellcome 59   While the date 1575 suits the appearance of the hand, it is probably that at which the lectures copied here were delivered. In Wellcome 778, by the same scribe, which contains various dates in 1579-80, he has noted at fol. 34 'Hic fecit finem …. die .9. xbris 1579', drawn a line, and resumed copying 'Die .2. januarij .1580. rursus cepit legere'.

Wellcome 86   The date 1463 is a later addition to this s. xiii MS of the Articella.

Wellcome 87   The date 1559 is not in the hand of the text of this German MS on artillery.

Wellcome 96   The date 1572 pencilled on the flyleaf of this collection of medical receipts and prescriptions is a much later addition.

Wellcome 107   The date 1588 is on the binding of the MS. While some of the engraved borders within the MS bear the date 1572, the alchemical texts copied are themselves undated.

Wellcome 113   While the date on the title page is 1570, the immediately following authorial preface to the reader of this 'Artznei Buechel' is dated 1572.

Wellcome 129   The dates 1563 and 1564 are probably those of the lectures copied in this MS.

Wellcome 136   Although intended for presentation to Elizabeth I in 1560, there is no such date in this MS of Pierre Boaistuau's Histoires prodigieuses.

Wellcome 178   The date 1517 is only that of a particular receipt in this collection of medical receipts.

Wellcome 181   The date 1561 on the title page of this 'Ercznei Buch' appears to be added.

Wellcome 192   The date 1584 refers to the date of the translation into French of the works of Christophorus Parisiensis, and not to this particular MS.

Wellcome 216   The dates 1538 and 1540 are those of the lectures copied here, not necessarily those of the MS.

Wellcome 218   The date 1596 appears to have been added to this collection of cosmetic receipts.

Wellcome 222   The date 1533 is that of the text not necessarily that of this collection of receipts.

Wellcome 244   The date 1564 applies specifically to a note on weights and measures and not to the whole MS.

Wellcome 260   The date 1560 applies to a specific receipt not to the whole collection.

Wellcome 266   The MS is datable rather than dated, the text ('Consilia', in German) being dated 1550 and the *ex libris* 1551.

Wellcome 269   The dates 1560-62 are those of the lectures copied here, not necessarily those of the MS

Wellcome 272   The date 1584 is that of the text ('Feuerwercken') and not that of this MS.

Wellcome 280   The dates 1537 and 1549 are those of particular receipts within this collection.

Wellcome 282   The date 1537 is that of the lectures copied here and not that of the MS. Foliation establishes it originally formed part of a larger volume with MSS 281 and 567.

Wellcome 304   The date (apparently 1428) of this copy of Gentilis de Fulgineo's Expositio in primam Fen quarti Canonis Avicennae has been tampered with

Wellcome 316   Although the date 1366 seems appropriate for the appearance of the handwriting of this commentary on Aristotle's Physics, the wording of the colophon ('Explicit primus tractatus huius summe per manus hainrici Feihtonis Reportata et per magistrum hermanum grabnerum in Nurnberg compilata ...') is such that 1366 could be the date of the text.

Wellcome 317   The date 1554 is that of the *ex libris* and not that of this 'Ertzney Buechell'.

Wellcome 332   Although the date 1515 occurs several times, it is that of letters copied within this compilation.

Wellcome 334   The date 1480 is that of the *ex libris* and not that of this Herbal.

Wellcome 359   The date 1563 is that of a particular receipt within this collection.

Wellcome 378   While the date 1419 suits the appearance of the handwriting, it occurs in the title to the first text in this medical compilation.

Wellcome 386   The date 1581 is that of an addition to this copy of Franz Joel's De morbis hyperphysicis et rebus magicis, dated on the title page '1579 Rostochij Typis Stephani Myliandrj' (*not* Mylionskii, as in Moorat, p. 256); that is, the MS was copied from an edition published by Stephen Möllemann, Rostock printer, 1561-1610.

Wellcome 394   The date 1589 is that of the text (on astrological geomancy) not that of the MS.

Wellcome 398   The date 1508 is the presumed date; there is no date in this German MS of surgery.

Wellcome 406   The date 1511 is that of the *ex libris*, and not that of this Leech Book.

Wellcome 433   Although the date 1480 suits the appearance of the script, this MS of the Consilia of Johann Lochner (for which see H.J. Vermeer, 'Johann Lochners "Reisekonsilia"', *Sudhoffs Archiv*, 56 (1972), 145-96) is datable rather than dated. It is a fair copy, and while a letter of 1480 from Lochner to his son (fols 15-16) is probably begun in his hand, it is concluded by the main scribe of the volume.

Wellcome 437   While the date, 1516, suits the appearance of the script, it is probably that of the text, Domenico di Lodi's Libro del modo de governar cavalli et medicar li.

Wellcome 440   The dates 1575, 1576, are those of the lectures copied.

Wellcome 470   Although the date, 1535, suits the appearance of the handwriting, it has been added to this medical MS.

Wellcome 476   The date 1520 is that of the text (Giovanni Martigegni's De morbo Gallico), not that of the MS.

Wellcome 478   The date 1585 is probably that of the lectures copied here.

Wellcome 485   The title page with date 1598 has been written by a hand other than that of the text (Theodore Turquet de Mayerne, Virtutes laudani).

Wellcome 509   Three different MSS have been bound in this volume. The date 1579 found in the third has been added by a hand other than that of the scribe of a letter on the Gregorian calendar.

Wellcome 519   The dates 1579, 1582, in this alchemical miscellany are added.

Wellcome 523   The handwriting of this alchemical miscellany looks later than the date 1430 (fol. 16). Moorat, p. 368, suggests this MS once formed part of a larger volume with MSS 418 and 707. All three MSS are the same size and the contents of the latter two agree with some of the contents recorded in MS 523, fol. 1 (by a s.xvi hand) which must once have been part of a larger volume. However, no single scribe occurs in any one of the MSS.

Wellcome 526   The MS is datable rather than dated, various dates between 1515 and 1527 being embodied in this collection of alchemical texts.

Wellcome 529   The date 1470 is that of a particular charm in this alchemical miscellany.

Wellcome 570   The dates 1576, 1577, are those of a plague at Monza of which the present MS contains an account.

Wellcome 593   While the date 1563 suits the appearance of the script, the wording of the title page, 'Büecher von vrsachen Zaichen vnd Curierungen der Kranckheiten avs dem Tartaro; Durch müeh vnd fleisz des fürteffenliche*n* Mans Adamj vo*n* Bodenstain an den Tag … nach laut der warheit publiciert Anno .1.5.63.', refers to Adam von Bodenstein's translation and edition of Paracelsus' text (publ. Basel, 1563; cf. K. Sudhoff, *Versuch einer Kritik der echtheit der Paracelsischen Schriften*, I, *Bibliographia Paracelsica* (1894), no. 54), rather than the present MS.

Wellcome 601 and 602   The dates, 1578 and 1579, in these two volumes, both copied by the same scribe, are probably those at which the lectures copied were delivered.

Wellcome 652   The date 1519 occurs within this collection of medical receipts.

Wellcome 695   The date 1565 is that of the lectures copied, not necessarily that of the MS.

Wellcome 696   The date 1536 is that of the *ex libris*. This collection of receipts is datable rather than dated, the date 1535 occurring in a heading to one of them (fol. 20).

Wellcome 698   The date 1559 refers to the date of cures effected by the owner of this Arzneibuch, not to the date at which he copied it.

Wellcome 765   The date 1596 and the name of the compiler of this Rezeptbuch are written in pencil by a later owner (s. xix) on one of the pastedowns.

Wellcome 788   While the date 1460 suits the appearance of the handwriting, it is scribbled on a pastedown by a hand other than that of the scribe of the text, an Italian translation of Vegetius' Ars veterinaria.

Wellcome 807   While the date 1296 suits the appearance of the handwriting, the colophon (fol. 260) does not make explicit whether Mr Bartholomeus Petrus was the author or scribe of this pharmacological treatise.

Wellcome 5650   The dating *c*.1440-60 for this medical compendium depends on the assumed tenure of John Marshall as Vicar of St Michael's, Appleby (colophon, fol. 28^v). While such a dating would suit the appearance of the script, and references to him range from 1444 (as chaplain, cf. J. Nicolson and R. Burn, *The History and Antiquities of the Counties of Westmorland and Cumberland*, 2 vols (1777), I: 328-9), vicar by 1447-48 (*Calendar of entries in the Papal Registers relating to Great Britain and Ireland: Papal Letters*, ed. W.H. Bliss *et al*. (1893-), X: 12) to 1458 (*CPR, Henry VI 1452-61*, p. 446), I have been unable to discover when he became vicar or when he died/resigned the living.

Westminster Abbey 38   Although *Liber Regalis* contains a recension of the coronation *ordo* probably due to Nicholas Litlyngton, abbot of Westminster 1362-86 (cf. W. Ullman, *Liber Regie Capelle: A manuscript in the Biblioteca Publica, Evora*, HBS, 92 (1961), 22-23), it is only supposition that the present MS was produced for the coronation of Anne of Bohemia in 1382. It is not included in the 1388 inventory of books in the vestry (cf. J.W. Legg, 'On an inventory of the vestry in Westminster Abbey, taken in 1388', *Archaeologia*, 52 (1890), 233-35).

Westminster Abbey 39   As Ker (*MMBL*, I: 414) states, the presence of the arms of Margaret Beaufort on fol. 1 and the occurrence of the Stanley jamb in decoration suggest that this MS Prayer Book was commissioned by the Lady Margaret for her fourth husband, Thomas Stanley (d. 1504). However, the couple married ten years earlier than Ker thought, in 1472 rather than 1482; see M.K. Jones and M.G. Underwood, *The King's Mother: Lady Margaret Beaufort, Countess of Richmond and Derby* (1992), p. 59 n. 70.

ADDENDA

A1 Congregational Library I.e.6   *1515*
[Brussels, Belgium]

Life and miracles of St Jerome, in Netherlandish

Parch. 175 fols. 205 × 140 mm. 1 col., 133 × 90 mm. 23 lines. Full-page mins (fols 2ᵛ, 154ᵛ) both pasted in, painted init. and border (fol. 15), col. inits, rubrics, ruling in purple ink. Bld-stamped bdg over boards, with two clasps.

Fol. 175ᵛ: 'Item Dit boec was volscreuen Int jaer ons heeren .m. vᶜ. ende .xv. sinte elyzabetten auent .xviij. nouember bij suster janneken van ophen Ende suster grietken van scaffele heesten becosten. ter eeren des gloriosen iheronimi .ten loue gods moet sijn. Eenen aue maria on gode'.
Fol. 175ᵛ (added by a hand contemporary with that of the text): 'Dit boec behoort Int regularisen clooster van sinte Elyzabeth op den berch van syon binnen bruesel [Augustinian canonesses of Ste Elisabeth-au-Mont-Sion, Brussels]', followed by two lines erased. On front pastedown 'R.M. Beverley LL.B 1817'.

A2 V & A L. 2223-1884   *1592 [Spain]*
Graduale Romanum

Parch. 91 fols, foliated in red (from present fol. 2) iij-lxxiij, lxxv, lxxvii-xciiij. 528 × 400 mm. 1 col., 460 × 280 mm. 18 lines. Col. inits, rubrics. Ruling in red. Whittawed leather bdg over boards, with metal bosses.

Fol. 91ᵛ: 'Acabose anno del .S. d. 1592'.

A3 Wellcome 8004, fols 5-74   *c.1454 [England]*

Medical miscellany, in English

Parch. 70 fols, modern pencil foliation as 5-30 [+ leaf omitted, 30*] 31-74. 205 × 143 mm. 1 col., 160 × 110 mm. 25-26 lines. Gold inits and borders, col. inits, rubrics. Vein man (fol. 18), zodiac man (fol. 39), diagrms. Kal. and tables in red and black.

Fol. 5 (in red): 'Tis [*sic*] calendere was begune in þe ȝere of our' lorde. Iesu cryste 1454'. A table of solar movements (fol. 28) runs from 1385-1469, and eclipse tables (fol. 29) from 1441-81. Fols 72ᵛ-74ᵛ blank. A following booklet (fols 75-99), written by the same scribe, contains an itinerary to Jerusalem in prose (beginning 'Who that wyll to Jerusalem gon' he must make hys chaunge at london' wᵗ þe lumbards ...') and two verse texts (Lydgate's *Dietary*, fols 83ᵛ-84, and *Storie lune* (*IMEV* 970), fols 85-98). Fols 98ᵛ-99ᵛ blank.
Fol. 1: 'Thomas Hill June 10th 1759'.
Christies's London Sale Catalogue, 29 November 1999, lot 9, with pls illus fol. 18 (enlarged) and fols 58ᵛ-59 (reduced).

INDEXES

Throughout the indexes reference is made to the serial numbers of the descriptions. Only in the Index of Dates is reference also made to plate numbers. Personal names are entered and cross-referenced thus:

ENTRIES

Family names where possible
(e.g. Frampton, Richard).
Names that contain *du* are entered under that name
(e.g. du Bosquet);

but

forenames are used for Italians
(e.g. Domenico Capranica)

and

forenames are used when the name contains
de, *di*, *da*, *von*, *van*, *of* (e.g. Ferry de Clugny);

and

rulers and princes are entered under their
territories or titles (e.g. England, Richard III, king of);

and

noblemen are entered under their title
(e.g. Arundel, Henry Fitzalan, earl of).

CROSS-REFERENCES

In case of doubt

always (e.g. Capranica, Domenico);

none;

always, from forename
(e.g. Richard);

always, from family name
(e.g. Fitzalan, Henry, earl of Arundel).

INDEX 1

Manuscripts containing languages other than Latin

English:	nos 1, 4, 6, 7, 11, 14, 22, 23, 25, 26, 27, 32, 35, 37, 39, 54, 68, 69, 70, 84, 87, 88, 90, 94, 96, 101, 108, 110, 111, 117, 118, 132, 134, 140, 145, 151, 159, 183, 185, 215, 258, 284
French:	nos 10, 12, 19, 20, 21, 22, 23, 24, 29, 31, 39, 88, 90, 101, 103, 105, 107, 109, 124, 131, 132, 150, 177, 201, 210, 235, 254, 264, 270, 277
German:	nos 112, 138, 162, 163, 164, 166, 167, 168, 169, 170, 181, 182, 193, 196, 216, 220, 221, 225, 226, 227, 228, 237, 252, 255, 273, 278, 279
Italian:	nos 113, 114, 147, 189, 194, 195, 230, 234, 236, 242, 256, 262, 268, 271, 275
Netherlandish	no. 264
Scots:	nos 41, 56, 73, 160

INDEX 2

Index of Dates

Manuscripts written in more than one year are entered under each year, with the exception of nos 37, 38, and 79, which were mainly written up annually over a lengthy period. Such annual entries are recorded, for instance, as 'annual entries 1425-1600'. Manuscripts written in two consecutive years are entered after the first and before the second year, in a sequence such as 1425, 1425 and 1426, 1426.

INDEX 3

Index of Authors and Contents

Works are listed under author's name or, if anonymous, under title; but see also the following general headings: Alchemica, Astrologica, Biblia, Cartularies, Chronicles, City of London Customals, Computus, Liturgical books, Miscellanea, Ordinances, Physicians' handbooks, Prayers, Questiones, Receipts, Regula, Registrum, Statuta, and Tracts, under which a number of anonymous entries have been classed together.

INDEX 4

Index of Scribes, Artists, and Binders

A.D.: no. 174
Abell, William, artist: nos 110, 154
Abiat, Bartholomeus Marcellus *see* Bartholomeus
Ago. Phi., of Rimini: no. 253
Agostino Cesareo: no. 114
Aloysius, an Italian: no. 198
'Ancilla Christi', of Diepenveen: no. 186
Andreas de Manzinis, OFM: no. 91
Antonius de Meer *see* A.D.
Anre, Johannes, OPrem., of Arnstein: no. 283

Baffi, Giovanni Battista *see* Johannes
Bales, Peter, writing master, of London: no. 26
Barret, Robert: no. 92
Bartolomeus (Bartolomeo)
   an Italian: no. 272
   Cynthius: nos 241, 259
   de Festoraziis de Belano: no. 233
   Marcellus Abiat: no. 219
   Sanvito, of Padua: no. 199
Battista da Cingoli: no. 267
   Parmense, engraver: no. 96
Benedeto: no. 262
Betson, Thomas, of Syon Abbey: no. 140
Bröll, Sigismund, of Nuremberg: no. 225
Browne, Lancelot, FRCP, of London: no. 137
Buck, Egghardus, cleric, of Bremen diocese: no. 44
Bukherst, Stephen: no. 117
Bürtzel, Johann, of Augsburg: no. 228

Calne, Richard, Aug. canon, of Lanthony II, Gloucs.: nos 76, 77
'Canevari bindery': no. 201
'Carmelite-Lapworth Master', artist: nos 51, 122
Carolus Guarnarinus: no. 208
Cesareo, Agostino *see* Agostino
Chell, William, B.Mus (Oxon): no. 85
Chesham, John, scrivener and notary, of London: no. 38
Cingoli, Battista da *see* Battista
Clement, prior of Lanthony I and II: no. 67
Cole, Robert, rent-collector of Lanthony II, Gloucs.: no. 120
'Considerans' scribe, an Englishman: nos 4, 161
Cosin, Richard: no. 71
Cossier, John, Master, Scriveners' Company, London: no. 38
Cotel, a Frenchman: no. 235

Culpet, Walter, scrivener and notary, of London: no. 38
Cynthius, Bartholomeus *see* Bartholomeus

Datis, Nicolaus Antonii de, of Visso *see* Nicolaus
Daunt, John, scrivener and notary, of London: no. 38
Dominicus Gallettus, papal secretary: no. 50
Duryvale, William, Clerk, Merchant Taylors' Company, London: nos 38, 111

Ebesham, William: no. 282
Egidius, Abbot: no. 203
Elias de Joneston, king's clerk: no. 129
Elmeley, Adam, procurator of Lanthony I, Monmouthshire: no. 118
Evesham, Alexander: no. 11

F.D., binder, an Englishman: no. 146
Fabyan, Robert: no. 35
Falck, Peter, of Freiburg: no. 182
Felicianus de Benis de Montone: no. 246
Flanderback, Gerhard, of Cologne: no. 138
'Flyleaf scribe', of Buildwas Abbey: no. 55
Frampton, Richard: nos 122, 125
Frater Ulmannus *see* Ulmannus
Freudenreich, Conrad: no. 16

Gagliardelli, Salvadore, writing master, of Florence: no. 195
Gallettus, Dominicus *see* Dominicus
Gasparo di Cagali: no. 230
Gilbert de Thornton, chief justice of the King's Bench: no. 106
Glover, Robert, Somerset Herald: nos 10, 13
Grove, William, scrivener, of London: no. 38
Guarnarinus, Carolus *see* Carolus
Guidotus, surgeon, of Vicenza: no. 209
Guttenberger, Eberhard, physician: no. 238
Gwynne, Jenkyn: no. 215

H.N., binder, of London: no. 85
H, William: no. 183
Hall, Anthony, skinner, of London, artist: no. 23
Haywarde: no. 70

Hebyn, John, cleric, of Swine, Yorks: no. 142
Hengler, Hainricus, of Isny: no. 252
Henricus de Geismar, canon of Bubeneč: no. 207
Hermannus Benedictus de Bulach: no. 229
Hert(z)en, Johannes, prior, of Ewig: no. 167
Heymandus de Veteri Busco: no. 239
Hieronimo Morescho, writing master: no. 189
Hooker, John *see* Vowell, John
Hunt, Hugh, gentleman, of London: no. 32
Hynton, Richard *see* Wyse

Johannes (Giovanni):
   Battista Baffi: no. 218
   Franciscus Genuesius, of Mantua: no. 200
   de Manga, OCarm.: no. 206
   di Piero da Stia, notary, of Florence: no. 265
   de Vitalibus, priest, of Brescia: no. 194
Jouffroy, Claude: no. 236

Kaczschicz, Tedricus, chaplain: no. 184
'King Edward and Queen Mary Binder': no. 86
Kom, Thomas: no. 75

Lake, John, of Furnival's Inn, London: no. 31
Lambarde, William: no. 179
Langenbach, Hainricus: no. 173
Lannkchamer, Stephanus, of Passau: no. 243
Lempt, Adam: no. 193
Leo, an Englishman: no. 52
Leonnardus de Wulp: no. 98
Leslie, John, bp of Ross: nos 41, 93
Lindner
   Johann, of Münchberg: no. 212
   Johann, of Wasserburg: no. 247
Lorenzi, Raffaelo Bernardo *see* Raffaelo
Lorenzo Guglielmo Traversagni, OFM, of Savona: no. 83

'MacDurnan Gospels Binder': no. 97
Machyn, John, kitchener, of Lanthony II, Gloucs.: no. 120
Maître du Remède de Fortune, artist: no. 190
Marshall, John: no. 49
   William, *Mag.*: no. 72

INDEX 5

People and places connected with the manuscripts

'ASRYDTOL' (?): no. 107
A. de Walsok, Aug. canon, of Barnwell
    Priory: no. 3
Abingdon (GB), Ben abbey: no. 45
Adgore, Gregory, Serjeant at Law: no.
    103
Adys, Miles, Warden, Goldsmiths'
    Company, London: no. 27
Aeton see Eaton
Afflyn, Annis: no. 284
Agard, Charles: no. 8
Alan de Thornton: no. 106
Alessandro Padovani, of Forlì: nos 136,
    209, 259, 272
Alicia de Eaton, prioress of Godstow: no.
    133
Allen, Thomas, of Oxford: no. 80
Amyes, Henry: no. 285
Andreas Stabilis: no. 275
Anford, William: no. 54
Antonius M de Castiliane: no. 190
Arden, Robert, of Warwick: no. 15
Armagh (Ireland): no. 97
Arnstein (Germany), Prem. abbey: no.
    283
Arundel, Henry Fitzalan, earl of: no. 47
Ashefeyld, Edmund: no. 56
Asolo (Italy): no. 208
Athelstan, king of England see England
Augsburg (Germany): no. 228
Avalle, W: no. 134
Ayscogh, Robert: no. 74

Bacon
    Sir Nicholas, owner (?): no. 5
    Thomas, B.A., B.D. (Cantab.), owner
        (?): no. 5
Bale, John, OCarm., later bp of Ossory:
    nos 5, 42, 50, 95
Banaff, Henry, OCist., of Whalley: no. 88
Bancroft, Richard, bp of London: no. 96
Banks, Richard, vicar of Crich: no. 64
Barkley, Sir Maurice, MP: no. 147
Barlow, George, of the Inner Temple,
    owner (?): no. 101
Barnwell (GB), Aug. priory: no. 3
Basel (Switzerland): no. 143
Bassyngbourne, John, OSB, of
    Westminster Abbey: no. 280
Beaufey: no. 80
Beaufort, Lady Margaret see Richmond
Becon, Thomas, canon of Canterbury,
    owner (?): no. 5
Bedford, William, prior of Barnwell:
    no. 3
Bellowe, Henry, Warden, Merchant

Taylors' Company, London: no. 111
Berckibel, Daniel, of Zwickau: no. 226
Bere, William, Clerk, Drapers' Company,
    London: no. 25
Besford, Joan: no. 185
Bingham, George, of Canterbury: no. 68
Blasius de Mulio, dominus: no.264
Bocher, William: no. 4
Boleyn, Geoffrey, Warden, Mercers'
    Company, London: no. 110
Bologna (Italy): no. 136
Bolzano (Italy): no. 162
Bozen (S. Tyrol) see Bolzano
Bradshaw, John, Rev.: no. 142
Braegel, March (?): no. 205
Brandenburg, Joachim, Margrave of: no.
    238
Braunau (Germany): no. 243
Bredeloe, Heinrich: no. 181
Bremall, Stephen: no. 192
Bremen (Germany): no. 181
Brigham, Nicholas: no. 95
Bröll, Johannes: no. 225
Brogreve, William, Warden, Drapers'
    Company, London: no. 25
Brown
    John: no. 24
    Richard: no. 133
Brümmers, Hanns, of Rottweil: no. 226
Bryce, Hugh, Alderman, London: no. 27
Bubeneč (Czech Republic): no. 207
Buccarini, Ottaviano, papal physician see
    Ottaviano
Buildwas (GB), Cist. abbey: no. 55
Bukberd, Ralph, Warden, Merchant
    Taylors' Company, London: no. 111
Burghley, William Cecil, Lord: no. 183
Burton
    John, Warden, Mercers' Company,
        London: no. 110
    Michael, of Wirksworth: nos 8, 9
Burton upon Trent (GB): no. 41
Bury St Edmunds (GB)
    MS written at (?): no. 14
    Ben. abbey: nos 5, 100
Buxheim (Germany), Charterhouse: no.
    276
Byrche, John: no. 40
Byrde, Roger, OSB, of Peterborough: nos
    149, 150

C S D D K, a German: no. 221
Calne, Richard, Aug. canon, of Lanthony
    II, Gloucs: nos 52, 57, 75, 76, 77
Cambridge (GB), Peterhouse: no. 43
    loan chests: no. 43

Canterbury (GB), Ben. cath. priory
    (Christ Church): nos 48, 58, 80, 97
Capranica, Domenico, cardinal see
    Domenico
Carew, George, earl of Totnes see Totnes
Carpenter, John, common clerk of the
    City of London: no. 24
Cecil
    Brownlow, earl of Exeter see Exeter
    William, Lord Burghley see Burghley
Chester (GB), Ben. abbey, MS written at
    (?): no. 30
Chichele, Henry, archbp of Canterbury:
    no. 51
Chomeley, William: no. 104
Claude d'Urfé: no. 201
Clifford, Thomas, OSB, of Westminster
    Abbey: no. 282
Clopton, Sir William: no. 185
Clough, Henry, Warden, Merchant
    Taylors' Company, London: no. 111
Cole, James, Jr, notary: no. 99
Cologne (Germany): no. 166
    Charterhouse: no. 205
    St Maria ad Gradus, collegiate ch: no.
        138
Constance (Germany): no. 227
Coote, Henry, Warden, Goldsmiths'
    Company, London: no. 27
Cope
    Alan: no. 83
    John, Bladesmith, of London: no. 183
Corkatenny (Ireland): no. 78
Cornelius, an Italian: no. 200
Corsaer, Thomas, priest: no. 4
Cotton, Sir Robert: nos 20, 21, 23, 90
Cranmer, Thomas, archbp of Canterbury:
    no. 48
Cremona (Italy): no. 189
Crich (GB): no. 64
Crusius, Daniel: no. 237

Dalton, William, OCist., abbot of
    Furness: no. 123
Danyell, John, OSB, prior of Lewes: no.
    72
Darcy, Edward: no. 68
Darrell, William, prebendary of
    Canterbury: no. 95
Daventry (GB): no. 124
De Meer family: no. 174
Derwayll, William, dominus: no. 79
Desford (GB): no. 156
Devon, William, prior of Barnwell: no. 3
Didacus Serrano, scribe in the papal
    chancery: no. 50

INDEX 6

Index of Rejected Manuscripts and of manuscripts in other collections cited

(R refers to an item in the list of Rejected Manuscripts)

Taunton, Somerset Record Office,
    DD/AH66/17: no. 47

Udine, Biblioteca Arcivescovile 83: no.
    208

Vatican City, Biblioteca Apostolica
    Vaticana
    Pal. lat. 1319: no. 241

Reg. lat.
    430: no. 268
    470: no. 66
Rossiana 1155-7: no. 44
Urb. lat. 455: no. 265
Vat. lat.
    3232: no. 197
    3283: no. 197
    11441: no. 83

Venice, Biblioteca San Marco, It. II. 173:
    no. 268
Vienna, Österreichischen
    Nationalbibliothek,
    Cod. 39: no. 267
    Cod. 5512: no. 207

Washington, DC, Folger Shakespeare
    Library, V.b.236: no. 185